Internet Management for Nonprofits

Strategies, Tools & Trade Secrets

TED HART
STEVE MacLAUGHLIN
JAMES M. GREENFIELD
PHILIP H. GEIER JR.

WILEY

John Wiley & Sons, Inc.

The AFP Fund Development Series

The AFP Fund Development Series is intended to provide fund development professionals and volunteers, including board members (and others interested in the nonprofit sector), with top-quality publications that help advance philanthropy as voluntary action for the public good. Our goal is to provide practical, timely guidance and information on fundraising, charitable giving, and related subjects. The Association of Fundraising Professionals and Wiley each bring to this innovative collaboration unique and important resources that result in a whole greater than the sum of its parts. For information on other books in the series, please visit:

http://www.afpnet.org

THE ASSOCIATION OF FUNDRAISING PROFESSIONALS

The Association of Fundraising Professionals (AFP) represents more than 30,000 members in more than 197 chapters throughout the United States, Canada, Mexico, and China, working to advance philanthropy through advocacy, research, education, and certification programs.

The association fosters development and growth of fundraising professionals and promotes high ethical standards in the fundraising profession. For more information or to join the world's largest association of fundraising professionals, visit www.afpnet.org.

2009–2010 AFP Publishing Advisory Committee

Chair: D. C. Dreger, ACFRE
Senior Campaign Director, Custom Development Solutions, Inc.
Nina P. Berkheiser, CFRE
Principal Consultant, Your Nonprofit Advisor
Linda L. Chew, CFRE
Development Consultant
Patricia L. Eldred, CFRE
Director of Development, Independent Living Inc.
Samuel N. Gough, CFRE
Principal, The AFRAM Group
Audrey P. Kintzi, ACFRE
Director of Development, Courage Center
Steven Miller, CFRE
Director of Development and Membership, Bread for the World
Robert J. Mueller, CFRE
Vice President, Hospice Foundation of Louisville
Maria Elena Noriega
Director, Noriega Malo & Associates
Michele Pearce
Director of Development, Consumer Credit Counseling Service of Greater Atlanta
Leslie E. Weir, MA, ACFRE
Director of Family Philanthropy, The Winnipeg Foundation
Sharon R. Will, CFRE
Director of Development, South Wind Hospice

<u>John Wiley & Sons, Inc.:</u>
Susan McDermott
Senior Editor (Professional / Trade Division)

<u>AFP Staff:</u>
Rhonda Starr
Vice President, Education and Training

*The editors and authors dedicate this book to the many volunteers and staffers
who work every day to support millions of charities around the world.
To each of them, we offer this book as a guide to making the most
of the Internet to bring together communities of supporters in service to others.*

Contents

Introduction

A Primer for Board Members and Nonprofit Executives: Increased Efficiency, Effectiveness, and Success through Use of the Internet

For those of us who work everyday to manage and govern charitable organizations, making decisions for how best to use some of the broad array of Internet technologies available can be a daunting task. Multiple online technologies are now available globally with expanding web sites linked to social networks in an increasingly mobile universe, all of which can be confusing to even to the most seasoned practitioner. This is why the comprehensive book, *Internet Management for Nonprofits: Strategies, Tools & Trade Secrets,* has been prepared, to answer both the "how to" along with "how to succeed" using an increasingly fast-paced, overly complex and always challenging asset, the Internet.

On some level we all know that managing the use of digital and Internet vehicles for marketing, communications, and fundraising purposes is essential to our ability to build the broad-based communities of advocates and supporters we require. We also know that mastering these techniques at some level is required to move toward the efficiency and effectiveness demanded in today's business environment. Yet, how to accomplish so much can seem a mystery beyond our organization's technical ability and fiscal constraints.

Using the voice of over 25 experts from around the world, this book is for board members, executive directors and CEO's, vice presidents and managers at all levels who know they must address channel confusion, must establish the return on investment (ROI) of any of these initiatives, and must know what measurements of success are possible and the path to get there using Internet, digital, and mobile services. The goal of this book is to help you to understand the tactical opportunities and to create outreach strategies based on objective analysis and audience development – not based on just the technologies themselves. Consider this book a "pitch free zone" where we are not promoting any services over another, but instead we are providing practical usable advice that both the expert and novice can use to better manage their organizations.

For managers in the large, well-established nonprofit to the smallest more entrepreneurial charity, the Internet has become an essential tool for managing marketing, communications, and fundraising alongside day-to-day operations. It is very easy to establish a web presence these days, but that is not enough. Build it and they will not necessarily come. It takes serious strategy to succeed online—just as a smart nonprofit manager or board member knows, it takes serious strategy to succeed offline as well.

Nonprofits who have carefully built brands and broad-based relationships offline risk damaging all they have created when they pursue ill-conceived Internet strategies. Yet every charitable organization cannot avoid the necessity of ever-increasing utilization of digital management for their organization if they want to compete successfully today and into the future.

This book has been prepared for all those who want to expand on the technological opportunities available to them and for those who want to learn how their organization can effectively and efficiently seize these opportunities.

The Internet provides every nonprofit three types of opportunities: 1) it links them directly to supporters, donors, and the larger community; 2) it lets them, even small ones, compete on a more level playing field because a smart strategy developed for a small charity has just as much opportunity for success as one developed by a much larger one; and 3) the Internet and mobile technology represent tools that can be used to develop and distribute services, information, and networking opportunities with multiple audiences not available through more traditional offline means.

As you prepare to use this book at board meetings, committee strategy sessions, and staff gatherings, here is a brief summary of the content prepared specifically for you by the international group of experts the editors have assembled.

World-renowned Internet expert Beth Kanter provides board members and charity managers a "users guide" to the Return on Investment (ROI) of social media in Chapter 1. Beth tells us, "Social media is propelling nonprofit goals to build a movement around a core advocacy issue, improve customer service or programs, reach new donors, and spread awareness of a nonprofit brand around the world." Yet, as you will learn, social media require a different skill set than do other more traditional forms of outreach for marketing, communications, and fundraising purposes. As Marnie Webb, co-CEO of TechSoup Global said, "Nonprofits can no longer ignore social media or they risk becoming irrelevant." In Chapter 2, Michael Sola and Tim Kobosko provide a unique approach to understanding the path to managing your charitable organization using online tools from the perspective of someone managing and/or governing a nonprofit. Unlike any other chapter in this book you are placed in the office as lessons are learned. Drawing heavily on these authors' experiences at the National Wildlife Federation (NWF), this chapter helps even novices understand the important steps needed to manage and succeed with your online resources.

E-Governance is a concept whose time has come, and our experts Dottie Schindlinger and Leanne Bergey help the reader learn how to improve board leadership through the use of online technology. In Chapter 3 this essential text helps board members and administrators learn exactly how they can bring the efficiencies they know exist to their own governance process to board recruitment and benchmarking to policies that successfully bring transparency to nonprofit operations that donors and supporters demand. Learning from Dottie and Leanne will help make succeeding in their efforts easier, more secure, and efficient for board members.

One of the "payoffs" all nonprofits can expect from increased use of the Internet is the ability to raise both more awareness for their cause and more money. The powerful team of Russell Artzt, John Murcott, and Mark Fasciano came together in Chapter 4 to guide us to strengthen our collaboration with staff members, board members, and volunteers. This strategy often can be scary to traditional minded managers and board members because collaboration often means letting go of control. But these three experts help us maneuver through those issues and help to maximize the time and money savings to be found in the hidden economies of scale and empowerment of the organization's stakeholders.

Loyalty and donor insight are two key strategies we learn to leverage, predict, build, and manage in the excellent Chapter 5 written by the legendary Roger M. Craver and Ryann Miller. Using prediction models, building strategy around those who can influence your outcomes and learning how to manage the new donor-centric world are techniques managers will now understand and implement. The main benefit in this chapter is to learn the strategic tools that can best turn donor insight into trust, loyalty, volunteer activism, advocacy, and a thriving bottom line.

Just when you thought you understood how to manage your organization along comes the Internet with its own language, tools, and metrics. Learning how to understand all the data can be mind numbing for even a seasoned techie. For the rest of us we just fear we either won't get it, or can't keep up. Fear no more. In Chapter 6 Blackbaud's Steve MacLaughlin brings his expertise to our desk. We already know that what we measure and how we measure it can spell the difference between successful strategy and failed initiatives. But through the use of easy-to-understand language and models, Steve helps us not only know what a click-through rate is or what benchmarks should be met, he helps managers and board members use data in a more powerful way that can inform the strategies that will lead to more efficient and successful initiatives.

Part II of this book has been specifically designed to focus our attention on fundraising and building the sort of online communities that can support our growing need for a stronger financial foundation.

It is always best to start at the beginning. In Chapter 7 Adrienne Capps provides a primer on tools and techniques for managing fundraising and building strong communities online. This is a must read for all board members who want to learn the opportunities available to their organization's management and for everyone in leadership positions at charitable organizations to expand their horizons as they seek to build the bridge between traditional and online fundraising and community building activities. Adrienne's advice is solid as it urges all nonprofits to take a step forward, not necessarily a leap toward building and outfitting their online efforts. She inspires and motivates as her skill helps you make sense out of the Internet that helps you raise more money.

No nonprofit can succeed for long without strong volunteers and capable leadership. Without a specific volunteer recruitment and retention strategy what is successful short term will be lost over time. No one knows this topic better than Walter "Bud" Pidgeon, the author of Chapter 8. We knew this seasoned executive and prominent author will help you leverage tools as diverse as e-mail to web sites to social networking. Bud helps you bridge from "old line" or more traditional approaches to the efficiencies to be gained by deploying Internet and digital methods to build a strong, well-connected network for recruiting and retaining volunteers.

If you are engaged in the use of social networks like Facebook, LinkedIn, MySpace, or others or even if you have just been thinking about them, questions that quickly come to mind are: "How do I know if this works?" and "How do I know if we are successful?" You are not alone in asking these important questions; experts Danielle Brigida and Jonathon D. Colman in Chapter 9 will help board members and managers alike understand that social media are not a waste of time, but can be an integral set of tools that can bring a great level of success to your communications and marketing efforts. Like any social situation, mistakes can be made when you don't know what is expected of you; Danielle and Jonathon will help you become online social butterflies. Measuring the impact of your success using the power of social networking and understanding how the tools, opportunities, and ideas all must be managed are presented as this chapter helps you learn to "improve, learn, reassess, and grow" through the use of social media.

Anyone involved with a fundraising strategy for more than five minutes learns about the traditional "Pyramid of Giving." Everything old is new again, because to succeed today we now learn in Marcelo Iniarra Iraegui and Alfredo Botti's Chapter 10 that success comes from understanding that the old pyramid has a secret hidden gate, a different entrance that can be accessed by making a donation.

The traditional pyramid also has an extra level that "admits nonfinancial, digital supporters who arrive via new media, web sites, social networks, e-mail and the increasingly popular short text messaging (SMS), or other wireless access points." Here is a new concept – those who try you out, before they give or even identify themselves. How to manage this level of contact and build on these nonfinancial relationships is one of the greatest mysteries for many nonprofits. This chapter leads you through the hidden gate to a new level of strategic success.

I have always thought that Philip King was a smart guy, but never so much as after he submitted Chapter 11 for this book on social networks. His chapter will help you understand that while I refer to the tools and techniques available through online platforms and social networks, the first step to making this all work is to internalize a basic truth that Philip brings to us: "Social media networks are not [really] tools; they are collections of people." People ready to be engaged, ready to take action, ready to be inspired. Hundreds of millions of people already are on social networks around the world and what comes with this engagement is a demand for honest self-assessment and conversation. As Philip points out, social media aren't just a new piece of technology; they're a new form of engagement. Harnessing this power can have dramatic effects on your outreach in marketing, communications, and fundraising initiatives.

The "shotgun approach" to fundraising never really succeeded offline and it is certainly not the path to success online. Lawrence C. Henze lives and breathes data and in Chapter 12 you can understand how to use prospect modeling and prospect research to develop a more informed fundraising strategy. So much rich data are available to nonprofits that can allow them to more easily target the prospects for support with the highest likelihood of success. Yet many nonprofits have barely heard of online giving analytics, demographic and lifestyle cluster data, data mining, predictive modeling, or any of the other methodologies available. Once you read this chapter and begin integrating these measures into your fundraising strategy (both online and offline), you will see a dramatic change in the ability to target your donors and execute your plans.

The editors of this book have developed a series of useful strategic approaches for board members and nonprofit managers around the world. Regardless of where you are located there is always some other place that can be described as "international" relative to where you are. Reaching beyond your own borders can be a successful way to fundraise for many charities, yet the cost to do so has traditionally been a deterrent. International fundraising experts Andrew Mosawi and Anita Yuen in their Chapter 13 share details on how your organization can harness the globalization of fundraising, as it expands along the trade routes of global "economic, technological, socio-cultural and political forces." This powerful duo demonstrates ways an organization can take advantage of this trend while leveraging the latest tools to fundraise internationally. Whether or not you plan to develop an internationally focused fundraising program, you must read this chapter, because it is a certainty that nonprofits outside your borders are targeting your donors and you must, at the very least, understand how they plan to do it.

Part III of *Internet Management for Nonprofits* provides expert advice on how best to make technology work for your organization. And it all begins with Chapter 14 where Allan Pressel shares the seven key components and five web site criteria necessary for success, and then adds such important topics as interactivity; site traffic; stickiness; return visitors; search engine rankings; and most important, results for your nonprofit. Allan also provides an analysis of how to manage these tools to help you accomplish all of them.

Now that you have developed a top-notch web site you also will want to make sure you have integrated fundraising tools that will maximize your chances of success. No longer is a "donate now" button enough; it takes a multichannel, integrated approach to succeed as Michael Johnston and Matthew Barr share from their years of experience in Chapter 15. They provide an analysis of multichannel effectiveness with accompanying case studies along with the staffing (human resource) issues you must address to manage your fundraising online efforts. Linking your online and offline fundraising strategies is key to long-term success.

The last thing anyone wants to happen is for their donor data to be stolen. The confidence and trust your supporters have placed in you will be compromised, in an instant, with the theft of sensitive and confidential information. Yet many boards of directors and nonprofit managers have very little knowledge and have given only passing thought to what is essential to protect their organization from violations of this sort. Catherine Pagliaro has spent years building her expertise in the ever-changing world of online and theft identity protection and in Chapter 16 she provides you with an 12-step primer on how to understand security issues that will protect your organization. Cybercrime is a serious and growing problem. "The Aberdeen Group estimates that more than $221 billion is lost globally every year to identity theft! Cybercrime is difficult to investigate and prosecute because it is borderless." Protecting your supporters using Catherine's advice is an important management topic.

The tragic earthquake in Haiti has increased the use of mobile giving, just as September 11, the Southeast Asia tsunami, and Hurricane Katrina put online fundraising and social networking at the forefront of all nonprofit board members and managers. A larger percentage of the world's population holds a mobile device than have access to high-speed Internet service. Ben Rigby's Chapter 17 will help you understand mobile technology and how it can be successful deployed by nonprofits. You will learn how texting can be used as an initial campaign hook, and then built into a successfully integrated online and offline campaign. And, although this topic seems new, Ben reminds us that it is already a primary method of communication between donors and supporters. Now is the time for you to learn how to "navigate the often-overwhelming variety of options" available in mobile giving.

The Internet also is richly designed for bringing together communities of supporters. Often activists for a cause are able to gather together, multiplying the effect of one man's voice to that of an entire community, sometimes even overnight. Frédéric Fournier shares the case study story of what the Nicholas Hulot Foundation learned of how to transform activists into donors. Fred details their dedicated event web site, targeted e-mail promotions, and the "power of thanks." You will learn the keys to their success.

It has been a privilege for me to work with my fellow editors Steve MacLaughlin, James Greenfield, and Philip Geier, along with our many authors and our friends at John Wiley & Sons to develop this book. We are all thrilled this book was chosen to be included in the highly successful AFP/Wiley Fund Development Series.

One last thought. We urge you to sign up for e-mail updates at http://www.p2pfundraising.org. As is pointed out in Chapter 10, given the new paradigms introduced by electronic media, perhaps Heraclitus, who was a Greek philosopher living on the coast of Asia Minor more than 2,000 years ago and couldn't possibly have imagined that his wise advice would still apply today, was right in saying, "There is nothing permanent except change." We believe this book provides an excellent background for everyone involved in charitable organizations to more effectively and efficiently manage them using tools, strategies, and techniques offered by the Internet, digital media, and mobile technology.

Ted Hart, ACFRE, Senior Editor
Washington, DC
February 2010

About the Editors

Ted Hart, ACFRE is considered one of the foremost experts in both online and traditional fundraising around the world. He is sought after internationally as an inspirational and practical speaker and consultant. He serves as CEO of Hart Philanthropic Services (http://tedhart.com), an international consultancy to nonprofits and nongovernmental organizations. He also created People-to-People Fundraising, a movement housed online at http://www.p2pfundraising.org. He is founder of the international ePhilanthropy Foundation. Hart has taken a leadership role in helping nonprofits become green by founding GreenNonprofits (http://www.greennonprofits.org). Hart has served as CEO of the University of Maryland Medical System Foundation and as chief development officer for Johns Hopkins Bayview Medical Center. He is certified by the Association of Fundraising Executives as an Advanced Certified Fundraising Executive (ACFRE).

Hart is the editor or coauthor of several books, including *Major Donors: Finding Big Gifts in Your Database and Online, Nonprofit Internet Strategies, Fundraising on the Internet, People to People Fundraising*, and *Nonprofit Guide to Going Green*. He resides in the Washington, DC, and New York City areas. He lives with his daughter, Sarah Grace, and son, Alexander Michael.

Steve MacLaughlin has spent more than 14 years building successful online initiatives with a broad range of Fortune 500 firms, government and educational institutions, and nonprofit organizations around the world. MacLaughlin is currently the director of Internet solutions at Blackbaud and is responsible for leading the company's development of online solutions for its clients.

MacLaughlin serves on the Nonprofit Technology Network's (NTEN) board of directors and supports its focus on both the growth and the professionalism of the nonprofit technology sector. He is a frequent speaker, an active blogger (http://www.blackbaud.com/connections), and writer whose insights have appeared in several nonprofit-sector publications.

MacLaughlin earned both his undergraduate degree and a master of science in interactive media from Indiana University.

James M. Greenfield, ACFRE, FAHP Jim Greenfield has served since 1962 as a fundraising executive to three universities and five hospitals on the East and West Coasts and in between. He retired from Hoag Memorial Presbyterian Hospital in February 2001 after 14 years as senior vice president, resource development and executive director, Hoag Hospital Foundation, where more than $120 million was raised during his tenure.

The author and editor of ten books and more than 40 articles and chapters on fundraising management, his books and articles on measuring fundraising results for effectiveness and efficiency are among the first to tackle these difficult and challenging issues. Recent books Jim has coedited with Ted Hart and others include *Nonprofit Internet Strategies: Best Practices for Marketing, Communications and Fundraising* (2005), *Major Donors: Finding Big Gifts in Your Database and Online* (2006), and *People to People Fundraising: Social Networking and Web 2.0 for Charities* (2007).

Jim and his wife Karen reside in Newport Beach, California where he continues to serve nonprofits and the fundraising profession with speaking, teaching, volunteering, and consulting services.

Philip H. Geier Jr., an advertising professional, became chair and CEO of the Interpublic Group of Companies in 1980. He retired from that position at the end of 2000. In February 2001, Geier formed the Geier Group to provide consulting and advisory services in the areas of marketing, communications, and venture capitalism. Geier also is a senior adviser for Lazard Frères & Co., and he serves on the boards of directors of AEA Investors and Fiduciary Trust International, and he is retired from the boards of Alcon Labs, Mettler-Toledo International, and Foot Locker. Geier's philanthropic director and trustee relationships include Memorial Sloan-Kettering Cancer Center, Save the Children, Autism Speaks, Columbia Business School, the Whitney Museum of American Art, and the International Tennis Hall of Fame. Geier holds a B.A. in economics from Colgate University (1957) and an M.B.A. in marketing and finance from Columbia University (1958).

PART I

Effective Management and Leadership Tools

CHAPTER 1

The ROI of Social Media

THE "I" STANDS FOR INSIGHT AND IMPACT

BETH KANTER

S ocial media is transforming how nonprofits do their work and their relationships with constituents. The early adopters that have embraced social
media with an approach of listen, fail informatively, and evolve are seeing results.
Strategic use of social media is actually helping measurably to reach new people
and is bringing added value to mission-driven work. Social media is propelling
nonprofit goals to build a movement around a core advocacy issue, improve
customer service or programs, reach new donors, and spread awareness of a
nonprofit brand around the world.

Nonprofits can no longer afford to take the stance that social media is "just a
bunch of hype" and continue with business as usual. The risk is playing a harsh
game of catch-up or even worse. Nonprofit leaders need to ask, what can our
organization do to make our Internet communications strategies and fundraising
more effective in these rapidly changing times?

The return on investment (ROI) of social media requires a different approach.
It is about replacing the word "investment" with new "i" words, "insight" and
"impact." This chapter will help demystify social media listening, measurement,
experimentation, and it will illustrate how nonprofits can effectively use these
techniques to help improve their social media strategies to see measurable results.

SOCIAL MEDIA ROI—A NEW APPROACH

Although social media tools have been available to nonprofit marketing and
fundraising professionals for several years, there is still debate about whether
these new tools are worth the time investment. With economic and financial
pressures always present, many nonprofit executive directors are highly skeptical

as to whether social media helps nonprofits reach their objectives. When staff members suggest incorporating social media tools and techniques into the media mix, executive directors ask the following: What are the tangible benefits? How much will it cost in staff time to implement? How do we measure success? And, of course, is it worth it?

Over the coming decade, social networking sites like Facebook and other social media outlets and channels will become as ubiquitous to nonprofit development, communications, and program departments as the phone, direct mail, and e-mail. This transition will happen gradually, as younger nonprofit staff members, who are fluent in the use of these tools, assume leadership roles. And as members of generation Y comes into their own as donors and new technical developments transform the web into a social space, the use of social media will become as commonplace as "air," says Charlene Li, a social media expert.[1]

Adding social media into the nonprofit marketing and fundraising toolbox does not mean abandoning proven marketing and fundraising methods such as e-mail marketing and direct mail. It does require some experimentation and a different expectation about short-term results. Finally, it means that organizations need to rethink and change their approaches, and that is easier said than done.

The Traditional Return on Investment Analysis for Nonprofit Technology

Many nonprofit organizations turn to a traditional return-on-investment process as a prelude to justifying a large investment in a mission-critical technology system or equipment. This might include new desktop computers, a video-conferencing system, a web site redesign that includes a new content management system, a customer relationship management (CRM) database, and the list goes on. Simply stated, the traditional ROI process is an analysis that looks at the benefits, costs, and value of a technology project over time. The analysis also includes financial projections that clearly show how the technology purchase will improve the bottom line. In other words, the analysis clearly connects the cost of investing in the technology to increased income or budget savings because the technology has made staff members more efficient in their work or has enabled them to better serve clients or stakeholders. Further, a traditional ROI analysis might also point out how staff time might be better spent, such as by illustrating how much more effective staff members are in their work because they can devote their attention to customers, clients, or program development rather than spend time on clerical tasks.

An ROI analysis is more than a simple mathematical equation that looks something like this:

Income from new technology − cost of new technology = ROI.

TABLE 1.1	TRADITIONAL ROI PROCESS, STEP BY STEP

Step	Description
1. Identify the objective	The organization identifies what it hopes to accomplish with the technology by identifying results.
2. Define the audience	The organization identifies the audience. It could be external audiences like donors or clients as well as internal audiences like staff members.
3. Benefits statement	The organization creates a benefit statement to identify how using the technology will help support its mission. Typically, benefits such as efficiency or effectiveness are identified. Benefits can also be intangible (can't be translated into a dollar amount and are usually behavior oriented) or tangible (those that can be translated into dollars or time savings)
4. Use metrics to translate into a dollar value	These are measures selected to translate the benefit into an objective measure. Data must be collected during this process, but only enough to answer decision makers' questions.
5. Calculate financials	The financial calculations might include comparing the cost of different solutions, comparing costs and benefits, comparing the cost of not doing, or identifying a small pilot to understand costs.
6. Communicate results	The ROI analysis is shared with key decision makers either as a prepurchase decision tool or postpurchase. It incorporates both numerical and qualitative data.

A traditional ROI analysis goes much deeper and involves a number of analysis steps, as shown in Table 1.1.

For a more robust and detailed understanding of the traditional nonprofit technology ROI process, please refer to chapter 3, "Measuring the Return on Investment," by Beth Kanter, in *Managing Technology to Meet Your Mission: A Strategic Guide for Nonprofit Leaders.*[2]

ROI and the Development and Marketing Departments

Development and marketing professionals have used ROI calculations to analyze the results of their Internet-based fundraising, membership, advocacy, and communications campaigns. Most e-mail and CRM software will capture standardized and universally accepted metrics such as open rates, conversion rates, and others. This can help nonprofit development and marketing professionals not only easily answer the question, did our campaign work? but also have confidence based on past experience of a certain level of results. In other words, there is less risk.

Over the past five years, the nonprofit field has begun to establish industry benchmark metrics for measuring the success of online e-mail advocacy and fundraising campaigns.[3] Nonprofit fundraising and marketing professionals use these metrics to compare their results to industry norms.

Nonprofit online fundraising and marketing professionals collect and analyze standard web site metrics from analytics software programs like Google Analytics. The software can crunch the data to clearly demonstrate an ROI (or not). In fact, Google Analytics has a feature that tracks revenue goals and can automatically calculate the dollar return of specific strategies. In addition, because web metrics have been in use for more than a decade, they are generally accepted and understood by executive directors. What nonprofit executive doesn't know the definition of a page view?

From Counting Eyeballs to Measuring Engagement

What is most difficult for many nonprofits to understand in their quest to measure and improve social media strategies or to justify getting started, is that social media not only requires defining success differently but also uses different metrics. Social media metrics are not all about page views. In fact, some social media experts go as far as saying that the page is view is dead or life support.[4] To measure social media success in the early stages, organizations need to measure intangibles such conversations and relationships. This can be a hard sell, especially when an executive director is screaming, "Show me the money!"

Social media requires not only a different approach to strategy but also a different mind-set from that of implementing e-mail, direct-mail, and other traditional communications and fundraising campaigns.

The social media measurement maven K. D. Paine, in an interview with the blogger Jason Falls put it this way: "Ultimately, the key question to ask when measuring engagement is, 'Are we getting what we want out of the conversation?' And, as stubborn as it sounds Mr. CEO, you don't get money out of a conversation."[5] At least in the initial stages of social media exploration, and as early adopters are discovering, engagement is leading to donations.

Reframing ROI from Investment to Insight and Impact

Should nonprofits be using an industrial measurement model in a digital age to measure the success of their social media efforts? It simply doesn't work. In the 1920s, ROI was created as a financial measure, developed by DuPont and used by Alfred Sloan to make General Motors manageable. It is an analysis that calculates business performance, taking into account not only whether the business made money but also whether that profit was good enough relative to the assets it took to generate it. Over past century, the ROI process has been refined and so deeply etched in business thinking that many view it as the only legitimate means of measuring business performance.

It is also important to remember that ROI was a measure of return on the total investment in the entire business. It was never intended to look at the ROI of a specific marketing strategy, program, tool, or any other isolated aspect of an organization.

Many social media gurus have challenged the notion of using a straight financial calculation to determine whether an organization should invest in social media before taking the plunge or evaluating the first forays. These experts are not saying to not use metrics or that social media isn't measurable. What the experts are saying is that organizations need to measure value, and that value isn't necessarily synonymous with dollars, especially in the early stages of social media strategy experimentation.

Perhaps the best recent illustration of why traditional ROI formulas should not be used for social media fundraising is the discussion that followed an article published by the *Washington Post* titled "To Nonprofits Seeking Cash, Facebook App Isn't So Green: Though Popular, 'Causes' Ineffective for Fundraising."[6]

The article, which proclaimed fundraising through Facebook's Causes application a failure, based its analysis of fundraising performance on a dollars-per-donor metric. The article created an uproar on nonprofit blogs, with many fundraising and social media professionals making the point that it is still too early to measure success in aggregate dollars per donor.[7] Allison Fine, author of *Momentum* and who blogs about nonprofits and philanthropy, pointed out that awareness, not dollars, is the right metric for success in fundraising on social networking sites at this point in time.[8] In addition, she argues that social fundraising applications such as Causes facilitate the spread of a nonprofit organization's message in a way that the nonprofit does not need to do the heavy lifting. Steve MacLaughlin from Blackbaud, a leading technology provider to the nonprofit sector, said, "If the reason why you want to use social networks is just to raise money, then stop now. It doesn't work that way. Causes is a friend raising tool, not a fundraising tool."[9]

The fundraising consultant Betsy Harman, principal of Harman Interactive, concurred and pointed out why fundraising on social networks requires time. "Any nonprofit who thinks they can simply create a Causes page on Facebook and wait for the money to roll in, doesn't understand networked fundraising. It's still all about building relationships, telling your story, and taking potential donors through the process of cultivation, stewardship and solicitation." Brian Reich, a marketing consultant and coauthor of *Media Rules! Mastering Today's Technology to Connect with and Keep Your Audience*, suggests that too many nonprofits have taken the "build it and they will donate" approach and that "simply by using the tools they'll raise a lot of money. They've forgotten that it's the relationship building and that takes time."[10]

The consultant Ivan Boothe said that Causes applications have been effective for organizing activists and keeping them engaged with a campaign. "Asking for and receiving donations has only ever been pursued on social networks as a way to reinforce this identity, not as a way to raise large amounts of money. It's about cultivating relationships with your most passionate supporters, giving them ways to speak in their own voice and connecting them with other people. Most young folks who are on social networks get this, since it is how they're relating socially on these networks already."[11]

It is important to understand that looking at the ROI of social media and social networking tools requires two new "i" words: "insight"[12] and "impact."[13] The concept of return on insight is something that the social media thought leader David Armano points out in his white paper "The Collective Is the Focus Group."[14] In the early stages, organizations need to approach social media implementation with more agility, which requires listening to and reiterating what works. He names this process "listen, learn, and adapt." The expectation of immediate dollar results is unrealistic, as many early adopters of nonprofit social media well know. It takes time to build relationships and more time to see results of social media efforts. As social media is largely experimental, it is imperative to measure quickly and make real-time course corrections and to figure out what is working. In this stage, learning and engagement are the value that social media offers to nonprofits.

The idea of impact on mission, which comes at a later stage, is to connect your social media objectives to specific organizational outcomes. As K. D. Paine, a thought leader in social media measurement commented, "We should reserve the term 'ROI' for impact on mission. For the Red Cross it's not about fans and followers or even money raised. It is about lives saved."[15] Paine goes on to say that if the social media strategists at the Red Cross can show that they helped more people in a crisis through Twitter, then that trumps all other metrics.[16]

Listen, Learn, and Adapt Defined

The best practice of listen, learn, and adapt has fueled the success of many nonprofit social media strategies. Of course, organizations need to first set an overall objective for a social media strategy and then identify the audience and tactical approaches (see Table 1.3 at the end of the chapter).

But before the organization establishes a presence or gets started using any tools, listening must be the first step. Listening means knowing what is being said online about an organization, its field, or its issue area. Listening involves the use of monitoring and tracking tools to identify conversations that are taking place on the social web. It is an important first step before engaging with audiences.

At its most basic, listening is simply naturalistic research, although it is more like a focus group or observation technique than a survey.

Listening is not simply scanning or data collection or a river of noise. The process involves sifting through online conversations from social networks to blogs—many voices talking in many places. The value of listening comes from making sense of the data and using it to inform your engagement strategy with stakeholders.

Learning means discovering what works once the strategy has been launched. It takes place in real time as the social media strategy unfolds and as an evaluative process at the conclusion. It's an aha moment that leads to moving in the right direction. Most important, learning is a reflective process that is done either alone or as a team to harvest insights. Wendy Harman, the social media strategist for the American Red Cross who has been using this approach for three years, says, "At first, I would do the reflection myself, using a journal to document the experiment and at the end of the project review everything I've collected. I'd think about successes and failures. I also kept an eye on what other nonprofits were doing in the social media space. This would inevitably lead to the design of the next experiment. Now that our organization has embraced social media, we do this as a team."

Adapting means using insights to make corrections to improve social media results in the next reiteration. It is much easier to adapt a social media project at a tactical level than to change or improve other areas in an organization that social media might shine a light on: customer service, programs, and services. And making changes in those areas may require rethinking staffing and work flow and, of course, involving leadership and others in the organization.

Overcoming Resistance

Depending on the organization's structure and culture, embarking on a social media strategy and using the approach requires a mind shift. Here are some typical concerns and how to address them:

- **What if they say bad things about our organization or program?** People complain. It is human nature. Social media, at the very least, gives nonprofits a chance to hear those complaints and act on them. A negative comment is an opportunity to improve the organization's programs or correct a stakeholder's misperception. Think of negative comments as an opportunity.

- **What if the organization only wants to see the numbers or "show us the money" in the initial stages of social media strategy implementation?** In the early stages, it is important to value insight and learning and to pick the right metrics for measurement. If the expectation is for an immediate dollar return, look to other channels. But also explore the lost-opportunity cost of starting to experiment and learn. The debate about what to measure does matter, and this should be part of the discussion. The hard data points or metrics should be focused on engagement and conversations (discussed in more detail later in this chapter) in the early stages.

- **What if our organization's style of working does not value or incorporate reflection time for fundraising or marketing projects?** Reflection and looking at what worked and what didn't in a formal way is essential to success. Begin with building brief reflection sessions into the project time line. More frequent, shorter meetings that look at what has been done as well as what there is to do are important. In the long run, this approach may even be more efficient.

THE ART OF LISTENING

Listening is knowing what is being said online about an organization, its field, or its issue area. Listening involves the use of monitoring and tracking tools to identify conversations that are taking place on the social web. This section of the chapter is a deep dive on listening techniques.

Understanding the Value of Listening

The value of listening goes beyond getting free market research, although listening through social media channels is priceless because it is a chance to hear what stakeholders are saying in a natural environment. Listening is typically used by nonprofits to provide better customer service, to correct misconceptions, and to point people to information resources. Nonprofits are also using listening to support improved program implementation, for example, by soliciting ideas from stakeholders or "crowdsourcing" for new programs ideas.[17] As one nonprofit social media strategist pointed out, "Paying attention to trends on the various networks and what people are saying is also incredibly beneficial because it makes it easier for your organization to be relevant. Listening helps you be less of a spammer and more of a service provider."

Kate Bladow, who works at LawHelp, a legal services nonprofit, says that listening has become a best practice for program management staff. She says, "I found out this week that a colleague and I both use the same keywords on 'legal aid' and 'pro bono' to listen because we want to know if anyone is reaching out and looking for legal aid." She directs people to the specific place on the organization's web site to find legal information. Bladow also listens to identify people who express an interest in taking on pro bono legal work and recruits them as pro bono lawyers. Finally, Bladow uses listening techniques for the blog as a way to build to a community of readers interested in legal aid, pro bono work, and other access-to-justice issues.[18]

Organizing Listening in Your Organization

An important consideration is how to organize the listening work flow. Will one staff person (or volunteer) in the organization do all the work, or will a team do it? Part of the preparation for listening includes determining what the response policy is. Organizations also need to think about how much time to allocate to the effort, which initially can take a minimum of five hours per week. Finally, listening isn't a matter of just collecting the data; someone will need to transform it from a river of noise into insights (see Table 1.2 for a checklist of listening questions).

Nonprofits use different approaches depending on their size, the scope of their listening, and the skill and experience of staff:[19]

Social media strategist as a professional listener: If the organization has a staff person responsible for implementing social media strategy, the listening task falls into this person's job description. The social media strategist becomes the organization's ears. The work flow, anywhere from five to ten hours per week, includes daily listening with free and paid tools, summarizing results, and distributing weekly reports to other departments. This person will also serve as the first responder in the social media space. Finally, the work flow includes tracking trends over time and mapping listening efforts to strategy implementation and metrics, as discussed later in this chapter.

Listening team: This model works for smaller organizations where there isn't a full-time social media staff function but social media is being integrated into the job description of a marketing or fundraising person. This approach works where there are senior communications people who are less facile with social media and younger, more junior staff members who are more comfortable with it. This approach will require a couple of weeks or even months of two-way mentoring, which begins with brief sessions learning about the tools and each other's work-flow needs. There needs to be a shared understanding of how to summarize the listening data, what requires a response and what doesn't, and what is an appropriate response, and senior staff need to take swift action.

Listening organization: In this model, the listening activities are not solely for marketing and outreach but also for other program departments that

TABLE 1.2 METRICS AND HARVESTING INSIGHTS FOR A BLOG

Metric	Definition	Analytics Tool	How to Generate Insights
Reader growth: RSS Subscribers Unique visitors	Subscribers have made a commitment to regularly receiving (and hopefully reading or at least scanning) blog content. Visitors are people who visit the blog. Unique visitors are visitors who visit the blog and can be specifically tracked.	Google/ FeedBurner Google Analytics	Look at monthly trends over time to gather insights about reader satisfaction with your content. Is the number of visitors and subscribers going up and to the right? If not, why? If yes, why? Think about your publishing frequency, length of posts, and mix of topics.
Engagement: Commenting Collecting Clicking Critiquing Sharing	Describes how readers are interacting with the content and sharing it with others.	PostRank	Review posts that scored a PostRank of 10: What are the topics? Are these posts longer and more in-depth or short and focused on a topic? Have they rounded up a lot of outside resources? What's the tone, formal or informal? Are they tips? What is the quality of the conversation in the comments? What did you learn from the conversation? If you have a group blog, are there differences between authors?
Bookmarking	A reader bookmarks posts, which means the reader is interested in retrieving a post later, which demonstrates value. This can also generate traffic.	PostRank	Review posts that scored a PostRank of 10. What is the format? Is the bookmarked post referring traffic?
Conversation index	Comments per post indicates engagement.	PostRank Joost Blog Metrics	What is the style of the writing? Do posts with more questions in the title and questions at the end generate more comments? Did you do any outreach to encourage commenting? Is there a conversation happening between people who comment? What do you do to facilitate it? What's the quality of the commenting—are you learning? Are the comments positive or negative?
Authority	The number of outside links to a post.	Technorati Yahoo Site Explorer Google Analytics	Look at the top 10 linked posts. Analyze the types of posts (content and format) that get linked and the impact of those links in referrals using Google Analytics. Are there any patterns?
Page views and referrals	The number of eyeballs per page	Google Analytics	How well are your blog-outreach efforts working? What generates views? What generates referrals?
Industry index	Comparison to other blogs in industry based on standard metrics	The Change List	Why is your blog increasing or decreasing in index number? What can you learn from the top-ranked blogs?

integrate social media listening into the work flow—for customer support, program development, research, and self-directed professional development. This requires identifying the right people, training them, and sharing the information across departments if appropriate.

Checklist of Listening Questions

- What is the schedule for coordinating who is responding to online conversations?
- How will the organization ensure that different team members don't send duplicate responses?
- Will the organization disclose who is engaging on behalf of the nonprofit? Where?
- How will the organization ensure consistency within a team in recording the various facets of conversations that the organization is tracking?
- How will conversations be recorded for future reference?
- How will the conversations about the organization or industry be reported?
- How will the team triage conversations for different types of response?
- Where are the limits? Which conversations will someone on the team respond to and which ones will not require a response?
- Is it important to have a set of standard Q&As to frame staff responses to common issues?
- Is there a common voice that your organization wants associated with its brand?
- What are the guidelines for response time to conversations?
- What process will the team follow when it encounters an issue for which it doesn't currently have an answer?
- Will the team use individual accounts on social media sites that require registration, or will it work from one organizational account?
- Will the organization permit or encourage the team to use personal accounts in the outreach?

Listening Literacy Skills

No matter what tools the organization uses to do the listening, the most important listening literacy skills are composing and refining keywords, analyzing patterns, and synthesizing findings.[20] There's also a fourth skill: effectively engaging. Listening is not just quietly observing—sooner or later, the organization needs to join the conversation. Working out when and how to respond is an important part of the work flow. At the very least, nonprofit organizations that want to do effective listening should set up searches on the basics. Some refer to this as "ego search." The items below provide a list of basic listening topics.

List of Basic Listening Topics
- Nonprofit name, including misspellings, acronyms
- Other nonprofit names in your space
- Program, services, and event names
- CEO or well-known personalities associated with your organization
- Other nonprofits with similar program names
- Your tagline
- URLs for your blog, web site, and online community
- Industry terms or other phrases

If the listening task is shared within the organization, coordination and policy issues need to be worked out. For many organizations, the basics will suffice. As a nonprofit organization begins to listen on a regular basis and scan results that are returned from the basics, it is a good idea to keep a spreadsheet of phrases or words that people actually use to describe the nonprofit organization. This provides a reality check and helps avoid assuming that audiences use the same words as the nonprofits' staff.

Carie Lewis, the social networking manager for the Humane Society of the United States, says, "I run keyword searches on current issues that people are talking about right now and that our organization is working on. Don't forget to search the names of individuals who oppose your issues."[21] Danielle Brigida, the social media manager for the National Wildlife Federation says, "It's important to listen to people based on their interests. For example, I create twitter searches for the phrase 'kids outside' which is related to our program Green Hour, http://www.nwf.org/playandobserve/, and is about encouraging parents to have their children spend more time outside enjoying nature. I compliment parents."[22]

Another valuable source of keywords is to run a search engine referral report (the words that people type into Google or other search engine to find an organization's web site). Analyze the keywords that people are using to tag or identify the organization's web content or blog posts in social bookmarking sites like Delicious or StumbleUpon. Apollo Gonzales, the social media campaign manager for the Natural Resources Defense Council (NRDC), conducted an analysis of keywords used to tag his organization's blog posts on environmental issues and was able to identify a lexicon used by people for or against the issue. This helped NRDC hone its social media keyword searches.

Finally, as Wendy Harman, the social media strategist for the Red Cross, advises, "You may not know what is not worth searching until you try searching on it and revise it based on what you see. Don't assume that you'll get it right on the first try, either. It takes fine-tuning of those key words before you get it right."

Tools

There are a variety of free and fee-based monitoring and tracking tools available for the listening process. The most important tool, however, is an RSS reader, software that grabs fresh content from blog posts, web sites, and Twitter, and facilitates "ongoing Google searches"—all of which are essential to the listening process. With RSS, it's possible to check for new content in one place without running all over the web to see if sites have been updated. Most RSS readers are free. (For additional tutorials and tips on using RSS readers, see the Nonprofit Technology Network's [NTEN] WeAreMedia ToolBox at http://www.wearemedia.org/.)[23]

Listening tools consist of monitoring, tracking, and analytics software. Many nonprofits begin listening using free tools. There are two important reasons to migrate to professional tools. The volume of results from the listening effort is so large that it is impossible for one human to synthesize and condense the findings into actionable information. The professional tools are designed to facilitate a team's work flow as well as to reduce time-consuming cutting and pasting. It is important to remember that the skills needed—composing keywords—are the same when using both free and paid tools. At the time of writing this chapter, this category of monitoring and tracking tools was changing very quickly, with new tools being added and free ones disappearing. (For a comprehensive list of social media tracking and monitoring tools visit http://socialmedia-listening.wikispaces.com/Tools.[24])

Nonprofits will need to consider fee-based services when it becomes impossible to manage a high volume of mentions. Professional tools and services, such as Radian6, BuzzLogic, Trackur, and Filtrbox can help analyze and understand the magnitude and sentiment of conversations around a nonprofit's brand, which would be extremely labor intensive if done manually. Services start out at free trial for a month and shoot up to thousands of dollars for large institutions with multiple users. When considering a paid service, nonprofits should do their due diligence for the different vendors and select the one that best matches their needs.

The number of professional listening tools has grown rapidly over the past year and will continue to grow as more companies adopt social media and begin with listening.[25] When the nonprofit's listening activities have become established and the need for professional software has become obvious, the social media team needs to decide whether it wants software for tracking conversations or to hire a consultant to do the tracking and provide a report. The difference is a trade-off between the time required for the do-it-yourself approach or the cost of hiring a consultant.

Listening as the Gateway: American Red Cross Case Study

The American Red Cross entered the social media space as a relative early adopter, just after Hurricane Katrina. The Red Cross knew there were negative blog posts about its disaster-relief efforts related to the devastating hurricane, but it had no capacity to respond, let alone monitor. In 2006, it hired Wendy Harman, a social media integrator, to "combat" bloggers and to increase organizational transparency.[26]

As Wendy Harman, whose current title is social media manager, says, "It felt like we were going to war. There were concerns about negative comments, fear even." Harman's first task was to get a handle on the existing conversation. There were hundreds of mentions across social media platforms each day. Also, "There is an exponential increase in times of disaster, nature, man-made and PR varieties. We monitor and track all of it, and try to respond to a lot of it."

The American Red Cross started a listening program prior to a social media campaign because it wanted to correct misinformation, to be informed about public opinion, to track conversation trends, to identify influencers, and to build relationships. Wendy Harman notes, "We needed to listen and engage first before we could do anything successfully with social media."

Listening to bloggers initially, and later to Twitter and other sources, has given the Red Cross the ability to successfully correct misinformation. Says Harman, "We have the ability to track conversation in great detail. For example, most people who blog about their blood donation experience also mention the type of cookie they receive and other intimate details of the experience. These conversations inform advertising and outreach to increase blood donations, which of course is one metric for success."

What surprised the staff at the Red Cross, and even Harman herself, was that most of the conversations were positive. Harman notes, "Instead of combating bloggers, we found that most are passionate and positive and want to help. Social media offers us a way to engage them and tell their stories about their experience with us to others." Perhaps the biggest benefit that the Red Cross reaped from its listening efforts is that they drove internal adoption of social media use and eventually informed the organization's overall strategy of social media presence. Wendy observes that others on staff, including senior staff, are no longer afraid of negative comments or posts. "The opposite of hate is indifference; if someone bothers to post a negative comment it means they care." The organization now views negative comments as an opportunity to educate and improve what it is doing.

Listening has also led to improvements in customer service. For example, a blogger write a post complaining about a Red Cross class at a local affiliate that the blogger thought was less than satisfactory.[27] Harman forwarded the comment to the local chapter director, who contacted the blogger. As the blogger mentions in a follow-up post, "Someone found my blog post and told the local chapter director. He called me to talk about it honestly. They care about me and they're willing to go the extra mile. This gives the American Red Cross *huge* points. I am now significantly more likely to take another class than I was before."

What started in 2007 as a series of listening and engaging experiments has now begun to pay off. In December 2008, thousands of Facebook members helped leverage a $50,000 donation from the Western Union Foundation by voting for the American Red Cross and its disaster-relief efforts on Facebook. The $50,000 donation contributed to a broader American Red Cross goal to raise $100 million for disaster relief.

Wendy Harman notes that employees at the Red Cross were initially blocked from accessing social networking sites, like Facebook, from work. Recently, a change in policy has allowed access, in part, because of the listening work undertaken with Harman's leadership.[28]

Harman, a self-described professional listener, spends approximately 10 hours per week listening. She has a daily routine. She notes, "We started with the free tools. It isn't rocket science, just keyword searches across social media platforms, adding additional keywords to track if there are special circumstances." Harman also culls and compiles daily mentions on blogs into a one-page update that is distributed widely to internal staff at the American Red Cross and affiliates.

Because she has been able to demonstrate the value of listening and how a professional tool can save valuable staff time, the American Red Cross is now using the professional listening and analytics tool Radian6 along with free tools. Notes Harman, "Listening is about 25 percent of my job and in the beginning it took a little bit longer because I had a learning curve."

As the professional listener on the Red Cross staff, her main challenge is dealing with the tsunami of information to analyze. "The professional tools get rid of a lot of cut and pasting, so that has helped. Also, we're looking at ways to represent the information visually. For example, I've bookmarked posts about people talking about the Red Cross and ran it through Wordle.com, a tool that creates a visual tag cloud."

The key metric Harman uses to help guide whether the organization should comment on a blog is the number of readers and Technorati authority ranking, which determines the blogger's influence. As Harman notes, "Authority matters but is not everything. Sometimes the most compelling story or most pressing issue comes from social media user with smallest influence."

Harman says that responses typically fall into several categories. These include relationship building (someone is saying something nice about us and we say, "Thank you") or there is a customer service issue or perception that needs to be addressed. Harman also reviews reports over time to look at different trends and to evaluate areas where people find their interaction with the Red Cross compelling enough to write about it on a blog or share it on Twitter. This information not only fuels the Red Cross's social media strategy but also informs program design, fundraising, communications, and virtually the entire organization.

Harman says that it is very important to document anecdotal evidence when making the case for the ROI of social media, especially feedback from staff members about how the listening process supports their work. She also documents how external stakeholders have engaged with the Red Cross by sharing screen captures of the actual Twitter "tweet" or blog comment. This drives adoption. Says Harman, "Now, everyone on staff wants the feedback. Documenting the successful one-on-one outreach with stakeholders has really built the groundwork for social media fundraising and communications campaigns."

Over time, the organization has come to appreciate and value the listening reports. And the Red Cross community knows that the organization is listening, and the conversation has changed and relationships have deepened. Most recently, engagement has also led to dollars. In May 2009, the Red Cross was 1 of 10 organizations selected by Target to participate in a Facebook competition where supporters voted for a share of the corporate philanthropy budget of $3 million.[29] The Red Cross was able to leverage a donation of $750,000.

As Wendy Harman sums it up, "Social media listening has become the gateway drug of the organization."

LEARNING FROM MEASURING

Learning means using experiments with metrics and the right questions at the right point to understand what works and what doesn't. Learning takes place in real time as the social media strategy unfolds and as an evaluative process at the conclusion. Most important, this is a reflective process—either alone or as a team—to harvest insights.

The secret sauce to social media success lies in careful experimentation. That means that nonprofits need to create a safe (or safer) place to fail. In the early stages of social media implementation, there will be mistakes, blowups, and malfunctions. This can be a difficult cultural shift for some organizations that are risk averse. The best approach is to start small, think big, and reiterate over and over again. As Clay Shirky said during the NTEN Nonprofit Technology Conference in San Francisco in April 2009, "We spend more time figuring out whether something is a good idea than we would have just trying it."[30]

Observes Wendy Harman of the Red Cross, "With social media, you must launch small 'proof of concept' experiments as part of an educational process for creating an effective social media strategy."[31] She advises identifying a project that won't take too much time and that relates to the nonprofit's communications goals. She suggests, "As you implement, document your successes and challenges. Be sure to interview those you connect with to see if they think your listening or outreach was valuable. Then rinse and repeat."

Fast, Flexible Learning

It is important to be intentional about learning, and this requires thinking like a scientist and keeping a journal. For social media, this translates into documenting and tweaking as the campaign unfolds. The process of real-time learning can help improve communications and messaging, the identification of influencers, and many other important elements of a social media strategy.

Scott Henderson, the cause marketing director for Media Sauce, who recently spearheaded the HungerPledge Campaign on behalf of Share of Our Strength, "Our primary metric was the number of people signing the pledge and secondarily the dollars contributed. As the campaign was unfolding, we watched those numbers like hawks. It was how we identified one of our super activists, a supporter from Missouri, who single-handedly generated over 500 signatures. We shifted some of our tactics as a result."[32]

Picking the Right Metrics

"You can't manage what you don't measure" may be an old management maxim, but no place it is more accurate than in implementing a social media strategy and measuring to get better results. To improve social media strategy results over time, it is imperative to know whether a result is getting better or worse according to a specific metric. In the first 18 months, the key learning task is to compare social media strategy results against set metrics for engagement and to ask guiding questions to harvest insights.

The most important step is to pick the right hard data points or metrics that enable you to measure the social media strategy objective. The metrics used are quite different from web site metrics, as shown in Table 1.2. And remember that numbers alone are meaningless unless they are used to harvest insights and look for trends.

Reiterate and Adapt

The definition of adapting is using your insights to make corrections to improve social media results in the next reiteration of your campaign strategy.

Reframing Mistakes

Reiteration is very important, but it may be difficult because it means reframing mistakes and failure. This can be difficult if the organization's culture embraces only perfection.

It is much easier to adapt a social media project at a tactical level than to change or improve other areas in an organization that social media might shine a light on—customer service, programs, and services. And making changes in those areas may require rethinking staffing and work flow, or involving leadership and others in the organization. Wendy Harman recalls, "We were hearing some people complain about getting more than one reminder to donate blood from some chapters. We investigated and learned that the complaints had to do with a software system issue and that it was wasn't something that could be fixed overnight."

It may be that the organization's social media strategy and implementation is housed in the wrong department. Danielle Brigida, of the National Wildlife Federation, initially started in the membership department, but the organization quickly discovered that education was a more appropriate place for the organization to begin its exploration of social media. The organization understood the opportunity costs of not implementing a social media strategy. It understood that if engagements and relationships were at the heart of social media, then starting off the strategy in the education department would be best. Brigida is now serving as internal consultant for other departments in how to incorporate social media strategy.[33]

Humane Society of the United States—Learn and Adapt to Bring in Dollars

In February, 2009, the Humane Society of the United States, an early adopter of social media, launched an online photo contest in honor of Spay Day.[34] The contest combined wisdom of the crowds with person-to-person, or rather dog-to-person, fundraising. Humane Society supporters could upload a photo of their pets for the contest and had the option of creating a customized fundraising page where they could reach out to their friends for donations.

The organization's social media strategy helped make its second annual Spay Day Online Pet Photo Contest a resounding success. It raised more than $600,000 from more than 40,000 entrants. Carie Lewis, the society's social networking manager, says, "Facebook was the number one referrer to the photo contest web site, and the Facebook app had a utilization rate of 60 percent. Also, only 42 percent of the entrants came from existing HSUS members."

Over the years, Lewis, an early adopter of social media for her organization, has become an example of how listening, learning, and adapting ultimately leads to dollars. In 2007, the Humane Society implemented its first photo petition campaign to protest Wendy's and the restaurant chain's treatment of animals. It tracked the number of photo submissions but also listened carefully to the responses from participants.

As Lewis mentions, "Since this was our first run at a photo petition, it was difficult to get across exactly what we wanted people to do without writing a book. So every person that wrote in and needed help was answered personally. This gave us a good idea of how to more clearly explain ourselves next time."[35] This particular photo campaign had many technical glitches, and ultimately the number of submissions was less than impressive. Did the Humane Society proclaim that photo competitions were a waste of time? No.

The next photo contest iteration was LOL Seals, which made it as easy as possible for people to participate. That's what the organization had learned from the first campaign. The first contest required that supporters upload and tag their photos manually, which meant that contest participants had to create a Flickr account and understand how tagging works. This proved too much of a barrier for participation. For that contest, the Humane Society used the Flickr Application Programming Interface (API), which made entering, uploading a photo, and captioning automatic. The Humane Society had about 3,000 submissions and captured about 2,000 new e-mail addresses. As Lewis notes, "We looked at the cost of acquisition of these email addresses as well as the life time value and there was definitely an ROI."

The secret to the Humane Society's success with social media is not only using metrics to learn what works and what doesn't but also reiterating the strategy on the basis of fast and flexible learning. With some years of experience and knowing what works and what doesn't, the Humane Society can most definitely demonstrate impact and a dollar return.

Grace Markarian, the online communications manager for the Humane Society of the United States, described how integrating social media into the organization's communications, advocacy, and fundraising efforts has helped break down staff silos and introduce a new approach to planning. The team has daily nine-minute meetings, unless there is something very important that makes the meetings run a few minutes longer. These short briefing meetings have helped the team to be more efficient and effective with every aspect of multichannel campaigns, particularly social media.

The Humane Society looks at both the tangible and the intangible benefits provided by the social media strategy, as shown in the list that follows:

Tangible and Intangible Benefits of Social Media

Tangible:

- Increased e-mail database
- Obtained original content
- Obtained free public service announcements
- Raised money
- Recruited new donors
- Recruited members, fans, friends

Intangible

- Raised awareness about issues
- Engaged people to participate in the issues
- Generated discussions on our issues
- Received buy-in from the top
- Received recognition and media attention (online buzz)

As the Humane Society well knows, it is important to get buy-in from the organization's leadership and to move past fears of losing control of messaging.[36] The Humane Society has accepted that it takes time listen and build a network of supporters before seeing dollars. Through months and months of experimentation and learning, the Humane Society has learned the following: (1) Integrating social media into a nonprofit's marketing and fundraising campaign can help build buzz and online actions (like donations) slowly, although it requires using other channels; (2) social media allows the organization to reach audiences it may not reach through other channels or at all, but resources must be allocated to monitor and communicate with those audiences to sustain success; and (3) participating on social networking sites allows the opportunity to experiment with new technologies but requires constant willingness to learn. This list shows some metrics used to measure success and make strategy improvements.

Metrics Used to Measure Success and Make Improvements

- No. of submissions/comments
- No. of friends, fans, members over time
- No. of new names added to e-mail file
- No. of donations/amount of donations
- No. of video/photo views
- No. of subscribers (RSS, blog)
- No. of blog and wall comments

- No. of voting participants
- No. of blogs linking to us/covering our story (consider quality)
- No. of friends recruited
- Frequency of bulletin reposts on MySpace
- Content of keywords, comments (what are people talking about?)

CONCLUSION

Social media is not a fad: It will become an increasingly important part of the nonprofit toolbox—not only for fundraising and marketing but also for program

TABLE 1.3   SOCIAL MEDIA ROI, STEP BY STEP

Step	Description
Step 1: Establish goals	Clear and measurable Link to organization's communications or fundraising plan Generate a set of learning questions that help you understand how to improve
Step 2: Identify the value	List how social media will solve a problem Identify the value it will offer–how will it help move forward other goals? Value might include customer service, new donors, new prospects, market research, and program improvement
Step 3: Pick the right metrics	Is your goal to build relationships? Use engagement metrics Is your goal fundraising or communication? Use dollars, acquisition costs, or new donors
Step 4: Find your audience	Who are they? What about your organization or issue is important to them? Where do they hang out on social media spaces?
Step 5: Listen	Set up your listening and monitoring system Listen and use what you learn to inform your strategy and initial engagement Let others in your organization know what people are saying Establish a response policy before you begin
Step 5: Get started	Engage with stakeholders and supporters Identify and work with influencers Set up presence Get others to remix and spread your message Build your network or community Document your strategy as it unfolds, tweak, and refine. Don't forget to get qualitative information like screen captures and quotes
Step 6: Measure	Use analytics tools to measure results using metrics against goals
Step 7: Reflect and reiterate	Review your metrics data and your documentation and reflect on what worked and what didn't Design the next project applying those learnings

delivery. As social media practices, techniques, and analytics mature, social media analytics software and agreement on standardized metrics are in the embryonic stages.[37] Savvy nonprofit leaders will consider the opportunity cost of not getting started soon. As Marnie Webb, co-CEO of TechSoup Global, said during a panel at the Craigslist Foundation Nonprofit Boot Camp on the future of technology for nonprofits, "The past, present, and future of nonprofits has been connecting people. Facebook is better at organizing people than nonprofits. Nonprofits can no longer ignore social media or they risk becoming irrelevant."[38] As Carie Lewis of the Humane Society says, "You have to take the time to build trust, and really roll up your sleeves and get dirty. Social Media takes a lot of time and efforts, but if done right, it can really pay off."[39] Whether a nonprofit engages deeply on many social media channels or takes a selective approach, it is time to get started or risk being left behind. The ROI steps are shown in Table 1.3.

Beth Kanter is the author of Beth's Blog: How Nonprofits Can Use Social Media (http://beth.typepad.com), one of the longest-running and most popular blogs for nonprofits. Beth is the coauthor of *The Networked Nonprofit*, to be published by Wiley in 2010. She has contributed chapters to several books, including *Managing Technology to Meet Your Mission: A Strategic Guide for Nonprofit Leaders*, published in 2009. A much-in-demand speaker and trainer at nonprofit conferences, she has been invited to present at some of the leading social media industry conferences, including O'Reilly's Graphing Social Patterns, Gnomedex, SWSX, Blogher, and PodCamp. In 2009, *Fast Company Magazine* named her one of the most influential women in technology and *BusinessWeek* named her one of its "Voices of Innovation for Social Media." She is visiting scholar for social media and nonprofits for the Packard Foundation. She lives with her husband and two children, Harry and Sara, in California.

CHAPTER 2

Path to Managing Your Organization Using Online Tools

MICHAEL SOLA AND TIM KOBOSKO

Premise: You are an executive director or CEO, perhaps even a member or head of a board of directors, and the topic of online tools is all you hear, day in and day out. You need to know about this topic, at the heart of all good business models, to properly manage the organization and bring it to greater levels of efficiency and success.

Social networking just happens to be one of the many tools at your disposal with which you can connect your organization to a much broader audience. You can use these tools to be more efficient and successful—but there lies the rub, as the cookie-cutter approach simply doesn't work. All we can do is follow the three "L"s—look, listen and learn.

FRANK INTRODUCTIONS

I'm going to be totally up front, honest, straightforward—nothing up my sleeves, frank. There is one simple fact: There is no silver bullet, no one-size-fits-all approach. What works for me may not work for you.

Neither of us are journalistic majors or marketing gurus; we are technologists who shout, "Tech from the mountaintops!" with hopes that those in the trenches and valleys below will listen. Any technologist worth his or her salt needs to understand the business needs, or we can't survive.

What I can tell you about the path to managing your organization's online presence is this: This chapter takes a page out of the writing experience relayed to me by the writer-producer David Simon. Back in early 2007 while attending a public forum at Loyola College in Maryland, Simon, an author or producer of the acclaimed HBO programs *The Wire*, *Generation Kill*, and *The Corner*, shared his views on the end of the American empire.

Simon was addressing mostly journalism majors in the room. He was quick to offer the disclaimer that he was no expert: He claimed he was a C student in school, which got quite a laugh from the three thousand or so attendees. What he did offer to those wanting to know was the formula for telling a good story, one undeniable, hard-learned lesson: Write what you know.

There is a ton of material available on this and that business model and the pitfalls and benefits of Web 2.0, 2.5, and dare I say 3.0. But all we can do here is relay our experiences and what we have done to introduce online tools into our respective organizations. We are going to write what we know, so welcome aboard.

Go Left; No, Go Right

My experience in the implementation of technical solutions has really taken a turn, and although we can point to the nature of the industry as our constant driver, I have to admit that, today, we're heading in a most welcome direction.

What is the goal, and how do we get there? I hear those questions a lot. Focus on the goal, but more important, know the goal. It's like that great line in the movie *Caddyshack* when Chevy Chase's character has blindfolded himself. As he's putting, he says, "Be the ball." We need to identify the ball.

As I write this chapter, I am into my seventh month as lead technologist for the well-respected National Wildlife Federation (NWF). In my second week, I was thrust headfirst into the organization's deep end of the tech pool, where implementation of a SharePoint platform had been started. This was a platform that would become the face our public would eventually interact with.

The intent was to use SharePoint as a launching point of content, to capture polling information, to use RSS feeds to collaborate and engage not just members but also affiliates and partner organizations—to harness some Web 2.0 tools into a single platform that kept institutional knowledge and data internal to the organization and not sitting in the "cloud."

I was excited to see NWF move in this direction, but as I began the process of looking and listening, I started asking questions. Trying to be the ball wasn't simple. In fact, the more I tried to be the ball, the more I realized that the ball had no chance of going into the hole. The hole was nowhere to be found:

- During polling, it became clear that the organization had a bad taste of SharePoint from a previous attempt.
- We didn't have infrastructure in place at our field offices to allow for staff to easily access the portal.
- We were a whole version behind in Microsoft Office.

- Hardware and memory upgrades were required.
- The rather outdated Novell GroupWise was in place instead of Outlook or Exchange.
- There hadn't been any training.
- The budget was allocated for this fiscal year but not the next, and the clock was ticking.

The realization for me in this case was that the organization's intent was solid, but getting there was going to be a challenge, not just technically but also culturally. The journey was going to be rough ride, and for the road ahead, we needed not only a well-thought-out map but also acceptance and buy-in from the very top. Without that, we were headed for a dead end in trying to move into an interactive, two-way conversation mode of operating.

WHEN IS IT SAFE TO GO DOWN THAT ROAD?

The challenge of moving into Web .x is looking not only to the outside but also to what's inside, or rather, what's behind the curtain.

Most technologists will agree that integrating as much of the data that an organization collects is the only way to get a true sense of the business. If you can't track what your clients are doing or saying, then how on earth can you provide what they want?

You probably cringe when you see departments or organizations heading down a path without considering how a consolidated data plan will either streamline the collection of data or maintain institutional knowledge.

At NWF, almost a quarter of the organization participates in a Yammer group (www.yammer.com) that has become a go-to place of sorts for distributing links and information that would normally get lost in the e-mail shuffle of the daily workload. The group members effectively started their own internal, unified collection of data.

But the data, the comments, the links, the biographies—all of that resides outside of the organization, and at any point of time, they could become unaccessible if Yammer decides to call it a day and pack up its playground. And here is a scary question: Do you really know who is mining all the data that "free" services like Yammer, Facebook, etc., are collecting?? How free is free?

KNOW THY CLIENT

With respect to customer needs, I want to share an excerpt from my blog (http://michaelsola.posterous.com/know-thy-audience) that I posted after returning from the annual Blackbaud Target User Forum held in Boston in 2009:

> We've all been caught up in the concepts of trying to put a return on the numbers as we work towards finding the right tools to fit into the strategies that organizations are trying to utilize on the social networking front. And it occurred to me as I was putting together some research for this book chapter that sometimes numbers for numbers' sake isn't the be all/end all for business to look at, especially on the tech front. Implementing the right tools to track, slice, dice, segment, while important, doesn't mean much if all we are doing is cultivating followers—rather shouldn't we be looking to engage our "tribe" to take on a leadership role? Wouldn't having more leaders translate into more action? More followers?

But are we asking the right questions to find out who our leaders are? If so, what are we doing with the answers?

At the forum, there was a session called "Navigating the Multi-Channel Challenge," headed up by Beth Isikoff, senior director of business development at Merkle Inc. Isikoff shared some illuminating personal experience about how she became as a member of and donor to six different nonprofit organizations by using different points of engagement, which she documented to gauge the nonprofits' relationship-building techniques. She challenged the group to ask the following: "At what point in the relationship do marketers cross channels and begin to communicate with our 'tribes' by not asking the usual questions? Because asking the right questions is invaluable if you hope to engage and cultivate your followers into leaders."

Halfway into the presentation, Isikoff started talking about how a staff member of one of the nonprofits she had joined over a phone call started asking her a series of polling questions. Halfway into that conversation, Isikoff started asking her own questions, like "Why are you asking me that?" The questions didn't resonate or connect her with the mission of the organization, and they did nothing to empower her to do more for the group. That made Isikoff realize that we don't ask the right questions. She used this story as an example of not just asking the right questions but also getting at what matters. She asked the room, filled with about 85 development folks, the following:

- How many of you are pet owners? Three-quarters of the room stood.
- If you have given your pet a treat, something other then just food, please remain standing. About two-thirds remained standing.
- Of those standing, how many got the treat for your pet as a present either for a holiday or for an event? Half of those remained standing.

- Of those still standing, how many of you gift-wrapped your pet's present? Two-thirds of those still standing sat down.

We had gone from 60 pet owners to about 10 real pet enthusiasts, and all because we had asked the right questions. The few folks remaining were obviously the hard-core pet lovers, the movers, the shakers, the ones who would carry your banner into battle. Those are the folks we want to be our leaders, the ones we are going to get the most out of and cultivate to that next level. We want to spend the majority of our time on that group, because in the end, it's not about large quantities of followers; it's about a small handful of leaders.

Knowing who you can transition from follower to leader has been the focal point of many strategy sessions, and it is key to moving an organization into the digital age. As the author and well-known speaker Seth Godin stated in his book *Tribes*: "Followers who do nothing but mindlessly follow instructions, let you down."

Social networking gives you an opportunity to cultivate and engage potential leaders at a much higher level and quickly, but it has to be more then just following or showing up. For a successful program, you have to empower them to take action and become part of your movement or cause. Don't you want to know who's gift-wrapping a dog bone?

WHEN PERSONABLE IS GOOD

The NWF has gone after a new audience and is doing so across digital channels. The organization still cultivates existing members to engage digitally, not in an aggressive way, but it does try to capitalize on the opportunity whenever it comes up.

During a recent phone bank, operation staff called members to ask them to call their respective representatives in order to push for the passage of climate-change legislation. The NWF used the hosted software service Activate (http://www.talkupactivate.com), which not only automatically dialed calls on the basis of the NWF's data but also showed staff a script, the name and phone number of the member's legislator, and biographical information for the member. Here are some benefits of Activate:

- The NWF could not only flag responses but also capture more information that may not have been on file, such as e-mail addresses.
- The NWF had the ability to direct members to a specific web page where they could learn more and take further action.
- The NWF added the captured data into the record and updated it to primary storage.

Activate was a very easy-to-use program, and one that allowed more than 25 staff members to contact more than 1,000 NWF members within an hour. The exercise resulted in some very positive outcomes. When the bill later passed, the NWF followed up with members who took action to thank them and inform them of how their actions helped.

The NWF was able to capture results of the exercise and cross department lines. It was an organizational endeavor, and that formula results in the building of relationships. The proof is in the numbers, and it's in the personal feedback and comments that the NWF received in reply.

Who Wants to Play in My Sandbox?

We have all heard that if you build it, they will come. Well, there is little doubt that in today's tech climate that statement is a falsehood. If the *Field of Dreams* strategy doesn't work, then who is it we are really trying to reach, and why don't they want to play in my sandbox?

Part of implementing what I call Nonprofits 2.0 is creating a process that houses the tools that engage members and allow organizations to manage that incredible asset that we in the tech world call data. I want my sandbox to have the tools to capture data and reports on those data. I want to play in it along with our base.

Nonprofits 2.0 mean two-way dialogue. Two-way dialogue is a sentiment I have heard about in many conferences and seminars. This generation is made up of digital natives. They live and breathe tech. They are online looking for an opportunity to speak and not just be spoken to. We want them to play in our sandbox.

Every Blog Counts

When I started writing a tech blog in early 2007, the goal for me was simple:

- Document a project.
- Share with the vendor the progress of the project.
- Share the experiences of the tech program's implementation with my nonprofit peers.
- Highlight the members of my team.
- Showcase my organization's role as an early adopter of a new direct marketing management software.

Over the years, I have become well known for implementing solutions and working inside the organization to partner with my peers. Many of the technical solutions required the acquisition of funding, as the IT coffers were typically bare. Partnering was key if I was to implement technology to fit a need. So the opportunity to share that experience and do it using tools I had been promoting was very compelling. It would show how storytelling could be engaging. It was time to put up or shut up, as they say.

What made my blog stand out from the standard company blog was that, for the most part, it was void of any environmental message. In fact, I made the point early on that, though I would tie in how tech was working with the organization's programs, I would not necessarily get into the details of how nitrogen reduction and oxygen depletion were harming the Chesapeake Bay. Those things were important to the organization's programs, but I didn't think they translated into an exciting blog. My approach was not necessarily well received, and at times, it was a source of great contention with management, as they had not bought into a personal approach to blogging.

At that time, most blogs regurgitated press releases and read like a police blotter in the local paper. Of course, not every post back then was void of emotion, but the idea of being personable was not the norm. That wasn't the fault of those who were posting; there simply wasn't a focus on doing anything more then using blogs as another means to promote press.

Fast-forward a few months to a roundtable discussion with a variety of vendors that my team brought together in an attempt to brief 20 or so web-oriented stakeholders in the organization about best practices for Web 2.0 tools. During the Q&A session, the panel pointed out my tech blog as an example of how a more casual personal style can help form a connection. I remember actually yelping "Woohoo!" Was the personal approach the right one? I don't know. The numbers of hits and comments were never huge, but they were respectable. Of course, those hits might just have been from my mother, so it's hard to say.

A personal approach clearly resonates across networks. Take Twitter, for example. Twitter gives users 140 characters to connect with others and build a relationship. That's not an impossible task. But you can't regurgitate press releases and quote company slogans over and over again. So how on earth can you connect when you really need to engage your followers so they respond and become leaders?

The year 2009's annual nonprofit CIO for Good Summit discussed the use of Twitter and how it affected policy and best practices. All the members were asked whether they "tweeted": 90 percent raised their hands. When asked whether they tweeted just business news, 90 percent of the first group kept their hands up. When asked how many tweeted about personal happenings, just 10 percent raised their hands. There were interesting responses to the question of why people didn't tweet personal information but just one resounding theme, and it starts at the top: policy. Policy and best practices forbid anything of a personal, unsanctioned nature to be shared publicly.

That being said, you might ask, Why? Why restrict what your staff is permitted to say? Can you really control what is said about your organization? If you think you can, please put the book down now—the train hasn't left without you; it never even stopped at your station.

Are You Hearing Me Now?

If you aren't out there representing the good the bad and the ugly of your organization, have no doubt that someone else most assuredly is. For many of us who implement technical solutions, it falls on us to enact and enforce policy. For example, a blogging policy can't be written in a vacuum. If so, when it's distributed at departmental meetings, it will meet so much resistance that it will have to be quickly shelved.

The NWF is having discussions about a separate policy on the use of social media. Such policies seem inevitable, even though many organizations rely on having staff follow existing policies. But if existing policies are weak or outdated, then it's time to revisit them. For example, many current communication standard practices are probably broad and were written before the advent of social media tools like Twitter. So it makes sense to fine-tune policies. It's important for legal, web, finance, communications, and tech staff to review any policy, but like all policies, a social media policy still comes down to enforcement and monitoring.

Members of nonprofits want to be communicated with. So you should provide as many options as possible; sit back; and then look, listen, and learn to find out what their needs are. You can do so through content, data collection, data processing—just realize that it's about connecting and cultivating the content that brings your network together. Otherwise, you'll have a ton of followers but few leaders.

I Love Italian, and So Do You

My first team exercise at NWF was an eye-opener: "Building Sustainable Communities through Network Building," or network weaving, as we called it. The session pulled together more than 20 program leaders from the national offices; stakeholders from headquarters; the chief operating officers; and me, the new guy. I wasn't sure what I could or would contribute, but I was quickly surprised and engaged almost from the word "go."

As part of the one-day retreat, we each had to conduct interviews with several people whom we would consider leaders (formal or informal). The idea was to learn about their views on weaving a viable network together for a specific cause that didn't have to be related to the organization. We were simply getting ideas.

We sat down as a group and began a discussion on the barriers to an effective community network and what was enabling us to be successful. Our facilitator was Dave Schrader from LeadingWork (http://www.leading-work.com), who led the group in listing the enablers and barriers to building networks. After the discussion, we broke into groups of four. On each group's table were red-and-white tablecloths and paper and markers. I was very excited—and reminded of Romano's Macaroni Grill decor. The idea was to have a 15-minute conversation at the table. Then one "host" would stay at the table and the three others would move to the next table. In this way, we didn't just talk about the concepts of building networks; we actually had conversations that continued to take shape even after some participants moved on to the next table.

Schrader calls this the world-café approach (from the book *The World Café: Shaping Our Futures through Conversations That Matter*, by Juanita Brown and David Isaacs), and it was a resounding hit. People at the table came from different programs, different levels of understanding, different parts of the country, and different backgrounds. Yet in the end, everyone walked away with a clear understanding of how important community building was, and how it would further the mission of the organization. The approach gave us a road map.

In that one-day retreat I learned almost as much about the organization as I had after being exposed to it for a month—now that's the power of networking! Bringing such a wide range of stakeholders together worked in large part because of who was tapped for the group. Picking the right people to be part of the process was as important an investment as the tools used to implement social networking in the organization. The participants would become the organization's leaders and early adopters.

SHOW ME MY MONEY

So you have your stakeholders, your players, your leaders and adopters, and hopefully a mission or a passion you are looking to promote and connect with your members. Now comes the part we all dread on the management side of the house: measurements. "Return on investment" (or ROI) is a dreaded phrase for some nonprofit executives. Although ROI is routinely used in the for-profit world, it has become a more common term in nonprofit boardrooms. In a down economic climate, the term is often tossed around even more frequently. As revenue streams are challenged and every expense line questioned, the question of ROI keeps popping up.

In its strictest sense, ROI refers to the ratio of money gained or lost on an investment relative to the initial investment. The amount of money gained or lost may be referred to as either profit and loss or gain and loss. This ROI methodology is used every day in the business world. But in a perfect world, ROI would be easily measured. If the cost of a project can be accurately accounted for and the benefit of the project determined, all projects could be approved or disapproved accordingly. The reality of projects, though, especially ones involving technology and the online world, is that they are very hard to measure and predict. Throw in other variables, including economic conditions and constituent behavior, and the ROI question becomes even more difficult.

KEEPING UP WITH THE JONES

The online world evolves and changes at such a fast pace that the variables you intend to measure can change in short order. Our constituents visit and do business with nonprofits online but also with the Amazons and Googles of the for-profit universe. It seems that nonprofits get measured against the for-profit world in terms of ease-of-use and end-user experience.

Constituents really don't care if nonprofits have limited resources in terms of budget and staff compared to the for-profit companies they do online business with. The user experience should rival what you get when you visit Amazon or Google, at least in the eyes of the constituent.

Online giving, or the ability to donate to an organization via a secure web site, is one of most common ROI issues for nonprofits. Most organizations understand that they need to facilitate online giving. The question becomes whether to develop the application in-house or to outsource it to a vendor that specializes in collecting donations on behalf of organizations.

Simply stated, an organization must calculate the total cost of implementing an online-giving solution and then the total amount of online gifts expected. The total cost should be an all-in cost, meaning it should include every expense, such as labor (of the application's developer and gift processing), software, secure certificates, bandwidth, server time, marketing efforts, and merchant fees related to online donations.

Fundraising consultants and vendors can assist in predicting the number and size of gifts. Organizations of similar size and mission may share their online-giving trends. Last, nonprofit organizations and publications might have research or other documentation to assist in developing a reasonable estimate for online gifts.

EXCUSE ME, DO YOU HAVE THE TIME?

Your organization should agree on a realistic time frame for measuring ROI. To fairly measure the ROI of an online initiative, it must be active for a reasonable amount of time. Given that most of the expense occurs in advance of the initiative being available and running, a substantial amount of time needs to pass before a measurement can be taken.

Another way to think about ROI is according to the soft gains or losses that a nonprofit might experience. "Soft" gains or losses refer to items that are not easy to calculate or measure. Hard gains or losses usually relate to investment in terms of dollars.

An example of using ROI to measure the success of a project is as follows: A nonprofit decides to invest in web-based software that allows for constituents to self-report address, phone, and e-mail information. This information is then automatically imported into the back-end database. This database is the source for mailings, outbound telemarketing, and e-mail messages. The database quality improves as the software is implemented. And the quality and accuracy of the data incrementally improve as more and more constituents update their information.

Over time, with more accurate data, the ability to communicate with constituents increases. The increase may not directly achieve more hard gains in terms of revenue (e.g., memberships, donations), but it could result in soft gains in terms of educating constituents or increasing their awareness of a subject near and dear to the organization.

ONE FOR YOU, ONE FOR ME; TWO FOR YOU, AND ONE, TWO FOR ME

Another way to think of ROI is not in terms of a revenue increase but in terms of the ability to mitigate expenses. In the previous section, we saw how an organization can reduce expenses as its database becomes more accurate. This would manifest in lower return postage costs for mailings, more phone calls answered during telemarketing efforts, and increased penetration and open rates for e-mail.

With these figures in hand, an ROI calculation can be made and presented as a savings rather than a gain. In some cases, an initiative may increase revenue as well as decrease an expense.

At NWF, I have been able to postpone the ROI discussion for social media and networking projects. At NWF we believe that we need to engage in some social media projects regardless of the payback. This decision is based on an effort to develop two-way communications with our base of supporters.

In summary, calculating ROI is a useful exercise for understanding the true costs and benefits of an endeavor. Like most things in life, you get better at calculating ROI the more you do it and come to understand how to better forecast costs and revenue.

WHOSE SANDBOX IS THIS?

If you have a desire to move your organization into the online world, one of the most basic questions that you must address is staffing. Who will "own" the online strategy and execution? What department or function will be responsible for online activity? Who does the president or CEO turn to when he or she wants to know the status of online initiatives?

Many nonprofits have existed since before the Internet and e-mail became part of everyday life. Such organizations "grew up" with traditional departments like finance, human resources, development, membership, communications, marketing, and information technology. When the boss declared that he or she wanted a web site (probably in the 1990s), there was not a department that could claim responsibility. Responsibility for that initial web site could have resided in several departments, including marketing, communications, information technology, or even development. In many cases, because the executive leadership team did not understand the resources required to manage an online presence, the responsibility was assigned as a collaborative duty.

That collaborative duty, regardless of which department was tasked with the assignment, may have gone to a younger employee or to someone who had experience with web sites. In some cases, organizations looked outside for vendors or consultants to host a site.

Vendors who offered to host a site usually produced sites that looked eerily similar and were static in nature. If you had to make a content update, it took a few days for the change to post. There was no such thing as real time.

It should be noted that there was probably not a direct connection to the back-end database or customer relationship management (CRM) system of the organization. That connection would follow in due time, but in the initial stages, there either was no database associated with the site or, if there was one, it was most likely independent of the fundraising or membership CRM.

Eventually, web management evolved into the creation of a webmaster position. This position's responsibilities vary widely among organizations. It was rare for any two nonprofits to manage their web sites in the same way. Webmasters managed the web site, and their domain stretched from content creation and deployment on the web to programming and application development to allow interaction between the front end (the visible web site) and the back end (the CRM database).

As the online world became more popular and constituents demanded more and more from their organizations in the virtual world, the role of webmaster became incredibly complex and unwieldy.

GOVERNANCE—WHAT IT TAKES TO GET THERE

There are many ways to staff for the online world. Because your organization's web site "touches" your constituents, you need an overall organizational strategy for what you want the web site to do for your organization.

For that strategy to work, an organization must have a framework for the company to understand and adhere to. If everyone on staff were allowed to create and post content without a template or a boilerplate to go by, it would probably lead to a chaotic and poor user experience on the web.

That is not to say you want to stifle staff creativity and enthusiasm for using the web to connect with your constituents. The web is a great way to connect with your members and donors, and every organization should do its best to leverage an online presence. But organizations should do so in such a way that it comes across as a coordinated and tightly integrated platform.

To achieve this, many parts of the organization come into play. Its web presence is as much skilled based as it is personality based. It requires team players who know their job, can work well with others, and are well versed in the organization's online strategy.

In the old days, content alone may have been good enough. After all, a web site was just another way to post the same collateral that you sent via the postal system or e-mailed to your constituents. Nowadays, the online presence must be more than just content.

How much more? That is the question faced by every nonprofit executive. At a minimum, you need to facilitate transactions on the web site. These could be donations or gifts, membership sign-ups, event registrations, or enlisting of volunteers.

It is imperative that whoever takes the lead with the online strategy understand how doing business on the web affects finance. There is the relatively simple task of finding a vendor to help you collect credit card transactions and other transfers online. There are many vendors that can do that for you and do it well. The secret to success is in the collection and disbursement of the monies as well as the proper reconciliation of each and every transaction.

IGNORE THE MAN BEHIND THE CURTAIN

Behind the scenes, there may be business intelligence that delivers content based on the individual. An application developer, database expert, or programmer would be responsible for that customization.

Whether you host your web site yourself or outsource it to a capable vendor, you must have the bandwidth to support users visiting the site. In addition to sufficient bandwidth, end users expect the proper security to be in place so they can have complete confidence when they decide to purchase a good or service or make a donation. Usually, a network engineer or system administrator will handle these duties if the organization hosts the site itself. If you use an outside agency, it will have the same expertise on staff.

No transaction will ever go through if the site is not designed to accommodate such activity. Good web design is part art, part science. When it works, users find what they need and can navigate easily. The colors, fonts, pictures, and video are all pleasing to the eye, and the entire experience is pleasant.

But we have all been to sites where you can't begin to find what you are after, and the look of the site gives you a headache. Web site design is incredibly important and should translate your brand to the web. Because technology and software change so quickly, it is really important that your web design team members stay up to date with current best practices and continue to evolve their skill set.

There's No "I" in "Team"

If a nonprofit cannot afford a web designer or believes that there is not enough work for a full-time web designer, there are many companies that can assist. If this is the route an organization must go, be careful to choose a partner that understands your business. Meetings with staff, key stakeholders, and constituents can ensure that the vendor better understands you and the business you are in. As design work begins, focus groups and usability testing are great tools to gauge how well the design will work with your constituents.

Now that many of the functions of online tools have been delineated and briefly explained, who should be in charge of the online effort? If someone in your organization understands how complex and interdependent the web site is, that is a good start. The leader must be a true team player and understand all facets of the organization and the mission. He or she must have the trust of the president or executive director and be respected by all of senior management. He or she must also be seen as an innovative and independent thinker across the organization. The leader will have to be an inch deep in all of the technical aspects of the online strategy and smart enough to ask an expert when he or she does not have an answer.

Does this someone exist in your organization? The perfect candidate may not be on staff. If that is the case, your organization is not alone. Finding a person with knowledge in all these areas and the right personality and management skills is extremely difficult.

As alluded to earlier in the chapter, a cross-functional team comprises subject-matter experts from across the organization. The number of members is important to consider. You need the team to be large enough to encompass all the skills mentioned herein. If you have too many players on the team, it will be harder to make decisions and get work done in a timely manner. The right number of players will allow the team to make all the decisions without going outside the team for advice.

A high-performing cross-functional team should meet regularly with specific agenda items and the ability to dive into the details of all ongoing projects. These meetings also can serve as brainstorming sessions and a chance to get together to discuss the ever-changing world of web initiatives.

As you analyze the strengths and weaknesses of each candidate, keep in mind how you can best set those candidates up to succeed. Look at attitude before aptitude. If the person is ready for the challenge and a go-getter, then you can surround him or her with good people to ensure success.

Whoever is in charge of the online strategy will feel pressure from all parts of the organization—seniors and subordinates. In addition, the online strategist will be exposed to parts of the organization that he or she never paid attention to in the past. You are looking for a mature and respected leader who is a good listener but willing to be decisive in decisions regarding the web.

Strengths and Weakness—Cue the Music

A word about strengths and weaknesses: The online strategy leader should be supplemented in areas where he or she is short in knowledge and expertise. A cross-functional team ensures that all the right skills are under the direction of a leader. Members of the team can come from finance, communications, marketing, information technology, development, and anywhere else in the organization. What is most important is that they can positively contribute to the effort, work well with others, and be comfortable in an environment that is probably less structured than they are used to.

Even in a less formal environment, team members want leadership and decisiveness. If everyone is comfortable with a cross-functional model, they won't be shy about offering their opinion, and they'll understand that there is one person who will make the decision.

Leading and participating in cross-functional teams is professionally and personally rewarding. It expands your horizons beyond what you would experience in a typical siloed organizational environment. Doing so exposes you to different ways of thinking, points of view, and personal preferences. You will learn to adapt to different styles of thinking, managing, and leading. With the right attitude and willingness to learn and share, the organization will benefit from the synergetic efforts of the team.

In my mind, a cross-functional approach is well suited to strategies that are in their infancy and subject to changes as technology moves and improves. Certainly, an organization's online strategy falls into this category.

PROJECTS, PROJECTS, PROJECT MANAGER

Although the departmental stakeholders are important, so is the concept of project management. Regardless of where the project is managed, the concept of project management (sometimes referred to as program or portfolio management) has begun to emerge in nonprofit organizations.

Project management can serve as the liaison between the business line (e.g., membership, annual fund) and the technology department. A dedicated project management emphasis will increase the chances of a successful online project. Technology-based projects have a high failure rate by default. But adding a project management component outside of the core tech component mitigates the risk.

In a typical nonprofit, a dedicated project manager is a luxury that not all can afford. Project management can start as a collaborative duty until the benefit of the position has a chance to prove itself over time. If the project management function increases the successful completion of online projects and adds some discipline and rigor to the management process, it can only add value to the enterprise.

With a project manager on staff, he or she can provide a fact-based approach to discussing the value of moving forward. It is vital that these discussions take place and at the appropriate level.

RISKS OF AN ONLINE STRATEGY

Is your online strategy still relevant? That is the first question that comes to mind when assessing risk in an online world. If your strategy is dated and lags the latest and greatest technology innovations, your constituents may consider you behind the curve. As the Internet continues to evolve and social networking and collaboration tools appear on the market, your online strategy is always at risk.

You should always go back to the basics of why you are online in the first place. Everyone needs a web site. But if you don't list your URL on a business card or reference it in printed collateral, your constituents will probably have a lower opinion of your organization.

What is in question is the strategy of having an online presence in the first place. Did you start a social network or online community on your site to compete with Facebook? Or did you build that capability to deepen the relationship between your constituents and your cause in an exclusive way? You have to think like one of your donors and understand their constraints and desires.

Do your followers really want to join another social network? If so, what is it that differentiates you from competing sites? What makes you unique? What drives traffic to your site? Can your content be found elsewhere?

It's Not an Illusion but Magic

The magic is figuring out how to play nice with Facebook, MySpace, and so on while offering some value-added services or products from your site. Most nonprofits cannot expect the volume of users that those sites generate.

Taking the long-tail approach, find your niche and build a strategy that supports it. If you try to be everything to everybody, chances are that you will fail. Stick to your mission, listen to your followers, and be nimble and agile enough to adjust as you go down the road.

The more time you spend on online initiatives, you'll find that it becomes more appealing to off-load basic functions to more experienced vendors. A great example is the data center. In a perfect world, we would all like to have our servers in an environmentally controlled data center—but most of us may not be able to afford it.

Start investigating whether certain core IT functions can be outsourced. Look at your internal IT environment, especially at functions that are utilitarian and not adding value in the way they might have in previous years. The data center, virtualization, and cloud computing are all fine examples of core tech functions you might be able to move from inside the organization to competent vendor partners. Obviously, you need to pick your partners carefully, understand the total cost, and build in very strong service agreements.

Outsourcing can help mitigate and eliminate some risk of infrastructure. Nonprofits can no longer afford downtime, and our constituents expect that everything will be operational around the clock. I certainly see the wave coming: More users will want more content and more interactivity. I think we are at a point at which in-house staff and infrastructure cannot scale up quickly enough to meet demand.

As an example, the NWF recently switched to storing popular video and picture galleries at Amazon Web Services (AWS). The organization uploads content to AWS, and end users access that content from their servers. End users will probably never know that we use AWS, and their experience has been upgraded in terms of load time. With a strong service level agreement in hand, we are confident that the content will always be accessible to our users. In addition, the pricing model is very favorable for the cost-conscious nonprofit.

You Have the Right to Remain Silent

You cannot have a discussion about risk without our mentioning privacy and user rights. We are all sensitive to this issue and take measures to ensure privacy. No one is exempt from this, and nonprofits are held to the same standards as for-profits in this regard. It's always best to default to the safest settings with regards to privacy.

In the case of opt-ins, we will not opt in a constituent unless he or she volunteers to do so. We also offer customized ways to opt out of e-mail and other electronic communications. By listening to the user base, we have found that it is better to give as many choices as possible with regard to sharing their data or hearing from us. The strategy has paid off for the NWF: The opt-in rate is very high and the organization is proud of its ability to electronically communicate with its base. The NWF takes the privacy issue seriously and has an outside law firm review the usage policy, privacy policy, and general web guidelines on a regular basis.

Another risk involves social networking and allowing and encouraging two-way dialogues between constituents and the organization. Like most nonprofits, the NWF visitors can post comments on articles and videos on the web site. After much discussion, the NWF decided to not require that users log in to post their points of view.

The commenters will tend to police themselves in this regard. There have been vulgarity and slanderous remarks posted to the site, but the organization removed them once it was made aware of them. In general, the back and forth has been professional and courteous. It's notable that most posts (about 90 percent) have been attributed, meaning that posters voluntarily identify themselves when making a comment or post.

The comments have not only been professional and courteous but also are starting points for continuing discussion between visitors. It is fascinating to watch constituents from different generations go back and forth on a topic. If one of the goals of the site is to engage constituents with one another and the organization, then the NWF's initial efforts are paying off.

Why Technologists Get Paid the Big Bucks

Technologists are tasked with promoting the use of technical solutions. They bring an organization together. There will always be the need for a working infrastructure, cohesive solutions, adequate reporting, and a willingness rather than a desire to use our technical knowledge for continuing good. In the modern world of social networking, we need to have a solid approach before we start shouting from the mountaintops.

Technology is always moving, barreling forward. We know the risks and rewards of implementing solutions that promote and connect not just people but also those who support and want a piece of our action. That conversation happening out there in the cloud is what drives us to listen. Listening is an act of love. In short, a lead technologist must have the vision, the passion, and the backing to keep nonprofits moving forward. In many cases, technologists are the train, the tracks, the ticket sellers, the porters, the engineers. The nonprofits decide on the destination, and technologists help them get there.

Michael Sola, a graduate of the State University of New York at Delhi, is a more-than-20-year technology veteran. He broke into the tech industry under the renowned authors and training pioneers Mark Minasi and Pete Moulton. As part of the Moulton, Minasi & Company team, Sola began supporting and training large groups of clients at the early stages of the tech industry. He has a mix of for-profit and nonprofit experience, with almost 10 years at the mid-Atlantic Chesapeake Bay Foundation. He recently moved into the role of senior technologist with the National Wildlife Federation. There, Sola introduced many technical improvements and established partnerships and priorities, and he has encouraged collaboration between programs and industry partners that built on the concepts of social networking. He is an active blogger, Twitterer, and speaker at Blackbaud conferences as well as workshops related to the nonprofit environment. He is a member of the national CIO 4 Good and the Maryland CIO Roundtable.

Tim Kobosko is vice president and chief information officer for the United Service Organizations (USO) in Arlington, Virginia. Kobosko is responsible for creating and managing the digital and information environment at the USO. He was previously with the U.S. Naval Academy Alumni Association, where he was vice president of information services. Kobosko earned his B.S. from the U.S. Naval Academy, his master's in administrative science from Johns Hopkins University, and his M.B.A. from Loyola College in Maryland.

CHAPTER 3

E-governance Is Good Governance

IMPROVING NONPROFIT BOARD LEADERSHIP
THROUGH ONLINE TECHNOLOGY

DOTTIE SCHINDLINGER AND LEANNE BERGEY

Picture the ideal board of directors, one that is fully engaged in the steward-ship of the nonprofit's mission—a board that is interactive in its governance role, without relying solely on printed reports for business intelligence. This board would be informed well in advance of each meeting on the key issues to be discussed and resolved. Members would collaborate between meetings and inform the agenda. They would have quick access to current financials, perfor-mance benchmarks, policies, and other information. They would be confident that the information they see is accurate, current, and reliable. Their decision-making process would be transparent, and members would be accountable for individual and collective actions.

WEB 2.0 ENTERS THE BOARDROOM

At its core, the concept of e-governance is about good governance. With the widespread adoption of e-governance in the nonprofit sector, there is a paradigm shift as boards move from passive consumers of historical data to active partici-pants in knowledge creation and management. With e-governance, nonprofits have the potential to cultivate the ideal board.

E-governance is paving the way for this evolution in much the same way that Web 2.0 changed the way we communicate. Gone are the days when we relied solely on snail mail to share information—we now regularly share photos and videos online; we blog, podcast, chat, and post messages on others' "walls." E-governance begs this question: With the wide variety of online, real-time collaboration people enjoy at home and at work, why would boards of directors still rely only on traditional methods of communication? Organizations are asking themselves this question, and the industry is responding with online tools—such as board portal technology—and strategies designed specifically to support good governance.

What Is E-governance?

Although the initial use of the term "e-governance" dates back to the late-1990s Internet boom, the concept continues to evolve in the wake of widespread use of Web 2.0 technologies. In its earliest iteration, e-governance referred to the use of the Internet to deliver government information and services to citizens—particularly in remote regions of the world—as a means to increase access to services as well as democratic participation.[1] With the advent of Sarbanes-Oxley legislation in the United States, many corporate boards began adopting similar principles to increase organizational transparency. Now, with governance-specific online technologies in use across the public, private, and not-for-profit sectors, "e-governance" can be defined as the strategic, conscious use of web-based technologies—particularly board portals—to improve governance.

Board portals offer a cohesive collection of web-based tools designed specifically to address the needs of boards of directors (Figure 3.1). Most board portals are online software-as-a-service solutions in which board members can store and retrieve documents, access real-time information, and connect with one another, thus allowing them to spend less time on routine tasks and more time focused on strategy and policy. Portal solutions offer the ability to meet virtually, as well as to enhance the productivity of face-to-face meetings. Although board portals range in terms of their features and pricing, all board portals have a common goal: to provide boards of directors a platform for achieving good governance by making their work more efficient and transparent.

This screenshot is of a typical board portal. The portal enables board members to share documents, communicate, and collaborate online through a web-based interface.

E-GOVERNANCE IN THE NONPROFIT SECTOR: WHAT'S HAPPENING NOW?

BoardEffect and the Alliance for Nonprofit Management teamed up in May 2008 to conduct a survey on alliance members' use of various online technologies to facilitate board governance.[2] The data collected tracked current board communication methods, the usage and adoption rates of different tools, and the effects that technology is having on board engagement. The results provide insight into a shift currently under way—as more nonprofit organizations

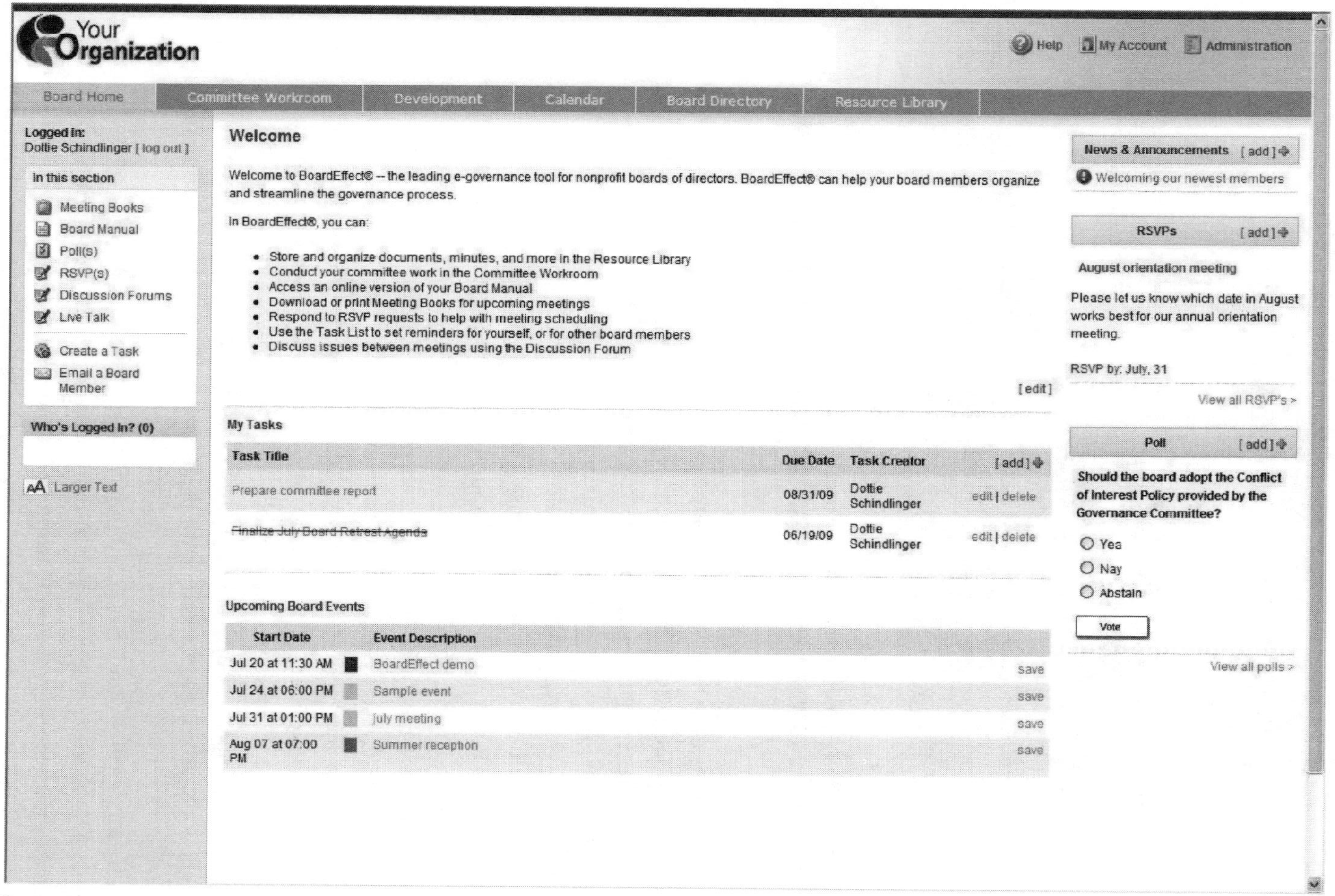

Your Organization

Help | My Account | Administration

| Board Home | Committee Workroom | Development | Calendar | Board Directory | Resource Library |

Logged in:
Dottie Schindlinger [log out]

In this section
- Meeting Books
- Board Manual
- Poll(s)
- RSVP(s)
- Discussion Forums
- Live Talk
- Create a Task
- Email a Board Member

Who's Logged In? (0)

AA Larger Text

Welcome

Welcome to BoardEffect® – the leading e-governance tool for nonprofit boards of directors. BoardEffect® can help your board members organize and streamline the governance process.

In BoardEffect®, you can:

- Store and organize documents, minutes, and more in the Resource Library
- Conduct your committee work in the Committee Workroom
- Access an online version of your Board Manual
- Download or print Meeting Books for upcoming meetings
- Respond to RSVP requests to help with meeting scheduling
- Use the Task List to set reminders for yourself, or for other board members
- Discuss issues between meetings using the Discussion Forum

My Tasks

Task Title	Due Date	Task Creator	[add]
Prepare committee report	08/31/09	Dottie Schindlinger	edit | delete
Finalize July Board Retreat Agenda	06/19/09	Dottie Schindlinger	edit | delete

Upcoming Board Events

Start Date	Event Description	
Jul 20 at 11:30 AM	■ BoardEffect demo	save
Jul 24 at 06:00 PM	■ Sample event	save
Jul 31 at 01:00 PM	■ July meeting	save
Aug 07 at 07:00 PM	■ Summer reception	save

News & Announcements   [add]
- Welcoming our newest members

RSVPs   [add]
August orientation meeting

Please let us know which date in August works best for our annual orientation meeting.

RSVP by: July, 31

[edit]

View all RSVPs >

Poll   [add]
Should the board adopt the Conflict of Interest Policy provided by the Governance Committee?

- ○ Yea
- ○ Nay
- ○ Abstain

Vote

View all polls >

FIGURE 3.1   **Board Portal** *Source: BoardEffect.*

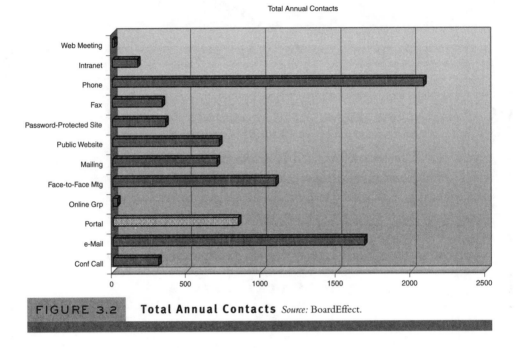

FIGURE 3.2   **Total Annual Contacts** *Source:* BoardEffect.

begin adopting e-governance, they are realizing gains in their boards' level of efficiency, productivity, and engagement. Of the 17.6 percent of Alliance members who participated in the survey, 61 percent work for nonprofits; another 33 percent were from for-profit organizations serving the nonprofit sector; and the remaining 6 percent were from other organizations, including consulting firms with both nonprofit and for-profit clients.

The survey asked what methods respondents were using regularly to communicate with their boards (Figure 3.2), ranging from board portals to e-mails and face-to-face meetings. The results show that nonprofits still rely mostly on e-mail, phone calls, and face-to-face meetings to facilitate board communication. However, although the percentage of nonprofit boards using board portals was small, the number of annual board contacts made via board portals was higher than via conference calls, public web sites, password-protected sections of web sites, online groups, mailings, and faxes. Figure 3.2 shows the number of annual contacts nonprofits have with their boards using various communication vehicles.

The survey also found that board portal-driven communication happens more frequently (at least once per month) than other methods (see Figure 3.3). This indicates that the organizations using board portals have a greater level of interaction with board members than those relying solely on other methods of communication. Figure 3.3 shows the frequency of contact nonprofits have with their boards using a variety of communication vehicles.

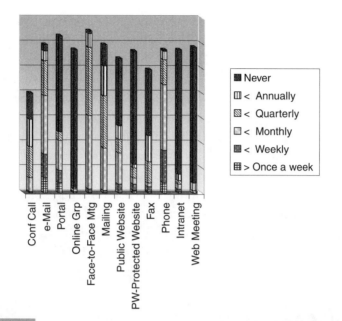

Never
< Annually
< Quarterly
< Monthly
< Weekly
> Once a week

Conf Call
e-Mail
Portal
Online Grp
Face-to-Face Mtg
Mailing
Public Website
PW-Protected Website
Fax
Phone
Intranet
Web Meeting

FIGURE 3.3   **Frequency of Board Communication, by Method**
Source: BoardEffect.

In terms of the types of organizations using board portals, the survey found no significant correlation between the size of the organization, average age of board members, or the size of the organization's budget and board portal usage. In other words, the perception that an organization's budget is too small or its board members or the organization itself too old to implement a board portal solution does not seem to be accurate.

The survey also asked respondents to estimate their time and expenses to manage the board's work. The weighted annual cost came in at $7,500, and the estimated cost in terms of staff time to facilitate the board's work was even greater. For example:

- About 70 percent of organizations require the efforts of two to five staff members to prepare board documents.

- More than 60 percent of nonprofits report that at least 10 hours per month of staff time is spent on managing the board's work.

- Approximately 20 percent reported spending more than 20 hours per month of staff time managing the board's work.

Even the most routine task, scheduling meetings, was reported to be labor intensive. More than half of all respondents reported that rescheduling meetings takes two days of staff time, and another 18 percent reported that it takes between

7 and 14 days. The high cost—in terms of staff effort and the expense of creating and disseminating board materials—is of great concern to many organizations, particularly in this era of heightened scrutiny and limited resources.

In addition, the survey found that information security—perhaps the most pressing concern in corporate governance—is becoming an issue in the nonprofit sector, as well. Although one-third of respondents reported concerns about the privacy and security of their board's information and documents, most respondents also distribute information to the board in e-mail attachments, a method of sharing information that is notoriously unsecure. The majority of the respondents who are concerned about information security rely primarily on e-mail, faxes, and mailings to distribute information to board members; none of these respondents used a board portal. The indication is that, as information security concerns continue to rise, nonprofits are likely to seek out more secure communication methods such as board portals.

Board Portals: A Brief History

As with many online technologies, board portals began to fill a specific need, namely reducing the personal liability of corporate directors in the wake of the Enron and WorldCom scandals early in the 2000s. New rules and requirements being handed down from every regulatory body—from the Securities and Exchange Commission to the U.S. Senate—meant that directors suddenly found themselves overloaded by information. Companies quickly realized they would need a way to manage and organize documents, track communications among directors, and filter important information so that it wouldn't get "lost" in directors' e-mail inboxes. Directors also needed to know that they were protected—that the information they had access to was of high-enough quality that they would be able to be accountable should something go wrong.

Beginning in 2002, several voices in the United States began to clamor for similar changes in the nonprofit sector. A study by McKinsey & Company in June 2002 calculated that the nonprofit sector could leverage an additional $100 billion a year by improving efficiency.[3] Soon after, the U.S. Congress, the Internal Revenue Service (IRS), and a panel on the nonprofit sector comprising nonprofit leaders from across the country began issuing recommendations for ways to improve nonprofit management and governance, focusing on transparency, accountability, and efficiency. In 2008, the IRS implemented a new version of Form 990—the form many nonprofits are required to file annually to the IRS—which required nonprofits to disclose their policies on conflicts of interest, document retention and destruction, and whistle-blower protection, and to identify whether the organization has a separate audit committee.

Nonprofit organizations now face increased scrutiny, tougher requirements to keep their charitable status, and heightened public interest in how dollars are spent. As early as 2003, nonprofits began seeking technology solutions that could help their boards govern more effectively. Some nonprofits, such as Gulf Coast Community Foundation of Venice, developed their own solution by adapting existing intranets.[4] At the time, the cost of hosted online governance solutions was perceived as too high for the nonprofit sector to absorb, with entry fees for board portals hovering around $25,000 per year.[5] However, with the recent advent of lower-cost board portals and the increased availability of nonprofit-specific options, more nonprofits began taking the leap, with an estimated 5 percent of the sector using board portals by June 2008.[6]

Board portal usage is on the rise in general—recent studies show that the number of companies using board portals grew from 12 percent in 2005 to roughly 26 percent in 2007.[7] Recent articles and workshops offered by BoardSource, a nationally recognized capacity-building agency specializing in nonprofit board governance, demonstrate that more nonprofits are beginning to take notice of e-governance and to investigate the options available.[8] The usage of this new technology in the nonprofit sector is likely to increase at rates similar to those in the corporate sector over the next three to five years.

Board Portal Features and Functionality

Although board portal software ranges widely in terms of price and industry focus, the features and functionality portals offer tend to be similar. The following sections discuss common features.

Personalized Dashboards and Alerts   Most board portals offer a variety of strategies to keep directors updated on current issues, discussions, documents for review, action items, and financials. A common feature is the personalized dashboard, which shows board members the items waiting for their time and attention the moment they log in to the portal. Items on the dashboard might include personalized to-do lists, meeting scheduling requests, news items, upcoming events, messages from colleagues, and the most recent documents added to the portal. Automated or manual alert systems are typically tied to e-mail—not to distribute board-related materials (which would bypass the security measures built into board portals) but to alert board members that something is awaiting their attention in the portal.

Meeting Materials and Policy Documents   As compliance regulations and accountability requirements have increased for board members, board portal companies have focused heavily on document management solutions. With few exceptions, board portals provide strategies for uploading and downloading, organizing, archiving, editing, and deleting documents securely through the web. Board members log in to find materials for the next meeting and are able to read, annotate, and download or print the files as needed.

Online Collaboration and Virtual Meetings   Most solutions include a variety of collaboration tools designed to enable directors to enhance the productivity of face-to-face meetings by allowing purely routine work to happen between meetings rather than at meetings. Online discussion forums, private workrooms for committees, shared calendars, resource libraries, and group editing of documents can be used both during and between meetings to help board members complete their work. When virtual meetings do occur, web conferencing, chat, and instant messaging can be used to help individuals interact more effectively, especially as online meetings often occur without the benefit of eye contact and body language.

Electronic Voting and Record Keeping   Although the rules on electronic voting for nonprofit boards differ state by state, most board portals offer some form of electronic voting functionality. For organizations in states that accept electronic voting, the board portal can assist in disseminating the motion, collecting and recording the votes, and exporting the results into the official minutes.

Security and Data Recovery   Selecting an online, hosted solution typically offers the benefit of redundant data storage, regular backups, and data recovery in the event of an accidental loss of data. The security options often increase with the cost of the board portal, with the most expensive solutions providing dedicated servers, restricted Internet protocol addresses, and rotating access credentials for users. Still-secure, but less expensive options focus on secure-sockets-layer (i.e., SSL) encryption, unique usernames and passwords for users, and security certification for the hosting facility. Options to add security to specific documents and secure messaging is also offered in some board portals.

Board Portals: Promise and Pitfalls

Boards that have implemented e-governance are reporting satisfaction in meeting their governance goals, but as with any technology, there are challenges. A study conducted by the Society of Corporate Secretaries and Governance Professionals (summarized in Table 3.1) highlights some of the benefits and challenges of organizations that have implemented e-governance solutions.[9] This study, along with articles in publications such as *BusinessWeek* and the *Wall Street Journal* point out that, though board portals offer a great deal in terms of increased efficiency, their adoption can be a slow process.[10] Critical to success is having a concrete

TABLE 3.1	ADAPTED FROM SOCIETY OF CORPORATE SECRETARIES AND GOVERNANCE PROFESSIONALS' RESEARCH

Benefits	Challenges
<ul><li>Real-time collaboration and communication among board members</li><li>Efficient facilitation of scheduling, organizing, and distributing information for corporate board meetings</li><li>Quick and easy access to the latest corporate information and company updates; current and historic company records; and key contact information</li><li>Cost and time savings by eliminating the need to create and distribute last-minute updates to board binders</li><li>Instant access to all proposed and approved minutes and resolutions</li><li>Flexibility to facilitate the delivery of information to board members during unexpected or unplanned travel</li></ul>	<ul><li>It takes time to see true efficiencies in the process; implementing a board portal can require more work up front.</li><li>Content has to be selected carefully; some documents don't lend themselves to online review.</li><li>Usability is key - the portal has to be intuitive for members to use, and providing training is a must.</li></ul>

Source: Society of Corporate Secretaries and Governance Professionals, New York, NY. "Developing a web Portal for the Board: A Research Paper from the Corporate Practices Committee," originally conducted in 2005 with updated data collected in 2007.

plan for implementing e-governance that clearly identifies the needs, goals, and core group of users and that introduces the new technology in stages.

Successfully Implementing E-governance

Making any significant change, particularly a change to long-standing group processes and procedures, takes time. Implementing an e-governance solution successfully requires strategic decisions and careful planning. There must be alignment between the needs of the board and the technology selected. Organizations that randomly select an e-governance solution without planning the implementation process are not likely to realize large gains.

Developing a Plan

Research on the best practices for implementing portals shows that the most successful ventures are those that were carefully planned, researched, rolled out in phases, and then evaluated against the original goals.[11] Figure 3.4 shows this

**Utilizing a cyclical planning process
to implement e-governance successfully**

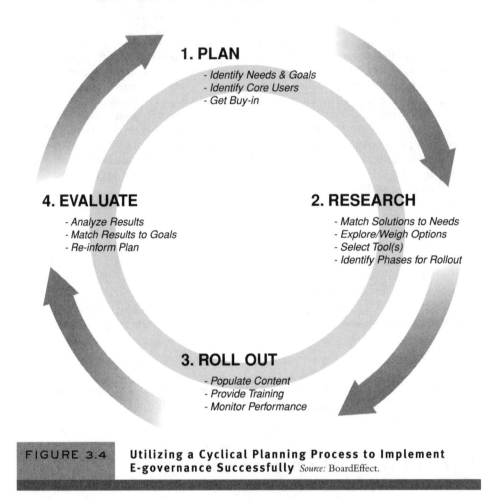

1. PLAN
- Identify Needs & Goals
- Identify Core Users
- Get Buy-in

2. RESEARCH
- Match Solutions to Needs
- Explore/Weigh Options
- Select Tool(s)
- Identify Phases for Rollout

3. ROLL OUT
- Populate Content
- Provide Training
- Monitor Performance

4. EVALUATE
- Analyze Results
- Match Results to Goals
- Re-inform Plan

FIGURE 3.4   Utilizing a Cyclical Planning Process to Implement E-governance Successfully *Source:* BoardEffect.

approach as an ongoing cycle involving four steps that are repeated every two to four years, depending on the time line for implementation (see Figure 3.4).

Step 1: Plan   The board of directors and executive staff should work together to identify the specific needs and goals for an e-governance solution. Asking core users about their pain points—specific processes that are onerous to undertake, are inefficient, are difficult to achieve in a timely way, or are otherwise in need of improvement—can provide a list of measurable goals that the e-governance solution must meet. For example, a goal might be to reduce the amount of staff time devoted to preparing board-meeting materials by 50 percent within a year. The more specific and tangible the goals, the easier it will be to evaluate e-governance options.

Equally important is identifying the core users for the e-governance solution—most often, the organization's board members and staff members who serve as liaisons to the board. The core group of users should review the goals to ensure they fit reality. At the end of the day, the core group of users will determine the success or failure of the e-governance solution—their buy-in to the concept of e-governance in general, and to a specific solution in particular, is critical to success.

Step 2: Research   Once the goals and needs have been identified, list them in a chart to assist in evaluating specific e-governance solutions (see Table 3.2). Weigh the specific options available against the list of goals and needs to find the best fit.

While you narrow the options available, have the core user group sit in on one or two short product demos. This is an important step to ensure that the solution truly fits their needs and gain buy-in for a particular solution.

Step 3: Roll Out   As the research process wraps up, a plan for the rollout should be in place. Time should be allocated to populate the new e-governance solution with content that is meaningful and valuable to the core users before it is introduced to the entire board. Content may include news items, policy documents, meeting materials, forms needing to be completed, calendar appointments, user contact information, topics for discussion and more. What is uploaded prior to the rollout should in part be determined by the goals identified during the planning phase. For example, if one of the goals was to provide more timely access to proposed meeting agendas, then focus energy on uploading meeting materials.

The best rollout plan introduces specific features and functions of the e-governance solution in stages—combined with appropriate training—to address the most important and urgent goals (see Figure 3.5). Other features should take a backseat and be introduced at a later date, once the most pressing needs have been addressed.

The example in Figure 3.5 of a phased rollout plan demonstrates how board portal features can be introduced in stages for a smooth implementation.

Step 4: Evaluate   Use the data collected during rollout to evaluate the advantages or limitations of the e-governance solution; compare the actual measurements (e.g., staff time preparing meeting materials) with goals to determine how they measure up. Be careful not to confuse the technical performance of the e-governance solution with the board's ability to use and adapt to new processes. For example, if the e-governance solution fails to reduce the staff time required to prepare meeting materials, examine the specific steps involved to determine how the e-governance solution supported or inhibited the process.

TABLE 3.2   E-GOVERNANCE SOLUTION RESEARCH, WORKSHEET

NEEDS	SOLUTION 1: _Sample____ _	SOLUTION 2: _____	SOLUTION 3: _____	SOLUTION 4: _____
Time required for setup and rollout	Initial setup is 5–7 business days; another 3 weeks on our end to populate content			
Training or documentation provided	Training provided for administrators, training for the board for an extra fee; user manual included in price			
Able to reduce amount of staff time required to create meeting books	Meeting books can be created from various documents and compiled into a single PDF; able to create a template for future meeting books to save time			
Shared calendar integrates with personal calendars	Web-based calendar; able to save appointments to Outlook			
Meeting scheduling capabilities	RSVP feature where members can vote on dates and add comments			
Private work space for committees	Committee workroom for just committee members; includes meeting book functionality and calendar for committees			
Works on different browsers and platforms	Explorer versions 6–8, Chrome, Firefox (all versions), Safari; PC, Mac, Linux			
Able to be customized	Customization available for additional fee			
Able to be rolled out in phases	All functionality is turned on; we can introduce functions in phases			

Source: BoardEffect

Board Portal Implementation Plan

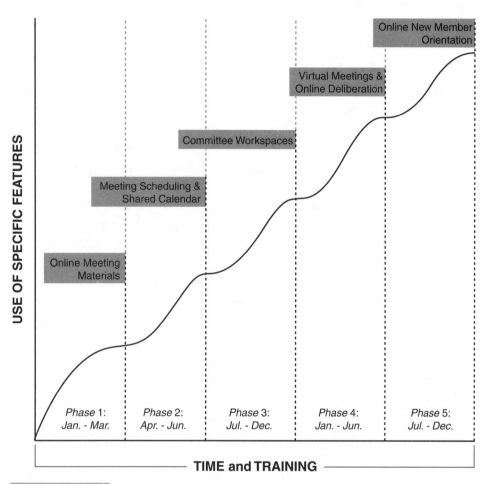

FIGURE 3.5   **Board Portal Implementation Plan** *Source:* BoardEffect.

Armed with more information on the outcomes of the initial e-governance implementation, the original plan should be revisited to assess if there are any new pressing needs. Invariably, as board members cycle off the board and new members arrive, new priorities will make themselves known. Use the cycle approach of planning, research, rollout, and evaluation to ensure that the return on the organization's investment can be maximized.

E-GOVERNANCE AND BOARD ENGAGEMENT: WHAT TO EXPECT

Despite the newness of e-governance in the nonprofit sector, organizations are already beginning to see an impact on their boards' ability to govern well. In recent interviews with nonprofits that have implemented board portals, respondents identified an increase in their boards' efficiency, improvements in communication, and a recommitment to best practices in governance.

Increased Efficiency and Effectiveness

The creation of meeting materials, board manuals, and reports can be labor intensive and inefficient. The traditional process, typically coordinated by staff, can take weeks as written reports are assembled into a meeting book that numbers in the hundreds of pages. Board members might receive this information as late as the day before the meeting as staff scramble to collect and collate the documents. With only hours (or minutes) to review copious information, boards often dedicate meetings to walking through meeting book content to get directors up to speed. By the time the documents have been reviewed, there is typically little time left to perform the governance role: that of careful oversight, deliberation on strategic issues, and policy setting.

It was this type of experience that led the Enterprise Center (TEC) to implement a board portal solution.[12] The Enterprise Center, founded in 1989 by the Wharton Small Business Development Center, provides a portfolio of business-acceleration services designed to better position minority enterprises to compete in the local, regional, and global economies. Like many nonprofits, TEC is underresourced and understaffed. Demands on staff time are great and, remaining true to its mission and constituency, TEC prioritizes program delivery above all else. Subsequently, administrative and managerial duties can be difficult to manage. Among the first of the tasks TEC sought to trim were document management, planning, and communications for TEC's board of directors. These labor-intensive activities at times demanded the full attention of both TEC leadership and administrative staff.

Now, with a board portal solution fully implemented, meetings are scheduled, RSVPs are tracked, meeting books are distributed, and online votes are held— all through the portal. The subsequent savings in staff time has allowed TEC to completely reorganize its administrative staffing structure, and board relations and communications no longer require a significant portion of any one staff person's work portfolio. Further, direct costs including express delivery of documents, paper, and publishing have been virtually eliminated. Management estimated a 660 percent return on the annual investment. According to TEC's president, Della Clark, "Basic board engagement has been reduced to a few points and clicks of the mouse. When we now spend time with our board, we can spend that time on substantive topics and decision making, not document review."[13]

Secure, Targeted Communication and Group Collaboration

Board portals have the potential to change the nature of conversations with the board. Once routine needs are being met in a more efficient way, board communications can focus on more significant issues. As Olivia Selinger, Director of Governance for the Girl Scouts of Eastern Pennsylvania, put it, "[Our board portal] did not necessarily foster more communication, just made communication more efficient. The portal has changed the content and quality of communication between board and staff."

Communication between board members and staff at nonprofits can be very time consuming. In our survey of nonprofits on board communication practices, we saw that even the most routine communications, such as scheduling meetings, can take hours, days, or even weeks of staff time. Because most nonprofits use one-to-one phone calls as a primary means of communicating with their board members, who often number in the dozens, we estimate that nonprofit staff people spend several weeks of every year engaged in routine communication with the board. In addition, the communication methods that nonprofits rely on, especially one-to-one phone calls, circumvent group deliberation and put the onus on one or two individuals to report on what was said and heard. E-mail communication, though it has the potential to be more egalitarian, can quickly lose its edge when one person decides not to reply to all and the thread of a conversation is eternally lost.

E-governance offers a way out of this trap. When board members have equal access to information and equal opportunity to comment, discuss, and review others' ideas, they have a greater ability to collaborate. Board portals also help take some of the sting out of routine communications by offering meeting scheduling functions, group polls, online discussion forums, real-time meeting capabilities, and an easy way to connect with the entire group. Conversations held in board portals can be archived and maintained for future reference rather than languishing in a single board member's e-mail inbox.

Transparency, Accountability, and Renewed Engagement

In this era of increased scrutiny and accountability, e-governance offers a way to improve not just the efficiency of the board's work but also the quality of its actions. As Olivia Selinger points out: "Changes in the [IRS Form] 990 and increased public attention to governance matters have enhanced consciousness and raised awareness of board responsibility. Through [our board portal], we're fostering best practices by making it easy [for board members] to stay organized and see current information well before meetings.... Our investment in e-governance tells board members that we value their contributions and involvement in governance."[14]

In addition, TEC found that using a board portal helped increase the organization's transparency and ability to manage knowledge transfer; staff turnover no longer affected board relations and communications. As the board has a portal, not a liaison, more sensitive documents could be shared than through e-mail, and specific documents could be further protected and viewable only to selected committee members. As S. Jonathan Horn, former co-chair of TEC's board of directors and principal at Deloitte Consulting, wrote, "We've seen a real increase in board activity and commitment in the last year. We've been doing a lot of things to make that happen and [our board portal] really facilitated the increased activity."[15]

The Girl Scouts of Eastern Pennsylvania have also seen how a board portal allows the organization's board to be more accountable to policies set at the national level. Olivia Selinger was particularly concerned with finding ways to ensure her board members could remain updated even as policies are changing: "[Our board portal] makes it easier [for board members] to know what they need to know when they need it. For instance, [they] don't need a 100-page board manual in front of them. . . . If you provide a hard-copy board manual to a new board member, it either requires constant updating or it will be two-years-old by the end of the director's term. Both we and our national organization update policies regularly, so [we] change files [in the portal] to ensure they're up to date whenever board members might look for them."[16]

E-governance, as realized through board portals, has the potential to create a paradigm shift away from the idea that board members merely review information and toward the idea that information is the fuel that powers good governance. With e-governance, the ideal board is easier to picture; e-governance is good governance. When board members are empowered with a platform designed to make their job easier, more secure, and efficient, increased effectiveness is a natural outcome. When given a secure environment to sharpen and deepen their communication and collaboration, they can capture the essence of great ideas, which will later grow into thoughtful substantive plans. When the tools for interactivity are carefully and consistently introduced, an enlivened, fully engaged board is within grasp. E-governance is more than just the next makes-sense technology; it is the next logical step in the nonprofit sector's quest for great governance.

Dottie Schindlinger, Vice President of E-governance for BoardEffect Inc., is an expert on the impact of e-governance in the nonprofit sector. She has worked in the nonprofit sector for more than 15 years, first developing projects for the Pennsylvania Humanities Council and later certificate programs for the Nonprofit Center at La Salle University. She joined Verve Internet Solutions in 2005 to help nonprofits meet their missions more effectively through online technology. During her tenure, Schindlinger was instrumental in developing BoardEffect, a secure online portal and information management system for boards of directors. She is a frequent national and international presenter and writer on e-governance in nonprofits. She received her bachelor's degree from the University of Pennsylvania and holds certificates in nonprofit management and board leadership from the Nonprofit Center at La Salle University's School of Business.

Leanne Bergey, Chief Strategy Officer for BoardEffect Inc., is a national expert on emerging trends in online technology for mission-based organizations. An entrepreneur and lifelong educator, she lead the research and development process for BoardEffect. She founded Verve Internet Solutions in 1996, an Internet-solutions company that served nonprofits in the Greater Philadelphia region, leveraging her background in marketing, strategic planning, and technology to transform business processes in the nonprofit sector. For her success in growing Verve and establishing BoardEffect, Bergey received the prestigious 40 Under 40 award from the *Philadelphia Business Journal*, which recognized her accomplishments as a successful leader and entrepreneur. Bergey earned her bachelor's degree at Dickinson College.

CHAPTER 4

Social Collaboration and Productivity

HOW WEB 2.0 TOOLS HELP RAISE FUNDS AND AWARENESS MORE EFFICIENTLY

RUSSELL M. ARTZT, JOHN MURCOTT, AND MARK FASCIANO

As a nonprofit leader, you're responsible for driving the projects and campaigns that generate funds and awareness for your organization. Success requires input and support from many constituents. Within your organization, you must collaborate with staff members, board members, and volunteers. Externally, you are in constant contact with volunteers, key beneficiaries, leaders from other nonprofits, and representatives from the community you serve. Beyond your involvement, the community of individuals who care about your cause are in constant contact with one another.

You need to collaborate with others to help achieve your goals, especially when you are trying to manage multiple projects simultaneously. Some of the key barriers to collaboration are geographically dispersed constituents, project time constraints, and different organizational cultures.

Collaboration often means letting go of control. This can be scary, but today, leaders need to evaluate not only how they can leverage the efforts and skills of their teams but also how they can open those efforts to a broader audience—the network of volunteers, supporters, and their personal connections. Collaboration ultimately saves time and money, uncovers hidden economies of scale, and empowers all stakeholders to help your organization meet its maximum potential.

Even when organizations have embraced the concept of collaboration, managing the collaborative process has historically been difficult. This problem has led to the development of a wide variety of tools and services for collaboration that are designed to improve organizational efficiency. The first collaboration tools were designed for the corporate world, which faces market pressures and has deep pockets. Implementations were both complex and expensive and typically involved large teams and focused on managing multiple projects. After an initial investment, the commitment would eventually pay off as internal adoption led to a measureable impact on the bottom line.

Unfortunately, the intensive cost, time, and training requirements meant that such tools were initially out of reach for most nonprofits. As technologies were proved in the corporate world, the systems would be adapted, refined, and simplified over time. Vendors begin to make lite or open-source versions of tools. This allows them to be adopted by the nonprofit sector, which can enjoy the benefits with less expense and lower risk.

Although the topic of business collaboration tools is frequently highlighted in case studies, best practices, and how-to books, there is comparatively little information about the unique challenges of nonprofit collaboration. Nonprofits push requirements to the limit. We have few IT resources, so we need software that can be installed quickly and easily. Our collaborators are everywhere, so we need tools that can be accessed anywhere, anytime. We rely heavily on volunteers, so we need extremely easy-to-use solutions that can be introduced with limited training. We need to save every penny raised to support our causes, so we cannot afford expensive products or services.

Luckily, the pace of innovation has put corporate-strength tools within our reach, and Web 2.0 technologies have dramatically broadened the concept of who can help with the collaboration process. This chapter highlights new collaboration tools that are easy to implement, easy to access, easy to use, and inexpensive or free. But before we get started analyzing individual tools, it's important to understand some key concepts and terminology.

THE WEB 2.0 LEXICON

The development of Web 2.0 technologies over the past few years has led to a wealth of new applications centered on user-generated content. The ability to easily and instantly share content has made sites such as Facebook, Wikipedia, and YouTube extremely popular. The Web 2.0 framework has also ushered in a wave of tools that enable organizations to collaborate across barriers and borders more quickly, easily, and cheaply than with traditional collaboration software.

The world of Web 2.0 moves fast, and definitions are ever evolving. A whole chapter could be dedicated to this discussion alone. For the purposes of this chapter, we use the following terms and meanings: "Web 2.0" refers to the second generation of web development and web design that facilitates information sharing, interoperability, user-centered design, and collaboration on the World Wide Web. The advent of Web 2.0 led to the development and evolution of web-based communities, hosted services, and web applications. Examples include social networking sites, video-sharing sites, wikis, blogs, mash-ups, and folksonomies.[1]

"Social media" describes relatively inexpensive and accessible tools that enable anyone to publish or access information on the Internet. In contrast to traditional media like newspapers, television, and film that communicate in a one-directional monologue from one source to many readers, social media enable the flow of information and content from many creators (even private individuals) to many readers. Examples of social media include blogs, wikis, Flickr, Twitter, and social bookmarking sites like Digg and Delicious.[2]

Social networking services focus on building online communities of people who share interests and activities, or who are interested in exploring the interests and activities of others.[3] They enable you to connect and keep up with friends in ever-expanding ways and enable us to find new friends and connections. The tools are largely inexpensive, easy to use, and give users their own stage, microphone, or soapbox. Popular destinations are Facebook, MySpace, and LinkedIn, but there are millions of niche communities to explore, making it possible for anyone to find like-minded communities and friends.

Social collaboration is the process that helps multiple people share information by using interpersonal and social networks to achieve any common goal. Social collaboration moves beyond the social networking activities that have become the calling card of Web 2.0. Although social networking concentrates mostly on communication and sharing among like-minded people, social collaboration is marked by an emphasis on goal-oriented activity in which multiple parties contribute toward reaching an objective, whether it be completing a document, organizing an event, or taking action of some kind.[4] Record or document management, threaded discussions, audit history, and other mechanisms designed to capture the efforts of many into a managed content environment are typical of collaboration technologies.

Software as a service, or SaaS, is a new software-delivery model that has greatly reduced the cost and complexity of implementing new software. Now, users don't have to download or install any software; they simply go to a web site and access the program via a username and password. This offers a number of advantages for nonprofits—there is no need for technical support to install any software, upgrades and updates are handled automatically behind the scenes, and you can access the tool from any browser at any time. There are financial advantages to SaaS models, as well: the software is leased on a monthly basis and usually does not require a large up-front payment. The costs are also usually reflective of usage, not a complex licensing model.

Web 2.0 Tools for Social Collaboration and Productivity

There are numerous tools that can help your organization improve collaboration—whether with other organizations, inside your own organization, or with your community—or enable your community to collaborate among its own members. This chapter reviews tools covering a continuum of complexity and cost but with an emphasis on helping you achieve your two most important goals: raising funds and raising awareness. As you explore each one, keep your goals in mind, and evaluate each in terms of how it can help you solve collaboration challenges.

Project Management Tools

Project management typically focuses on the time lines, deadlines, and milestones of group activity, with a specific focus on assigning individual tasks to team members. The first technologies that addressed this were designed for large corporations managing sizable internal teams and multiple projects. The technology includes tools like document sharing, project deliverable management, threaded message boards, and online work spaces.

Project portfolio management (PPM) is the process by which project investment decisions are made—selecting, prioritizing, and monitoring project results. The primary objective is to improve efficiency and drive down costs. The software provides management with a view into multiple projects, allowing management a bird's-eye view of investments and how resources are being used.

There are a wide range of tools available in the marketplace to fit any organization's size and budget. We start with some of the early movers in the space who have focused on the corporate market, and then focus on lower-cost options for smaller nonprofits.

Clarity   The gold standard in project management software is Computer Associates' product Clarity (see Figure 4.1). Clarity enables organizations to seamlessly manage services, projects, products, people, and financials through any web browser. Users can get started quickly with essential functionality, including education and implementation—usually in just a week. One of Clarity's strengths is its flexibility: Organizations can significantly customize the solution to adapt the product to existing processes.

Clarity offers larger corporations like Kellogg the ability to manage a $20 million human resources transformation project by creating a centralized project management solution. Kellogg is using Clarity Project and Portfolio

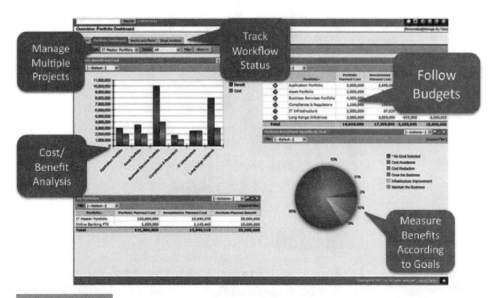

| FIGURE 4.1 | **PPM Standard: Clarity from Computer Associates** |

Management to track all aspects of the human resources project, from time and resources to financial information. The solution has been deployed using the SaaS deployment option, which meant that Kellogg could start using Clarity within just 10 days and without any capital outlay. Using Clarity to manage its human resources project will help Kellogg improve productivity, time-to-market, and cost control.

Knowing that smaller organizations also have a need for project management tools on a smaller budget, Computer Associates has created Clarity PPM On Demand Essentials, a lighter SaaS version of the product. At the entry level, implementations can be achieved in as little as five days and involve lower risk and investment.

Basecamp For smaller organizations with simpler needs and smaller budgets, there are a variety of online tools to manage projects and collaborate with the team members associated with each project. For example, Basecamp offers a very affordable basic plan and is currently used by nonprofits like Amnesty International and the World Wildlife Fund. With it, you can assign tasks to stakeholders, share files, track time spent, and help everyone meet deadlines. It's usable and visible to everyone you need to get on the same page, whether they're in your office or across the country. Basecamp has a companion iPhone application called Outpost that pulls in the current status of projects so you can keep track of everything while you're away from your desk.

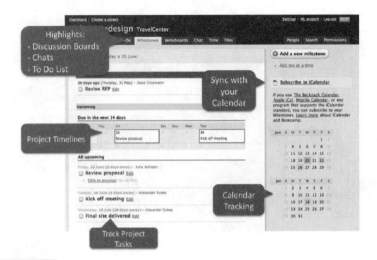

FIGURE 4.2   Basecamp: A Lightweight, Low-Cost PPM Solution

Imagine that your organization is planning a fundraiser and you have several teams, such as event planning, honoree selection, and promotions, working on various aspects of the event. Each of these teams has a number of tasks to perform, but many of the tasks cannot begin until another is finished. For example, the promotions team cannot create flyers until it knows the theme of the event (decided by event planning) or who will be honored (handled by the honoree-selection team). Even within a team, there are various tasks that must be assigned, as when the promotions team needs to decide on creative elements: name and theme, production of flyers, updates to the web site, invitations, and registration forms. Basecamp allows you to manage all three teams through a simple user interface (see Figure 4.2). The first step is to lay out the tasks, assign them to team members with corresponding deadlines, and indicate which tasks are antecedents (i.e., which tasks must be completed first).

After the tasks and time lines are established, each user can update his or her status as the tasks are completed. The tool provides an easy-to-understand dashboard to see the overall project status and view the updates from each team member. Because the tool is web-based, all members can update their activities online even if they are located across the country.

Wikis

> *If HP knew what HP knows, we would be three times as profitable.*
> —LEW PLATT, FORMER CEO OF HEWLETT-PACKARD[5]

Most Internet users have heard of Wikipedia, the online collaborative encyclopedia, but not everyone knows that the term "wiki" simply means a collection of pages that visitors can read and edit live and that individuals and organizations can create wikis of their own that are public or private. Think of wikis as a limitless whiteboard on which people post and respond to information. The persistent and ever-growing nature of wikis makes them a perfect format for a knowledge base, or a repository of information on topics that concern your organization.

Wikis offer many advantages over a traditional intranet. They can capture information that would otherwise be in team members' heads or inboxes. As wikis are easy and fast to edit, people quickly catch on to adding content—and mistakes are easy to fix. Organizations can use wikis to post information for new employees or volunteers, to capture requirements for future projects, and to record and track news about your cause.

Before you select a wiki engine for your organization, ask yourself a few questions: How tech-savvy are the users? You can find wiki programs that use markup language or have a what-you-see-is-what-you-get (called WYSIWYG) editor. Some also offer the option to retain past versions of your pages so you can view changes or roll back if necessary. Private wikis are password protected, so they are accessible only by your community and can be used to organize and document internal projects. For those wishing for the top level of security and privacy, a wiki like those offered by MediaWiki, which are hosted on your own servers, may be the best option (see Figure 4.3).

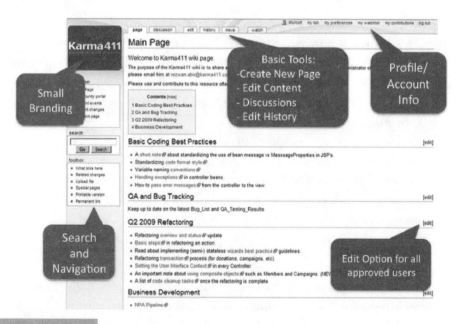

FIGURE 4.3   **MediaWiki: An Immediate Intranet or Extranet Site for Collaboration**

It's important to designate a wiki facilitator in your organization; such people have an important role and a fine line to walk. For a project-based wiki, before you begin, give stakeholders a tutorial on how to add, change, and complete tasks. For a knowledge-base-type wiki, it's best to begin with some content so the blank page does not intimidate anyone. However, don't categorize information too rigidly; you want participants to take the reins and feel like equal owners in the endeavor. Users will enjoy being able to search for previously asked questions and archived reports or presentations and the ability to add new pages or content without the trouble of going through a webmaster.

Real-Time Collaboration Tools

There are two modes of collaborating with fellow team members: synchronous and asynchronous. Tools like Basecamp and wikis are asynchronous, which means that contributions are added and saved for later review by other team members. There is permanence to the data, because discussion threads, project statuses, and wiki page content remain on the site until they are removed.

When teams need to communicate in real time, or synchronously, other tools take center stage. These tools allow people to talk, text message, or present data while others view and respond. These tools are as close as you can get in the virtual world to having people in the same room, but because of the nonlinear nature of in-person discussions, the content of these interactions is rarely saved for future reference.

Voice-over-Internet-Protocol When face-to-face meetings are not possible, voice is the next best thing. To avoid extreme phone bills, voice-over-Internet-protocol (VOIP) can be a significant cost-saving solution. Popular vendors include Skype (see Figure 4.4) for making calls via your computer and Vonage for making calls via a landline.

There are considerable business advantages to using Skype. For computer-to-computer discussions, there is no charge for unlimited usage (the only expense is the Internet connection that you already have). There are low-cost options for making direct calls to standard phones. Beyond VOIP, Skype offers text messaging and video conferencing, as well. There is also an asynchronous element to Skype because the discussions can be stored on your computer for use later.

Instant Messaging Instant messaging can be a useful tool for organizations in several ways. First, it enables quick communication when it would otherwise be difficult to schedule a full meeting or phone date. Second, instant messages can be a great back-channel communication method to privately discuss what is going on during a conference call and agree on next steps before speaking

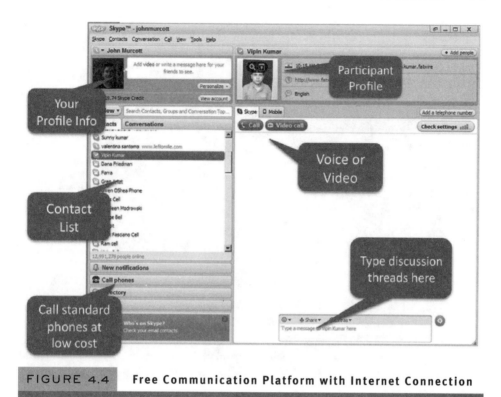

FIGURE 4.4   **Free Communication Platform with Internet Connection**

aloud. Third, it's extremely useful for sending links that would otherwise take forever to read aloud.

Two instant-messaging categories exist: synchronous (you're chatting in real time) and asynchronous (you leave messages for one another, only occasionally finding one another live). Examples of synchronous chat include Yahoo, AOL Instant Messenger, and MSN. Services like Trillian allow you to use one program to log in to and manage all of your chat identities. Need to get more than one person in on the conversation? Try a chat-room service like Meebo.

If your team enjoys Twittering—where you send real-time short messages out to all of your friends—then Yammer is the organizational equivalent, providing enterprise-level privacy and security.

Asynchronous messaging—or persistent chat—is akin to having a war room. Imagine a space in which you can leave messages for the team members who will see them when they pop in. You'll read messages when you have time—but, occasionally, you'll end up in the room with another teammate and have a real-time conversation. Services like Skype and Campfire make this possible.

Presentation Software   Entrenched in PowerPoint culture? If you frame your thinking in slide format, you can still share ideas and generate audience

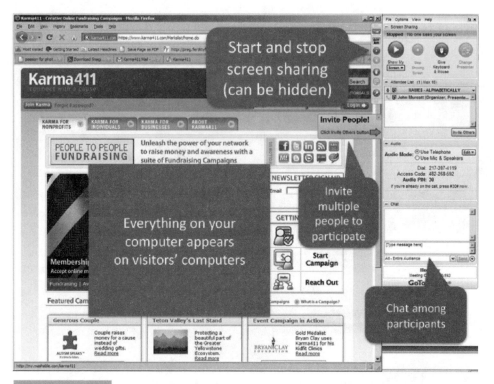

FIGURE 4.5   **Share Your Screen with Invited Participants Using GoToMeeting**

participation via any number of web conferencing tools. WebEx is the industry leader, with enterprise-level software and services. For those with smaller budgets and more occasional needs, look to providers like ReadyTalk and GoToMeeting (see Figure 4.5).

There are many benefits of adding web conferencing to your technology mix. Web conferencing is not just a one-directional communication channel; users can share desktops and collaborate in real time. For presentations you do over and over, like training new employees and volunteers, presentations can be recorded and watched any time.

Not only is web conferencing a much more cost-effective way to get everyone in the same (virtual) room, but it's essential for green organizations in reducing their carbon footprint. The WebEx client Positive Outcomes, a corporate-social-responsibility advisory firm, was able to dramatically reduce the number of miles its employees flew in the first month of use, and it plans to cut its overall travel in half. Positive Outcomes is now truly able to walk the talk about going green and save time and travel expense in the process.[6]

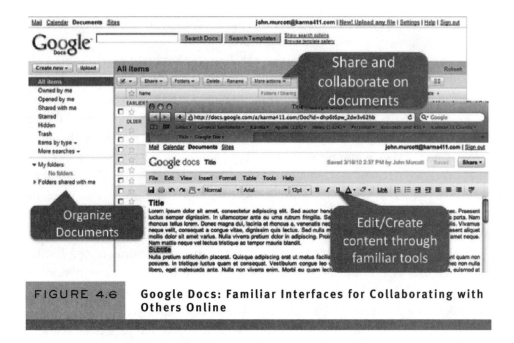

FIGURE 4.6   Google Docs: Familiar Interfaces for Collaborating with Others Online

Document Editing   Most organizations create a lot of documents during the course of daily work and communications. Situations in which multiple people must contribute to a document, such as during strategic planning, create serious productivity sinkholes. When multiple document drafts are circulated via e-mail or kept on a shared drive, it's very easy to lose track of the latest information and waste the team's time duplicating efforts.[7]

Several online collaboration tools allow multiple users to work on a document while they keep track of users, changes, and updates. Google Docs is a leader in this space—it's free, powerful, and offers unlimited storage (see Figure 4.6). Teams can upload, share, and edit documents in real time. For complex projects, you can keep a list of open issues, assign responsibilities, and track status using a related tool, Google Spreadsheets. Thanks to integration with Google Talk—Google's chat and VOIP tool—teams can communicate via instant messaging and even voice while editing. The system will show you when another team member logs in so you can collaborate in real time while editing the document.

Once a document is finalized, it can be locked and kept online for others to view. Having a central repository of key documents in a collaboration work space is useful, as it constitutes an agreed-on platform for starting for future work—no need to start from scratch.

Google Wave   New online collaboration tools are being developed all the time. Google Docs will soon be outperformed by a new collaboration application. Google Wave—the beta version launched in September 2009—promises to be Google's answer to every online collaborator's dreams. This was the beginning of a new way to view online communications.

Google Wave is a free, open-source collaboration tool that revolutionizes the way teams communicate online by taking existing tools to a new level. Google Wave allows multiple users to join together on a "wave," in which they can write and reply to one another while seeing each character appear in real time. New participants can be invited to the discussion and can play back the entire group's interaction at any time.[8]

Waves can be used by organizations to create documents, allow multiple editors to work at the same time, track who made the edits, and view the finished document at any stage. Conversations and documents can be enhanced with richly formatted text, photos, videos, maps, and more.

Google Wave can integrate with other social media including blogs, Twitter, and organizational intranets. Because Google Wave is open source, developers around the world will be adding new functionality and applications on an ongoing basis. Google Wave is both easy to use and customizable, which ensures its ability to grow with your organization and evolve at the rapid pace of technology.

SOCIAL NETWORKING GROUP FUNCTIONALITY

We've explored a number of tools your organization can use to collaborate internally. However, nonprofits cannot survive without collaborating with the outside world—both the community it serves and the community of people who support it. They are online, and they are already talking about your issues. Your approach to social collaboration should embrace the growing Web 2.0 revolution—that is, it should leverage the personal, powerful, and immediate aspect of networking sites so your constituents can speak loud and clear in support of your cause.

Swimming with the Big Fish—Nonprofits and the Big Social Networks

Initially, people used social networks like Facebook and MySpace to share information about their lives and keep in touch with their connections. Organizations quickly got on the bandwagon, setting up fan pages, where they can post about recent initiatives. Because it's free and so many people are on these social networks, this strategy has become big for nonprofits. In a recent survey, three-quarters of respondents representing nonprofits of all sizes and from multiple vertical segments reported having a presence on Facebook, and 30 percent have one or more social networking communities on their own web site.[9]

In addition, the social networks enable your own constituents to talk about your cause directly to their personal networks. Now, any user can organize an advocacy group via Facebook Causes. Cause administrators can post announcements to the cause and communicate with members through e-mail and on-site notifications. Members can discuss the issues, share their experiences, post media, and sign petitions. Causes can fundraise by selecting a beneficiary organization to receive donations; the donations are automatically delivered monthly.[10]

YouTube is the second most popular social networking site on the Internet and is filled with every kind of video under the sun. Recently, the organization All for Good responded to President Obama's call for Americans to engage in service and launched the Video Volunteers program on YouTube. It asks people to connect with the nonprofits they care about, identify their needs and the key points they want to get across, and make videos in support of the issue. Then, they upload the video to their channel and spread the word to their networks. It's a very real way to leverage the talents and networks of your constituents, and to put a personal face on your fundraising efforts.[11]

After Facebook and YouTube, Twitter is the third most popular social networking site.[12] Posts, or "tweets," are limited to 140 characters, including URLs. Nonprofits like the Red Cross, the American Civil Liberties Union, the American Cancer Society, and the Humane Society use Twitter to send updates about their issues to their followers. Examples include the latest media coverage of a key issue, updates on the progress of ongoing efforts, and replies to followers' questions. If you manage several Twitter accounts, the free applications TweetDeck and Nambu let you manage multiple identities in one place, and conduct searches to track what's being said about your nonprofit and issues.

Michael Gilbert, of the web site Nonprofit Online News, reminds us not to spend precious resources on social media for its sake alone—it's only useful when you do it for the relationships. Don't do it because your peer organizations are doing it or because it's hyped in the media. Use these tools judiciously to reach out and connect with your constituents, to enable them to speak on your behalf, and to listen carefully to your stakeholders.[13]

DEDICATED COMMUNITIES FOR YOUR CAUSE

Although the large social networks are full of people, they are also very fragmented. When someone is checking his or her Facebook page or Twitter account, that person is in a social mind-set, so it is not always the best place for collaborating with your community. To collect together your passionate community members, sometimes you have to create a destination just for them. Ning is a tool that enables communities to establish their own online headquarters—complete with discussion threads, a live chat room, audience polls, and a fully customizable interface that can be designed to blend into your existing web site.[14]

When seeking to attract more active members to your community, social networking sites designed for social good are the ideal place to find giving-minded people. Karma411 combines the social aspects of sharing personal stories with collaboration tools that enable nonprofits to maximize their community's energy and effectiveness.

Karma411 puts passionate individuals in the driver's seat—they can set up a profile and indicate favorite charities, write about their interests, and run their own fundraising campaigns on your behalf. Directing your volunteers and activists to such destinations puts the necessary tools at their fingertips while ensuring that their messages fall on attentive ears. Even in a networked world, the personal request remains the most powerful motivator for donations, so when members of the group invite their friends, it helps grow your support base exponentially. Photographs, videos, and personal stories enhance the appeal, and a real-time thermometer measures the campaign's progress to date.

For nonprofit leaders, Karma411 lets you collaborate with your community on a more intimate and immediate level and empower them to help achieve your goals. You can poll them, ask for feedback on various initiatives, update them on your progress, invite them to attend events, and even allow them to purchase tickets and sponsorships.

Case Study: R Baby

Founded in 2006, the R Baby Foundation works to reduce infant mortality through improving pediatric emergency care in the United States. In 2009, it established an annual Mother's Day run/walk event in New York's Central Park. Although the event itself held many opportunities for families to participate, the online collaboration tools R Baby used enabled maximum involvement before the event even began.

R Baby partnered with Karma411 (see Figure 4.7) to build a registration web site that would allow visitors not only to register for the run/walk but also to collaborate in ways that make the experience personal and compelling. The event itself was in New York City, but the web site made it possible for people everywhere to get involved. Supporters could form or join virtual teams or make a difference by signing up to cheer others on.

The cornerstone of this campaign's success was the formation of teams and the empowerment of the individual. With big budgets and clout, corporate sponsors were an integral part of the campaign; companies formed large teams, and each

FIGURE 4.7   **R Baby Fundraising Page on Karma411.com**

team set ambitious fundraising goals. In addition, related nonprofits and activist individuals established fundraising teams of their own.

Each team automatically received its own online fundraising page, where team leaders could share pictures and stories to help recruit new team members. The system tallied donations in real time and measured them against the fundraising goal. The fundraising efforts of each member of the team are reflected in the total.

Each team member could contribute to the team page but also got a personal fundraising page where he or she established a personal fundraising goal, told his or her own personal story through words and images, and sent invitations through the system asking friends to support his or her participation in the event. For those unable to be in New York on Mother's Day, the option to make a virtual walk allowed people to create fundraising pages as if they were walking or running, and they could likewise send them to their contacts to raise funds and help spread the word.

The key success factor was that the appeal for donations came not from R Baby, nor from the corporate team, but from the individual. The cycle perpetuated as donors who became educated and energized about the event registered themselves or sent the message to their own friends via the system or links to Facebook asking for additional participation (see Figure 4.8). The result

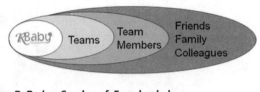

FIGURE 4.8   **R Baby Cycle of Fundraising**

of this multitier effort was an in-person event with almost 10,000 participants and $659,000 raised online.

Allowing event registrations online not only helps raise money; it is simply good service. According to the State of the Nonprofit Industry survey, 59 percent of nonprofits say that their organizations expect fundraising contributions from events to increase this year, and 26 percent expect that revenue to hold steady. Only 10 percent get no funding at all from events or don't hold events. So, 90 percent should be allowing registrations on the web versus the 43 percent that do. At a minimum, the 78 percent that advertise events through other direct-marketing channels could almost certainly see an improvement in event participation and associated gifts by allowing interested parties to learn more and register online.[15]

ENCOURAGING ADOPTION OF TECHNOLOGIES

We've reviewed many Web 2.0 tools that leverage social collaboration to increase your productivity, awareness, and fundraising. It's a great time to get started, because many tools are inexpensive or free, are easy to use, provide real-time results, and are constantly evolving. They also present new ways to leverage your supporter base, to include those people in the collaboration process.

Yet no matter how good the collaboration tool, it may take some effort to change your processes and facilitate adoption. The following recommendations will help:[16]

- Keep your ultimate goals in mind when selecting tools; don't allow bells and whistles to distract attention away from your core objectives.
- Nurture team members and help them grow with a natural affinity for the social collaboration sphere.
- Roll out functionality on a small scale and allow a core team to develop a proficiency before a full deployment.
- Train your team, allow team members to practice, and train again.

- Develop standard operating procedures and make collaboration tools an integral part of them.

- Include collaboration tools in job descriptions and performance reviews.

- Budget for training, upgrades, maintenance, and associated creative tasks.

You needn't change every aspect of your collaboration process at once. Identify your greatest need and search for a tool that will help you the most. Start with one small step and get most engaged constituents on board—you'll be surprised at how quickly it seems like second nature. Once your productivity jumps to the next level, you'll be looking for the next hot application!

STAYING ON TOP OF DEVELOPING TECHNOLOGY

The very nature of Web 2.0 is that it is always evolving, and the nature of a book is that it represents a snapshot in time. Stay abreast of new developments in the nonprofit technology space by reading industry papers and related blogs and by remaining active in your own online communities.

The Internet is rife with information that is good, bad, and useless. Search engines do not discern usefulness as well as someone who may have been looking for the same things you are. Communities have established useful ways to find the content particularly relevant to them through the use of tags. The collaborative nature of today's Internet means that, as people browse, they classify and rate content as they go.

On Twitter, you may have seen tweets or status updates with hash tags—words with the hash (# sign) in front of them. This allows Twitter Search to track all the tweets related to that term. The same principal applies to the Internet; people tag content using social bookmarking services like Delicious or Digg, effectively filtering the best and most relevant content on any topic for the rest of the community to enjoy.

The nonprofit technology community has adopted the tag "NPTech" to mark any web resource, blog post, or photo that has to do with nonprofit technology. When community members find helpful web pages, they tag them; as a result, the Delicious NPTech page is a great collection of resources that anyone can access. In addition, when these people blog about nonprofit technology, they tag each post with NPTech; a glance at the Technorati page for NPTech reveals all kinds of blog posts about nonprofit technology.

Thanks to RSS, you don't have to visit Delicious or Technorati every day to keep track of all these great resources. Feed readers like Google Reader, FeedDemon and NewsGator allow you to subscribe to the RSS feed for the

NPTech page in these services, and they let you read all tagged content in one place.[17]

CONCLUSION

Nonprofits are used to hard work and stretching every resource to the limit. It may seem impossible to achieve all of your goals, but through collaboration and the tools to enable it, you can both spread the effort and keep track of it.

Make it a habit to stay aware of new technologies, noting what has worked for the business world, and then leverage those best practices. Become the connectivity champion for your organization; you'll become closer to your team and the greater community involved in your cause.

As with any campaign effort, establishing traction takes time, but the results are worth it. Once you can eliminate the time and difficulty in planning in-person meetings and the coordination costs of thousands of phone calls, e-mail, and online meetings among your constituents, you can focus on your real goals—raising money and awareness for your nonprofit. Get everyone aligned using social collaboration tools and watch your productivity improve.

Russell M. Artzt is vice chair and founder at Computer Associates, playing an instrumental role in the evolution of the company's enterprise IT management vision. With more than 30 years of IT industry experience as a technology leader, consultant, and executive, Artzt also provides counsel in the areas of strategic partnerships, product development leadership, community and public affairs, board relations, and corporate strategy. Artzt is a recognized expert in software development and project management. He serves as chair of the Advisory Board of Stony Brook University's Center of Excellence for Wireless and Information Technology and is a member of the board of directors for the Advanced Energy Research Group. In March 2008, Artzt was inducted into the Long Island Technology Hall of Fame. Artzt is also active with many charitable organizations. He is the founder and sponsor of a research group at Mount Sinai Hospital in New York City involved in researching cures for liver diseases, is a major sponsor of the Juvenile Diabetes Research Foundation International and is a major supporter of North Shore University Hospital. In addition, he is a member of the Queens College Foundation board of trustees. Artzt received a bachelor's degree in mathematics from Queens College and a master's degree in computer science from New York University.

John Murcott runs products and strategy at Karma411. He is responsible for product development and runs the engineering and Q&A efforts on the site. He has worked with nonprofits such as the United Way, the Boys and Girls Clubs, and Mothers Against Drunk Driving to get them started with their Web 2.0 strategies and reach out to their supporters. Murcott was a cofounder of FatWire Software in 1996. He led the FatWire products group and engineering team and was responsible for product strategy and direction. Murcott has lectured on topics ranging from social networking to Web 2.0 technologies and content-centric applications. Murcott received his M.B.A. from the University of Maryland with a concentration in information technology and operations management and earned his undergraduate degree from Tufts University. Murcott and his wife, Gretchen, had their first baby boy, Jake, on May 23, 2008.

Mark Fasciano is the CEO and cofounder of Karma411, a social networking site that raises funds and awareness for nonprofits. Fasciano brings together his expertise in Web 2.0 technology with his entrepreneurial experience as founder and CEO of FatWire Software to help Karma411 members connect to a cause. Fasciano has worked on enterprise deployments with customers such as Ford Motor Company and GM, JP Morgan Chase, Best Buy, and the *New York Times*. He originally helped build the early versions of FatWire's first content management system, but as CEO, he focused primarily on the strategic business, including raising more than $30 million of venture capital. Articles about Fasciano and his work have been published in the *New York Times*, the *Wall Street Journal*, *Long Island Business News*, *USA Today*, and a number of software trade magazines. In 2000, he won Ernst & Young's Entrepreneur of the Year award. Fasciano graduated from Cornell University with degrees in English and computer science, and he received his M.S. and Ph.D. in computer science from the University of Chicago. His doctoral thesis from the Artificial Intelligence Lab at Chicago described a system for planning and acting in real-time, uncertain worlds.

CHAPTER 5

Insight Tools for Surviving and Thriving

ROGER M. CRAVER AND RYANN MILLER

Make no mistake. The global financial crisis that started in 2008 and is ongoing is not the cause of diminished financial performance and effectiveness on the part of many nonprofits, nor should it be used as some convenient excuse for avoiding the stark reality that the world of nonprofit fundraising and communications has changed dramatically—and forever.

The key trends over the past five years—which began long before the current global crisis—are clear and sobering:

- Despite overall population increases the number of donors contributing to nonprofits has actually declined.
- The blindly loyal World War II generation of donors that formed the bedrock of nonprofit giving over the past 30 years is now in the minority, supplanted by a new majority of donors—the more skeptical baby boomers and increasingly the younger generations X and Y.
- The tsunami-like flood of online information and the rise of social media—blogs; forums; and social networks like Facebook, LinkedIn, Twitter, and dozens of others—have supplanted and threaten to replace the conventional communications channels with a degree of fragmentation and democratization never before seen.

The result? Increased cost and difficulty in acquiring new donors, declining loyalty and retention rates, increased competition and fewer barriers to entry thanks to the web, and a bewildering array of communications channels. In short, a markedly changed fundraising and communications landscape in which the old rules, old ways, no longer pertain.

Don't Panic—There's Good News

Fortunately, at the very time that the good old days and their old ways are evaporating, there's been a remarkable surge in technology and technique, which we believe will make the new days even better than the old ones. These new tools, this new reality, this cacophony of channels and mediums, represent a new standard for nonprofits that we call the new nonprofit paradigm.

Thus, this chapter and its explanation and exploration of fundamental tools that every nonprofit executive, fundraiser, communicator, and campaigner should employ without delay. If you're a nonprofit executive, pay special attention: as with any new paradigm, the new nonprofit reality requires outstanding leadership. We talk of tools, but implicitly included in this discourse is the need for nonprofits to be communicative, integrated, real time, and networked; to be more grassroots 2.0; to listen to supporters and stakeholders and respond accordingly; and to collect data to turn that into insight, with an eye toward ongoing benchmarking. And it's up to management to define an organization's role as leader or follower.

Our insights and recommendations are based on surveys and tools developed for the clients of DonorTrends, a new company designed to help nonprofits listen to their donors and other constituents and take specific actions that will immediately and sustainably affect their bottom lines, whether the bottom line is money, campaign results, loyalty, or identifying and inspiring missionaries and recruiters to help swell their ranks.

In addition, we've tapped into the research, shared experiences, and practical advice provided by the editors and readers of the *Agitator* (http://www.theagitator.net), our daily information service that tracks trends, tips, and cutting-edge developments in the world of fundraising, advocacy, and communications.

In the sections that follow, we've focused on skills and tools that improve listening. Why? Because in the new donor-centric world, as opposed to the old organization-centric era, you will survive and thrive only if you know what your donors are feeling, saying, and doing—not just where your organization is concerned but across a range of the donor's lifestyle actions and events, all of which have an impact on you!

Specifically, we believe that there are three areas that deserve your immediate attention if you're going to help your organization grow and succeed in the fast-changing future:

1. Building loyalty

2. Effectively using social media and Web 2.0

3. Increasing your share of the competitive wallet

TIME FOR A MIND SHIFT

Today, most fundraisers continue to set strategies and measure results using a set of principles developed 50 years ago and improved only in incremental ways since. Yet the market has changed in so many ways that the old principles may no longer pertain, no matter how sophisticated they are.

Whether you're using the printing press and post office or are heavy into Web 2.0, if you're still using age-old fundraising and communications principles and evaluating those approaches by more or less old-fashioned metrics, you're simply not going to get the results you want and need.

The old-reality principles are based on acquiring donors in a mass way; retaining them using a standard set of best practices; and communicating with them through a small and identifiable number of channels, most of which involve pushing information from the organization to its donors or other constituents. Top down.

The new reality requires listening to individual donors and understanding what they're doing (e.g., giving, taking advocacy actions, recruiting) not just with your organization but also with your competition, seeing what other things define them, and then understanding which of their preferred interests and communications channels can best be used to involve and inspire them.

To put it another way, donors no longer just depend on one or two organizations to learn all about the issues and causes they care about and the involvement they seek. Today, and even more in the future, your organization will be given life and definition by the thousands or tens of thousands of your donors and their friends through their social networks. This creates a situation in which nonprofits are outsiders who must earn their right to respect and positive acceptance—new challenges and new opportunities.

Mercifully, the new generation of tools and approaches facilitate the shift from the organization-centric past to the donor-centric present and future. Welcome to the new safety net!

FOCUS ON THE NEW ROI

The traditional metric of return on investment (ROI) is still very important. But frankly, there's another ROI that's even more critical: return on insight. There's no question in our minds that knowing what your donors are doing, beyond the mere transactional data reflected in your contact with them and their response to your top-down or push messaging, is more important than ever, but it will be essential tomorrow.

Remember that we're focused here on listening and on the tools that will help accomplish that. All the conventional approaches to fundraising provide some insight into some important parts of behavior like who (the person who bought a product or made a gift) and what (the object of their beneficence). But the essential ingredient that all the conventional data and analyses don't provide is the one critical variable: when!

For a moment, put yourself in the position of the marketing strategist for a leading brand that defleas dogs. You can easily buy data identifying dog owners. And you can survey for the problems that dog owners are most concerned with—you might assume that flea problems are right up there.

What you can't buy, rent, or find from analyzing a database is the "when" factor. When will the dog and its owner experience a flea attack, and when will the owner want to take action? Just imagine if your company or nonprofit could find out exactly when your customers or prospects have a heightened concern about an issue.

Well, you can. And more important, if you organize the listening tools available to your nonprofit, you can find out what your donors are concerned with and when they're most concerned, and so most open to becoming more involved with your organization. Now you're in a position to positively involve donors at exactly the right time.

Our goal in this chapter is to outline the immense potential of some new technologies and suggest how to make the most of them. We begin in the following section with the most important factor in organizational sustainability and growth—loyalty.

LOYALTY—THE HOLY GRAIL OF FUNDRAISING

A high degree of loyalty is essential to the financial growth and efficiency of any nonprofit. This is especially true when the costs of acquiring new donors are rising.

Failure to hold on to newly acquired donors means that, the lower is your retention rate, the actual cost of recruiting a new donor becomes higher. In fact, at some point, it becomes nearly impossible to recover the acquisition investment. Thus, if you're trying to pour the water of new donor acquisition into your organizational bucket, you want as few leaks as possible. That's what loyalty or high retention is all about and why it's the number-one job for virtually every fundraiser and nonprofit executive.

We use the term "loyalty" here as a catchall for "retaining," "upgrading," and otherwise increasing the value of a constituency. Here we focus on fundraising, but you can also apply our ideas to advocacy, volunteerism, or any other measurable activity that advances the mission of your organization.

Consequently, any nonprofit intent on surviving into the future must focus on loyalty because it must steer its fundraising and communications investments in the most efficient way to hold on to those donors who are most likely to be there for you tomorrow and for years to come.

There are two essential steps to building a truly effective loyalty program:

1. Understand just how loyal your donors, members, or constituents are and why, and measure that against a national or sector benchmark.

2. Identify those who are most likely to be loyal in the future and focus your attention and investment of time and money disproportionately on them.

First, Do a Reality Check   Almost every organization we've ever worked with assumes that all active donors (defined as those who've made contribution in the past 12 months) are valuable. And yet we know this isn't true. The truth is that, even though you might classify them as active donors, there are large clumps of active givers who only break even (their contributions just pay for the costs of fulfillment and servicing) and many who actually lose money.

So, even before focusing on loyalty, do a reality check on profitability and be prepared to jettison those donors who cost you money. Of course, there may be other reasons, such as advocacy or sheer size of donation, that you may want to keep them, but we're focusing on raising money here.

Figures 5.1 and 5.2 show a quite normal distribution of donor profitability, ranging from the highly profitable to the money losers. Take the time and do the analysis to see how your organization compares.

Fundraising strategies should be implemented to protect the profitable segments and upgrade or eliminate donors from investment levels.

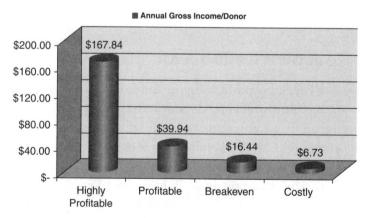

Step 1: Calculate the average annual cost to renew a donor. In this example the cost to renew a donor is $16/year.

Step 2: Evaluate your return on investment by calculating the average gross annual income per donor minus the total annual cost to renew.

FIGURE 5.1   Distribution of Donor Profitability

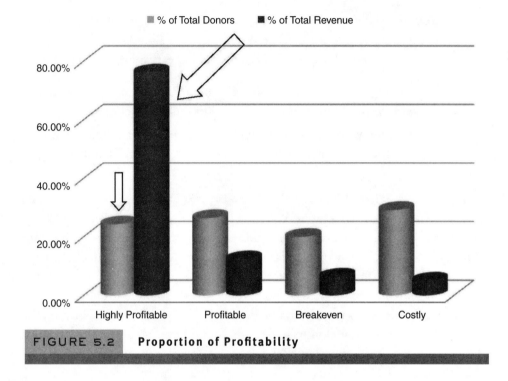

FIGURE 5.2   **Proportion of Profitability**

In Figures 5.1 and 5.2, note how 50 percent of the entire group of active donors accounts for 80 percent of the money, whereas the remaining 50 percent just break even or cause the organization to lose money. Is this happening in your organization? In all probability, the answer is yes. Creating an effective, future-oriented loyalty program requires a basic shift in the mind-set of most organizations. The reality is that, when it comes to making investments in loyalty, not all donors should be part of that investment.

NEXT, FOLLOW THE DOLLAR

With the reality check on profitability in hand, focus next on a plan to build loyalty among the most profitable donors and a plan to move the break-even donors into the profitable range and to discard the costly donors.

Don't make the mistake of assuming that those who currently give you the most money will be the same ones who do so in the future. Sadly, life and fundraising don't work that way. Instead, build your loyalty plan by identifying those donors who are most likely to maintain and increase their giving over the next 36 months.

Why Is Predicting Future Loyalty So Important?   In the end, it all comes down to money and the return on investment. Why spend precious funds on folks who aren't going to be with you in the end? It's the difference between dating and going steady.

The problem with today's conventional approaches, like the use of recency, frequency, monetary value (RFM), is that they focus on the past and present and do not predict future loyalty. So how do you factor in the future? How do you know which new donor is worth spending money on and whom you should simply ignore? The answer isn't simple, but here's our advice:

- Make an investment in a predictive loyalty system model. If you're not sure where to find one, look to DonorTrends. The DonorTrends Loyalty Predictor will spot—with 93 percent accuracy—those donors worth spending money on and those who you should pass over.

- Establish your own definition and prediction of what's likely to constitute future loyalty. Consider factors like size of first gift; time between the first, second, and third gifts; length of time for regular giving; and upgrading and downgrading.

THE ONE LOYALTY MYTH TO AVOID

There are lots of theories about what factors best predict loyalty. Frankly, you're pretty safe in taking them all into consideration. But the one myth that will lead you astray is what we call the net promoter myth. This is the belief that, if a donor is willing to recommend your organization, that somehow makes him or her more loyal than other donors. It doesn't. We wish it did.

For years in the commercial world, the net promoter theory held sway. Today, it's largely been disproved. In fact, in all the DonorTrends loyalty system research we've done, the theory simply doesn't matter. Period.

The theory is called the net promoter score because detractors are subtracted from promoters to provide the estimate of how many more promoters than detractors the organization has.

The problem with this widely accepted myth is that loyal donors don't always act as advocates for the nonprofits they give to. In fact, our DonorTrends research shows over and over that they seldom do.[1] So if word of mouth is actually more constrained than conventionally thought, how exactly does the net promoter concept work? Well, it doesn't. And for heaven's sake, please don't rely on it heavily as a measure of loyalty—you'll be led astray.

ENOUGH THEORY—WHAT DO I DO?

Having identified the most loyal and least loyal donors, put together and execute a loyalty plan. Specifically, we recommend that you do the following:

- Identify and specifically address likely defectors.
- Tell your success story to existing donors.

- Put your leader in front of your donors.
- Effectively manage the issue of trust with your donors.
- Monitor the competition.
- Deliver a sense of belonging by capitalizing on a prime trait of loyal donors—their propensity to use online engagement tools.

Next, focus your communications and stewardship programs on those donors you've identified as the most likely to remain loyal and increase their giving. Pay particular attention to those who have been with you the longest, those with the highest gifts, and those new donors who show extraordinary activity compared to the rest of the pack. The following list sets forth a list of practical and sensible communications tips sent by Lisa Sargent of Sargent Communications, to the *Agitator*:

- **Gift reminder:** If donor Jane sponsors a cat-dog acre of rain forest for her nieces and nephews, send her a reminder next year and make it easy for her to repeat the gift. Such gifts are often last minute, so perhaps send your message a week earlier. Somewhere in this sequence, why not ask donors whether they'd like to add more special dates—then you can automatically send them reminders. For example, May 5 is Johnny's birthday and August 22 is Fido's.

- **Progress reports:** When donors can sponsor practically anything, that just begs for updates! Tell donors about a sponsor dog: Is he making friends? Getting new training? If a donor has sponsored a child, does she read her new book night and day? Is it summer where she lives? Or in another case, is the donor's acre of rain forest now linked to 200 others, and is it a prime neighborhood for poison dart frogs? Even general info is relevant: changing seasons, annual migrations, aerial photos, and so on.

- **Tips targeted to individual interests:** If Greta gives to support breast cancer, chances are pretty good that she knows someone who has it or has it herself. Is there something new about breast exams that would help? A breakthrough on who should get breast cancer genetic testing? For other causes, you might send pet-care hints, dog-training tips, low-sugar recipes of the week, or monthly action tips for greening your house.

- **"Invented" event acknowledgments:** The anniversary of an online gift is an obvious event to acknowledge. Why not give the animals in your sponsor program birthdays when they arrive, and then send a thank you to a donor on his or her pet's birthday? How about a sponsor child's first day of school?

- **Share your stories:** Who doesn't want to hear stories of hope in this crummy economy? E-mail your donors and offer them an opt-in to a Monday miracle story, true tales from the rescue case files, field report archives, video links of the week, and so on. But don't turn it into a pitch fest: share the story; add relevant donate, about, share, and video links; and stick to it. You might consider creating some cliffhangers with two-part stories.

- **Wild cards:** How about surveys? Or a fun quiz for visitors to test their knowledge about a certain topic. You might include audio links, such as allowing visitors to listen to a whale's song, kids in your sponsor child's village at play, or morning feeding time at the zoo.[2]

Barb Perell, of Avalon Consulting, suggests, "If funds available for executing your loyalty plan are limited, concentrate your resources on activities aimed at the most loyal donors. After all, this is where you'll get the greatest return on investment. However, if you do have extra funds, you should also take steps to hold on to those donors who are about to defect."[3] The following list sets forth some basic intervention strategies for the not-so-loyal group, the likely defectors:

- Identify likely defectors (e.g., by decreasing gift size or frequency) and vary communication.

- Meet the performance test by retelling donors your story—have outsiders look at your communications and make donors feel part of your accomplishments.

- Introduce your organization's leader in person, such as through online video messages, blogs, podcasts, or live town hall meetings or membership meetings.

- Monitor and respond to high-profile reputation casualties—for example, if an ethical lapse has occurred, underscore your organization's ethics. If you leader has blundered, bring forth your Rock of Gibraltar.

SURVEYING AND BENCHMARKING LOYALTY

Among the most important insight tools is the loyalty survey of your organization's donors. When you use a loyalty survey to gauge your own stakeholders, in conjunction with a comparative loyalty benchmark survey (which benchmarks against loyalty in other organizations), you not only will learn the strengths and weakness related to loyalty among your donors but also can see how you're doing compared to other nonprofits nationally or in your specific sector.

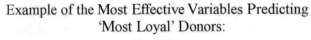

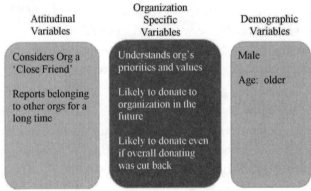

Example of the Most Effective Variables Predicting 'Most Loyal' Donors:

Attitudinal Variables	Organization Specific Variables	Demographic Variables
Considers Org a 'Close Friend' Reports belonging to other orgs for a long time	Understands org's priorities and values Likely to donate to organization in the future Likely to donate even if overall donating was cut back	Male Age: older

FIGURE 5.3   Predictive Variables

Ideally, we recommend that you begin the process with both a survey of your own donors and a benchmark comparison of other organizations' results. Then you should periodically update your survey and benchmarking to constantly monitor your progress toward achieving a higher loyalty score among your constituents. Given the financial value that increased loyalty brings to a nonprofit, a loyalty survey with comparative benchmarking is one of the best investments you can make.

The omnibus and organization-specific surveys we conduct at DonorTrends help identify the key factors in predicting loyalty among a large group of donors. By identifying the most effective predictive variables, an organization can steer its messaging and donor communications to increase loyalty. Figure 5.3 sets forth the attitudinal, demographic, and organizational factors most predictive of loyalty for a hypothetical organization.

Donor loyalty surveys also provide vital information for fundraisers and executives. Such surveys not only can help spot problem areas but also can signal whether a particular group of donors is likely to increase or decrease giving in the near future.

Figure 5.4 reflects the attitude of our hypothetical organization's most loyal donors toward future giving. When compared with the national benchmark sample, the organization's donors are slightly less likely to give again to the organization than are donors to other nonprofits. If the results had been much lower than the national benchmark, the organization's management would be alerted to a potential problem that they would need to address.

In survey after survey conducted by DonorTrends, we have found that the issue of trust is among the most important factors in predicting and ensuring

How likely are you to donate in the next 12 months?

Survey Answer	Total	0-12 Month Donors	Super-Loyal Donors	National Benchmark
Definitely	12%	20%	27%	31%
Probably	38%	48%	47%	46%
Probably/ Definitely Not	49%	31%	25%	24%

FIGURE 5.4   **Likelihood of Contributing in the Next 12 Months**

donors' loyalty. A properly constructed donor loyalty survey can help guide an organization's messaging and the tone it sets with its donors around the essential issue of trust. Figure 5.5 illustrates a few of the questions that help inform fundraisers, communicators, and executives how their organization is currently perceived.

THE VALUE OF LOYALTY-INSIGHT TOOLS

Loyalty-insight tools can help ensure your organization's future in the following ways. First, loyalty surveys tell you how your donors perceive you and help identify key attitudinal and demographic factors that predict future loyalty. They

How Respondents View Organization A

Survey Answer	Total	0-12 Month Donors	Super-Loyal Donors	National Benchmark
Like a close friend whose value I share	22%	20%	30%	28%
Like an acquaintance I admire	58%	56%	54%	52%
Like a relative I feel obligated to support	13%	11%	12%	19%
Like a panhandler who pesters me until I give	5%	2%	1%	4%

FIGURE 5.5   **How Donors View Your Organization**

help identify problems and inform the best approaches to solving them. When benchmarked against other organizations in your sector or against a diverse group of nonprofits, they let you know how you're doing up against the competition and alert you to problems and opportunities.

Second, loyalty scoring and predictors help you steer spending more effectively to ensure maximum net income from an increasing base of the most loyal donors. These tools, rather than the old RFM approach, which deals only with the present and past, help you focus on the future and take appropriate actions toward greater and greater profitability.

Insight Tools for Social Media and the Online World

Just as we were putting the final touches on this chapter, the Pew Internet Project released its latest figures on home broadband penetration in the United States. Break out the champagne because broadband penetration is increasing most dramatically in the population segments that form the best donor groups for most nonprofits. In brief:

- Broadband usage among adults age 65 and older grew from 19 percent to 30 percent.

- Among adults between the ages of 50 and 64, broadband usage increased from 50 percent to 61 percent.

- Of respondents living homes with annual household income of $20,000 or less, 35 percent have home broadband, compared with 53 percent of those with household income of $20,000 to $30,000 and 85 percent penetration for those with household incomes of more than $75,000.

- Among adults whose highest level of educational attainment is a high school degree, broadband adoption grew from 40 percent to 52 percent (compared to broadband penetration in 83 percent in homes where a college degree or more is highest level of education).

Why is this information important to nonprofits? From a fundraising and issue-education standpoint, more and more of the boomer and older population—the current demographic sweet spot for fundraising—has broadband. Internet-usage studies have indicated consistently that access to broadband significantly increases both the amount of time users spend online and the range of online activities they engage in (e.g., more searching for information, watching videos, giving online, and using social networks).

Speed and the always-on aspect of broadband really count! According to Ray Mitchell, of Trident Communications Group:

> There is little doubt, in my own view anyway, that broadband penetration into U.S. homes, and the continuing explosion of web-based communication, means that every nonprofit organization wanting to survive must have or begin developing a corporate-constituency communications plan that includes a preeminent, online component. To ignore this reality is to risk failure in an organization's efforts to communicate effectively and have any impact on the larger, external audience. An audience, by the way, that is being bombarded with information (and "noise") every single day! Since building and cultivating loyal, supportive and generous constituencies begins with and is based on a core foundation of communication, the equation is clear—particularly in the case of baby boomers and the others who possess so much of the resources. To get to them with a compelling message on mission and make an equally compelling case for their financial support, a nonprofit has to pursue them where they are (or will be)—at the keyboard of a computer![4]

At Last! Expectations Delivered

For years, fundraisers have bemoaned the fact that the glorious expectations of online fundraising have yet to materialize. To this day, the funds generated online are a fraction of those from direct mail. But each year the online portion increases and increases dramatically.

What's even more important to your nonprofit is that, increasingly, donors now get their basic information and news online and are stampeding toward social media and social networks. Facebook saw its 35–54 age bracket blow up by 276.4 percent between June 2008 and January 2009. The 55-and-older contingent grew 194.3 percent in the same amount of time. The total number of Facebook users over the age of 35 in October 2007 totaled just fewer than 845,000; as of January 2009, their combined might totaled nearly 8 million, or 18.9 percent of the total Facebook pie.

The might of this important fundraising demographic extends beyond Facebook, too. More than 60 percent of baby boomers consume socially created content, according to a recent Forrester report. Though they might not create content as willingly as the average 22-year-old—the report notes they aren't as likely to start a blog or upload a video to YouTube—this group of 43- to 63-year-olds instead wields more disposable income and constitutes a bigger generational segment.[5]

So pay attention, because that group has no problem consuming social content. In Forrester's survey, 62 percent of boomers aged 53–63 and 66.7 percent of boomers between the ages of 43 and 52 said they could be found "reading blogs, listening to podcasts, watching user-generated videos, reading forums, or reading consumer ratings."[6]

Facebook and YouTube aside, who better to cater to these emerging social network addicts than AARP? In 2009, the nonprofit advocate for the 50-and-older contingent revamped and relaunched its web site, including an online community boasting 400,000 registered users (see Figure 5.6). Community membership is free and members can create personalized profiles and post photos, video, and blogs.

According to AARP, older members of its community are getting their bearings just fine. "More than ever, our users are becoming more comfortable talking to each other, creating blogs and commenting on articles," says an AARP spokesperson.[7]

So, now that key fundraising audiences are online in a big way and user-generated content (e.g., blogs, social networks, Twitter, wikis, news sites, podcasts, video-sharing sites) is proliferating at warp speed, a key question is, What are the insight tools that smart fundraisers and communicators should be using?

INSIGHT TOOLS FOR WEB MONITORING—A CRASH COURSE IN WHY, WHAT, AND HOW

One thing is certain: Gone are the days when a clipping service—online or offline—was sufficient and timely for monitoring what was said in the media about your organization, your issues, and your competition. With more than 50 million actual or prospective donors reading blogs, with more than a half billion individuals registered on one or more social networking sites, and with millions and millions of individuals using microblogging services, it is increasingly vital to monitor what's happening in the online world in order to influence how your organization's reputation and issues are dealt with.

Many nonprofits have instituted at least a rudimentary routine of using Google search or Yahoo! Alerts in some combination with other services like Technorati or Digg in an effort to follow what's being said about their organization and their issues in the online world. These services have the advantages of being free but the disadvantages of being time consuming and woefully inadequate for gathering meaningful intelligence.

Whatever approach or technology you employ, it needs to be able to deliver on what we call the five "musts" of nonprofit intelligence for survival in the Web 2.0 world:

1. **Who is doing the talking and what's that person's influence?** Quickly identify the key influencers, and then get detailed information about their sex, age, industry, and interests.

2. **What are people talking about? What are the key conversations?** Monitor the conversations to see what is being said about your organization and issues and about your competitors. Identify the major themes and issues being raised not only in the social media landscape but also in the mainstream media.

3. **When did these conversations happen? Was there a lot of activity?** Learn more about when these conversations happen—both historically and in real time. Look at and compare the buzz generated over time.

4. **Where did these conversations happen? Was there a lot of activity?** Access geodemographic information to see where conversations

are taking place around the nation and the world—right down to a town or city.

5. **Why are conversations happening? Are they positive or negative?** Determine whether conversations are because of seeds you've planted or are independent of your organization. See whether what's talked about is positive, negative, or neutral, and determine the impact on your organization.

Here are the key features that a sophisticated monitoring and measuring tool should provide:

- Instant access to a comprehensive and spam-free archive featuring billions of conversations (and counting) and dating back at least one year.
- Continually updated content from blogs, social networks, microblogging services, wikis, message boards, video-sharing sites, and traditional news sources (e.g., CNN, *New York Times*)
- Geographic and demographic (e.g., age, sex) information
- Automated sentiment to assess whether conversations are positive, negative, or neutral.
- Text analytics to identify key themes, emerging topics and trends, and context
- Measurable metrics about popularity, geography and demographics, and authority
- The ability to compare reach, share of voice, and brand impact with those of competitors.

With the foregoing features, insight tools will be able to do the following:

Listen: The social media landscape is busy and filled with plenty of noise. This makes it a challenge to identify and hear the conversations on blogs, social networks, forums, microblogging services, news sites, and more. You need the ability to listen to millions of conversations about your organization and issues in real time.

Measure: Instantly track and measure your organization's campaigns, your nonprofit's brand, and the issues you work on by sentiment. By analyzing results over time and making comparisons with competitors, you can build context and optimize messaging.

Understand: Get insight into conversations taking place about you or your organization, who's involved, and where the conversations are taking place. You can then determine the impact on your organization's campaigns, issues, and reputation, and if needed, make adjustments to your communications, campaigning, or fundraising plans.

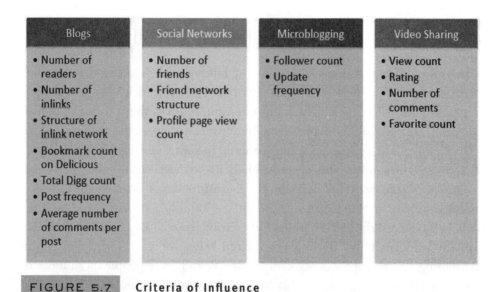

Blogs	Social Networks	Microblogging	Video Sharing
• Number of readers • Number of inlinks • Structure of inlink network • Bookmark count on Delicious • Total Digg count • Post frequency • Average number of comments per post	• Number of friends • Friend network structure • Profile page view count	• Follower count • Update frequency	• View count • Rating • Number of comments • Favorite count

FIGURE 5.7   **Criteria of Influence**

Engage: Identify the people driving the conversations, and understand who they are, their interests, and their authority and relevance to your organization and its issues. This lets you engage with key influencers and opinion leaders to build, nurture, and steer relationships.

Figure 5.7 illustrates the various attributes used to rank or identify the most influential social media sites.

The ability of whatever insight tool you employ to determine and measure influence is critically important if you are to harness the true power of social media for your organization and its campaigns.

By identifying those bloggers, Twitterers, and social network members with the most influence, you will be able to focus your time and resources on those who will have the most profound effect on the mission of your nonprofit.

Knowing what and who is talking about you is crucial. Listening and reacting to these conversations is what separates sector leaders from the rest. In the new era of online democratic communications channels, the user (or donor) is king. Gone are the days when communication was top down and a web site was the message.

Organizations have a challenging but important opportunity ahead of them. Ask yourself what you want to track and measure and why, what questions you want answers to, and how that will affect the mission of your campaign or organization. Without having your destination in mind, the path will never be a straightforward one.

IDENTIFY AND INVEST IN THE RECRUITERS

There's lots of buzz around social networks, but how can you turn that buzz into donations and other actions such as advocacy and recruiting? We know many fundraisers are still struggling with this question. Frankly, the conversion of buzz into actual results isn't a mystery. The same process that applies to offline forms of fundraising and campaigning apply online. In short, identify, cultivate, solicit, and involve those folks who are most likely to be most valuable to you in your online work, that is, those folks in your constituency who are super users of online social networks.

Why? Because those people have the most friends. Because they can potentially bring or enlist above-average-sized teams for your social networking fundraising events and advocacy campaigns. We call these people recruiters, and we classify them, along with highly loyal donors, as super donors.

Table 5.1 is from a DonorTrends 2009 report on super donors. Just take a look at how much more recruiters give each year, and you'll quickly see why they're worth paying special attention to.

In the online world, recruiters distinguish themselves from all other types of donors because of their online behavioral patterns. Table 5.2 shows how different these behavioral patterns really are when it comes to charity and cause-related online behavior.

IDENTIFYING THE RECRUITERS

There are a number of ways to identify recruiters. Carefully analyze the online transactions and activity of your constituents or survey them to find behavioral patterns similar to those in Table 5.1.

TABLE 5.1   SUPER DONORS

	Loyal Donors	Nonloyal Donors	Recruiters	Nonrecruiters
Annual giving to charities	$2,221	$467	$1,080	$749
Annual giving to issue advocacy	$108	$61	$103	$62
Annual giving to political campaigns	$113	$36	$166	$22
Total annual giving	**$2,442**	**$564**	**$1,349**	**$833**
Will give more in next five years	54%	40%	55%	39%
Will give less in next five years	5%	11%	9%	10%
Have a will with charitable gift	13%	6%	18%	5%
No will yet but anticipates including a charitable gift	35%	36%	42%	34%

| TABLE 5.2 | BEHAVIORAL PATTERNS OF RECRUITERS |

	Recruiters (%)	Nonrecruiters (%)	Loyal Donors (%)	Nonloyal Donors (%)
Purchase online using a credit card	45	35	39	36
Read a blog	33	16	26	18
Frequently put themselves on online newsletter lists and info alerts	32	18	26	20
Publish on social networks like Facebook and MySpace	31	14	17	18
Visit another person's profile on a social networking site	31	16	19	19
Research a nonprofit online before giving	27	10	20	12
Urge a friend online to take action on an issue	27	8	20	10
Watch a charity or cause-related video online	15	4	11	5

An easier and more accurate method is to use a screening service that will identify potential recruiters for you.

An effective approach to screening begins by identifying which social networks your donors or prospects are involved in. Then you'll know which of your donors you should spend more time and money enlisting for your organization's online activities. It never ceases to amaze us how many people can be found in donors' social networks.

CONCLUSION

Insight tools are essential for succeeding in this new era of fundraising. Of particular importance are tools that help you identify and predict loyalty. For example, media monitoring tools give you clarity about how your organization is viewed and by whom in the sometimes-swirling, murky world of the Internet. Other tools give you an online edge when it comes to identifying and enlisting social network leaders among your donors and activists.

In the new donor-centric world, donor behavior online and offline is your vital concern. What are they saying? Where else are they giving? Who is the most loyal or potentially loyal, and how do you communicate with them in ways to produce the highest ROI? How many friends do they have, and can they recruit their friends to your cause? How can you best turn donor insight into trust, loyalty, volunteer activism, advocacy, and a thriving bottom line?

Looked at as a whole, insight tools represent the opportunity to create a new nonprofit paradigm. However, techniques, technology, and new channels of communication are not enough: they alone can't improve your bottom line, can't stop the bleeding of donor attrition, and can't make your organization the darling and recipient of a slick online social network campaign. The insight tools described in this chapter can help you answer the question, What should we do now that we see the opportunity?

Roger M. Craver is editor in chief of the Agitator, a daily information service on fundraising and communications (http://www.theagitator.net) He is also founder of Craver, Mathews, Smith & Company and cofounder of DonorTrends (http://www.donortrends.com), which monitors donor behavior and motivation and provides actionable recommendations to the nonprofit community. Craver has been a fundraiser for 40 years and has helped build some of the household names in social justice and citizens movements, including the American Civil Liberties Union, Greenpeace, Habitat for Humanity, Common Cause, the National Organization for Women, and Amnesty International in the United States.

Ryann Miller is managing director of DonorTrends. She is also a specialist in integrated fundraising and campaigning, with special emphasis on online media and social networks. Miller has served as a consultant to Greenpeace International; the International Campaign for Tibet; Amnesty International; and a variety of humanitarian and relief, environmental, and health-based organizations. Formerly a senior fundraising consultant with HJC, Miller likes to help nonprofits leverage the Internet as one of the tools in the nonprofit fundraising, advocacy, and marketing tool kit.

CHAPTER 6

Demystifying Online Metrics

UNDERSTANDING THE HITS, CLICKS, AND ERRORS

STEVE MACLAUGHLIN

Metrics are an omnipresent part of our daily lives. Although we may not devote a lot of time to thinking about them, there would be chaos without them. Imagine no distances on the road signs or not having the right measure of coffee in your cup. The sensors on everything from planes to trains and automobiles would not function. Even the local clock tower or your alarm clock would be useless without metrics. The direction of the wind or changes in the stock markets or the ebb and flow of the tides all depend on metrics to help guide us.

We live in a world measured and moved forward by metrics—perhaps at times a little too much so. Although what we measure and how we measure it continues to change, the importance of metrics has only increased. This is true of the Internet, and it is true for how nonprofits are leveraging this medium to create dynamic interactions with their constituents. The Internet brings with it a host of new and evolving set of metrics that nonprofits must understand and embrace.

METRICS OVERVIEW

Understanding the key metrics for managing online initiatives allows nonprofits to measure their performance and to benchmark themselves against other peer organizations. This includes using metrics related to web sites, e-mail marketing, online advocacy, social media, and online fundraising. As these metrics programs become more mature, there is a natural progression toward using benchmarks to understand how the nonprofit is performing relative to other organizations.

Building a successful metrics program also requires building a culture that understands and embraces the importance of measuring progress and performance toward important goals. These areas will each be explored in more detail to demystify the purpose and power that online metrics can bring to nonprofits as they focus on fulfilling their missions.

What Is a Metric?

A discussion about metrics should begin by defining the term. A metric is a standard unit of measure. It is an established and accepted measurement of a particular item. A metric might be a universal standard agreed to by kings, queens, scientists, and governments or something very obscure that is used only by a small group. Metrics tell us things like how big; how small; how fast; how slow; and other measurements of space, time, size, shape, and distance.

They also help us establish qualitative and quantitative measurements of how well something is performing. Metrics provide us with a time machine that gives us insight into things that happened in the past and present and that can help predict the future. Nonprofit metrics exist in categories that range from operational to programmatic, financial to fundraising, and the host of communication and engagement channels they use with constituents.

Why Are Metrics Important?

Metrics give nonprofits the ability to measure and manage their progress toward organizational goals and objectives. If you can't measure those things, then you can't manage them. Metrics remove the guessing about how things are going and the direction they are going in. Metrics give nonprofits an important tool to improve their results and get the most out of their various initiatives.

All of this provides a framework for what to measure and how to measure it in meaningful ways. It also helps reveal why people take an action, how often, and under what conditions are things less favorable for results to happen.

It should also be noted that nothing causes a stir like a discussion about metrics. Bring up measuring results and people often react in extreme ways. People get defensive. People get argumentative. People put up walls. People get downright rude. Statistics and benchmark reports often create widespread discussion in the industry. Some engage in debate over the findings or the sample size or the source of the findings or a host of other variables related to the metrics.

There are a few reasons the discussion of metrics causes such strong reactions. First, many programs and departments in nonprofits are measured on their performance. Budgets, jobs, and careers are all subject to how good, bad, or ugly performance is over time. It can hit close to home when a metric shows that you are underperforming in an area or compared to peer organizations.

This explains the innately human reaction to metrics that either support our work or question our results. Creating a culture in which metrics are understood and leveraged to improve the entire organization will require a change in how we approach performance measurement.

It has been said before that not all things that count can be counted, and not all things that can be counted count. There is a natural apprehension to letting metrics tell the whole story or establish the value of an initiative in totality. Establishing what is being measured, how it will be measured, and how this data will be turned into valuable information is the cornerstone of any good metrics program.

Having a healthy dialogue about how much weight metrics should have in an organization's decision-making process is recommended. But do not fall into the trap of not leveraging all the positive capabilities of online metrics because the news may not always be rosy. Focus on how metrics can help the organization improve the ways it serves its constituents and increases its ability to fulfill its mission.

Truth be told, there are good metrics and there are bad metrics. Good metrics are simple, measurable, actionable, relevant, and timely. These characteristics form the basis for the online metrics that will now be examined in more detail. The next section begins with a review of common web site, e-mail, online advocacy, social media, and online fundraising metrics.

Web Site Metrics

Despite countless books and seminars on the topic of web site metrics a lot of confusion still remains. The field continues to evolve and change as new technologies are introduced that allow for better monitoring on the web. It should also be noted that measuring what happens on a web site is an inexact science. This makes it all the more important that nonprofits understand what they are measuring, why it matters, and what to do with the information.

Hits, Runs, and Errors

When it comes to web site metrics, less is more. Having more data does not mean having more insight or value. In fact, the most valuable web site metrics do not have mounds and mounds of data. They are finely tuned pieces of information that tell you what is happening on your web site in meaningful ways. There is a simple hierarchy to understanding the basics of web site metrics. It is based on a series of commonly collected pieces of data that can be captured and analyzed to measure results (see Figure 6.1).

Hits

A hit is the building block for web site statistics and accounts for most of the volume of data in web site metrics. It is also a very misunderstood, misinterpreted,

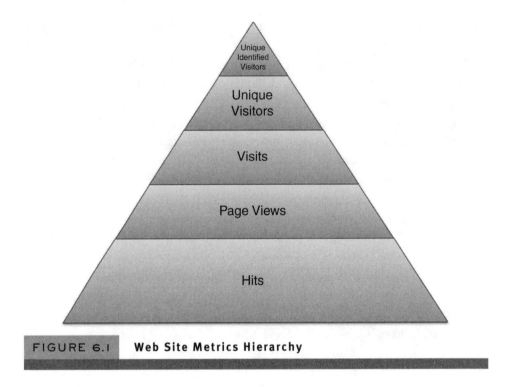

FIGURE 6.1   **Web Site Metrics Hierarchy**

and overused term. A hit takes place when a request for a file from the web server takes place. This happens when a visitor to a web site goes to a page and everything on that page is loaded and presented to him or her. A single web page typically consists of multiple files. A hit is registered for the page, every image, and any other files present on that page. Some of these files may be entirely hidden to the user and can distort the statistics.

This means that visiting a single page can generate dozens of hits and produces a lot of web site metric data. You can quickly see why a hit is not a useful metric other than a way to measure the totality of all the things being presented to visitors of your web site. People who brag about getting 5,714,285 hits to their web site either don't understand what it really means or are hoping you don't. It is worth noting that in the web metrics business, the word "hits" is said to stand for "how idiots track statistics."

Page Views

A page view is the next web site metric in the hierarchy. A page view is a request to load a single web page. Unlike a hit, this counts just the entire page itself. This happens when visitors to a web site types in a URL or clicks on a link that takes them to a page. It is possible that, in some cases, multiple pages are being framed or otherwise loaded to appear as part of a single page.

Page views are a useful metric for looking at the entire web site or specific content. Total page views for the site can give a big-picture view of trends, and page views for specific pages can be very helpful in fine-tuning what is working and what is not on the web site. Page views can be looked at over periods of time or for a specific event to look for results. Be sure to note how marketing efforts or e-mail campaigns have an impact on page views during that window of time.

Visits

A visit is when someone goes to the web site during a set period of time. It is important to note that not all site-tracking tools measure this period of time in the same way. In some cases, the measure could be 30 minutes or several days. Be sure to see exactly how your tools measure this important metric. A site visit contains one or more page views and acts as the next tier in the web site metric hierarchy.

Visits help you understand what people do when they visit your web site. Are they viewing just a single page or multiple pages? Are there common patterns to what they are doing? Looking at visits also opens up several other tracking options like visits by day of the week, time spent on the web site, geographic location, browsers being used, and bounce rates that can be very useful.

Unique Visitors

A unique visitor is tracked by a cookie or other scripting techniques. This happens when a visitor views the web site from the same computer or device during a period of time. Tracking unique visitors can be affected by a variety of factors that decrease the reliability of this method. This includes the fact that people may use multiple computers or devices, and there is not a way to track them across the different contact points. It should also be noted that many companies routinely block or delete cookies from machines, and this will skew statistics or the ability to target certain content reliably.

Unique visitors can help distinguish new and repeat visitors to the web site. If the site is good at attracting people but not very good at getting them to return, then this can be a problem. Understanding the behavior of specific users can provide valuable insights into what people are doing or not doing on the web site. Looking at patterns among unique visitors over time is one way to see how changes to the web site are making an impact. They also allow an organization to test different scenarios, tasks, or navigation options and view how distinct visitors respond.

Unique Identified Visitors

A unique identified visitor is the ultimate web site metric for measuring behavior. A unique identified visitor is tracked through information stored in a central database. This happens when the visitors log in or are automatically signed into a web site they visit. The ability to measure unique identified visitors used to be both costly and technologically challenging, but most of those barriers have now been removed for nonprofits.

Measuring unique identified visitors eliminates a tremendous amount of web site metric guesswork and error. It also enables nonprofits to segment, test, and personalize content to known audiences and measure the results with incredible accuracy. This metric proves out the idea that less is more when it comes to web site metrics. You may have a smaller group of data to look at when it comes to unique identified visitors, but the information gained has much more value than raw or anonymous data.

Other Web Site Metrics

The core web site metrics represent a solid foundation for building a measurement program. The ever-changing nature of the Internet also means that other metrics are more specialized in nature and not necessarily applicable to all situations or nonprofits. These include referrers and in-bound links, the bounce rate from the site or pages, the click density of certain areas of the web site, and the page-view duration.

Tools of the Trade

There is a web site metrics tool for every shape, size, and budget. These include the large enterprise-reporting solutions such as Webtrends, Omniture, Click-Tracks, and NetTracker. They have a lot of functionality and customization options but typically have higher costs. Newer tools like Mint and Woopra are lower-cost options that provide valuable statistics. Also, many content management systems provide some level of web site metrics reporting out of the box. Be sure to verify the reporting capabilities that you have today and whether they support the ability for measuring the core metrics.

Google Analytics has become a very popular choice for web site metrics because of its ease of use and detailed reporting on a number of key metrics. Google Analytics has also become widely used in the nonprofit community because it is free. All that is required is the creation of an account and the placing of some specific embedded code within your web site. This tool has helped make web site metrics more accessible to people who do not live and breathe statistical analysis. Google Analytics is a very useful tool and a good place to start improving your web site metrics measurement.

Putting It Together

Web site metrics can be a mind-numbing display of numbers, lists, charts, dials, and graphics. Understanding what metrics really matter and which ones only add to the noise level is important. The availability of affordable and even free web site metrics tools should give your organization the ability to measure and manage its online presence.

Begin by reviewing the performance of your web site based on current metrics and establish a baseline for how things measure up today. Continue to focus in on the high-value metrics and begin to adjust and test different types of content and user scenarios. Be sure to communicate what is working and not working on the web site to a broader group in the organization. Managing the message can be just as important as managing the metrics.

E-MAIL METRICS

Successful use of e-mail for communication, fundraising, and advocacy purposes is both an art and a science. Consider this section as the science lesson behind how e-mail metrics work and how you can use them to measure your results. This is not intended to be a review of the best practices of all the things that go into creating a good e-mail message. There are numerous books and blogs that cover that topic in great detail. Instead, the focus here is on how to measure what happens to an e-mail message after you push the "send" button.

Open, Clicks, and Conversions

Any discussion about e-mail should begin by noting that not all e-mail are the same. The type of message, the target audience, and a number of other factors influence the metrics and results. Your e-mail marketing strategy should clearly identify the type of e-mail being sent. Those groups of e-mail can then be viewed both individually and collectively.

There are a few common e-mail types that nonprofits use regularly. Acknowledgement e-mail are typically automated and sent to people after they have taken an action on a web site. This might be something like an e-mail acknowledging a donation or confirming an event registration. Measuring metrics for these types of e-mail may not yield a lot of insights unless you also embed additional calls to action in the messages. Another e-mail type is the retention message. These are typically newsletters and other communication-only messages in which a call to action is not the primary purpose of the e-mail. Measuring metrics for such e-mail can produce valuable insights into what kinds of content viewers are interested in enough to click-through to the web site or when people unsubscribe for a variety of reasons.

The e-mail type with the most emphasis on metric analysis is the acquisition or action-oriented message. This might be a direct fundraising appeal message, an advocacy call-to-action alert, promotion for an event or membership, or a peer-to-peer fundraising message. Significant insights and results can be achieved by the careful measurement and management of the metrics for this e-mail type.

As with web site metrics, there is a hierarchy of e-mail metrics that is important to understand. These metrics represent the cornerstone of an effective e-mail measurement program for your organization. Understanding each of them individually and how they tie together can help you improve your results. Figure 6.2 shows the e-mail metrics hierarchy that can be used to measure your results.

Deliverability Rate

The deliverability rate measures the percentage of e-mail that are successfully sent and delivered to the intended recipient. Measuring the deliverability rate is an inexact number because not all Internet service providers (ISPs) report delivered e-mail. When you send an e-mail message to a group of targeted constituents, there is often a difference between the total number of intended recipients and those who actually receive the message. E-mail addresses that are no longer valid

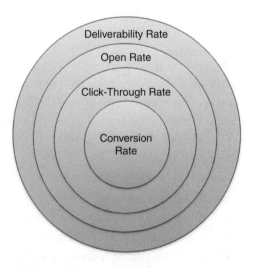

FIGURE 6.2   E-Mail Metrics Hierarchy

will hard bounce, e-mail accounts that are unreachable or over quota may soft bounce, and some ISPs may block your e-mail for a variety of reasons.

Deliverability is important because if your messages never reach people, then none of the other metrics or actions mean a thing. Most reputable e-mail providers or software packages that include e-mail tools will handle important deliverability best practices on your behalf. These include proper handling of hard and soft bounces, avoiding blacklists and spam filters, and managing your overall e-mail reputation. It is not enough to ask about deliverability rate; you also need to know how they stay on top of things. This is a constantly changing area because spammers are always trying new tricks and ISPs want to stop them. Being a good sender is the first step in making the most of e-mail marketing for your organization.

Open Rate

The open rate measures the percentage of opened e-mail that were actually delivered. Measuring the open rate of an e-mail is not an exact science because the tracking method does not always work. The open rate is tracked by placing a small image in the message. This is sometimes blocked by e-mail systems or completely ignored by plain text readers, like those on many mobile devices. Preview panes on some e-mail systems may also record false-positives depending on where the image is placed in the e-mail message. There will always be a margin of error for your e-mail open rates.

The e-mail open rate is still an important metric despite the fact that it is never 100 percent accurate. Most successful nonprofits look across multiple e-mail appeals and campaigns to establish average open-rate metrics. Drastic changes in one direction or another signal that recipients are favorably or unfavorably reacting to your communication with them. Open rates are often used to measure the effectiveness of different e-mail senders, subject lines, the day of the week or time of day, and other message-testing changes. The tests focus on improving results by adjusting how and when the message is initially viewed rather than the actual content of the message.

Click-Through Rate

The click-through rate (CTR) measures the percentage of links clicked by unique individuals in an e-mail. Measuring an e-mail message's CTR requires that you place links to web sites within the body of the message. Also, the CTR is highly dependent on the quality of the segmentation, content, and design of your e-mail messages. Make sure that you include both unique CTRs and unique individual CTRs in your metrics. These can be a sign that recipients are using your e-mail more than once to click to a link. Most e-mail tools provide the ability to see CTRs and the links being clicked on a per-message basis.

Click-throughs are the first e-mail metric that have a high degree of reliability. They are very important in tracking what people are doing with an e-mail message once it has been delivered and opened. This is why making links inside the e-mail should be clear, consistent, and focused on a call to action. Looking at CTRs for e-mail appeals and e-mail newsletters will give you insights into the types of content that are resonating the most with recipients. Deeper analysis of the links being clicked will also allow you to measure how much recipients are scrolling down in your e-mail messages and taking action. CTRs should also be used to improve your web site content. Make sure those commonly clicked links have pages that are kept up to date or fine-tuned on a regular basis.

Conversion Rate

The conversion rate measures the percentage of delivered messages that resulted in an action. The action may be a donation, event registration, survey response, membership purchase, advocacy alert, or other action driven from the e-mail message. Some e-mail tools may also calculate the conversion rate from opened messages and click-throughs as well. These variations may prove useful to improve your performance as long as you continue to use them consistently. The conversion rate on your e-mail will vary depending on whether the message is an acquisition, retention, or acknowledgment e-mail.

The conversion rate is the ultimate measure of the success of an e-mail campaign. This requires that each and every e-mail message sent by your organization has some type of call to action in it. Do not miss the opportunity to further build your relationship with constituents while you have their time and attention. This call to action does not have to always be financial in nature. It could be a call to action that simply asks for feedback or to perform an advocacy action. The conversion rate is an integral part on measure return on investment as well as return on engagement for your organization.

Other E-Mail Metrics

There are some other e-mail metrics that need to be taken into consideration. One of the most important is looking at the unsubscribe rate and overall e-mail list churn. Increases in the number of unsubscribers from your e-mails is an indication that the messages may not be relevant or appropriate to the recipients. A certain amount of list churn is healthy and to be expected over time. According to the 2009 eNonprofit Benchmarks Study, the average nonprofit annual list churn rate has hovered around 20 percent.[1] This is a combination of unsubscribes and e-mail addresses lost to spam complaints, e-mail bounces, bad or no longer functioning addresses, and other losses.

Another metric used with e-mail is the form-completion rate. This metric looks at the percentage of visits to a page that result in a user completing a form where a call to action is present. This could be a donation, survey, advocacy action, or event-registration form. This metric can be tracked by looking at the number of unique click-throughs to a page with a call to action and comparing that with the number of unique completed actions. The form-completion rate helps show the success of landing pages, the call-to-action form, and the originating message.

Tools of the Trade

There are a number of e-mail marketing tools available in the market. The lines are blurred between solutions built specifically for companies and non-profit organizations. Tools designed mostly for nonprofits typical bundle the ability to accept online donations, build a web site, integrate with a constituent-relationship-management system, and other capabilities.

Putting It All Together

Keep in mind that all the best e-mail metrics in the world do not help you if you are not following basic e-mail best practices. If you don't segment your lists, carefully craft your content and links, test your messages, and continually refine your campaigns, then these metrics will tell you only so much. But doing all these things and not paying attention to the metrics and results is criminal. Place a greater emphasis on metrics like click-throughs and conversions in cases when the reliability of these measures is much higher.

Start by measuring yourself against your own results before comparing things to industry benchmarks. Continue to test additional elements, including subject lines, the day of the week and time of day that messages are sent, and different call-to-action options for the targeted segments. Be sure to integrate your e-mail communication efforts with the other fundraising channels, and don't forget to follow up and steward constituents over time.

ADVOCACY METRICS

Online advocacy has been a very useful tool for nonprofits for many years now. Its use among nonprofits in the United States has grown and matured over the past few years. This mobilizing tool is also becoming more popular in other countries across the globe.

Several of the metrics associated with online advocacy are shared with web site and e-mail metrics. This is because e-mail is the basis for many advocacy communication campaigns, and open rates, click-throughs, and actions are the metrics that matter most. The form-completion rate is another important advocacy metric because most systems require that users provide additional information to respond to an action alert.

Activists, Actions, and Web Forms

There are some additional advocacy metrics, such as total number of action takers; total number of messages sent around an action alert; and number of messages sent via e-mail, faxes, and web forms. In the United States, members of the federal legislature use special web forms to receive online messages from their constituents. Advocacy tools are able to submit information through these web forms to ensure message delivery.

Tools of the Trade

Advocacy tools typically fall into two major categories: point solutions and integrated solutions. The point solutions handle only advocacy-related activities, such as by displaying legislative information, creating action alerts, sending advocacy-related e-mail messages, and managing web content. Integrated solutions combine advocacy tools with more robust web content management, e-mail marketing, and customer relationship management (CRM) capabilities. Nonprofits that are just beginning their advocacy efforts or that do not have a fundraising focus tend to use point solutions. Organizations that have advocacy as part of their total communication, engagement, and fundraising strategy often choose integrated solutions.

Putting It All Together

Organizations that use online advocacy to engage constituents must combine the best practices of web site and e-mail metrics. Monitoring and measuring how activists respond to specific issues, which messages result in a greater number of actions, and how often those individuals continue to respond over time is very important to a successful advocacy campaign.

Social Media Metrics

The growth and importance of social media continues to transform how nonprofits engage and interact with their constituents. Today, there are popular sites like YouTube, Flickr, MySpace, Facebook, Twitter, Second Life, Orkut,

FriendFeed, Digg, Blogger, 12seconds, Plurk, Ning, and Yammer. There are several other chapters in this book devoted to covering how best to use these tools and to build awareness and meaningful relationships online.

Friends, Followers, and Diggs

Keep in mind that what is hot today may not be all the rage tomorrow. It is also likely that some of current tools will not even exist in the future. We are in the very early stages of a rapidly evolving set of new media channels, and there are bound to be some giant splashes and some epic crashes. Think back to the 1990s when new search engines were popping up all the time. Sites like AltaVista, WebCrawler, Magellan, Infoseek, Excite, HotBot, Yahoo!, Lycos, Ask.com, Northern Light, and Google generated a tremendous amount of traffic, interest, and buzz. Today, the market has matured and only a few major services have emerged.

This does not mean that nonprofit organizations should sit on the sidelines to see how things shake out. Fortune favors the bold, and metrics can play an important role in that. When a new technology tool or trend emerges, there is a tendency to throw all the traditional rules out the window. This is a shortsighted mistake, and nonprofits should keep in mind the basic principles of metrics and measurement. Focus on the metrics that are simple, measurable, actionable, relevant, and timely when it comes to social media.

Most of the social media sites have measurable data that mirror both web site content and e-mail metrics. For example, a video on YouTube gives you metrics like number of times it has been viewed, how many sites link to that video and number of click-throughs from those links, how many times people have marked that video as their favorite, any video responses, and the number of text comments about the video. These can be very effective in measuring results and comparing trends across different social media campaigns.

Successful nonprofits have learned that integrating their social media efforts into their broader Internet and organizational strategies is the best path to take. One way to look at social media is as an extension to your existing online efforts. These are different contact points out on the Internet that allow people to take action. They can also be used to funnel traffic to your existing web site (see Figure 6.3).

Tools of the Trade

The majority of the social media web sites, tools, and aggregators have embedded reporting within them. This is a glimpse of the future of integrated reporting and metrics. These tools rely on good metrics reporting, given the potential

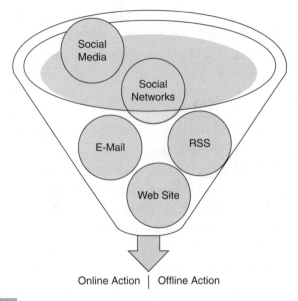

Online Action | Offline Action

FIGURE 6.3   **Social Media Funnel**

high volume of users and information. Over the next few years, there will be more mainstream applications that bring together social media data from across multiple sources.

Despite the many embedded reporting capabilities in such services, you should track them in a central location. This might be as simple as a spreadsheet or as advanced as storing them in a database. This is because many sites store data for only a limited period of time. In some cases, historical data is kept for only three or four months. This means that data are constantly dropping off—they should be collected beforehand to keep a complete record.

Putting It All Together

The use of social media and social networking web sites continues to grow. If the past is any predictor of the future, then expect many of these sites to disappear and a certain amount of consolidation take place. This makes having a strategy for what you want to achieve and how you plan to measure it so important to success.

Online Fundraising Metrics

There are countless fundraising metrics that nonprofits measure and monitor in their organizations. Many of the same traditional fundraising metrics can be

TABLE 6.1   USE OF DATA

	Year 1	Year 2	Percentage Change
Total constituents	250,750	255,890	2.05%
Total donors	170,362	172,391	1.19%
Online	5,366	5,803	8.14%
Offline	163,633	165,071	0.88%
Online and offline	1,363	1,517	11.31%
Total gifts	182,650	185,528	1.58%
Online	10,594	12,059	13.83%
Offline	172,056	173,469	0.82%
Total revenue	$82,476,355	$84,765,190	2.78%
Online	2,490,786	2,627,721	5.50%
Offline	79,985,569	82,052,704	2.58%

applied to online fundraising. There are some basic calculations that you can use to evaluate where you are today and what it would take to meet your goals for tomorrow.

To get a comprehensive understanding of your online fundraising metrics, it is important to look at them alongside your traditional fundraising metrics. Examining where gifts are coming from, the percentage of the total constituent population being engaged online, and how they are trending over time should be part of an online fundraising metrics program.

Gifts, Ranges, and Renewals

Knowing basic information about your total constituents, donors, gifts, and revenue can quickly produce valuable information about trends in your organization. Table 6.1 illustrates how this data can be used.

Using just these few data points, you can calculate a number of metrics and trends. Table 6.2 illustrates several important metrics.

How much of your existing constituent and donor base is giving online, the volume of giving and the revenue coming from online channels, and trends around average gift size are important to measure. This type of metrics monitoring could also be broken down on a quarter-by-quarter basis to look at trends in a given year.

Another important online fundraising metric is the distribution and range of your online gifts. The average gift amount provides high-level insights, but looking at the entire range of gifts should also be part of your metrics program. These metrics can be measured across all online giving and on a per-donation-form basis for more granular statistics.

TABLE 6.2   METRICS AND TRENDS

	Year 1	Year 2	Percentage Change
Constituents who are donors	67.94%	67.37%	−0.84%
Constituents who are online donors	2.14%	2.27%	5.96%
Constituents who are offline donors	65.26%	64.51%	−1.15%
Constituents who are online and offline donors	0.54%	0.59%	9.07%
Donors who are online donors	3.15%	3.37%	6.86%
Donors who are offline donors	96.05%	95.75%	−0.31%
Donors who are online and offline donors	0.80%	0.88%	10.00%
Gifts from online gifts	5.80%	6.50%	12.07%
Gifts from offline gifts	94.20%	93.50%	−0.74%
Revenue from online	3.02%	3.10%	2.65%
Revenue from offline	96.68%	86.80%	−0.19%
Average online gift amount	$235.12	$217.90	−7.32%

Keep in mind that several factors can skew your analysis. Using a single donation form versus multiple donation forms can affect results. Allowing donors to enter an "other" donation amount rather than using fixed donation amounts will influence ranges and averages. The use of anonymous donation forms versus targeted donation forms should also be taken into consideration. It is recommended that you remove the highest and lowest gift amounts to get a more accurate picture of giving patterns.

Other Online Fundraising Metrics

There are some other online fundraising metrics that may require additional data and calculations. These metrics focus on analyzing the role that new donors, retained donors, and reactivated donors play in the overall fundraising mix. These metrics include the following:

- Total new donors
  - New donor revenue
  - Revenue per new donor
  - Retained new donors
  - New donor retention
- Total retained donors
  - Retained donor revenue
  - Revenue per retained donor
  - All-donor retention rate
  - Multiyear donor retention

- Total reactivated donors
  - Reactivated donor revenue
  - Revenue per reactivated donor
  - Donor reactivation rate
  - Reactivated donor retention

Peer-to-Peer Event Fundraising Metrics

Peer-to-peer event fundraising, also referred to as friends asking friends, is a special type of online fundraising that has become very popular with nonprofits in recent years. This type of fundraising involves individuals creating personalized web pages that allow them to accept online donations and send e-mail appeals to friends, family members, peers, and other personal contact. Organizations then are able to centralize reporting and event management.

The majority of these fundraising programs are based around events (e.g., marathon, walkathon, swimathon), but some nonprofits also use the approach for campaign fundraising, missionary fundraising, and other nonevent types of giving programs. There are some specific metrics associated with this type of event fundraising that nonprofits should use. There are some common metrics used for measuring peer-to-peer fundraising results. Table 6.3 illustrates how these data can be used.

On the basis of the information in Table 6.3 you can calculate a number of metrics and trends. Table 6.4 illustrates several important peer-to-peer fundraising metrics.

Additional analysis can be performed by breaking down fundraisers into team captains and team members. Some tools also allow administrators to view how

TABLE 6.3   USE OF DATA

	Year 1	Year 2	Percentage Change
Total event participants	16,851	17,913	6.30%
Total fundraisers	7,641	8,415	10.13%
Online	4,964	5,790	16.64%
Offline	2,677	2,625	−1.94%
Total fundraiser e-mail sent	34,910	37,810	8.31%
Total gifts	25,587	28,761	12.40%
Online	19,280	22,568	17.05%
Offline	6,307	6,193	−1.81%
Total revenue	$1,709,670	$2,078,916	21.60%
Online	$1,486,532	$1,857,614	24.96%
Offline	$223,138	$221,302	−0.82%

TABLE 6.4   METRICS AND TRENDS

	Year 1	Year 2	Percentage Change
Constituents who are fundraisers	45.34%	46.98%	3.60%
Constituents who are online donors	64.97%	68.81%	5.91%
Constituents who are offline donors	35.03%	31.19%	−10.96%
Gifts that are online donations	64.97%	68.81%	5.91%
Gifts that are offline donations	35.03%	31.19%	−10.96%
Revenue from online donations	86.95%	89.35%	2.77%
Revenue from offline donations	13.05%	10.65%	−18.44%
Average revenue per fundraiser	$223.75	$247.05	10.41%
Average gift amount	$66,82	$72.28	8.18%
Average gift amount per e-mail sent	$48.97	$54.98	12.27%

often fundraisers log into their personal pages, how many of them have met their fundraising goals, and other important metrics.

It is very common in peer-to-peer fundraising that 80 percent of the revenue raised is from 20 percent of fundraisers. There are also cases in which this is more extreme, and even fewer fundraisers represent the vast majority of total revenue raised. Focusing in on these individuals and teams to understand why they perform so well should be done through follow-up surveys, phone calls, and other outreach efforts. Measuring the retention rate for these high-performing teams is a critical metric for long-term peer-to-peer fundraising success.

BENCHMARKS

Once you gain comfort and confidence with your own metrics, then it is time to graduate on to using benchmarks. The best analogy for understanding benchmarks is this: if a bear is chasing me and you, then I wouldn't try to outrun the bear. I would focus on trying to outrun you. That's benchmarking. The purpose of benchmarking is to compare the same metric across a number of organizations and establish a level of performance for specific period of time and set of conditions.

You, Me, and the Bear

It is very important that benchmarks are used in combination with your own metrics and do not substitute for measuring your own progress. This point cannot be stressed enough. The value of using benchmarks is tied directly to knowing your own performance. For example, if the current benchmark for e-mail open rates is 14 percent, this is helpful only when you know your own open rate.

Knowing whether your own performance is above or below the benchmark can provide a useful reality check.

Benchmarks help nonprofits understand how changes in technology, the economy, and user preferences affect online performance across peer organizations. There are often trends specific to your organization's sector that are covered in benchmark studies. For example, international relief organizations may have different benchmarks than higher education institutions. Nonprofits heavily engaged in advocacy may not have a lot of use for benchmarks about membership renewals. Take these potential differences into account when comparing your own metrics to those published in benchmark studies.

There are a number of online benchmark studies specifically published for nonprofits every year. Most of them are available at no cost, but even those that involve a fee have value that easily trumps the cost. Be sure to read and review the actual reports, and resist the temptation to rely on just excerpts or snippets republished elsewhere. Benchmarking reports usually provide information about the types of organizations in the analysis, the definition of the metrics used, the sample of the participants and data reviewed, and other relevant criteria that were used to establish the benchmarks.

The most relevant benchmarks are those in which you are an active part of the analysis. Pursue opportunities to participate in benchmarking reports or engage with other nonprofits to compare similar metrics and results. This will involve providing a complete and comparable set of data to the individuals doing the analysis. Participating in these studies on a regular basis will help reinforce the discipline to stay on top of your metrics program on a continual basis.

Nonprofit E-Mail Benchmarks

There are some established benchmarks for e-mail performance in the nonprofit sector. These metrics often differ dramatically from benchmarks found in the for-profit world. This is also a maturing area of the nonprofit sector, and over time, more detailed benchmarks will become more commonplace.

The most established e-mail benchmarking report is the eNonprofit Benchmarks Study, which has been published for several years now by M+R Strategic Services and Nonprofit Technology Network (NTEN). Table 6.5 represents benchmarks from both the 2008 and 2009 studies.[2]

The eNonprofit studies include the page-completion rate metric in their analysis. This is calculated as the number of people who completed a form divided by the number of people who clicked on the link to get to that form. Response rate is calculated as the number of people who took the main action requested by an e-mail message divided by the number of people who received the e-mail message. "Response rate" and "conversion rate" are often used interchangeably.

TABLE 6.5	BENCHMARKS FROM THE 2008 AND 2009 STUDIES

E-Mail Fundraising Appeals Benchmarks

	Open Rate	Click-Through Rate	Page-Completion Rate	Response Rate
2008	14.5%	0.6%	19.0%	0.13%
2007	14.8%	1.1%	16.5%	0.13%
2006	17.3%	1.2%	17.2%	0.17%

E-Mail Newsletter Benchmarks

	Open Rate	Click-Through Rate
2008	15.0%	2.1%
2007	17.6%	3.6%
2006	21.8%	4.3%

Advocacy-Alert Benchmarks

	Open Rate	Click-Through Rate	Page-Completion Rate	Response Rate
2007	16.0%	2.1%	88.0%	4.5%
2006	18.9%	3.6%	85.3%	8.6%
2005	23.8%	4.3%	88.5%	7.5%

The studies highlight the performance of e-mail fundraising appeals sent by nonprofits. To be clear, the studies also look at separate metrics for e-mail newsletter and advocacy-alert messages. The three-year trend for e-mail shows a drop across the board, with the exception of page-completion rate. Open rates can be deceptive, but click-through rates and response rates are very telling. They tell us is that 99.88 percent of these fundraising-focused e-mail failed to result in a gift.

E-mail is not direct mail. Although many of the same strategies apply, comparing the two is like comparing apples and iPhones. E-mail communication has more robust segmentation and personalization capabilities. It has faster response cycles; it is more cost effective to test; and combined with higher average gifts, it can have better return on investment (ROI) than traditional channels. E-mail isn't the perfect marketing tool or the holy grail of marketing tools, but having success less than 1 percent of the time shouldn't be acceptable for your organization.

Online Fundraising Benchmarks

Online fundraising has continued to grow at impressive rates for many years now. For more mature nonprofits, the online revenue channel has helped them continue to grow when traditional methods are down or flat. For newer nonprofits, the Internet has become a vital source of fundraising revenue because they do not yet have mature direct-mail or major gift fundraising programs in place.

From an analysis of several reports, studies, and published data, a clearer picture has begun to emerge about the amount of online fundraising being done. There are several reputable reports and studies that have tracked online fundraising among nonprofit organizations.

The Center on Philanthropy at Indiana University noted in the Summer 2007 Philanthropic Giving Index that 29.6 percent of the surveyed nonprofits reported that online donations accounted for 6 percent or more of the organizations' total donations. The same report noted that 47.4 percent of nonprofits reported that online donations account for 1 percent to 5 percent of their organizations' total donations.[3]

Blackbaud's 2007 *State of the Nonprofit Industry* report surveyed more than 1,100 nonprofit organizations. Nonprofits indicated in the survey that an average of 6 percent of their donations come from the Internet.[4]

In 2009, Target Analytics released the 2008 *donorCentrics Internet Giving Benchmarking Analysis*. The report examined the online and offline trends of 24 large direct-marketing-focused nonprofit organizations and an aggregate of 9.5 million donors. The report found that organizations averaged between 10 percent and 11 percent of total revenue from online fundraising.[5]

The *Chronicle of Philanthropy* has tracked online giving trends since 2002 and publishes information from across several nonprofit organizations annually. In 2009, *Chronicle* published information for approximately 170 nonprofits, including the percentage of contributions that came from online fundraising. Table 6.6 is a breakdown of this information by different nonprofit sectors.[6]

There is so much variance in the percentage of fundraising that comes from the Internet that establishing a single benchmark would be difficult. But there is a range of performance that nonprofits should benchmark and measure themselves against. Figure 6.4 is a recommended online fundraising range based on data from numerous studies.

Nonprofits that raise less than 1 percent to 3 percent of their total fundraising contributions online are considered to be underperforming the rest of the sector. Organizations raising between 3 percent and 7 percent of contributions online are considered to have average performance. Those nonprofits that raise more than 7 percent of their total fundraising revenue online are considered exceptional performers.

Some sectors of the nonprofit industry may experience different results over time. There is a trend among organizations with more direct-mail experience to have an easier time increasing online fundraising than nonprofits with established major giving programs. It is always recommended that you track your own performance and use it as a reality check against other industry metrics.

TABLE 6.6	ONLINE FUNDRAISING AS A PERCENTAGE OF TOTAL CONTRIBUTIONS	

Sector	Percentage
All verticals	2.35%
Arts and cultural groups, public broadcasting	0.81%
Colleges and universities	0.97%
Community foundations	0.40%
Education	7.42%
Environmental and animal welfare	4.17%
Health	4.43%
International	3.36%
Jewish federations	0.78%
Religious	3.62%
Social service	2.77%
Youth	0.65%
Other	6.55%

Source: The Chronicle of Philanthropy

METRICS CULTURE

Until now the focus of this chapter has been on demystifying what to measure and what those metrics mean. But what hasn't been addressed is how to actually start measuring and monitoring these things in your organization.

The data are really just one part of what successful nonprofits look at to measure an aspect of their online initiatives. The reality is that organizations need to take a more comprehensive look at the ways they interact with supporters.

The Who, What, and Why

People get excited and engaged about metrics only when they are tied to people and things important to the organization. An e-mail conversion rate might not get a lot of attention, but that same conversion rate for lapsed donors will get a lot more interest, even from those in the organization who don't understand all the technical mechanics involved in the measurement process.

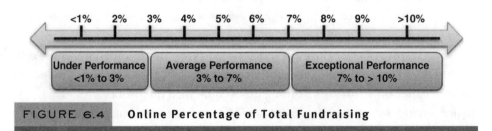

FIGURE 6.4	Online Percentage of Total Fundraising

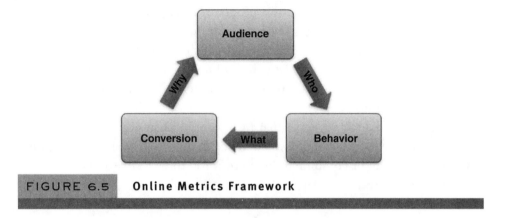

FIGURE 6.5   Online Metrics Framework

Part of developing a culture for measurement and metrics is having a framework (see Figure 6.5). Focusing on the audience, their behaviors, and conversions is the basis for a solid metrics framework that nonprofits can start using immediately. Use this framework as a basis for creating a strategy and building a culture within the organization that values metrics.

Audience

Who are you targeting? Is it donors, alumni, members, activists, subscribers, volunteers, parents, lapsed donors, journalists, board members, grant makers, event fundraisers, or a host of other supporter types? Knowing the audience and who you want to learn more about is the first step in building a metrics framework. A simple group exercise would be to write down all of the potential audience groups that your organization interacts with or wants to interact with. For some nonprofits, the list may only be a few groups, but for others, the list can grow to be extensive.

Think of this as a segmentation exercise to bring to the surface different audiences from across the organization. You may be surprised to see groups listed that interact with only limited areas of the organization. The quantity of the audience types doesn't matter as much as the quality and the genuine relevance of the groups.

The next step is to begin to prioritize the list of different audience types. It's not reasonable or even expected that you measure metrics for every one of these groups. Your resources and priorities will help determine how many groups you focus on first. Start with the top-three audience types and then go through the rest of the framework components. Expand over time or adjust the audience groups when you are able to devote the right amount of resources to measuring them.

A good CRM system or database program should be able to produce data sets for each of the audience groups. Be sure to establish a baseline or initial measurement of how many people belong in each group. Start with the known constituents first and then estimate the unknowns last. You will have much greater success with identified audience members than with trying to track masses of anonymous people.

There are bound to be people that fit into more than one group, but try to avoid this whenever possible. If two audience groups have a lot of overlap, then consider redefining or combining them. Your top three to five audience groups should have little to no overlap in them.

Behavior

When you know who you are trying to measure, then you need to move on to what is being measured. This next piece of the metrics framework is all about measuring the behavior of people in each audience group. This is where each of the various web site, e-mail, social media, online fundraising, and advocacy metrics come into play. Using an active approach rather than a passive approach to engaging with constituents will make tracking behavior much easier.

The next step is to try and establish a baseline for each of the key online metrics if you have not already done so. This may or may not be tied directly to each of the high-priority audience types. Of course, knowing the baseline for a metric across the board and for specific audience types can be very useful. For example, if your click-through rate across all e-mail newsletters is 27 percent but is 39 percent for younger donors, then that is very valuable information. Reviewing the most popular content and testing different links for these groups may boost results.

If you are just getting started, then it is entirely possible that you can establish few baselines. This means that you will need to keep a closer eye on changes during the first few weeks and months of your metrics program. The more you already know going into measuring behaviors will allow you to gauge what is happening sooner.

Having both audience and behavior information should already begin to give you a clearer picture of what constituents are doing. There may be a few "whoa!" and "wow!" moments when the first sets of data come flowing in. Resist the temptation to start guessing why things are happening.

Conversion

Everything comes together when you add conversions from behaviors for known audience groups to the metrics framework. Remember that conversions are the ultimate measure of success. Tracking people and their behaviors without something to convert is like a lab rat running down cheeseless tunnels. Conversions also form the basis for ROI calculations. Conversions are often the "return" in ROI. As noted previously, conversions are not always financial in nature. They can be any call to action in which information or feedback is exchanged and traceable to individuals.

Measuring conversions allows you to connect the dots between distinct constituent groups and the behaviors they exhibit over time. If you have followed the framework up to this point, then the insights should begin to unfold. Reviewing conversions also might cause a certain amount of frustration, as many efforts often do not produce a high percentage of results. This is why focusing on a target audience, as opposed to random efforts, is so important to being successful with your online initiatives.

Understanding why certain audience behaviors result in conversions is the last part of the metrics framework. A combination of metrics analysis and follow-up surveys is one way to gather additional insights into why constituents take action. Another growing tactic of nonprofits is to telephone or mail certain constituent groups to get feedback on why they chose to donate, take an action, or register for an event online. Given the potential long-term value of the constituents, it makes perfect sense to use multiple changes to get additional information.

Putting It All Together

If you and your organization are relatively new to using online metrics, then using this framework should help get things started. For organizations that are looking to improve their programs, then this framework should help provide a larger strategic context for the role of metrics.

Also keep in mind the frequency of monitoring metrics and grouping them together. Web site and social metrics can be grouped into weekly, monthly, and quarterly cycles. E-mail metrics can be grouped into individual messages and newsletter issues—and then rolling up to e-mail campaigns and how they perform compared to traditional fundraising channels. Advocacy metrics can be grouped into individual action alerts and across the entire campaign.

Online fundraising metrics should be monitored on a monthly, quarterly, and annual basis. For peer-to-peer fundraising activities, special events, or time-sensitive fundraising cycles, this monitoring may be grouped into daily and weekly reviews. Going back and retrieving as much historical data about online fundraising performance will help establish better baselines and metrics for future growth patterns.

Conclusion

Good metrics are based on a clear understanding of what is being measured and the ability to apply those findings to the decision-making process. It is never too early or too late to start an online metrics program in your organization. Keep in mind that measuring something is more important than measuring everything. Start with the core metrics. Expand over time and begin to test different scenarios with different audience groups. Share your results internally and with other nonprofit organizations. Focus on lessons learned and how to improve results by turning raw data into useful information.

The Internet has created a whole new frontier of metrics to be measured and mastered. The pace of change and technology adoption will only increase as we move into the future. The importance of a good metrics program will be critical to understanding how constituents are engaging with nonprofits online. The evolution of web sites, e-mail, advocacy, social media, and online fundraising is already extending itself to mobile devices. Look for more points of interaction to become available that increase how nonprofits can interact and engage with their supporters online. More benchmarks and studies will become available, and this will give nonprofits greater insights into how their performance compares with that of similar organizations and across the entire sector. The future is right now and it is happening every single day. Take your first step or your next leap toward knowing the exciting developments that are there to greet you at every turn.

Steve MacLaughlin has spent more than 14 years building successful online initiatives with a broad range of Fortune 500 firms, government and educational institutions, and nonprofit organizations around the world. MacLaughlin is currently the director of Internet solutions at Blackbaud and is responsible for leading the company's provision of online solutions to clients. He is a frequent speaker at nonprofit conferences and events. MacLaughlin serves on the Nonprofit Technology Network's board of directors and supports its focus on both the growth and the professionalism of the nonprofit technology sector. He is a frequent blogger (http://www.blackbauds.com/connections) and writer whose ideas and opinions have appeared in several nonprofit-sector publications. MacLaughlin earned both his undergraduate degree and a master of science in interactive media from Indiana University.

PART II

Managing Fundraising and Building Communities Online

CHAPTER 7

Managing Fundraising and Building Communities Online

ADRIENNE D. CAPPS

Quite a basic and important need of any nonprofit organization is raising money so as to be able to serve out its mission. Fundraising at its very core is about building relationships between people in the organization and those external to it. Increasingly this work is being done via computers and the Internet and to a very effective degree. Entire direct-mail campaigns are being replaced by very specialized online campaigns where potential donors receive multiple, targeted e-mails, texts, or messages via a social media outlet. Nonprofits are also moving their traditional fundraising events and galas online by staging auctions and selling tickets. Some very creative organizations are even raising funds over the web by shopping, posting video campaigns, and using social media outlets.

There is also another side to using the Internet for fundraising and that is by building communities of people that may not be supporters yet, but that get to know you via web. This is called friend raising in this chapter. The concept behind friend raising is that your organization provides opportunities for people to get involved with your nonprofit, perhaps as volunteers. Volunteer participation allows for both parties to get to know each other better, and if there is a match between your organization's mission and the individual's passions and interest, then the fundraising will naturally come from the relationship. Currently, many nonprofit organizations are friend raising online with e-mail, their web sites, and social media outlets and by integrating all these techniques.

This chapter describes the many ways nonprofit organizations can fundraise and friend raise online and provides real-world examples from organizations, small and large, located across the country and internationally. The following content aims to inspire, motivate, and supply new ideas for you and your organization and help you make sense of the Internet and how powerful it can be to help you succeed in your efforts.

One special note here is that some of these techniques require technical assistance. If you are not well versed in the back-end or technical side of sending out a mass e-mail solicitation to thousands, building online giving pages on your web site, or tracking your response rates, you will need to hire an IT consultant to assist you. An equal number of the methods described here can easily be performed using the tools of existing companies, consultants, and web sites that have done all that back-end legwork for you. Just be sure to understand what you are getting into and what technical requirements, like security issues, spam, and so on, are necessary to get started, lest you run into difficulties, delayed time lines, and unanticipated costs down the road.

FUNDRAISING ONLINE

It has been only in the past decade or so that nonprofit organizations have taken advantage of the Internet to raise money. When I look back at my own professional fundraising career, which began in 1998, I am astonished at how things have changed. I recall using the Internet only to send e-mails and conduct research online about various prospective businesses or foundations, and that was about the extent of it. At that organization, we did a traditional direct-mail campaign; fundraising events with silent and live auctions and invitations, all conducted offline; and letters of inquiry and grant proposals that were mailed off. We sent letters, met in person much more frequently, and used the phone more often than sending an e-mail. The receptionist had a typewriter, and there was no scanner for putting things up on the web or creating PDFs. Today, most of these activities can be done online, if not all of them.

This section is divided into several subcategories of ways your nonprofit organization can use the Internet to raise funds. Each subcategory will have examples of real nonprofits that are using the online fundraising method described. It includes their successes and challenges along the way. The subcategories of online fundraising methods are direct e-mail, auctions, events, shopping, social media outlets, integrated online and offline, and a catchall category that provides examples of organizations using creative techniques to raise funds online.

Direct E-Mail

Direct e-mail or e-mail solicitation is, in effect, conducting your traditional direct-mail campaign online instead of through the post office. This is a simple concept that most organizations are familiar with and may even have firsthand experience with. The current challenge with direct e-mail is two-fold: (1) older donors, who are most comfortable with mailed solicitations and not as technologically savvy, do not respond to e-mail solicitations or do not even have an e-mail address; and (2) securing an e-mail address for every individual in your database and keeping those addresses current and accurate is time consuming, expensive (or both), and just about impossible.

The Gillette Children's Foundation, based in St. Paul, Minnesota, conducted an internal assessment of its fundraising efforts in 2007 (Figure 7.1). Traditionally, the foundation had focused on major gifts, but it wanted to turn to building a robust annual fund to help support its efforts. Board leadership, however, was concerned about conducting an annual fund campaign online. Would direct e-mail be perceived as obnoxious, rude, and undesirable? Would the patients and the patients' families who opted in to receive communications from the foundation be turned off by an e-mail approach? Would this all damage the foundation's brand in the community?

The foundation hired an outside consultant to guide it through the process and address some of these concerns. With the help of the consultant, the professional staff spent the first few months in open discussion with board leadership to address their concerns and develop a plan that allowed everyone to feel comfortable about the e-mail campaign.

Prior to implementing the e-mail campaign, the foundation had a database of about 70,000 prospects and donors that it mailed to but only 1,080 e-mail addresses. They mailed a newsletter four times per year and had just one direct-mail appeal annually.

To start the e-mail campaign, the foundation sent a simple welcome e-mail to those for whom it had e-mail addresses to introduce itself as the Gillette Children's Foundation. The e-mail included a message that it wanted to start communicating online and via mail. It allowed for an opt-out option but also asked for e-mail addresses of friends, family members, and colleagues to be added to the lists if the receiver thought it would be of benefit. Several weeks later, the foundation sent a second e-mail asking individuals to get involved by donating or volunteering. The foundation then began sending an e-newsletter twice per month with information about the organization and a soft sell asking for donations.

After four months, the foundation combined forces with another local organization and sent a promotional e-mail to both groups' constituents offering the option of a raffle prize. They asked people to forward it to family, friends, and colleagues. This effort was the single most successful e-mail the foundation did at the start. Within two months of the raffle campaign, the foundation's database of individuals with e-mail addresses grew from 1,080 to 5,412—more than 400 percent growth, and all new prospects!

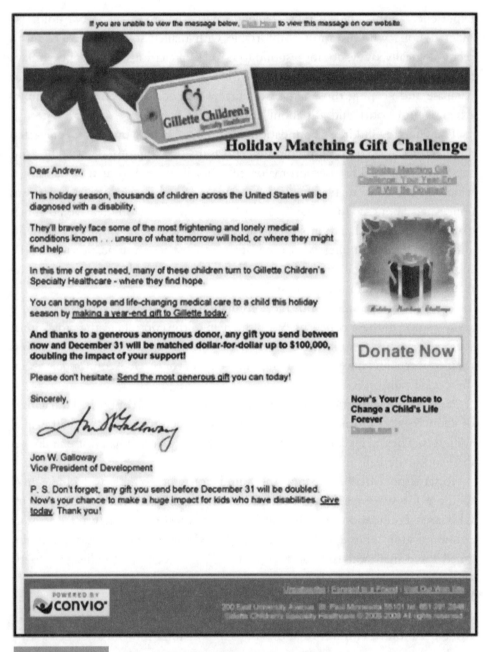

FIGURE 7.1   The Gillette Children's Foundation

With some small successes under its belt, board leadership and staff felt confident and reassured by their efforts, so they planned a holiday e-mail solicitation
campaign targeted at 20,000 of the 70,000 offline individuals and the 5,412
individuals with e-mail addresses on file. They designed two pieces: a snail-mail

version of the solicitation and an e-mail solicitation, both of which were branded with the same look, images, and messaging. They mailed the traditional solicitation to everyone, including those for whom they had e-mail addresses, and then followed up with an e-mail to the group for whom they had e-mail addresses. The last component was a telemarketing campaign.

The result of the hybrid campaign was astounding! In total, the holiday campaign raised $50,013 via mail and more than $11,000 online, whereas for the 2007 holiday campaign, the grand total was $32,972, an increase of more than 51 percent. The foundation received donations of more than $9,200 by mail: each one enclosed a check along with the printed e-mail demonstrating that people were reading and responding to the online campaign as opposed to the direct-mail piece. They also received gifts from previously disengaged major donor prospects and have begun to reconnect and continue conversations with these individuals.

Nearly 12 months later, the foundation has seen a 61 percent increase in online donations. For those who are solicited by e-mail, donors give 8.6 percent more per year, and the average gift is 116.3 percent greater than those who give via snail mail. And the consultant's fees were paid back within 11 months of starting the campaign.

Auctions   We are all familiar with online auction sites where an individual can buy or sell goods in a fixed period of time. The winning bid is the highest received at the end of the time allotted. More recently, nonprofit organizations have been getting into online auctions as a fundraising technique. Many are familiar with auctions because they have been a component of fundraising events or galas. Now organizations are taking these online and with great success. Women Helping Women (WHW), based in Cincinnati, Ohio, organizes a large gala event that typically draws 300 to 350 people each year to a themed party with live and silent auctions, raffles, hors d'oeuvres, and drinks. In any given year, the event raises about $70,000 to $75,000—and then there was 2009.

In 2009, WHW decided to take the auction online. Two weeks before the event, it put the 75 silent auction items that had been secured online through one of the many companies offering these services. It also previewed the live items that were to be bid on at the event. Individuals could also buy tickets to the event through the auction site.

The WHW e-mailed information about the online auction to its database of more than 1,000 prospects and donors. It also included a link to the auction on its web site, in the event's invitation, and on its Facebook Cause page. The WHW teamed up with magazines and other event marketing groups in the city to publicize the auction. These groups sent out e-mail to their constituents and ran ads in exchange for ad space at the event.

Following the initial announcement of the online auction to its constituents, the WHW sent a second e-mail one week later, then another two days before the event and then the day before. In the end, they sold 59 of the 75 items and took the remaining 16 to the event and sold them all.

Looking back, the WHW is pleased with the outcome. In 2009, it raised nearly $83,000, a 6.4 percent increase from 2008. It has seen examples of how other organizations have expanded their online auctions, and it plans to do the same, namely by concentrating on securing a larger e-mail database over the next year.

Events At the heart of a fundraising event is an experience. Certainly, the guests feel good about supporting charity, but they are also looking for an experience, whether networking with friends and colleagues, getting some great deals on auction items, or just having a fun night. This experience will probably always keep the traditional fundraising event from being a true online candidate. However, many parts of the event, including online auctions as described previously, can be taken online. This section describes one creative organization that has created an integrated online and offline series of fundraising events that offer opportunities for involvement at many different levels and for many different audiences.

Catholic Charities (CC) CYO in San Francisco offers a set of programs and services for the HIV/AIDS community focused on housing issues. After years of traditional fundraising events, CC decided its approach was getting stale and that it needed to broaden its audience to include opportunities for young people. In a tough economy, it also wanted to offer opportunities to get involved, participate, and donate at many different levels but also not forget its core base of supporters.

As a result, CC developed Red House 2009, which had three event components between June 17 and June 1, 2009: (1) a traditional cocktail party for its major donors, (2) a nonevent called Stay@Home, and (3) a way for anyone interested in raising money for CC by hosting their own parties called Red House @ Your House (Figures 7.2. and 7.3).

The major donor cocktail party was by invitation only to CC's largest donors. It was to serve as the kickoff for Red House 2009 and was hosted by a board member. There was a special speaker, and CC gave an award to recognize a longtime major donor. The night was a low-cost event at which CC could cultivate and steward high-end donors in an intimate atmosphere.

Stay@Home was conducted as a traditional nonevent fundraising activity: CC mailed invitations to its prospects and donors asking them to stay at home. Considering everyone's busy schedules, the number of events people get invited to, and the cost of throwing such elaborate parties, CC offered them a chance to stay at home and simply send in a donation using the invitation's response card.

facebook   Home   Profile   Friends   Inbox   Adrienne D. Capps   Settings   Logout

🗓 Red House at Aventine
Happy Hour to benefit CCCYO HIV/AIDS Services

R E D 🏠 H O U S E
CATHOLIC CHARITIES CYO

Host:	Maria Sullivan
Type:	Party – Benefit
Network:	Global

Date:	Wednesday, June 17, 2009
Time:	6:00pm – 8:00pm
Location:	Taverna Aventine
Street:	582 Washington
City/Town:	San Francisco, CA
	View Map ▾

Phone:	4159811500
Email:	marialsullivan@gmail.com

Share ➕   Export 🔲

Your RSVP

○ Attending
○ Maybe Attending
○ Not Attending

Other Information

- Guests who are not attending are hidden on the guest list.
- Guests are allowed to bring friends to this event.

Description

Please join me for an evening of drinks and hors d'oeuvres at Aventine to benefit CCCYO's five HIV/AIDS Programs in San Francisco. These programs include Assisted Housing & Health Services, Derek Silva Community, Peter Claver Community, Leland House and Rita de Cascia. CCCYO was one of the first organizations to respond to the HIV/AIDS crisis in San Francisco beginning in 1985 and has a long-standing tradition of caring and providing for those affected by this disease.

$10 cover at the door – all proceeds will go to CCCYO AIDS/HIV Services. We will also be raffling off several fabulous prizes – 1 raffle ticket for $5 or 5 for $20.

Other Invites

Maybe Attending (35)   See All

Justin Roja   David Cohen   Ryan Wagner

Awaiting Reply (125)   See All

Joe G-b   Katie Wallace   Joshua Horowitz

Links

Displaying 1 link   See All

🖼 REDHOUSE Event Page
Source: redhousesf.wordpress.com

Ok all, the kick off of REDHOUSE 2009 is upon us. The 11th is only 3 days away and we are working hard to get more great Auction and Raffle Items in. But please read on to find out what great things we have so far!!! (FMV= Fair Market Value)

Posted by Maria Sullivan

Event Type

This is an open event. Anyone can join and invite others to join.

Admins

- Meghan Monahan Livingston

Confirmed Guests

This event has 36 confirmed guests   See All

Karen Sung   Noël Moossa   Mark Kniesche   Raymon Cancino   Nicola Fraser   Ye-Hui Lu   Stacey M Gordon   Richard Ling

The Wall

Displaying all 8 wall posts

RSVP to this event to post

Heather Elizabeth Keane (Lewis & Clark) wrote
at 10:30am on June 17th, 2009

Hey Maria I can't make it but keep up the good work and thanks for the invite!

Report

Marti Sullivan wrote
at 7:25am on June 17th, 2009

Maria, I am going to try to bring Alex Abela from Peter Claver to say hi and thanks to the group. His client story is pretty amazing!

Report

Maria Sullivan (UCLA) wrote
at 5:14pm on June 16th, 2009

Can't wait to see you all tomorrow! Complimentary appetizers, great raffle prizes and support of an AMAZING cause. Please come out for a drink or two and bring your friends!

xo Maria

Report

FIGURE 7.2   **Catholic Charities CYO's Red House**
Source: Catholic Charities CYO of the Archdiocese of San Francisco

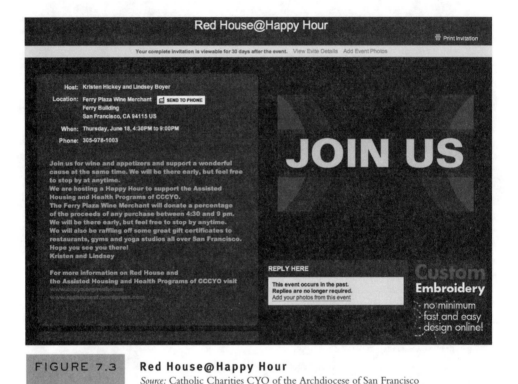

FIGURE 7.3	**Red House@Happy Hour**
	Source: Catholic Charities CYO of the Archdiocese of San Francisco

The most intriguing component of the campaign is the Red House @ Your House, which offers an opportunity for young people to get involved. With this component, CC encouraged people to volunteer to host a party at their own homes or at a nearby restaurant. When there, volunteers set up a laptop that guests could use to make a donation via CC's web site. The donation page requires a user to create a log-in profile, so CC also collected information about party guests as potential new donors or volunteers. Some that volunteered asked a local restaurant to host and give them a portion of the cover charge or bar sales that night to donate back to CC. Then CC also provided interest cards that guests could complete if they wanted more information. They offered raffle prizes to host volunteers to give away to one lucky person who completed an interest card. The interest card was a second way for CC to collect information about party guests.

In April 2009, CC launched Red House @ Your House with a mail and e-mail campaign. It also posted a host kit online that gave party volunteers the tools they needed to organize a party. The host kit included information about using e-invitations, recipes and recipe blogs, and links to a blog where volunteer hosts could exchange ideas about their party planning. It also started Facebook and Twitter feeds to allow volunteer hosts find one another and discuss their party plans. Within a month, CC had eight parties being planned.

The concept of Red House 2009 is in sharp contrast to concepts of the past. The traditional event held in previous years was at a restaurant, and a predinner awards ceremony with major donors and board leadership was followed by a cocktail party open to all ticket buyers. The cocktail party had an auction and a raffle. In 2008, the event netted about $18,000. In 2009, Red House 2009 generated $23,000 in donations and cost CC $5,400 in total, including all the events and efforts, a slight drop in revenue.

However, the event series generated at least as many people involved in planning and attending the events in 2009 as the 150 in attendance at the restaurant in 2008. Also, CC reported a significantly increased web presence and that it had engaged a much different constituency of young donors that the organization had not seen before—great potential for the future. Of course, the organization did not raise as much as it had at the 2008 event, but in general, it felt that, considering the economy, it was the right direction to go in. In addition, there are two more Stay@Home events planned for the coming months, so momentum continues.

Shopping   More recently on the Internet, nonprofit organizations have been using web sites where a portion of consumers' online purchase goes back to support a charity of their choice. You might be familiar with iGive.com, where a shopper visits a virtual mall, chooses a store, buys something, and a certain percentage of the purchase (usually less than 1 percent) is donated to a charity that he or she chooses. Personally, I do this with every purchase I make online – booking hotels and airfare, buying clothes and a digital camera, and even buying printer ink. I started in 2000, and in nine years, I have raised nearly $400 for a variety of causes. I know that $400 is not a lot of money, but for some of the smaller nonprofits I support, and combined with other supporters shopping, it can add up to big bucks.

Online shopping for charity appears to be embarking on the next generation—a Shopping 2.0 of sorts. Nonprofits continue to promote iGive.com and other shopping sites, but a few organizations are creating their own shopping malls to support and promote specific causes. One such shopping portal, Innovative School Funding, was created about two years ago to help schools raise money on their own.

Innovative School Funding (ISF, at http://www.innovativeschoolfunding. com) creates a web site for the individual school with its own unique web address that can be used in marketing and promotional materials (Figure 7.4). Once on the school's site, supporters can choose from more than 400 stores from autos to flowers to travel. Then ISF negotiates a certain percentage to go back to the school with each individual business, usually between 1 percent and 3 percent. Moreover, ISF maintains the web sites for the schools, works with the

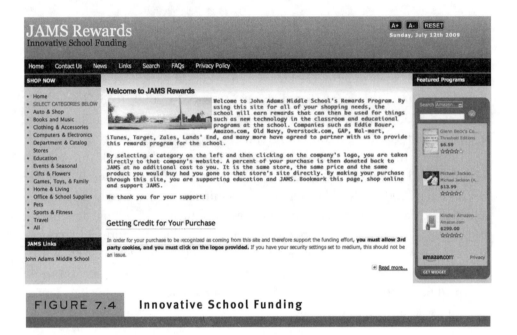

FIGURE 7.4   **Innovative School Funding**

businesses, and maintains the funds generated by shopping. It then sends a check to the school each quarter. In the end, ISF passes along 80 percent of the funds generated, reserving 20 percent to maintain the web sites, work with businesses, and for administrative purposes.

Besides creating and hosting the shopping web site for the school, ISF also promotes itself and the schools through social media and works with the schools to create flyers and news articles that schools can use to market the program. It's starting small, but in the past two years, ISF has recruited 12 school partners from across the country and is beginning to get the interest of local churches. Attributing its success to keeping new content fresh and the use of social media, after one year page visits have grown from 40 hits per day to more than 840. In total, ISF has raised more than $1,300 for its partners. For 2009, ISF hopes to be able to launch a direct link that supporters can put on their desktops so they do not have to go to ISF's web site to find the school before starting to shop. Instead, supporters can simply click the link and go directly to the shopping page—no more multiple clicks or having to remember lengthy web site addresses.

Social Media   The Nonprofit Social Network Survey Report released in May 2009 concluded that, though a great majority of nonprofit organizations had a presence on social media outlets, such as Facebook, MySpace, Twitter, and LinkedIn (74.1 percent), few were raising money (39.9 percent via Facebook), and a good percentage of those (29.1 percent) had raised just $500 or less over the past 12 months.[1] This may be true, but certainly social media is a new phenomenon, and users, individuals, companies, and nonprofits are still working to determine how best to use these sites for marketing, business, and fundraising purposes. I think the survey is too quick to dismiss the potential power and the fact that this technology is so new that many people are still not quite sure how to use it. Perhaps by the time you read this, we will all have a better handle on social media use and how to use it effectively and in an integrated way with other marketing and fundraising components.

There are several successful nonprofit stories that have hit the media, but most, as the survey demonstrated, are raising few dollars. There is one small nonprofit organization, however, that is a real-world success story. It has raised a few thousand dollars via Facebook, generated interest from new constituents, and all without the staff and financial resources of a big nonprofit.

The local San Diego chapter of the Young Nonprofit Professionals Network (YNPN) was motivated to use social media outlets, like Facebook, because it was small and without many resources. Social media offered a cheap way for the chapter to get up and running, to recruit volunteers and participants, and to raise money. It also had a great commitment to being green and so wanted to use the Internet as way to be more socially responsible.

With a budget of about $10,000 annually, YNPN San Diego is run by an all-volunteer group of nonprofit professionals who are just getting started themselves in the nonprofit sector. At its start, the group quickly recruited 15 board members and organized themselves into eight committees. Board members and volunteers stay connected by e-mail and, increasingly, via social media sites like Facebook and LinkedIn. What the organization quickly discovered after its inception in April 2008 was that the network of emerging leaders in the nonprofit sector in and around San Diego was virtually nonexistent. Naturally, to build awareness and to fundraise for YNPN San Diego, the group turned to the tools it had been using itself to communicate, namely social media sites.

First, YNPN created a Facebook group, and in January 2009, after receiving its 501(c)(3) status, it started a Facebook Cause. The goal was to raise $1,000 on Facebook within four months, by the organization's first anniversary in April 2009—and people started to get creative. One of the volunteers pledged $100 if 100 people joined the organization's cause. A few board members paid their board dues of $100 per year through Facebook by either paying it themselves or raising the funds through friends to raise awareness and publicize their support of YNPN San Diego to their Facebook friends. The first donation for the campaign came in on January 19, 2009, and YNPN San Diego surpassed the $1,000 goal on March 18, 2009—one month ahead of schedule. As of July 1, 2009, YNPN San Diego had 238 members of its group and 113 people had joined its cause, for a fundraising total of $1,507.

In April 2009, YNPN San Diego completed its first fundraising plan, which includes many references to conducting the fundraising program in the most green manner as possible and to continuing to raise funds in creative ways through Facebook. An excerpt from the "About YNPN San Diego" section outlines the group's commitment to green fundraising: "YNPN San Diego continues to use its Listserv, Facebook, LinkedIn, and Twitter as its primary modes of communication focusing on being a 'green' organization." An excerpt from the "Online Networking and Resources" section explains the group's goals in greater detail:

> YNPN San Diego uses the latest and greatest technology to help man-
> age our internal communications and network with our members. This
> multi-faceted strategy is fun and green, as well as time and cost-efficient.
> YNPN San Diego continues to examine new communications technolo-
> gies and at this time you can find YNPN San Diego using the following
> tools: listserv, blog, Facebook, LinkedIn, Twitter, Idealist and more. The
> use of social media has helped YNPN San Diego spread like wildfire and
> become a model organization for nonprofit social media use. Through
> its website, YNPN San Diego also provides pages on resources related to
> next gen nonprofit issues as well as career information. We believe that
> these resources provide support to our members by creating a small clear-
> inghouse of information for our membership that helps to strengthen the
> San Diego nonprofit community.

Integrated Online and Offline   The previous examples make use of one on-line technique, whether an e-mail solicitation, an online auction, or a shopping site. Dartmouth College is an example of a highly sophisticated organization whose online fundraising efforts have become well integrated. According to a report published by the *Chronicle of Philanthropy* in 2008, Dartmouth was No. 1 in the average gift per donor at $58.99 and No. 8 overall in dollars raised in fiscal year 2007 among all colleges surveyed. In this Online Fundraising 2.0 example, Dartmouth offered a look at one specific integrated online and offline campaign that gives plain reason for its successful efforts, which currently raise more than $6 million online each year (Figures 7.5–7.7).

In one month, Dartmouth sent numerous strategically crafted and placed solicitations according to the following schedule:

- June 9: E-mail solicitations to affinity groups
- June 11: Campaign launches on web site with home page main image focusing it
- June 15–16: Campaign direct-mail drops
- June 15: *Dartmouth Alumni Magazine* mails with two-page ad of campaign

FIGURE 7.5   Dartmouth College Fund

- June 15: Video on web site, YouTube and home page main image changes to link to video
- June 15: Facebook ads driving to video on home page
- June 18: E-mail solicitation driving to video on the web

Who's Made a Gift?

Visit the honor roll to see who from your class has made their annual gift. Give by June 30 to add your name to the list!

FIGURE 7.6   Dartmouth: Who's Made a Gift?

From: Dartmouth College Fund <dartmouth.college.fund@Dartmouth.edu>
Subject: **You Wouldn't Run a Business This Way (Test 3)**
Date: June 16, 2009 9:34:12 AM EDT
To: karlynmorissette@gmail.com
Reply-To: Dartmouth College Fund <dartmouth.college.fund@Dartmouth.edu>

If you are having trouble viewing this message, see it in your browser.

"Dartmouth creates a world-class product, discounts the price 54 percent, gives an additional discount for certain buyers...then begs for money." —Ernie Parizeau '79

Ernie's got it right. That's Dartmouth's business model in a trim twenty-two words.

How and why does the Dartmouth business model work?

Watch the 2-minute movie, "You Wouldn't Run a Business This Way" and learn for yourself.

Share it with others. E-mail it to a friend. But first...enjoy!

Thank you.

Give Online

This message sent to karlynmorissette@gmail.com by dartmouth.college.fund@Dartmouth.edu.
Dartmouth College Fund - 6066 Development Office - Hanover, NH 03755
You opted in to this list from: Dartmouth Alumni
Unsubscribe

FIGURE 7.7   **Dartmouth: You Wouldn't Run a Business This Way**

- June 18–19: Green line mails with articles on campaign and video, helping make it go viral with social media
- June 19: E-mail to volunteers with link to campaign and video and ideas and instructions for helping video go viral
- June 25: E-mail to "Every Year since Graduation" segment, e-mail to reunion alumni who came to reunion, e-mail to all other reunion alumni, e-mail to nonreunion alumni
- June 30: E-mail to all nondonors and open pledges, last chance

This comprehensive, integrated campaign generated 43 percent of all gifts received during the month (2,120 online gifts and 4,899 total cash gifts from alumni and parents). The campaign also resulted in gifts totaling $1,316,768—about 11 percent of the dollar total of $12,066,495—and 76,605 page views, which was 8.69 percent of the web site traffic received in the month. Although your organization may not command the staff and financial resources to organize and execute such a large campaign, I've included this example to demonstrate the effectiveness of strategy, planning, and using multiple communication media (and soliciting multiple times) with prospects and donors. The key is thinking more globally, integrating your efforts, and being creative when planning your fundraising campaigns.

Other Online Fundraising   There are also a great number of nonprofit organizations using the Internet for fundraising purposes that fall outside the typical methods already described. They are examples of nonprofits and for-profits supporting charity and capitalizing on new technologies and creating fundraising opportunities from them. Three such unique examples are described subsequently.

Launched in December 2008, Heart Card of America (http://www.heartcard. com), allows users to buy a gift card in any amount that recipients then spend or give to their favorite charity. Any charity can apply to be a Heart Card donor recipient, but charities must first be vetted. Heart Card checks nonprofit status and, for now, all charities must be U.S. based. Currently, Heart Card adds two to three organizations each day to its list of recipients.

You can purchase cards directly from Heart Card's web site to give as gifts, or Heart Card has a display program. If your organization signs up to house a brochure display, and if folks who pick up brochures buy gift cards, of each $1 they give, $0.15 comes back to your organization, $0.73 supports the charity of the recipient's choice, and $0.12 pays for the administrative costs of the Heart Card. A card purchased online still supports the Heart Card's administrative expenses at $0.12 on the dollar, and the remaining $0.88 is donated to the recipient's charity.

Heart Card also works directly with nonprofit organizations like the Girl Scouts, where it can fit right into an existing fundraising infrastructure. When Girls Scouts go door-to-door or set up tables in your community, they can also sell Heart Cards. Supporters can buy cards and funds will go back to the Girl Scouts.

For museums and art galleries, the Statue of Liberty–Ellis Island Foundation offers another creative fundraising approach (Figure 7.8). The organization has millions of visitors each year. It was felt that with so many annual tourist and visitors a souvenir or memento would be a successful revenue generator and would strengthen the emotional ties to the Statue of Liberty and Ellis Island.

The AMERICAN
FLAG *of* FACES™
at The Ellis Island Immigration Museum

Brought to you by
The Statue of Liberty-Ellis Island Foundation, Inc.

LIBERTY ELLIS ISLAND

Add your Photo to the Flag   Search the Flag of Faces   More about the Flag of Faces

The American Flag of Faces is an exciting
new way to honor your family in America, at
historic Ellis Island in the shadow of The
Statue of Liberty.

All Americans are eligible to post on our
Flag, whether it's a picture of your ancestors,
your family today, even yourself!

The American Flag of Faces will be a permanent memorial - viewable for posterity - of
the people you choose to honor. Be part of
this spectacular tribute to our nation and the
individuals who make it great. Take your
place on the American Flag of Faces at Ellis
Island, our cherished National Monument
to freedom, welcome and opportunity.

Just add your favorite family or personal
photo. It's easy to get started. **Click on the
Flag to begin.**

Learn more about Ellis Island

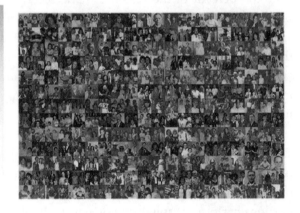

*Add your photo to the Flag
of Faces to support Ellis
Island and become part of
the great American tapestry.*

Intro to Flag of Faces

FIGURE 7.8   Statue of Liberty–Ellis Island Foundation

And because the foundation gets no government funds and little corporate support, visitors offer a great fundraising opportunity.

Along with selling gifts at an online gift shop, running a traditional annual fund and direct-mail campaign, and charging a nominal fee for audio tours, the foundation launched the Flag of Faces website (http://www.flagoffaces.org) in March 2009. For a $50 donation, you can upload a photo of yourself, your family, or your ancestors that will be electronically displayed at Ellis Island. The concept is similar to the current Wall of Honor that is displayed at Ellis Island. Individuals buy a brick space for a $150 donation to honor a family member who came through Ellis Island. After 10 years, the wall is running out of spaces. The new Flag of Faces becomes a permanent memorial because it is virtual and can continually be added to, unlike the Wall of Honor. A computer display shows the Flag of Faces on site at Ellis Island, and it can be viewed online.

The foundation presented Flag of Faces a few months later at its annual Heritage Awards held on May 19, 2009. The event was attended by such celebrities as Joe Namath, Jerry Seinfeld, and Candice Bergen. It also sent more than 2 million e-mail to supporters and visitors who had signed up for news and information about the foundation. The campaign is still in its launch phase as of this writing, so no statistics about giving and participation have yet been determined. However, the computer display at Ellis Island will be in place by the time the museum expands in 2011.

Each year at the Graduate School of Management (GSM) at University of California, Davis, graduating M.B.A. students spend the last month cramming for exams, interviewing for full-time positions, and raising money for a class gift before they graduate. The class of 2009, a small group of 59 full-time students, was a unique bunch. The class-gift campaign committee filmed five very personal YouTube videos to create interest and urgency and to help their fellow classmates understand what the campaign was about and the importance of the class gift.

The first YouTube video was launched on March 31, 2009; sent by e-mail to the entire class; and posted to the class's Facebook page. The video was simply a fun top-10 list of ways to take the old school building "out in style," as the GSM was planning a move to a new facility across campus. It grabbed people's attention and introduced students to the YouTube concept for communications with fellow classmates. By the end of the campaign, the video had 255 views.

The second video launched April 7, 2009, again sent by e-mail to the graduating class and posted to the class's Facebook page. The video explained in a funny way what an endowment is and how and why the class-gift campaign, which supports the student endowment, is important. One of the students presented in the video wearing a homemade paper moustache and goatee. By the end of the campaign, the video had 133 views.

The third video launched on April 16, 2009, also sent by e-mail to the entire class and posted to the class's Facebook page. It was a save-the-date teaser for the class-gift campaign's kickoff party, hosted by the committee. The video offered comical reasons why students really did not have an excuse not to come to the party. Nearly 70 percent of the class attended the kickoff party the following Monday. At the event, the committee received 13 pledges—about 22 percent of the class. The video had 102 views by the end of the campaign.

The fourth video launched on May 14, 2009, and the group took the same steps as for the other videos. It was a funny video called "Terrence Jumps for Pledges" to inspire students to give to the campaign. One of the class-gift committee members "jumped" the school building on his moped. It was creatively and comically edited to appear as such. The video had 111 views at the end of the campaign.

On May 22, 2009, the graduating class reached 100 percent donor participation, only the third class in the history of the school to make such an achievement. The class raised more $10,000 for the endowment.

The fifth and final video launched June 10, 2009, as a thank-you to the class for pledging, and it was distributed in the same fashion as the other videos. It had 85 views by the end of the campaign. The thank-you included one of the committee members running until the class reached 100 percent participation, with the understanding that the other members hadn't told him they already had reached 100 percent. His classmates left him running while they went to celebrate at a pub crawl with their other graduating classmates.

Friend Raising Online

"Friend raising" has become a common term in the nonprofit sector to describe the process of developing a relationship and/or cultivating an individual or group for purposes other than fundraising—although financial investment may come at a later date. Friend raising may result initially in an individual or group volunteering, or working as a mentor for a program client, or helping build awareness and carrying the message of your organization's mission. The focus is on marketing, advocacy, and building awareness among new or existing constituents rather than on raising money.

The following sections highlight three ways to friend raise using online tools, including via your organization's web site, through social media, and in an integrated method using multiple online techniques.

Web Site   In these ever-changing, technologically advancing times, one might think that a web site is a must-have for informational and presence purposes but not something that would engage an individual or a community. Are web sites becoming obsolete in that sense? The two organizations described here do not think so, and they have the volunteers, expanding mission awareness, and online web site communities to prove it.

The Catholic Medical Mission Board (CMMB) in New York City was challenged with a name and brand that was not remembered or inspiring to its constituencies and communities (Figure 7.9). The organization wanted a way to engage new and existing donors, develop its brand, create an online presence, and build awareness for its mission. It developed a campaign that launched at the end of April 2009 called Packed with Love (http://www.packedwithlove.org). On the web site, users enter their name and e-mail address, and those data are immediately written on a care package of health-care supplies that will be sent to a needy community overseas. A user can literally watch the package be picked up by a lift truck and the scene goes to a page where the user can "tell a friend," donate, or see messages on Facebook or Twitter. Also at the page, care packages with others' names on them go by on a conveyor belt and the user can roll over the box and see where the box is going and what supplies are inside.

FIGURE 7.9   **Catholic Medical Mission Board**

Then, CMMB sends a welcome e-mail to the user that includes a thank-you and a story about where the package, along with other packages, is going. The e-mail is updated with a new story each month to keep the content and news up to date and fresh. Several weeks later, CMMB sends a second e-mail with additional information and asks specifically for a donation.

From April 29 to June 23, CMMB secured 2,160 new e-mail addresses through the Packed with Love campaign—about a 7 percent addition to its existing database. Table 7.1 is a chart of the campaign as of June 23, 2009. In addition to the new e-mail contacts it received, CMMB had significant increases on Twitter and Facebook.

The Trisomy 18 Foundation offers another example of a nonprofit organization that is using its web site to build community and offer a method for its constituents to connect. Trisomy 18 is a rare chromosomal defect that affects 1 in 3,000 live births. Because it is relatively unknown, families have had little support, information, and security in researching resources until the foundation created a robust support page on its web site that is filled with details of the disorder, offers resources, and provides opportunities to connect with other families.

TABLE 7.1   ONLINE METRICS AS OF JUNE 23, 2009

Action	No. of People Taking Action
Send a box (total) . . .	2,160
Via Facebook ads	182
Via Change.org	1,310
Via Google Search, content, and banners	30
Via CMMB web site or e-mail	101
Via direct traffic, Facebook Links, e-mail	537
Join CMMB on Twitter	167 (increase from 0 to 167)
Join CMMB Facebook group	406 (increase from 128 to 534)
Tell a friend	94
Donate	$524 (the bulk of sign-ups have yet to receive the solicitation e-mail)

One of the best features of the site is Legacy Pages. There, families can create their own unique page to talk about an unborn child that has just been diagnosed and struggles and challenges during pregnancy and/or remember a child who passed away from complications. Families can tell their child's story; post pictures; and have other family members and friends sign their book with thoughts, prayers, and encouragement. Legacy Pages can also serve as place for inspiration and support for other families.

In its first three years, nearly 450 families have created a Legacy Page. The foundation confirms that these pages are the most heavily used on its site. Unlike posting these stories on other, very public, social media sites, the Trisomy 18 Foundation provides a more secure and private experience for families because the site is not nearly as heavily viewed by the public (Figure 7.10). More recently, the foundation added a function that offers a unique web site address for a Legacy Page, so if a family wants to post to social media sites, they can. In addition, "donate" and "volunteer" buttons appear on each of the Legacy Pages so family and friends can also give to the foundation in support of research and finding a cure.

The Trisomy 18 Foundation also maintains a database of key dates for the family, such as birth date and, in many cases, date of death. On these especially meaningful dates, the foundation sends a personal e-mail to the family members and includes an opportunity for them to send in honorarium and memorial donations in their child's name. Through these efforts, the foundation hopes to maintain lasting relationships with families and create opportunities for them to support the foundation's mission. These efforts have helped the foundation raise more than $115,000 in the past three years.

Social Media   There is a lot of attention focused on social media today and how to understand it and capitalize on it to garner financial and volunteer

FIGURE 7.10   The Trisomy 18 Foundation

support. This section addresses using social media outlets for secure volunteer support, building awareness, and promoting advocacy for nonprofit organizations.

Just Tell (JT) is an organization created to encourage youths to speak up about sexual abuse (Figure 7.11). The nonprofit does not provide services but offers a safe space for children suffering with sexual abuse in their lives to tell an adult who can help them find the help they need.

In August 2006, JT created a MySpace page—one year earlier than it even had started a web site. As the social media wave has evolved, Facebook, LinkedIn, and Twitter have overshadowed MySpace, but it continues to have a strong presence with tweens and teenagers, which is just the population that JT is trying to reach.

Three years later, the MySpace page for JT has seen more than 50,000 hits, has more than 3,000 friends, and has received more than 6,000 messages on the page. Adult survivors of sexual abuse have also left messages thanking JT for its work, saying that they wish JT had been around when they were children, and asking what they can do to help the organization. Teens who have befriended the MySpace page have also put the organization's banner on their own MySpace page to build awareness and advocacy for the organization.

Just Tell also uses LinkedIn and Facebook, but it is not as successful on those fronts. The organization finds adult professionals who have helped with various volunteer needs on LinkedIn and have raised a small amount of money on Facebook, but the organization says it finds the Groups application on Facebook too cumbersome for users—just too many steps to find the Group, the Cause page, and how to donate.

However, the organization continues to make great progress with young people through MySpace. Through messages and communications with teens who want to help the organization on their MySpace page, JT has organized 11 street teams in eight states since October 2008 and has a New York City–based advisory group and one that was formed on MySpace. These groups and the street teams design all the marketing and promotional material that the organization uses to directly peer-to-peer, and it seems to be working. Recently at a youth conference with 90,000 in attendance, JT distributed more than 35,000 flyers, bracelets, and T-shirts. In the future, JT hopes to convert many of its followers and supporters to donors and secure their e-mail addresses so they can send them news and event information.

Integrated Online Friend Raising   In conducting research for this chapter, one small organization stood out like a star with regard to effectively making use of multiple online techniques to connect with people across the globe, to mobilize volunteers, to raise awareness, and to build an advocacy campaign: the

FIGURE 7.11   Just Tell

Uganda Rural Fund (URF). The URF is run by one individual working on a volunteer basis, but it has accomplished amazing results in the past four years to friend raise and fundraise for projects in Uganda.

John Mary Lugemwa started URF when he was a sophomore in college in 2005, but he has managed to build an orphanage for 22 kids, build a school with a 125-student enrollment for children from poor families or who are orphaned, create an after-school program for area children, start the Women Empowerment Program to teach women how to start small businesses and otherwise be entrepreneurial, create a microfinance program run by the women in the empowerment program, and organize community seminars.

As he has been a full-time student ever since the organization started (Lugemwa is currently in graduate school), he has had limited opportunities to travel, so he does most of the marketing and researching resources online. Over the past five years, URF has found partners online to help with various projects. It has partnered with Engineers without Borders at University of Minnesota and Virginia Tech for water, sanitation, and solar-energy projects for the school in Uganda. Engineers without Borders has put in an underground well to provide clean water for students and the community. Last summer, the Virginia Tech team installed solar panels at the school.

The URF has also connected with Architecture for Humanity online, which is helping Lugemwa with designs for new buildings to expand the school. The organization has made designs for new classrooms, computer labs, a library, a community center, a medical clinic, and student dormitories.

Lugemwa is achieving all this through an integrated online approach that promotes URF on various social networking sites such as Facebook, MySpace, Razoo, Development Crossing, Ammado, Causecast, Idealist, Ning, KIDS Worldwide, and more. These networks have helped him spread the word about URF's work. He has raised some money through networks like Causes on Facebook and GiveMeaning and secured equipment and computers for the school through online postings on LinkedIn and Facebook.

In addition, Lugemwa has recruited more than 90 volunteers from all over the globe, from countries such as Canada, the United States, Australia, Spain, Holland, Sweden, Norway, Ireland, England, and Scotland. He coordinates the volunteer program remotely over the Internet and via phone. He secures volunteers who are on the ground in Uganda building and running programs to people in Europe providing financial assistance to some in the United States who help him write grants. He has established a volunteer application process and reviews the volunteers and arranges their placements in Uganda—all online. He has been able to harness the power of the Internet to market URF and network with individuals and groups that he would never have been able to reach considering his limited resources and time constraints.

The URF has also networked with eight college campuses that have contributed to the cause in various ways. A breakdown of what the organization has achieved since 2005 is available at http://ugandaruralfund.org/our-achievements.htm. Lugemwa is truly a leadership example of the power of the Internet and is doing tremendous things with the few resources in his command.

CONCLUSION

In conducting research for this chapter, only the most inspiring, thoughtful nonprofit organizations were chosen as examples. That is to say that there are many, many more across the country and across the globe that are achieving exciting results for their organizations, whether by adding 10 new e-mail contacts or raising $25,000 through a great variety of online techniques and tools. I hope you have found a new nugget of knowledge—something to help improve your own organization's fundraising and friend-raising techniques online or to motivate your organization, whether small or large, to take on the challenge of a new way to secure volunteers, raise money, build awareness, and create advocacy online.

One last message: As you try new tools and techniques, I hope that you and your organization will be inspired to take a step, not a leap. As you prepare your next annual development plan, take a deeper look at one aspect of your fundraising portfolio, whether the annual fund, grant writing, events, or major and planned gifts. Next, think about how you and your organization can make changes to incorporate or improve your online strategies. Could you begin to secure volunteers online using Facebook or LinkedIn? Could you motivate donors and prospects through your web site? Could your organization share photos of the programs you have funded on a special web page or via Facebook? Could you try an online auction at your next event?

The idea is to take small steps continuously over a long period of time. This approach will help ensure success by creating buy-in from your constituents, allowing for changes to the course if things are not working out, and making everyone feel in control of the process. It will also allow you and your organization time and room to communicate changes with donors, volunteers, staff, and others; seek their input and feedback; and make them feel connected to your organization.

Resources

There are a tremendous amount of resources on the web about leveraging the power of the Internet to improve your fundraising and friend-raising efforts. Whether or not they are specifically geared toward the nonprofit sector, much of the information is applicable. The following is a list of resources for nonprofit organizations that I found in the process of researching and writing this chapter:

Grassroots.org: Equips nonprofits with the most current resources by leveraging modern technologies and best business practices. It currently serves more than 1,100 501(c)(3) organizations located in all 50 U.S. states. Each organization has access to a suite of services valued at approximately $24,000, including web design, graphic design, search engine optimization, and domain registration. http://www.grassroots.org.

Taproot Foundation: The Taproot Foundation exists to close the gap in the lack of operational resources nonprofits need to be effective and to ensure that all nonprofits have the infrastructure they need to thrive. Every year, hundreds of nonprofit organizations rely on the foundation's award-winning Service Grant program to provide millions of dollars worth of pro bono marketing, human resources, IT, and strategy management consulting services that better equip them to tackle our society's toughest challenges. http://www.taprootfoundation.org.

The Foundation Center: The Foundation Center is a national nonprofit service organization recognized as the nation's leading authority on organized philanthropy, connecting nonprofits and the grant makers supporting them to tools they can use and information they can trust. http://www.foundationcenter.org.

Network for Good for Nonprofits: Network for Good makes it as easy to donate and volunteer online as it is to shop online, and it makes it simple and affordable for all nonprofits, of any size, to recruit donors and volunteers via the Internet. http://www.networkforgood.org.

Idealist.org: Idealist is an interactive site where people and organizations can exchange resources and ideas, locate opportunities and supporters, and take steps toward building a world in which all people can lead free and dignified lives. http://www.idealist.org.

TechSoup: TechSoup.org offers nonprofits a one-stop resource for technology needs by providing free information, resources, and support. In addition to online information and resources, it offers a product philanthropy service called TechSoup Stock. Nonprofits can access donated and discounted technology products, generously provided by corporate and nonprofit technology partners. http://www.techsoup.org.

Karma411: Karma411 is a social collaboration tool for nonprofits to raise money and awareness for their cause. Karma411 focuses on people-to-people fundraising, which means that nonprofits not only can run their own online appeals through the site but also can encourage their supporters to do the same and directly ask their friends, colleagues, and family members to help support the cause on their behalf. http://www.karma411.com.

Convio: Convio provides marketing, fundraising, advocacy, and donor database tools to help organizations take advantage of the inherent effectiveness and efficiency of the Internet to motivate donors and other supporters. http://www.convio.com.

Vacation Homes for Charity: Vacation Homes for Charity is a luxury and high-end rental company that secures a week's rental for charitable auctions from its clients. As of July 1, 2009, the organization had helped 26 nonprofit organizations, auctioned 16 houses (some homes were donated multiple times), and helped raise $153,100 for charity. http://www.vacationhomesforcharity.org.

Adrienne D. Capps has spent her career committed to the nonprofit sector in serving as a professional fundraiser. She has raised nearly $20 million for a variety of causes, including at-risk youth, mental health, and higher education in Virginia, New York, and California. A certified fundraising executive since 2004, Capps has published several articles in *Advancing Philanthropy*, the most recent of which is "Gastronomy and Giving." She is coeditor of *The Green Nonprofits Handbook* and authored the chapter on green fundraising. Capps is a member of the Council for the Advancement and Support of Education as well as the Association of Fundraising Professionals where she served on the board of the Greater New York chapter, and she is a frequent guest speaker for both groups. She serves as treasurer of S.W.i.S.H, a New York City–based gay-straight alliance, and she recently launched the social venture Vintners Charitable Cooperative, where nonprofit supporters can drink charitably by joining a wine club that gives 50 percent of profits to charity (http://www.charityvintner.org). Capps holds a B.S. in business administration, with honors, and a B.A. in leadership studies from the University of Richmond, a certificate in fundraising administration from New York University, and an M.B.A. in financial management, with honors, from Pace University in New York City.

CHAPTER 8

The Nonprofit Leader's Volunteer Recruitment and Retention Strategies

WALTER P. PIDGEON JR.

There is an explosion of new and truly exciting ways to reach volunteers and donors through the ever-expanding electronic road map. Nonprofit leaders, as well as people working in many other facets of the community, are weighing in on what have become the most dynamic advances in history in how to attract and retain people's interest. In my book *The Not-For-Profit CEO Workbook: Practical Steps to Attaining and Retaining the Corner Office*, I included a message to volunteer leaders. That message emphasized the importance of having a close relationship between volunteers and nonprofit leaders. I noted that "the quality of relationships depends on the level of trust that is attained and the communications level that is maintained between the manager and volunteer."[1]

The methods that nonprofit managers use to communicate with volunteers need to be chosen wisely to fit each individual relationship.[2] The challenge, however, for nonprofit leaders is to determine both the best tools to use and how to use them effectively. To address these important management decisions, leaders need to do the following:

1. Approach their decision from a historical perspective.
2. Conduct research to determine what's out there.
3. Match organizational needs, including budget limitations.
4. Learn how other groups are taking advantage of the electronic revolution
5. Create a marketing plan that will meet needs and maintain standards.
6. Put in place an evaluation process to measure worth, reveal refinement opportunities, and guide future use.

HISTORICAL PERSPECTIVE

One cannot approach philanthropy and volunteer recruitment and retention without an understanding of the origins of the nonprofit community and the vital role that volunteers play. Acts of volunteering can be found throughout recorded history. Ancient Egypt yielded perhaps the first evidence of works of charity: the first written documentation praising those who fed the hungry and gave water to the thirsty can be found in the *Book of the Dead* from 4000 BC.[3]

Volunteering, for practical reasons, first became organized in the United States, following European traditions, during colonization. During that time, acts of goodwill filled a service void that Old World governments had traditionally provided.[4]

Robert H. Bremner, in his classic book *American Philanthropy*, noted, "The real founders of American philanthropy were men and women who crossed the Atlantic to establish communities that would be better than, instead of like or different from the ones they had known at home."[5]

From the very beginning of our nation, the founding fathers designed a government of limited power separate from religious influence. As a result, philanthropy and volunteerism had a natural breeding ground to flourish.[6] Many of the significant events and activities of our nation have been the result of volunteering: the Underground Railroad is a wonderful example. Volunteering in the United States is a history of common people's combined efforts to accomplish tasks, provide social outlets, and promote a sense of community.[7]

Alexis de Tocqueville noted, "To study the operation of American Society, it was necessary to analyze the operation and function of the volunteer associations."[8] Those who pioneered the nonprofit sector lived through much greater challenges than we have or will face. Yet they not only survived, they flourished. The secret, I believe, was both the passion they held for the causes that they championed and the ability to wisely use the resources at hand (see appendix 8A).

THE UNIVERSAL BENEFITS OF VOLUNTEERING

A decade ago I authored the book *Universal Benefits of Volunteering*. The book was based on the National College Graduate Survey on Volunteering, which I had conducted. The study's findings documented that those who volunteered (88.43 percent) received return value, including personal benefits such as self-satisfaction and career benefits such as a better understanding of ethical and moral standards and the ability to work with different constituencies. The most significant finding of the study was that more than 90 percent of those who volunteered gained leadership traits.[9] The findings of the study provide nonprofit leaders with vital data to attract and retain volunteers. Managers not only can encourage volunteering on the basis of performing good works but also can encourage community service for the return value that volunteers receive from the experience, such as the following:

- Opportunities to work with leaders and others in the community
- New contacts
- The ability to work with different constituencies
- The satisfaction of helping provide a service to others
- Committee and board experience
- A better understanding of social patterns
- Development of a strong sense of personal mission
- Becoming more concerned about the future of society
- Strategic planning experience
- A better understanding of ethical and moral standards
- Increased willingness to take risks
- A sense of personal power

   Source: Pidgeon, Walter P., College Graduate Study on Volunteering, 1991

Return value is also a practical tool for encouraging business executives to institute and sustain in-house volunteer programs. Such programs not only fulfill community service goals but also bring back to the workplace measurable value that could lead to increased productivity.

INCREASED CHALLENGES FACING NONPROFIT ORGANIZATIONS

The increased challenges that nonprofit volunteer and professional leaders face call for new strategic measures that will attract and retain quality volunteers in all aspects of the nonprofit community. It is particularly important that managers put into place a plan that emphasizes the universal benefits of volunteering, relationship building, and instilling passion in volunteers. This plan should encourage volunteers to become involved in every aspect of the organizations that they lead, including in raising the funds required to fulfill its mission.

Volunteering makes it possible for a nonprofit to dramatically expand capacity to better serve its constituents. Unfortunately, some nonprofit professionals consider volunteers more of a nuisance than an asset. These managers tend to rely on full-time employees to do most of the work of the organization. They are not students of the nonprofit process, and they do not understand the historical origins of the sector. If they did, they would understand that:

1. Almost all nonprofits were created by volunteers.

2. Members, donors, and volunteers are the true owners of an organization.

3. So much more can be accomplished if volunteers are used efficiently in conjunction with full-time staff.

What's Out There?

The answer to the question, "What's out there?" can be summarized in one word: "plenty." With the sheer numbers of media channels emerging every day, it would be unrealistic to attempt to use them all. Managers need to selectively choose the channels that suit their not-for-profit's needs.[10] Therefore, the major challenge that nonprofit leaders face is to keep up to date with emerging marketing applications and, more important, on how such channels might apply to their nonprofit organizations. This can be accomplished by conducting research, testing, and evaluation. One of the best ways to stay up to date is to keep in contact with your constituents and determine what they are using to communicate with one another.

There are also a host of online sites that can keep you informed. Relative to online resources, particularly with the advent of social networking, these are two of the best:

1. Mashable.com, which is the most comprehensive and its material is updated regularly. If anything, the site may provide too much information, but it is well worth your time. The site includes news updates on the top social networking sites, such as Facebook, MySpace, Twitter, and YouTube.

2. Social Media Today (http://www.socialmediatoday.com), which is designed for those who wish to enter the social media field. It includes a moderated discussion board with entries from bloggers, marketers, and other professionals.

Obtaining and Using Information

It is likely that it is not the lack of information on the subject but the proper filtering of information that is required to make a sound decision based on an organization's need. It is also important to keep in mind that organizations must be flexible in their approach, because social media and networking tend to be ever changing, with individuals moving from one channel to another at breakneck speed. Nonprofits will need to become change agents if they wish to stay timely with their key target audiences.

Nonprofit leaders, therefore, need to be kept informed and able to measure both current and emerging applications on the basis of need and adaptability. To accomplish this, a leader needs to create a standard for the organization. This standard should be based on need, communications style, and budget. The standard should measure existing methods to determine whether they are still valid and new methods to determine worth.

The key is to discover the right blend of both current and new applications. The challenge is that this is not a onetime exercise but a process that needs to take place constantly as part of a manager's ongoing overview of operations. New applications are coming online more quickly than ever, and they are also maturing rapidly. Faxing is a wonderful example of this. The fax machine was a major breakthrough when it was introduced, but it has quickly become a second-tier communication practice.

The key, therefore, to maintaining a successful volunteer marketing plan is to keep it comprehensive but flexible enough to adapt to new applications as they come online and as you drop outdated techniques. To attract and retain volunteers, therefore, you need to consider a blend of three categories of marketing:

1. Old-line practices
2. General electronic applications
3. Social networking

Old-Line Practices

Although many old-line practices may seem just that, many still perform well if administered properly and blended with newer techniques.

In-Person Contacts   Face-to-face contact remains the best way to influence an individual or group. This is particularly true when asking someone to volunteer or donate at higher levels. The major challenge, however, is the time and expense that it takes. This tends to limit our practice of in-person contacts to high-level prospects.

Speaking   Another way to project your message is to find ways to speak before groups that have targeted prospects in the audience. This is a wonderful way to open a door to a prospect with whom you may not have a direct contact. Often you can approach such a prospect after you speak to ask for advice or perhaps arrange a follow-up call. In some cases, the prospect may even approach you. It is very special when that happens.

Telephone   Personal calls by landlines or cell phone still provide a personal touch, particularly if you already have established a relationship with the person in question. Cold calls can be deadly and should be avoided. However, encouraging someone who knows the person to call first may help start a relationship.

Fax   Sending a fax is not used as much as it once was, but faxing a hard copy document is sometimes easier than scanning. Faxing can still provide a nonprofit a power punch, however, in the advocacy arena. When volunteers flood a corporate executive's suite or legislator's office with faxes, these messages tend to be more effective than e-mail simply because they tend to gain more notice. An e-mail, for example, can be simply deleted by an administrative assistant or aide. In one case brought to my attention, e-mail sent to a congressman were merely counted to note their position on a particular issue, but most people who faxed received a reply.

Mail   Direct mail continues to be an effective tool to reach targeted audiences, and one of the major uses of this tool for nonprofits is fundraising. A direct-mail approach to attempt to attract volunteers is not the best initial approach. However, direct mail used wisely can be very effective for many nonprofit applications. On the downside, it is expensive and time consuming, and the returns tend to be low. Tailored letters to targeted individuals, particularly those with whom you have a relationship, can be more effective. A personalized letter is becoming a lost art, and as a result, when they are executed properly, receivers will appreciate them. House organs, from newsletters to magazines, update recipients on the latest activities of the organization. These continue to be effective tools for maintaining relationships with existing members and donors. They are also a wonderful way to recognize and encourage volunteering.

General Electronic Applications

Electronic applications have become a key way for nonprofits to reach their audiences. This is particularly true for small to midsize nonprofit organizations.

E-Mail   Perhaps the most widely used electronic application is e-mail, which is a very effective way to contact both individuals and segmented groups. Response time from key players in nonprofits can often be quicker by e-mail than by telephone. E-mail newsletters are good ways to create an ongoing buzz with active volunteers and those who simply wish to be kept informed about your organization. The association I lead, the U.S. Sportsmen's Alliance (USSA), has a weekly e-mail newsletter that is simple in design and is very well received.

Our reach has expanded significantly because of the timeliness and predictability of the offering.

The USSA also has formed partnerships with other key entities to create the U.S. Sportsmen National Alert Network. The network partners agree to forward our materials to their e-mail list. Everyone who receives the alerts is kept informed and knows who is leading the charge. This has benefited both the USSA and its partners. The network has grown to more than 500,000 subscribers.

Web Sites   Most nonprofit organizations have web sites. Some web sites, however, are more effective than others. The ones that seem to be the most effective are those that are pleasing to the eye, easy to use, and provide open access. The most effective web sites also are linked to other sources of information from the organization, including social media outlets and outside sources. These links allow a certain degree of seamlessness among channels. Well-designed nonprofit web sites generally have a tab or button at the top of the web page to encourage users to donate, and users simply click it to be taken to a landing page that gives them various options for contributing. To encourage giving, it is advantageous to provide a breakdown of how funds have historically been spent on the landing page. This can be a simple overview or, as some groups do, can include links to copies of appropriate tax forms.

Volunteer-driven nonprofits also have a tab on their web sites devoted to volunteering, which takes users to a landing page with specific information on how they can become involved in advancing the organization's cause.

If a nonprofit organization offers e-mail services (e.g., an e-newsletter), a tab should be on the web site that encourages individuals to sign up. Keep in mind that capturing an e-mail can be the first step toward building a relationship. Some groups also work to create an active community through a comprehensive network of multiple web sites, blogs, and social networking opportunities. Depending on an organization's size and staffing, the group's main web site may include some social networking features in addition to connections to the standard social networking sites. Whether this is done (or is useful) depends on the type of audience and the ability to maintain an active user experience. If this can't be done, it is best to focus exclusively on the major social networking sites like Facebook, MySpace, and Twitter.

The good news is that nearly all nonprofits are committed to an Internet presence to support their various programs and causes. However, Leverus, a Canadian company that publishes the Internet Survey for Associations and Not-For-Profit Organizations has pointed out that 50 percent of respondent organizations reported being somewhat unsatisfied or very unsatisfied with the current design of their web sites.[11]

Nonprofits continue to upgrade their web sites to gain attention from both prospective donors and volunteers with steps such as the following:

- Making navigation buttons large enough to read easily
- Minimizing the number of navigation buttons to eight or fewer on any given level or section of the site
- Making everything accessible using just a few clicks
- Using an attractive color palette
- Incorporating graphics moderately
- Presenting a dynamic home page that puts the information front and center

It is an ongoing struggle for some, however, to find the right mix. Online donations, for example, still make up a very small portion of most organizations' overall fundraising programs—less than 1 percent of overall giving in 2007 as reported by the *Chronicle of Philanthropy*.[12]

Texting   Texting from cell to cell is a popular exercise among youths, but it is also an effective tool to converse quickly with your key players, particularly volunteers.

Social Networking

Social networking is the new media of corporate-customer interaction, so plan accordingly. Social networking focuses on creating online communities of people who share similar interests and/or activities. Facebook, MySpace, Twitter, and LinkedIn are among the most popular social networks. The following list shows four ways that social networking is changing the nonprofit world:

1. They are deepening relationships and engagements through empowerment, passion, and commitment.
2. Individuals and small groups are self-organizing around nonprofit causes; individuals can create a cause and run with it, and nonprofits reach more people than ever before.
3. More collaboration is occurring with facilitation and "crowdsourcing."
4. Social change is occurring behind the firewall because social media can help change the culture, speed up decision making, and improve programs and services.[13]

The trend seems to be moving toward smaller and more targeted offerings. For-profits, for example, are flocking to sites that attract individuals whose profiles are similar to their customer base. They are finding that their approach is more focused and the cost is less. Everyone from start-ups to Fortune 500 companies see the advantages of segmenting their audiences for future growth.[14]

Social networking is built on the idea of a joint conversation. Nonprofits need to join in on that conversation. The objective is to create awareness and promote your identity. Active participation helps you spread your message spread further and more quickly. However, you need to identify your target audience. You also need to be realistic. There are audiences that you can reach and others that you may not or at least cannot reach in a way that makes the expenditure of time and/or financial resources worthwhile. The following list includes four advantages of social networking sites for nonprofits:

1. They are generally free to join and easy to use, as opposed to having to create and maintain web sites, which may be cost prohibitive.

2. They allow nonprofits to connect with current and prospective donors or members while also keeping external entities and partners informed.

3. Social networking sites have the potential of reaching target audiences around the clock.

4. They help build a loyal following by keeping supporters up to date on an organization's activities.

Certain kinds of content seem to spread more naturally. Even if your organization's subject matter is hard to sell, there is always content that you can create that will gain attention. It is vital, therefore, to discover what content to use to promote your nonprofit organization. Also, remember that expressing interest in others does wonders for driving traffic to your web site and social networking profile. Sometimes, a simple profile story of another volunteer is enough to gain the attention of new potential volunteers and expose them to the mission of your organization.[15]

Social networking is becoming the key way that we communicate with one another at all levels. Shannon Buggs, in an article in the *Houston Chronicle* titled "Business of Giving: Nonprofits Should Make Use of Social Networking," noted that she posts what's interesting her and sends it to more than 190 contacts to let them know: "It works great when the source has up-to-date technology on their web sites to easily post information and photos on Facebook pages. But too often that technology, an RSS (Really Simple Syndication) formatted feed, is nowhere to be found, especially on web sites of nonprofits, to allow those interested to receive regular updates." Buggs also points out that nonprofits need to make it easy for their fans to pass on information.[16]

It is important to note that outsourcing your total social media program has benefits, but you need to realize that a personal touch is the point of the process. The customer wants to hear directly from you, and you can accomplish this by wisely using a number of social tools that you directly control. Here are a few examples:

- **Blogging**: Blogging has become an ideal way for key nonprofit leaders to promote the mission of the organization and reveal their passion.

- **MySpace**: MySpace is a social media site for those who wish to send and receive messages, browse photo albums, check out profiles, add new friends, read and post blogs, and so on.

- **Facebook**: Facebook, possibly more than MySpace, offers nonprofit leaders an opportunity to connect with those who are deeply interested in their cause. Facebook has more than 200 million users and myriad nonprofit pages. It is a social utility that connects people with friends and others who work, study, and live around them. Facebook encourages users to solve world problems through its use. In particular, the Causes application offers a gateway for prospective volunteers and donors.

- **LinkedIn**: LinkedIn is a site designed for professionals. Users can post contact information and résumés, form networks, find job openings, and pose questions. LinkedIn can also be particularly useful for leaders looking to discover potential talent.

- **Twitter**: Twitter is a free social messaging utility for staying connected in real-time messages that use 140 characters or less. It has become a key way to gain attention and open relationships. The media, celebrities, and businesses, for example, have embraced Twitter. The Wharton School professors Andrea Matwyshyn and Kevin Werbach note, "Like most of the big Internet success stories, Twitter has taken off because it serves the needs of many different communities."[17] Nonprofit leaders need to consider how best to use this media source to their advantage. Using Twitter as part of a marketing plan can change the way you use the web. With it, you have a research tool to tap into a diverse community to discover what they are thinking; you can evaluate your blog or even a hard-copy piece to tailor your message to your intended audiences; you can keep your brand out there and remind them that you exist and that you have other electronic venues; you can draw individuals to your point of view; you can become the authority in your area of expertise; and you can open up new relationships with potential donors and volunteers.

Other Social Media Opportunities

It would be impossible to list all the social media outlets that nonprofits can use to build relationships with current and potential donors and volunteers. Here is a sampling:

- **YouTube**: The leader of online video, sharing original videos worldwide through web experience. You can easily upload videos from web sites, mobile devices, blogs, and e-mail. Nonprofit leaders can update visual content by uploading videos of events or describing major issues.

- **Flickr**: A photo and video management and sharing application that has some interesting uses for nonprofits. It can offer a visual gateway for prospective volunteers and donors, particularly the younger set.

- **Qik:** Allows people to share moments live through mobile phones and provides the opportunity for instantaneous visual sharing of events.

- **Bit.ly**: One of several sites that allow users to shorten, share, and track links. Users can follow traffic to posted links in real time and see who's using a given piece of content developed by your organization.

- **Niche social networking sites:** Sites that cater to specific interests or causes, such as Blackplanet.com, an online niche serving the African American community, and MyCancerPlace.com, which offers networking opportunities for those suffering or recovering from cancer and/or their family members.

Your Organization's Needs

Once you understand the historical background of volunteering and the array of marketing outlets available, you need to determine the best applications for the organization you lead. Even large and well-funded nonprofits cannot afford to spread themselves too thin. Marketing, after all, continues to be a focused approach to gain the best results.

Most organizations should not abandon all old-line practices for electronic applications. A blended approach is far more effective. Managers need to keep in mind, as well, that some of their audience may wish to continue to receive information through those sources. In fact, old and new media work very well together and can be linked in a number of ways. If a nonprofit's public service announcement is well received on television, for example, a viewer might "tweet" a friend about it on Twitter, and that friend might pass it on. Just think of the possibilities if thousands of viewers did the same: millions of people could see your message. This is how many individuals communicate with one another, and nonprofit leaders need to take full advantage of this trend.

Creating Your Mix

How do you determine what you should and should not adopt? The simple answer is that it depends on your constituents' needs and how best to fulfill your strategic plan on the basis of those needs. To begin the process you need to

- Know your organization's core requirements
- Keep up to speed on what's out there
- Create an organizational standard by which to measure the worth of both traditional and new applications

Chances are that you are applying several appropriate approaches already and need only add or refine a few additional elements. Although each organization's mission and operations are different, there are standard needs that most organizations should field to attract and retain volunteers:

- A process to identify quality volunteers
- A flexible method to educate and train volunteers
- Avenues to communicate properly with volunteers on a regular basis
- An evaluation and renewal process
- Productive ways to recognize volunteers

The key objective, therefore, is to create a tailored volunteer plan for your organization based on need. The 2008 donorCentrics Internet Giving Benchmarking Analysis noted, for example, that online donors

- Have higher incomes and are younger than direct-mail donors
- Give larger gifts
- Can be an integrated part of the entire direct-mail program

Therefore, your relationship-building plan to attract younger donors and volunteers could begin online.

PROFILE OF A TYPICAL NONPROFIT ORGANIZATION

To illustrate my points in this chapter, let's take a look at a profile of a typical nonprofit organization. Some of the characteristics may differ from your organization, but many will be close enough that you find an idea or two to adapt to fit your needs.

On the surface, the Do Good Society seems healthy (see Table 8.1) The society is on budget and seems to have a diversified marketing plan in place. Yet it has identified a need to grow. In most cases, organizations must grow to maintain their momentum, and to do this requires increasing capacity to attract new constituents, volunteers, and funding.

TABLE 8.1	A SAMPLE NONPROFIT PROFILE FOR THE DO GOOD SOCIETY

Category	Basic Information
IRS classification	501(c)3
Age	35
Headquarters	Anywhere
Facilities	
Own or lease	Own
Appraised	$2.5 million
Other locations	Federal office, Washington, DC
Own or lease	Lease
Territory	National
Budget	$5 million
Expenses	$4.9 million
Reserves	$5 million
Endowment	$10 million
Staff	20
Volunteers	
Current	1,500
Total need	2,500
Roles	Board of directors, committees, task forces, activities based
Members	
Current	40,000
Total need	60,000
Donors	
Current	5,000
Total need	8,000
Support and marketing plan	House organ, web site, direct-mail program, e-mail program, social network and Facebook
Age of members or donors	
20–45	25% current, 35% total need
46–55	25% current, 35% total need
56–65	30% current, 20% total need
66 and older	20% current, 10% total need

The Do Good Society may be fulfilling its mission currently, but what will happen in 10 years if the organization does not attract new members and donors? Perhaps as much as a third of its member and donor base may be gone. The society has identified a goal, and it is vital that it meets that objective. Therefore, a relationship–building program needs to be a part of the organization's volunteer plan. The plan's objectives would attract quality volunteers in the key age brackets identified and call on dedicated volunteers in older age brackets to become mentors to the younger volunteers to ensure a smooth transition.

Identifying Needs

Identifying your organization's current and future needs is vital to creating a plan to fulfill them. The not-for-profit profile in Table 8.1 examined some of the core needs of the Do Good Society, but an actual organizational needs assessment would be far more detailed and unique. An organizational needs assessment is, therefore, the first step in creating a well-designed volunteer plan.

Bring Excitement into the Mix to Attract Quality Volunteers

A key aspect of attracting members, donors, and volunteers is the quality of the activities that not-for-profits stage to fulfill their mission. Many programs tend to generate little buzz, and as a result, they are somewhat difficult to sell to prospective customers. Almost all programs, however, can be refined to increase interest in them.

One of the areas often overlooked, for example, is government affairs. Non-profit managers tend to either treat this opportunity as a secondary issue or, in many cases, shy away from it all together. Even social service 501(c)3 organizations can engage in some facets of government affairs and should do so to the maximum that the law allows. The role that volunteers can play is substantial if managers introduce excitement into the equation. In fact, in many circumstances, volunteers are better suited to play the advocacy role than government affairs professionals.[18]

The Do Good Society's Volunteer Plan

The key to attracting quality volunteers for the Do Good Society is to create a marketing plan that combines old-line practices, new technologies, and social networking and that uses a common theme throughout the effort.

Old-Line Practices   For old-line practices, you can initiate in-person contact to grow the organization, and you can recruit volunteer leadership from the current pool of key players to address possible declining membership in the older age bracket. The two groups form a joint task force to identify potential volunteers, plan tailored approaches to each prospect, assign teams in a combination of older and younger age groups to recruit prospects, and guarantee success of the new volunteers through proper training and coaching. Next, develop two documents to present to prospective volunteers: 1) plan to fulfill the mission by growing the organization and 2) provide a detailed summary of volunteer opportunities. Use successful **old-line practices** including the following:

- **Speaking opportunities**: The joint task force finds avenues to speak that will help to educate members and donors and to identify new players.
- **Telephone**: A manager arranges personal phone calls to encourage volunteers to work on the plan and to attract additional individuals to volunteer.

- **Mail**: Promote the new volunteer plan by issuing personal letters to all members and donors when needed, using house organs to feature success stories, and having an ample array of recognition for volunteers.

New Technologies and Social Networking   Use some steps to incorporate new technologies and social networking into an organization's plan including the following:

- **E-mail**: Push to acquire e-mail addresses from all members and donors, launch a weekly e-mail newsletter to create buzz, and send e-mail alerts to volunteers to encourage progress and highlight successes.
- **Web site**: Refine the web site to focus on the key areas that will move the organization to a new level while continuing to fulfill the mission and serving current members.
- **Texting**: Use texting to contact volunteers to fulfill time-sensitive activities.
- **Twitter**: Use the campaign theme to create buzz that would attract potential volunteers from the society's target audience and direct them to more information on other society sources, including Facebook, the web site, blogs, and so on.
- **Facebook**: Use a theme to create buzz with more detail, and encourage target audiences to seek more information from the society's web site, blog, and so on.
- **Blog**: Create a blog written by the CEO to personalize the message, add strength to the campaign, and encourage the society's target audience to seek more information from the web site.

IMPLEMENTATION

Implementation is not always as easy as it seems. Nonprofit managers seem to struggle with what to focus on first: what is happening now or what needs to be put into place to prep for the future. Vijay Govindarajan, professor of international business at Tuck School of Business at Dartmouth College, notes that his management strategy involves the use of three boxes. He encourages leaders to constantly think about what goes in or stays out of all three boxes:

1. Box 1 involves managing in the present.
2. Box 2 involves selectively forgetting the past.
3. Box 3 involves creating the future.

Govindarajan recommends that managers spend more time and energy thinking about what goes in boxes 2 and 3.[19] That way, what nonprofit leaders do now to fulfill their missions may be important, but if managers neglect to prepare for the future, what they do now may have little meaning.

The Use of Social Networks

Implementing a social network plan requires internal involvement. To accomplish this, managers need to determine the following:

1. Who within the organization is currently engaged in social networking? These are the individuals who are potential key players to help implement the plan.

2. Of the key players identified, select potential leaders to help create a strategy and determine goals. The objectives should reflect the outcomes you wish to attain, such as increasing volunteer involvement, attracting new funding, creating a new program, and other related issues.

3. Once you have developed your plan, you can then determine the technologies to acquire initially.

Ed Schipul, the founder and CEO of Schipul, a web-marketing firm, suggests that one way to navigate the social web is for nonprofit leaders to attend local NetSquared meetings, an organization with chapters throughout North America. The following list provides some other suggestions for acquiring donors and volunteers online:

- **Secure the technology**: There is little point in acquiring prospects online unless you have the tools to build enduring relations with them.

- **Drive prospective donors to your web pages**: Search engine optimization (SEO) involves tweaking your web site and taking steps to ensure that links to your site appear near the top of searches that relate to your mission.

- **Persuade your site visitors to take action**: Convert initial interest into a tangible action by making it easier for site visitors to leave their e-mail address, make a donation, or volunteer.

- **Don't drive searches to your home page**: Instead, drive searches to an action page that relates directly to whatever visitors searched out in the first place.

- **Get permission to stay in touch**: Have an opt-in e-mail check box across your web site.

- **Find ways to encourage deeper commitment**.

- **Keep supporters informed through e-mail and newsletters**:[20]

EVALUATION

One of the major components of a nonprofit manager's relationship-building plan is the evaluation process. How a leader blends old-line practices with new technologies and social networking is the key. In many ways, this is all about the volume of people that you attract to read or at least open your sources, but basing your evaluation solely on that information will not tell you whether you received meaningful value from such engagements. Although various sources provide models for business evaluations, nonprofit leaders need to look at the evaluation process a bit differently, particularly in measuring long-term relationship-building benefits. The following list goes over ways that nonprofit leaders can measure the value of marketing methods through certain filters:

- **Usage**: The most obvious measure is actual use. This should include traditional and new methods as well, such as return rate to direct-mail pieces sent, income average per call, number of hits on your web site, and the level of comments on your blog and other social media outlets.

- **Point of entry**: As constituents and prospects move to new media venues to send and receive information, nonprofit managers need to adapt to meet that demand. It is vital that they track this movement and tailor nonprofit marketing plans not only to fulfill demand but also to stay ahead of the curve. Managers, therefore, need to measure the level of use of each point of entry and provide the support required to meet demand.

- **Passion**: Managers need to measure constituent passion for their nonprofits. This can be done through various survey methods. You need to determine why people are involved, what turns them on, and how best to keep their passion alive.

- **Activities and issues**: It is important to determine the activities in your organization in which your constituents have the most interest, are willing to volunteer for, and financially support. The profile of an individual who wishes to volunteer for a government affairs activity will be quite different from one who wishes to mentor a youth. Both roles may be vital, but your approach to each one will be quite different.

- **Brand identification**: Although most nonprofit leaders do not refer to their nonprofit organizations as brands, perhaps they should. After all, marketing efforts need to be directed, in part, toward increasing awareness and recognition of organizations. The greater the awareness of the brand among targeted audiences, the greater return will be achieved. Therefore, nonprofit marketing plans need to measure brand awareness.

Nonprofit Managers' Challenge

Leaders who are not engaging their nonprofit organizations in a comprehensive marketing plan that includes the right mix of old-line practices, new technologies, and social networking with clearly defined relationship-building goals, including donor and volunteer acquisitions, are in for a rude awakening. The playing field has changed, and organizations that hesitate will be left behind. Nonengaged managers need to stop debating the challenge to field such a plan or the costs. They need to focus on the immense opportunities that such a plan can provide to fulfill the missions of the organizations that they lead. For an example of creative marketing, note Appendix B to this chapter.

Walter (Bud) Pidgeon Jr. is a seasoned not-for-profit professional leader who has served in a number of key positions, including chief executive officer at four national organizations. He is a nationally recognized consultant in the areas of strategic thinking, volunteering, government affairs, and fundraising. Bud has also conducted research on various not-for-profit subjects. He has authored numerous articles for national publications and four books, including *The Not-For-Profit CEO Workbook* (2006), *The Not-For-Profit CEO* (2004), *The Legislative Labyrinth* (2001), and *The Universal Benefits of Volunteering* (1998), all published by John Wiley & Sons. Pidgeon received his B.A. in human relations from Salem University, in Salem, West Virginia, and his Ph.D. in philanthropy, leadership, and voluntary behavioral studies from the Union Institute and University. He is a certified association executive and a certified fundraising executive.

Highlights of America's Philanthropic and Volunteering Heritage

EARLY AMERICAN GOOD WORKS

- Almsgiving was established in Boston in 1662 and in Philadelphia in 1732. This was the beginning of institutionalized social welfare and the involvement of part-time to full-time assistance.[21]

- Several business associations formed before 1800 are still functioning today, such as the Chamber of Commerce (1768).[22]

- By the early 19th century, associations' nature and character began to change from religious organizations to causes and issue groups.

- By 1890, more than 124 secret fraternities had been established in the United States.

- By 1901, 366 societies had been formed, including the Odd Fellows and the General Federation of Women's Clubs.[23]

- From 1890 to 1930, foundations were formed to satisfy donors and fulfill focused missions. Most foundations were family-run institutions. Gradually, outside individuals were brought onto their boards.[24]

- In 1887, in Denver, Colorado, a Catholic priest, a Protestant minister, and a rabbi created a federated campaign that would become the United Way of America.

SIGNIFICANT GROWTH IN THE 20TH CENTURY

- The 20th century brought myriad help-related groups that involved volunteers as founders and supporters, such as the YMCA (1886), the American

Federation of Labor (1881), Rotary International (1905), Boy Scouts of America (1910), and Future Farmers of America (1928).[25]

- Dwight D. Mooney practiced a near-perfect, hard-hitting YMCA drive to obtain a dollar goal in a limited period of time. The campaign became a standard for fundraising and recruitment.[26]

- The Depression saw philanthropy fall on hard times.[27]

- During the Roosevelt administration, philanthropy's survival was even more questionable, given the new and more aggressive labor, Social Security, and tax policies of the time. Community Chest leaders helped change this by amending the Revenue Act of 1935 to permit corporations to deduct charitable contributions by up to 5 percent.[28]

GROWTH AFTER WORLD WAR II

- Immediately following the war, volunteerism became more commonplace and not-for-profits made upward pushes (e.g., the Ohio Society of Crippled Children became the National Society of Crippled Children).[29]

- National emphases on volunteering occurred during the Kennedy administration with the establishment of the Peace Corps in 1961. The emphases continued through the Johnson administration, with the Volunteers in Service to America program (Vista), and during the Nixon administration, which emphasized public service by combining the Peace Corps, Vista, and other programs under the Action program.

- In 1971, the Committee for Economic Development persuaded corporations to take a leadership role by instituting time-release opportunities for employees and creating a loan executive program to assist nonprofits.[30]

THE ADVENT OF THE 21ST CENTURY

- In 1989, President George H. W. Bush created the Points of Light Initiative to encourage volunteering. He noted that, "from now on, any definition of a successful life must include serving others."[31]

- Through both the Clinton and Bush administrations, volunteering continued to be emphasized nationally.

- The Obama administration, like past administrations, has also valued the role of volunteering and has emphasized its importance.

Creative Marketing Example

The nonprofit One International (http://www.one.org) provides an example of what it is doing to fulfill its mission through electronic marketing. One International is a grassroots campaign and advocacy organization backed by more than 2 million people who are committed to the fight against extreme poverty and preventable disease, particularly in Africa. Cofounded by Bono and other campaigners, One is nonpartisan and works closely with African policy makers and activists as described early in this chapter.

The organization features a page dedicated to volunteering at http://www.one.org/us/actnow. This is a one-stop-shop page with several ways to engage on global poverty issues:

1. Tips for writing letters to Congress

2. Tips on drafting letters to the editor

3. Tips for promoting local government resolutions supporting the issues of interest to the organization

4. Tips for organizing at the local level on university campuses and churches, and for creating one's own local event

5. E-mail sign-up that goes to local organizers to facilitate communication and logistics when setting up local education events.

The site also offers blogging opportunities for those who sign up to discuss issues or advertise events that they may be involved with hosting at the local level. Note the screen shot of the volunteer page (Figure 8B.1).

ACT NOW

What you can do right now.

SIGN UP

E-MAIL

ZIP CODE

JOIN ONE NOW

FEATURED ACTION

A GLOBAL GIFT:

It's not just the holiday
season -- when Presid
critical decisions impac
to Fight HIV/AIDS, Tub
Ask him to give a globa
$1.75 billion for the Glc
Fiscal Year 2011 budg

ACT NOW

FIGURE 8B.1   One International volunteer page

CHAPTER 9

How Successful Are Your Social Media Efforts?

DANIELLE BRIGIDA AND JONATHON D. COLMAN

The hardest thing about getting started is getting started.
—Guy Kawasaki, Entrepreneur and Former Software
Evangelist for Apple Computer

Social media is too often dismissed as a waste of time for nonprofits, a distraction from their mission, a luxury, and a dismissal of their donors' wishes that the organization operate efficiently. Development staff often have a challenge in raising funds for operations-related activities, as donors want to see their gifts go directly to on-the-ground projects, not to keeping the lights on.

Making the case for incorporating social media as a critical piece of the communications and marketing puzzle for your organization can make the difference between having no budget or resources and getting support to try more targeted campaigns. Just think of what an organization could accomplish if it prioritized social media in the same way as it did other media channels, such as television, radio, and print news.

In an effort to gain long-term support for social media to make it a sustainable strategy for your organization, we respectfully submit that social media is more than a one-off effort; rather, it should be seen as a central tenant of strategic communications and efficient operations in the following key areas (among others):

- **Media relations and opportunistic/crisis communications:** Social media offers a much quicker response system for real-time coverage of events than traditional public relations activities. Social media also helps your organization respond to unfortunate incidents such as scandals and other damaging events in the news cycle.

- **Information technology:** Social media offers a distributed infrastructure that supports a diverse range of technologies that may be untenable for a nonprofit to bring in-house or contract out to a third party. Furthermore, it provides the bandwidth and capacity to handle worldwide distribution and swift response to spikes in attention and activity. Often, all of this comes at little or no cost for the nonprofit.

- **Member and constituent engagement and stewardship:** At best, most organizations can offer only the most rudimentary experience of personalized communications on their web sites or e-mail lists. Social media offers the nonprofit and its constituents a chance to engage in both two-way communication (nonprofit to constituent and vice versa) and three-way communication (nonprofit to constituent, constituent to nonprofit, and constituent to constituent) or greater conversations.

When making the case for using social media in your organization, look to the multitude of examples that are available from the people and companies using it successfully. You won't be disappointed, especially when looking specifically at what nonprofits are doing and talking about. A great resource that talks about the leaders in nonprofit social media is Beth's Blog: How Nonprofits Can Use Social Media, written by Beth Kanter. Using information like this to couch your argument for why your organization should be participating is a great idea.

Some other great resources are the following:

- Mashable, at http://www.mashable.com (see Figure 9.1)
- Hubspot, at http://www.hubspot.com
- Nonprofit Technology Network, at http://www.nten.org

CONDUCT A SURVEY

Conducting a survey is a great way to get a sense for what people are feeling. Your reasons for using a survey to question your audience can be used either before implementing social media or after, to get a sense of how successful your presence is.

Things you can find out before you are on social media:

- Find out whether your organization's employees currently use social media.
- Ask your bosses which sites they've heard of or would like you to be on.
- Ask who would be willing to join you on the social media front.
- Ask your organization's members, volunteers, and constituents if they use social media.

FIGURE 9.1   Mashable.com Sample Resource

By collecting this data, you can properly gauge effective ways to both implement social media internally and get buy-in throughout your organization.

Use Competitor and Partner Data

If your competitors or partners are on a certain network, there's a good chance you should be, too. Look at what they are trying out, and don't be afraid to ask them what's working and what's not. Knowing what the status quo is and how you can get ahead of the curve is useful information when selling social media to your internal audiences.

There are many sites that offer free comparative data and general marketing metrics for any competitor web sites that you may be researching. Among these are the following:

- Alexa, at http://www.alexa.com
- Compete, at http://www.compete.com
- QuantCast, at http://www.quantcast.com

FINDING AND ENGAGING A CHAMPION IN LEADERSHIP

Find an ally. Trying to get buy-in from the top can be a tedious and long process, but luckily, as every day goes by, more and more organizations are understanding that social media is the new direction of media technology. If you can, identify an ally within the leadership of your organization who can help you champion the incorporation and implementation of social media. This step is important because even if you are going rogue, and exploring social media on your own, eventually you will need the support of your organization's leadership, even if its just on the level of you being an approved and trusted messenger.

Be an ally. If you're in a leadership position, support your staff and help them figure out their priorities.

MAKING THE VALUE CASE FOR SOCIAL MEDIA

When you're an adherent of a new trend, tool, or technology, it's often easy to fall into the trap of thinking that the value of the system speaks for itself. This sort of tunnel vision is a key problem for managers seeking to add social media elements to their marketing communications efforts. You may understand, intuitively, the value that real-time, online social interactions bring to the table of your organization. But remember that you're not trying to convince yourself or people like you—your goal is the leadership of your organization, possibly including those C-level executives and board members who may be resistant to technology investments and change itself.

The key to winning over resistance at this level of leadership is to link the value of Web 2.0 and social media with the larger goals that your leadership wants to achieve for the organization.

Increased Findability

Findability is "the quality of being locatable or navigable," and Google is by no means the only game in town when it comes to helping Internet users find what they're looking for. If you've been focusing exclusively on ranking well on Google, then what of Facebook's search engine? Engaging in social media can help your organization and its issues and services become more findable in all of these outlets, not just in standard or broad search engines.

Enhancing your organization's ability to be found online is beneficial for increasing traffic and attracting new supporters, but it really shines as a strategy during periods of crisis or opportunity. In the unfortunate case where a scandal is about to break at your organization—or in the more favorable scenario where your organization is being featured on prime-time television for a major success story—social media is a valuable tool to have in your arsenal.

Increased Brand Awareness and Engagement

What if everyone you knew was going to a party, and you were invited but decided that it would be too much work to show up? This illustrates the position of nonprofits when it comes to online social networking—they simply refuse to join in. But think of all the good things that happen at parties or at any social gathering: you make professional connections and find people who are interested and passionate about the same things you are. These sorts of parties—and social media—have a lot to offer nonprofits that are struggling to define themselves both for their existing audience as well as for the one they hope to reach in the future.

This clearly isn't just a party; it's a conversation involving hundreds of millions of people, many of whom fall into one of two categories:

1. They're already talking about your organization and its efforts, thereby establishing a personalized or localized representation of your brand for their connections and listeners.

2. They don't know that they're looking for you and your services, which means that they have the capacity to join the former category—if only your organization would engage them with compelling messages and opportunities.

Social media marketing isn't simply a framework for rigidly defining and protecting your brand and brand assets; rather, it presents smart, innovative managers with the ability to help their target audiences become part of that brand and experience it in new ways. When nonprofits are able to connect directly with their supporters, those constituents are able to redefine the brand story of the nonprofit by including themselves as part of it in a much more intimate way than by simply donating. And when your supporters feel that your brand includes them, barriers to activity are broken down, which leads to action.

Increased Influence with Target Audiences

Social media is fundamentally different from the static content on your organization's web site, even if that content is multimedia and includes audio, video, Flash programming, and other engaging forms of content. Content that is truly constructed socially is both dynamic in nature and, by definition, more engaging than content constructed and published by a hegemony of marketing staff back at the home office.

Although content localization and personalization offer emerging opportunities with the static content on your organization's web site, social media offers the savvy nonprofit organization an opportunity to leverage the passion and support of its constituents to directly aid the mission. That support can take the form of direct fundraising, but it's not limited by the barriers imposed by traditional communications, such as direct mail. Rather than just engaging in fundraising, smart organizations use engaging content to present opportunities that identify and activate their most enthusiastic supporters.

Constituents who are actively supporting your organization—by taking microactions, involving their contacts, disseminating your messages through their networks, and so on—are more likely to stay engaged with your organization over the long term and have the potential to give more and more often.

Increased Ability to Measure Results

Wouldn't it be great if you could find out how many people heard your organization's last radio public service announcement, how they found out about it, and what their demographics were? And wouldn't it be better still if you could record that information and then feed those same people content in the future that met their likes and dislikes based on actions they had taken in the interim? And what if you could figure out who among all those content consumers were the most active in offering feedback and forwarding your messages on to their connections? These are, essentially, the standard features offered out of the box to any organization that sets up a Facebook page.

The good news about this measurability is that you'll have no shortage of data and case studies to present to your colleagues and leadership. There's no need for statistical voodoo or cooking the books or otherwise relying on estimates of social media audiences and the impact of your campaigns. Your final step is to present your successes—and key learnings from any failures—to your organization in a way that secures their buy-in and continued investment and involvement with your future efforts.

LISTENING: THE KEY TO SOCIAL NETWORKING SUCCESS

> *To listen well is as powerful a means of influence as to talk well, and is as essential to all true conversation.*
>
> —CHINESE PROVERB

It wasn't that long ago that organizations had to rely on focus groups and direct feedback from their supporters to know exactly how they were perceived.

With the social web, all of this has changed. The web—and social media in particular—is all about people connecting and conversing with one another. These conversations are indispensable when it comes to understanding how people talk about your organization. Listening allows you to know where you stand with your strongest allies and your toughest detractors.

Listen First

Before strategy, before campaign planning, before staffing, before grant writing and budgeting, you must first listen. It is like many situations in life—look before you leap. By absorbing what people are talking about in relation to your organization or issue, as well as how they are talking about it, you can determine exactly how to enter a conversation. Know your audience: With countless conversations crossing different channels and media forms, social media allows a listener who is interested in a particular topic to find exactly what he or she is interested in.

People Are Already Talking about You—Find Them!

Monitoring how your organization is discussed in online conversations is a vital part to understanding how to continue outreach and engagement campaign efforts. Type keywords into search engines, observe Facebook discussions, or sign up to receive alerts in your in-box every time your company is mentioned. These tactics only scratch the surface of how you can harness the searchability of content on the web, such as blog posts, comments, and news articles.

With the power of knowing who supports you and who doesn't, you can more effectively message them and reward them in ways that benefit both you and them. Generally speaking, when people complain or praise online it is polite for you as an organization to respond. With this knowledge, you can properly determine how to communicate with people online, assuming they act in hopes of gaining attention from your organization.

Here are three tips for listening:

1. Use search fields: Develop a standard list of keywords that you search on a regular basis in search engines and any place you see a search field.
2. Organize your results: Use an RSS reader to pull in feeds that update your search-term results in real time. This will save you from having to go to the sites individually and search them.
3. Streamline whenever possible: Find ways to consolidate your search results—whether through an alert sent to your in-box or other tools like http://www.socialmention.com; find a way to make recovering your search results easier.

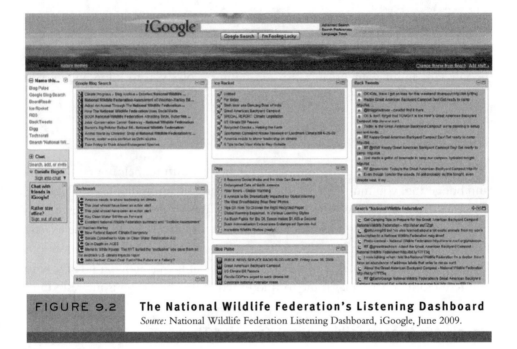

FIGURE 9.2   **The National Wildlife Federation's Listening Dashboard**
Source: National Wildlife Federation Listening Dashboard, iGoogle, June 2009.

Using iGoogle, the National Wildlife Federation tracks a number of mentions all over the web by searching key terms and pulling the RSS feeds into a one-stop location (see Figure 9.2).

Identify Influentials

While listening to conversations on the web, it's extremely important to pay attention to the influence people have in their specific community. Especially when dealing with the blogging community, influence is key. Here is a list of ways you can decide whether someone's influence is worth cultivating for a mutually beneficial relationship:

- **Ranking:** There are a lot of formulas and algorithms for measuring different types of influence on the web. This can help you put a person or site's authority into perspective. Some examples are PageRank for web pages and Twitter Grader for Twitter.

- **Comments:** The number of comments a person gets can be an important determining factor in deciding how influential a person is. Comments are a sign that the person knows how to facilitate conversation and is probably gaining interest among others.

- **Passion:** Keep track of people who are truly passionate about your mission. Regardless of their ranking or how many comments they get, if someone is already a firm believer in your mission, you should want to know him or her. Perhaps you can help each other out in some capacity in the future.

Acknowledging People Who Mention You

After you have found blog posts or web pages talking about your mission, your organization, or your issue, it's time to act. It's important to acknowledge people who are furthering the cause. Thanking them is a good way to start.

If you've found people who don't support the work that you do, it's also very important to consider engaging them in conversation, especially if they seem legitimately upset or are making honest points. Being smart about commenting on a frustrated person's blog might not change his or her overall feelings, but it can at least humanize your organization and potentially gain that blogger's respect. Many people think bloggers are just shouting to be heard, but more often than not, they are writing to initiate a conversation, and they are usually more than pleased when you respond or reach out to them.

Anytime you come across someone writing positively about the work that your organization does, it is important that you have some strategy set in place to thank them:

- **Give them access:** Sometimes just a comment post saying, "Feel free to reach me anytime," is a great way to start a conversation. When you show people that you are accessible as an organization and that the staff are available to help, it helps strengthen your relationship with them and gives them access they deserve as advocates for your organization.

- **Let them influence decisions:** Letting positive supporters have influence is another way to reward a loyal advocate. Ask them questions, approach them for feedback, and let them know their thoughts are actually being heard.

- **Acknowledge them:** Sometimes acknowledgment is the most time efficient and worthwhile way to thank people. Simply writing a comment, sending the author an e-mail, or pushing traffic to the mention is a great way to show appreciation to your web supporters.

Interpreting the Impact

In the social media world, there are a number of ways to interpret the impact you are having in your networks and beyond. Keep track of the following:

- **Mentions:** As the saying goes, any press is good press, and that is why tracking mentions—whether they are in the form of blog posts, Twitter messages, or general mentions—and knowing the number of people bringing you up in conversations, positive or not, is useful. That way you can tell what topics truly captivate your audience while learning what interests them less by the lack of mentions.

- **Sentiment:** Although any press is good, it is smart to note while tracking mentions how people feel about the mission you are working on and whether they are supporters of the work you do. Tracking your reputation in the community leads to a more conscious effort to bring about change.

- **Influence:** With limited resources, it is good to know who to target if you can reach out to only a few key people.

LEVERAGING YOUR SUPPORTERS TO INCREASE ENGAGEMENT

> *I've learned that people will forget what you said, people will forget what you did, but people will never forget how you made them feel.*
>
> —MAYA ANGELOU

Traditionally, communication coming from an organization has been very much like broadcasting. You share with your members information about the work you are doing, ask for money, and occasionally reach out for feedback. This is how many nonprofits communicate. Although that has worked in the past, the web offers an important means to doing this. However, many organizations see the web as an untamed jungle in which some attempts at campaigns go mysteriously viral and others fall on dead ears.

> Web sites and tools are creating new opportunities for communicating with the public every day. To successfully harness these opportunities, nonprofits can no longer convey messages in a top-down way. Your messages must be a part of a true conversation.

This does not mean nonprofits will no longer be a resource—all it means is that we have to make sure to listen just as much (if not more) than we talk. It is no longer about what we want *them* to do; instead, it is about how we can take something *they* want to do and make it easier for them. The sooner you learn this lesson, the better. It's not about your organization anymore. It's about the people. The following are some steps for successfully engaging people with social media:

- **Be present and active:** So many people I meet want to "leverage" Facebook. They have 20 ideas for doing so, but they are missing something— active accounts. The first step to understanding social media is being a part of it.

- **Strategically choose your involvement:** Don't sign up for every social network out there and overwhelm yourself. Prioritize which social media sites you like and then invest in them.

- **Motivate brand leaders:** Social media is especially helpful when it comes to locating and motivating brand ambassadors or leaders. By actively listening online, you can enter the conversation and find a way empower people.

- **They're just not that into you:** Trying to be someone for everyone is not the way to win the hearts of anyone. Some people just won't be that into you. It doesn't mean that you should spend your whole budget trying to win them over, however. Take care of your current audience, and they will spread the word that the work you are doing is good.

- **Date before getting married:** Getting to know your supporters should never be an afterthought. Before you swoop in with a donation ask, it is a good idea to get to know them and allow them to get to know you. For this reason, social media makes a great environment for "dating" potential supporters. You wouldn't propose to someone on the first date, just like you wouldn't swarm around potential supporters and immediately inundate them with membership appeals.

Know Your Supporters

If you already have established presences on the major social media sites (e.g., Facebook, Twitter), it is beneficial to survey these people, but maybe not with traditional methods. By observing how the fans in your different communities behave, you can identify what type of supporters they are and help them reach their own personal goals.

Novices   The novices in a social media community usually fit into three groups:

1. **Testing:** You can tell people who are new to the different social media sites by the completeness of their profile. If it looks like they are testing the waters and experimenting with different features, then they may be testing out the functionality and deciding whether they want to continue. Find these people and take them under your wing! They will appreciate you for it.

2. **Shouting:** People who first join a community and shout repeatedly about their mission or promote their blog exclusively are probably in the novice category. If they aren't novices, that means they are spammers, so don't be afraid to block them.

3. **Inactive:** Many people will join up as testers but lose interest. These people become pretty inactive pretty quickly. Or they are users who spent some time initially making connections online but otherwise got distracted. If these people are in your community, try contacting them with a personal note to see whether they are still even keeping tabs on the site.

Quid Pro Quo Supporters   Quid pro quo supporters will ask for favors and will expect you ask for them in return. Help them and they will help you. A great number of these people offer up loyal support so long as you reciprocate. For example, if you attempt to spread a message on a social news site like Digg, your quid pro quo supporters will be the ones thumbing up your story if you thumb up theirs.

Influencers   These are the people leading and participating heavily in the community discussion and are well respected. People listen to them. Whether you are joining a community or trying to reinvigorate your own, it's good to know the influencers. Usually, they are very approachable so long as you don't ask for something right away. Introducing yourself is a good start, and maybe initiating the conversation by saying that you would like to learn more about the community and the work he or she is doing for it.

Elite Supporters   The elite are usually the cream of the crop when it comes to community, and this status means they are harder to access and get the time of. They may be active in several communities. They may just have such a following that they are almost too busy to contact. These people are microcelebrities, and their support online is worth trying for, without putting all your eggs in their basket.

Barriers to Engagement

Part of successfully inspiring people is identifying the barriers that prevent them from taking action and engaging with your organization. Acknowledging that there are legitimate reasons why people cannot do more to further the cause, it is important to make the barriers smaller. Keep these barriers in mind as you build a community, to figure out what is reasonable to keep people coming back and participating:

- **Messages or actions are too complex:** Whatever you are working on, make sure to keep it simple. When you let the complexity of your asks get in the way of engaging people, then you aren't doing your job as a community organizer, and you certainly aren't helping empower people. Remember that simple campaigns and asks can be made fun with a little creativity.

- **Lack of time:** People are generally overcommitted. You have to somehow get on their agenda or you can kiss their participation good-bye. You just have figure out what they do with the time that they do have and help them get to know your cause. Usually, if you can give them a simple task and make them feel very good for doing it, you can start engaging them more and more.

- **Not passionate:** With all the issues out there to support, you will certainly come across people who are not passionate about your organization's issue. Activating these people can be truly inspiring, if only you can find a way to either teach them more about the issue or involve and empower them.

PLANNING YOUR OUTREACH AND ENGAGEMENT CAMPAIGN

To be successful in social media, remembering basic community-building concepts is key. But it is also important to be realistic with expectations. Beth Kanter has it right when she says, "Sometimes being a social media evangelist and only touting the benefits can backfire. It is important to explore both positive and negative perceptions and alternatives."

So while you are setting up your campaign, make sure you set realistic goals that don't include the word "viral" (no matter how hard people within your organization say that this is what should happen).

Set clear long- and short-term goals, revisit your previous outreach techniques, investigate, and read up on the research done on the most up-and-coming tools and methods. From there you can identify key audiences and potential partners for your campaign and begin the true outreach portion.

Steps for Your Outreach Campaign

1. Analyze your current campaign techniques.
2. Be sure to have both long- and short-term goals.
3. Do your research.
4. Pick your audience.
5. Pick your partners.
6. Engage your audience where they are active.

Although outreach is the initial extending of the hand, engagement is about reading what the community wants and needs and then servicing just that. Engagement comes from empowering your members to run with things while also lighting the way if you can give them a goal to organize around. While planning both engagement and outreach campaigns, it is ideal that you don't just have social media but that you incorporate your current marketing strategies and use social media to complement them.

MEASURING YOUR IMPACT

> *The only man who behaves sensibly is my tailor; he takes my measurements anew every time he sees me, while all the rest go on with their old measurements and expect me to fit them.*
>
> —GEORGE BERNARD SHAW

George Bernard Shaw's tailor has the right idea—we can never measure too closely or verify our measurements too often. And even though many of the old measurements that you might apply to other areas of your work can also be used with social media, new strategies and tactics require new measurements as well so you can better determine the progress you're making toward your mission.

Measurement and analysis are the tools we use to figure out how we're making a difference online as well as how we should adjust our campaigns to be even more effective in the future. Metrics help us determine not only the value of our work as a whole but also the value of our investments in that work. So if you want to increase your project budgets and staff levels for next fiscal year, measuring your impact online and sharing the results within your organization can help you make your case.

If you're just starting out in web metrics and analysis, the good news is that almost every action that a visitor takes online can be measured. There are free tools of nearly unimaginable power, like Google Analytics, that are relatively easy for your staff to implement on your site and that yield an astonishing amount of data about how your visitors are performing. Plus, many brand-name social networks like Facebook, Flickr, and YouTube now provide social media metrics for your campaigns.

Using Google Analytics (Figure 9.3), The Nature Conservancy National Wildlife Federation tracks interactions, engagement, and conversion on its web presences, including at http://www.nwf.org and at smaller sites representing particular campaigns that leverage social media for outreach and promotion.

The bad news is that all of this powerful technology and information comes with a side effect: It can seem much more difficult to analyze and make sense of all this data coming from multiple sources, and even harder still to make it actionable. In fact, you'll probably find measuring to be the easy part—interpreting your results and acting on them is the real challenge.

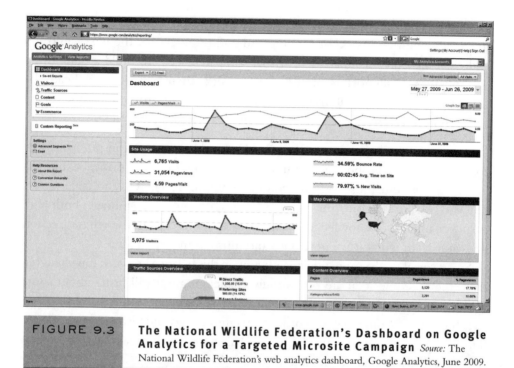

FIGURE 9.3	**The National Wildlife Federation's Dashboard on Google Analytics for a Targeted Microsite Campaign** *Source:* The National Wildlife Federation's web analytics dashboard, Google Analytics, June 2009.

Setting Success Measures for Social Media

One of the first steps that managers should take when considering a social media strategy is to determine what they want to achieve. Although these goals are often expressed qualitatively (e.g., we want to reach a new audience of young people), the best goals are quantitative in nature (e.g., we want to reach 5,000 new contacts comprising 20- to 35-year-olds in North America).

Setting realistic quantitative goals is an important and vital step in the formulation of any campaign, whether it's one driven by social media or another online strategy. Without firm, realistic goals, it's impossible to measure your success and accomplishments.

Short Term versus Long Term   Smart goals take into account the future state that your campaign will help bring about. Looking beyond today provides many benefits to your organization, including the flexibility to plan for and react to changes in technology (an all-too-common occurrence with social media). But it doesn't simply end there with tools—as you grow your audience online and learn more about what works for them, you'll need to plan for the sorts of impact that they can have when you help them work together to create social change.

Considering the future as part of your campaign-planning effort is also useful in laying the groundwork for funding and staff resources for the next campaign and even the one after that. If your first campaign seeks to build a core group of thousands of supporters on a social network, then you'd better already be thinking about how you'll manage that community as it grows over time. Every successful campaign should provide a bridge into what comes next.

Low-Hanging Fruit versus Stretch Goals   How can you inspire your staff to think outside the box and achieve new heights of performance while still ensuring that your most basic outcomes are within reach? Go too far one way and you risk burning out your team and colleagues, which encourages both high turnover and loss of knowledge and know-how; go too far in the other direction and your team won't learn new skills and innovation will suffer.

Smart social media campaign goals maintain this balance between low-hanging fruit, the outcomes that are only mildly challenging but still bring about some rewards, and stretch goals, which require new investments and creative thinking to achieve an outcome that is an order of magnitude beyond historical precedents. The first step toward striking the proper balance is often breaking your success measures down into strategies and tactics.

You can tie the tactics that help you pluck low-hanging fruit to the larger strategies that bring you long-term progress toward your mission. Goals formed around strategies tend to be more aligned with stretching your internal processes and changing the way you do business, which can be helpful for getting your team's creative juices flowing, even though the goals take much more time to complete. In contrast, you can measure your progress toward that strategic goal by breaking it down into a series of realistic, tactical steps.

Accomplishing smaller tasks helps keep up staff morale while creating steady advances toward your ultimate goal. It's important to recognize the little successes that your staff works toward and to remember that they're also footsteps along the path to bigger accomplishments.

Shared Goals with Other Parts of Your Organization   Managers often make the mistake of focusing too much on staking a claim to social media that prevents other groups in an organization from participating. This is a critical error when it comes to conducting social media outreach, because you lose the value that your entire organization can bring to bear. Although nonprofits typically treasure and embrace a degree of entrepreneurial effort (and rightfully so), the lack of coordination and cooperation with other teams can leave holes in your social media strategy as well as unfulfilled goals on your annual review.

Social media often becomes the purview of a development team, though sometimes it gets delegated to a person or team engaged in traditional public relations work, a membership team, or even an IT group. Regardless of who's charged with creating strategy and goals, think of all that these teams could accomplish if they worked together: a cohesive plan that takes into account marketing communications, technology, and fundraising.

Your teams and divisions already support one another in the bricks-and-mortar world, so why not when it comes to the online one, too? Partnering with internal teams and creating shared goals is an effective strategy because of its openness, accountability, and ability to scale over time to meet demand. When more people are brought into your efforts, there are more hands that can make light work.

What to Measure, and Why

Sure, you could measure the average length of your nose hairs as well as their rate of growth over time, but would that provide any insight into your credit score? When looking at the myriad metrics available for your social media campaign, it is important to ask questions that matter, not just to record data for their own sake.

Metrics provide detailed answers to specific questions, so formulating your question is of key importance so that you measure the right activity. It's not enough to ask broad questions such as, How is my campaign going? Rather, the overall patterns of user participation should be questioned to see how the campaign is performing against your goals, and those questions should reveal meaningful answers.

The following sections discuss four key areas that you can measure in your social media campaigns to determine your real-world impact.

Awareness   Your social media campaign may reach many people who already know the who and what of your organization. But connecting with your existing base of supporters is only the first step—what of the far larger population who has never heard of you, is unconvinced of the value your organization provides, or is completely unaware of your mission or entire area of focus?

You can measure the awareness that your social media campaign builds for your organization in a number of ways. More effective than just tallying page views and clicks is looking for meaningful actions. Rather than just counting measures of passive activity, such as a single visitor consuming content alone, you should measure actions that can be taken only once a visitor understands your mission and decides to do something in support of it.

Sentiment   What are the attitudes that your target audience has about your campaign and your organization as a whole? By studying the documentation of these attitudes and measuring them, you can see how your campaign influences people's feelings and perceptions over time. Sentiment can be measured in as simple a format as pure binary (positive versus negative), but it's even more helpful to measure the impact of that sentiment. You can determine this by considering factors such as the following:

- **Recency of sentiment:** Is this post, thread, or tweet current? When was the most recent update?

- **Sentiment-related activity:** Are many visitors commenting, voting, or otherwise engaged? What actions are they taking?

- **Intensity of sentiment:** How specific and strong are the feelings involved? Do the author and commenters advocate that visitors take any actions?

- **Affinity for sentiment:** How many other sites are interested and posting inbound links? Is the post accessible by search engines and ranking well?

For example, a long, negative rant about something your organization has done poorly on a blog that's rarely updated, lacks commenters, and that does not maintain a loyal audience has much less impact than, say, a long discussion thread about a major success of your organization that attracts many one-way, inbound links from a number of blogs.

Engagement and Depth   It's hard to capture someone's attention in the real world, and doubly so online, where there's always another LOLcat ready to whisk your target audience away right when they're about to click on your "Donate now!" button. So focusing your measurement efforts and analysis on the actions that your campaign participants take is of key importance for interpreting their overall engagement.

Campaign activity isn't a binary, all-or-nothing deal. There is often a spectrum of actions that participants can take, including the following:

- Simple (e.g., voting positively or negatively on a story)
- Moderately complex (e.g., commenting on a story already posted)
- Very complex (e.g., posting a story or media item that they've personally created)
- Direct support (e.g., actual donation and/or successfully recruiting donations from their contacts)

It's important for managers and analysts not just to focus measurement on this latter category but instead to appreciate all of the microsteps and other actions required to steward campaign participants toward direct support of your organization.

Data that can give you insight into your participants' engagement are often calculated metrics, that is, values that are composed of two (or more) individual metrics compared mathematically. For example, comparing page views alone is relatively useless, but looking at page views per visitor session is somewhat more informative, particularly if you are able to segment those visitors according to source or audience segment.

Measuring an external factor like re-tweets or Diggs per hour (or even per minute) and comparing them to inbound visitors from those sources over the same period can be helpful for performance modeling (something your IT staff will greatly appreciate) and will help you determine the targets you need to hit to achieve a viral effect in those networks.

Conversion   Social media campaigns tend to comprise series after series of microactions designed to help a visitor care and take action on particular issues. Because this presents a more complex framework of interaction, mangers need to employ a more complex system of measurement to understand what drives conversion and what doesn't.

Rather than relying on a single conversion metric, it's important to separate out conversion for segments of activities based on either the level of engagement required to participate or the barriers to entry that a participant needs to overcome to engage at a particular level of your campaign.

A key metric to focus on in regards to conversion is bounce rate, the visitors who come to your campaign or web site and then leave without viewing any other content. These single-page visits drastically decrease your conversion rate and are a key indicator that you're failing to engage that segment of your referred traffic. Although you can engage in testing to determine how best to reduce bounce, this requires that you lead your team in acknowledging that failures are learning opportunities and lessons in how to improve performance down the road.

Learning from Failure, and from Success

Many organizations fall into one of two traps when it comes to social media:

1. Moving from campaign to campaign without ever stopping to evaluate whether any true progress is being made toward the organization's mission.

2. Always testing small, tactical approaches without ever defining a true strategic framework or set of goals to be achieved.

As nonprofits that make promises to donors and have missions of social good to accomplish, they can't be so afraid of failure that they never rise to the challenge of participating. However, they can't become so obsessed with moving forward that they never figure out where they're headed or what's working well and what isn't.

Learning from our successes and failures in the world of social media helps us to create accountability for our actions and guides us toward becoming more effective marketers and advocates for our missions.

Reporting Back   As valuable as data are to your organization and as many insights as it offers, data do not speak for themselves. The failure to disclose information about campaign results—both to internal colleagues and leadership and to external participants and constituents—is a critical error when seeking to build long-term acceptance and support for your social media program.

By embracing a few key facets of accountability and openness early in the life span of your team's efforts, you'll help ensure that your efforts stay active and enjoy success for the long run.

- **Raw numbers don't tell the whole story:** Smart managers provide context with their results and focus on telling a story. Tie the online actions taken by your constituents with comparisons to real-world activities and settings that may be easier for your audience to understand.

- **Differentiate your value:** Show the minute details and evolutionary changes that your team makes to provide additional benefits to campaign participants to drive short-term activity and long-term engagement. Present reasons why and examples of how this campaign is specifically tied to the social media channel while highlighting your integration and synergy with other teams and their efforts.

- **Show, don't tell:** The language and media created by your constituents should play a central role in the story of your campaign and how you frame its results. Remember that your supporters' words and efforts are always more powerful and inspiring than your own. And they'll have a bigger impact with your leadership when you message them in pictures and through other visual vocabulary.

- **Thank your participants:** We often find ourselves focusing only on proving the value of our efforts internally without remembering who really drives our campaign effort: the people on the outside who are inspired by and support the mission. More than anything else, your supporters want to know that they're helping to make a difference and that the organization recognizes their impact.

Sharing results and key findings—even negative ones—internally while stewarding and rewarding your participants for their participation externally is a key facet of your analytics strategy and will help booster the profile of your efforts as well as your organization's reputation.

Conclusion

Incorporating social media into the DNA of your organization is no easy task. You can't just add a few staff people and make a new department that immediately falls into line with the rest of your structure.

Social media encompasses a veritable cornucopia of tools, opportunities, and ideas that can be incorporated into all of your departments and roles. Spreading that understanding is the key to making these new communications outlets work for your cause. It's an exciting challenge, and one in which you will always find room to improve, learn, reassess, and grow.

Danielle Brigida is social media outreach coordinator of the National Wildlife Federation, the nation's largest member-supported nonprofit conservation organization. The NWF is at the forefront of confronting global warming and protecting America's wildlife and habitat. Brigida is a part of NWF's internal Cool-It! Committee, which was formed in an effort to reduce the organization's carbon footprint and create a more sustainable work culture at its headquarters and nine regional centers. She is responsible for communicating the NWF's mission and message across the social media world. She has a B.A. in technical writing from Christopher Newport University.

Jonathon D. Colman has designed, developed, and promoted web sites for large nonprofit organizations and companies, including the Nature Conservancy, Conservation International, IBM, and Recreational Equipment Inc. (REI). Colman's web-marketing strategy and leadership helped earn the Nature Conservancy two Webby Awards for Best Charitable Organizations/Nonprofit Web Site in the 13th Annual Webby Awards, including a People's Voice Webby Award. He served as a Peace Corps Volunteer in Burkina Faso, West Africa, where he lived in a small village performing rural health development work, including education and health infrastructure capacity building. A runner, biker, tree-hugger, and eco-geek, Jonathon lives in Seattle with his wife, the glass artist Marja S. Huhta.

References

Andresen, Katya. *Katya's Nonprofit Marketing Blog: Getting to the Point*, http://www.nonprofitmarketingblog.com.

Armano, David. *L + E: Logic + Emotion*, http://darmano.typepad.com/logic_emotion/.

Bartholomew, Don. *MetricsMan Blog*, http://metricsman.wordpress.com.

Brogan, Chris. *Social Media Business Strategy and More*, http://www.chrisbrogan.com.

"Findability." Wikipedia: The Free Encyclopedia. http://en.wikipedia.org/wiki/Findability

Forrester Research Inc. *The Forrester Blog for Internet Marketing Professionals*, http://blogs.forrester.com/marketing/.

Interactive Insights Group. *Interactive Insights Group Blog*, http://www.interactiveinsightsgroup.com/blog1/.

Kanter, Beth. *Beth's Blog: How Nonprofits Can Use Social Media*, http://www.beth.typepad.com. See particularly, Beth Kanter, "Creating Your Organization's Social Media Strategy Map." http://beth.typepad.com/beths blog/2009/01/creating-your-organizations-social-media-strategy-map.html.

Kaushik, Avinash. *Web Analytics Blog: Occam's Razor*, http://www.kaushik.net/avinash/.

NTEN: The Nonprofit Technology Network. *NTEN Blog*, http://nten.org/blog.

The Pilgrim Network. *Marketing Pilgrim: Internet Marketing News*, http://www.marketingpilgrim.com.

Third Door Media. *Search Engine Land*, http://searchengineland.com.

TopRank Online Marketing. *Online Marketing Blog*, http://www.toprankblog.com.

Wild Apricot by BonaSource Inc. *Wild Apricot Blog*, http://www.wildapricot.com/blogs/newsblog/.

World Intellectual Property Organization. May 17, 2009, http://www.wipo.int/ip-outreach/en/tools/guides/planning/outreach_strategy.html.

CHAPTER 10

Social "Trysumers"

AND THE HIDDEN GATE IN THE PYRAMID

MARCELO INIARRA IRAEGUI AND ALFREDO BOTTI

Indiana Jones adjusts his hat, lowers his head, summons up all his courage, and pushes the sphinx. The entrance to the pyramid he'd studied for years opens up before his eyes. He reaches for his torch and steps into the labyrinthine passageway. He has discovered a new gate, one that has remained hidden from the sight of those who passed right by every day. The torch lights up the passageway. Suddenly, the echo from his footsteps becomes louder and a golden chamber appears before him revealing the pyramid's glittering treasure, its brilliance illuminating an unmistakable smile on the face of the archeological adventurer.

A hand, just like Dr. Indiana Jones's, is about to open another gate in a pyramid. . . . It hesitates for a moment, as if considering: "Why not? It's a good cause? Let's give it a try." A few seconds later, the index finger on the hand clicks the right button on the mouse and the "send" option changes color.

The data arrives at the organization in less than a second and the entrance to the pyramid opens up. A confirmation message, slightly less glamorous than Dr. Jones's treasure chamber, appears: "Thank you for subscribing to Save the Forests. Your details have been received."

And so began the article that we wrote for publication in the November–December 2008 edition of *Advancing Philanthropy*, an article that then inspired us to go on and write this chapter.

Every day, millions of people concerned about thousands of causes go through a new gate in the very same fundraising pyramid that has been described for years using the donor's pyramid (referred to hereon in as the traditional pyramid). This traditional pyramid describes an organization's donors according to rank, position, and type. The digital transformation of society, however, has led to the emergence of a new entrance to that pyramid and a new kind of relationship between organizations and supporters. Charities have yet to fully capitalize these new developments and nor have they been fully acknowledged in fundraising textbooks.

In this chapter, we will add to the traditional pyramid by introducing two new concepts. The first is that the pyramid has another gate, a different entrance from that which can be accessed by making a donation. In turn, the pyramid also has an extra space, an entire level that admits nonfinancial, digital supporters who arrive via new media, web sites, social networks, e-mail, and the increasingly popular short text messaging (SMS), or other wireless access points. The second concept is a new trend that emerges from the entry of these nonfinancial, digital supporters, or social "trysumers" to the pyramid. They try out the experience and determine the effectiveness of social organizations all over the world at no cost, before deciding whether to become a donor or whether to remain a nonfinancial, digital supporter by taking part in campaigns or participating in the organization as an online volunteer, etc.

This new, bigger gate allows us to incorporate a much greater volume of people into our social organizations who want to experience and participate in what the organization has to offer. This gate is a whole new paradigm for the social sector.

THE HIDDEN GATE

Andrew Grove, the former chair and CEO of Intel Corporation, said, "Success breeds complacency. Complacency breeds failure. Only the paranoid survive." Despite many successful years in the social sector, we have always been paranoid about losing our touch. A while back, we finally decided to find out exactly why we were getting such good results, and then we used that information to involve even more people in social causes.

THE TRADITIONAL FUNDRAISING PYRAMID

The traditional fundraising pyramid illustrates several things. For us, the following factors are the most relevant (see Figure 10.1):

1. **The income breakdown from our current individual donors:** Who donates to us? How much do they donate? How do they donate? We can easily distinguish low-value givers from those who donate greater amounts.

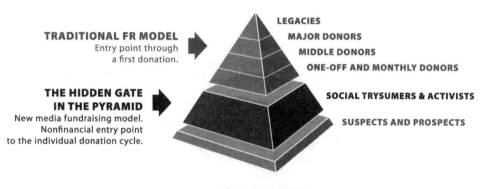

© Botti - Iniarra 2006

FIGURE 10.1   Traditional Fundraising Pyramid

2. **The aspirational path we would like our donors to transit:** We want donors to graduate from small amounts and low-frequency giving to greater amounts and higher-frequency giving, as well as other types of giving such as fundraising and legacies.

3. **The various levels of the pyramid show us the levels in the life cycle of the donor (one-off and monthly donors, middle donors, major donors, and legacies):** Some donors start by giving one-off gifts and move upward through an organization's upgrading programs. Organizations with a significant donor strategy will see their middle donors strongly represented in the pyramid.

Entry points refer to all recruitment techniques, from face-to-face, direct mail, door-to-door, member-get-a-member, the web, and e-mail. After all, all fundraisers can agree that, regardless of the entry points to the pyramid and the amounts donated, our main aim is to pursue as many supporters as possible and to have them donate as much as they can. This would mean seeing as many donors as possible escalate the pyramid.

The New Fundraising Pyramid

A new level has been added. The traditional fundraising pyramid permitted access to an organization only through a donation. This entry was generally accepted and respected by everyone. Entry could be gained by making a onetime donation; by becoming a monthly, middle, or major donor, or by leaving a legacy. It always, however, involved an initial financial contribution. Organizations enthusiastically invited prospective donors to enter the fundraising pyramid exclusively through the donation entrance (see Figure 10.2).

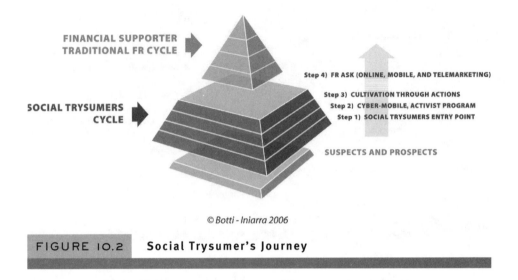

FINANCIAL SUPPORTER
TRADITIONAL FR CYCLE

Step 4) FR ASK (ONLINE, MOBILE, AND TELEMARKETING)

Step 3) CULTIVATION THROUGH ACTIONS
Step 2) CYBER-MOBILE, ACTIVIST PROGRAM
Step 1) SOCIAL TRYSUMERS ENTRY POINT

SOCIAL TRYSUMERS
CYCLE

SUSPECTS AND PROSPECTS

© Botti - Iniarra 2006

FIGURE 10.2   Social Trysumer's Journey

The pyramid in Figure 10.2, which clearly incorporates the existing one, can give us a new insight into how we can invite people to have a different type of relationship with an organization, an initial, nonfinancial, digital relationship.

This different type of relationship involves encouraging people to do things together with the organization before asking them to donate money. There are endless ways that organizations can engage with potential financial supporters, thereby generating a discrete and rich list of prospective donors.

WHO ENTERS THROUGH THE NONFINANCIAL GATE?

This new relationship is comprised by a diverse group of people, two "tribes." The first tribe comprises social trysumers, people who want to try out new experiences in the social sector via new media without incurring any costs. The trysumers concept was introduced by Trendwatching.com in March 2007. We have adopted the term here to describe those nonfinancial supporters who are in search of new and creative proposals for social change.

The other tribe is a more traditional group of social participants who enter through the nonfinancial gate in search of familiar experiences, which are made easier by new media access, and who want to be part of a digital movement, activism, or community. They want to form part of the organization but do not want to donate right away.

What Are Social Trysumers Looking For?

Social trysumers are those who want to have a personal and direct experience with achieving the aim or mission of an organization. Organizations want social trysumers to have that experience and say, "I love doing things for this organization." Then those people will respond to financial appeals by saying, "Sure! I'll financially support your cause because I know how important it is to fight for, how difficult it is to achieve certain goals, and I know that you will make the best out of my donation." To achieve this, organizations must involve people in what they do, bring them closer to the organization, and allow them to feel part of it—for free!

It is important to emphasize that this experience goes far beyond the power of branding. No matter how much an organization excels in transmitting its mission and vision through branding, no brand can transmit the feeling of intimacy or close relationship with an organization. So although branding is a key factor for every organization, we also want people to experience the real thing, to become one of us.

As with retail sampling, which enables potential consumers to try out a specific product for free that they later might purchase, social trysumers can try out and experience what it means to fight along with an organization for a cause, for free, and support them in a nonfinancial way. They can experience the obstacles that we face, find out why collective action is useful, and discover that we have a greater chance of achieving our goals if we work together. This not only will enable some of them to get to know us better but some of them may enjoy the experience, start to feel like part of the team, and go on to support us financially.

Digital Paradigms

New media has changed social paradigms. When looking at social transformations and their impact on day-to-day life, contemporary philosophy often helps us understand these new processes. Paula Sibilia, the Brazilian philosopher and author of *The Post-Organic Man: Body, Subjectivity and Digital Technologies*, focuses on the profound changes provoked by digital technology:

> With the decadence of an industrial society populated by disciplined, docile and useful bodies, certain figures such as that of the automaton, the robot, the man-machine, begin to weaken. These images have provoked so many metaphors and inspired fiction and reality alike throughout the past two centuries. Today, however, other ways of being preside. Far removed from logical mechanics, these contemporary bodies form part of a new digital regime and include data and code processing systems,

profiles and information banks. Due to the new rhythms of technoscience, the human body appears to have lost its classical definition, its analogical solidity. In the digital sphere, it has become permeable, predictable and programmable.

She then goes on to introduce a challenge: "Arts, sciences and philosophy have a challenge ahead: To break through the safety net of what has already been considered and dare to imagine new questions." That makes us think about the transformations that have already occurred, those that are taking place right now, and those that are yet to come. In the social sector, these changes have occurred gradually, if not sluggishly and slightly unwillingly. However, we are not going to get caught up in a debate over the reasons for the sluggish integration from analog to digital. Rather, we want to focus on understanding why these transformations occur and the behavioral changes they provoke in society. It is up to organizations to interpret these changes and discover how to use them to our benefit in achieving our organizational objectives.

A Look at Some Figures

Currently, 1.5 billion people in the world use the Internet and more than 4.2 billion people own a mobile phone.

According to a report from Wireless Intelligence, "It took about 20 years for the first billion mobile phones to sell worldwide. The second billion sold in four years, and the third billion sold in two." The communications revolution is speeding forward, and the mobile phone has been incorporated into every corner of the globe. This has had a massive impact on the way we communicate with one another and with social organizations.

To visualize these changes, let's look at two examples of communications models employed for Greenpeace rock concerts, In 1970, Joni Mitchell, James Taylor, Phil Ochs, and the band Chilliwack staged a benefit concert in Vancouver for the Don't Make a Wave Committee, which raised US$17,000 for what would eventually become Greenpeace. The communication strategy was typical of the time: word of mouth, leaflets, and posters, and perhaps mentions in local magazines and radio stations. In 2007, Greenpeace arranged for rock singer Fabiana Cantilo to give a concert onboard the *Arctic Sunrise* boat in Buenos Aires, Argentina. The concert was organized 24 hours in advance using a flash-mob communication strategy and mobile phones: an SMS was sent to the organization's list of mobile activists inviting them to the event. The SMS messages then functioned as tickets to get into the concert.

Since the emergence of new media, a new entrance to the fundraising pyramid has appeared—a nonfinancial, digital gate—and a new level where millions of people can begin to experience an organization.

In our work in various Greenpeace offices, we began to consider cyberac-tivists, e-newsletter subscribers, mobile activists, and other people who involved themselves in the organization as supporters rather than prospects.

It is useful to clarify that, for Greenpeace, the change really began when we started to consider the contacts in our e-mail lists not just as mere contacts but as people with an entrance to the organization who may go on to make a donation further along the road. However, many of those supporters will continue to engage with the organization nonfinancially through voluntary participation. This participation could include involvement through digital media by sending protest e-mails to governments or corporations or by staying informed in order to express activism in their day-to-day lives. When we presented this model, we often received criticism that it would only be applicable to campaigning organizations like Greenpeace or Amnesty that might find it "easier" to directly involve people in their work. However, we strongly believe that any charity can offer specific activities that would enable the public to join in.

But how did this new gate begin to emerge? And what transformed it into a large access gate for social organizations?

SOCIAL TRYSUMERS AND THE FREE-EXPERIENCE ERA

Digital transformations have been occurring before our very eyes, and we as organizations haven't even noticed. Many of us might still be surprised when we go onto Google to find a recipe for Greek food, click on "search," and then find thousands and thousands of links to Greek food information—all from the comfort of the couch in our living rooms in just a few seconds, and all absolutely free (see Figure 10.3).

The Wikimedia Foundation and its main project, Wikipedia, is a clear example of the vast potential that lies before us in the era of free experiences. Wikipedia

FIGURE 10.3   **Free-Experience Era**

revolutionized the concept of an online encyclopedia, encouraging its users to develop and expand content and to access for free a vast encyclopedia. However, when Jimmy Wales made a recent online plea for funding to keep the site running, people were so impressed by Wikipedia's model that the US$6 million goal was reached in just a few days. But how does this help explain the creation of a new gate in the fundraising pyramid?

If we want to find out the weather forecast in a small city on another continent that we'll be visiting in a few days, all we have to do is visit Weather.com or visit Windguru.com, and all the information is there for us to peruse. And again, for free! Or say that we want to talk to a friend who lives on the other side of the world. All we have to do is connect to our Skype account, and there we can have a conversation or a video conference with our friend, wherever he or she may be, and absolutely free of charge.

This free experience era does, however, involve a significant creative challenge when it comes to making money from initiatives. Perhaps the most revolutionary solution came from Google's sponsored-link program, which enabled the company to reach number 117 on the Fortune 500 list in 2008, with a turnover of US$21.795 billion and a US$4.226 billion profit.

Free access to organizational experiences has certainly been underestimated and underused by the social sector as a way to get people involved in causes. Some of the only free information available to potential supporters is that which can be found on their web sites, in free newsletters, or as tips. With the recent boom in social media started by MySpace and later maximized by Facebook and other networks, social organizations have reacted late, and with a certain degree of reluctance, to expanding their range of free experiences as a way to begin dialogue between themselves and those people interested in their causes.

FREE EXPERIENCES AND SOCIAL TRYSUMERS—SOME KEY RESEARCH

Although much of our work involves strategy development, we, Alfredo and Marcelo, consider ourselves to be, above all else, practitioners of social trysumerism, utilizing this concept to achieve our campaign goals in the fight for social causes. "The Happiness of Giving: The Time-Ask Effect," an article published in the *Journal of Consumer Research* by Wendy Liu, assistant professor of marketing at University of California, Los Angeles, and Jennifer Aaker, Xerox Distinguished Professor of Knowledge at University of California, Berkeley, focuses on how asking for time versus money can lead to two distinct mind-sets that affect consumers' willingness to donate to charitable causes.

According to Liu and Aaker's research, if individuals are asked how much time they would like to donate to a charity, as opposed to how much money they would like to donate, this ultimately increases the amount of money that they donate to the charity.

Consumption is about making people happier through purchases. Organizations must therefore focus on making consumers happy about giving. As people's perception of time is more closely associated with emotions than is their perception of money, Liu and Aaker conclude that asking consumers for their time rather than their money is likely to increase their emotional involvement in an organization.

Liu and Aaker also look at whether asking a question involving time versus donation intent resulted in different behavior. When consumers are asked about their intention to donate to charity, the process of answering that question may lead to changes in behavior. For example, consumers who answered a survey asking about automobile purchase intentions were more likely to purchase a new car in the next six months. The authors therefore claim that questions about donations lead to the consideration of economic utility. Yet questions about donations of time lead consumers to consider their feelings and the emotional meanings derived from an action.

Building Social Trysumer Databases

When we began working with the social trysumer model more than 10 years ago, we started with the construction of simple e-mail lists and went on to develop entire social media and mobile mobilization programs.

In each campaign, we took the knowledge acquired and used it to construct databases of social trysumers. Why did some actions succeed and others fail? Learning from this information is vital for social organizations. Perhaps we should all put up a big sign in our meeting rooms: "Failure is an option. It helps us to improve."

Some of the Lessons We've Learned

The most important lesson we've learned is to tailor our work to the needs of the supporter and not to the needs of the organization: Why do people do what they do? What are their needs? In general, we have focused on five supporter needs to construct our social trysumer databases (see Figure 10.4):

1. **Me! The social-hero generation**: Supporters are given the opportunity to become social heroes.
2. **I am a social hero:** Supporters are recognized for their actions by organizations and their peers.

FIGURE 10.4   Supporters' Needs

3. **Instant campaigning**: Instant campaigns ignite a rapid response chain.

4. **Positive approach**: Smile campaigns use available digital media (the web and mobile).

5. **Be part of something bigger**: Invites participation in a relevant action that brings people together (perhaps even millions of them!).

ONE LITTLE STEP FORWARD—THE CONVERSION FROM SOCIAL TRYSUMER TO DONOR

We now focus on how to convert social trysumers into donors and on how to maximize conversion rates and minimize cost. To achieve this, we must first study the point at which social trysumers enter the organization, the main channel of communication used to keep in touch with them, and their contact details that are on file. Because we intend to maintain a relationship with these people through digital media, we can assume that we at least have either their e-mail address or mobile phone number. The following list describes the main appeal and response channel for each type of data we have:

- E-mail: e-mail appeal and landing on the web
- Landline number: Outbound telemarketing
- Mobile phone number: Outbound telemarketing and/or SMS

Although the foregoing list clearly shows how to use each contact detail effectively, we should consider all possible combinations. First, we should begin with an e-mail appeal, as this is the cheapest option. Depending on the country in which your organization is based, return on investment (ROI) for e-mail conversion may significantly vary from the ROI for telemarketing conversion.

Second, if we have any supporters' phone numbers, we should also use these contacts. The first option is to call the mobile phone numbers, as the 90 percent contact rate is likely to be dramatically higher than the 25 percent contact rate with landlines – up to four times higher!

The ideal conversion campaign (assuming that we have the social trysumers' mobile phone numbers) would involve SMS. We can send an SMS to anticipate a great story that the social trysumer will then receive via e-mail. This generates expectation so that the open and conversion rates will be higher. This type of campaign can be fortified (or weakened) depending on the send time. If people with third-generation mobiles receive SMS and e-mail on their mobile phones at the same time, this could affect results.

Many organizations will prefer to ask for microgifts through the various payment alternatives offered by mobile technology over beginning a conversation online via e-mail. Ideally, we should use all available communication methods to prepare social trysumers for the ask and to increase their willingness to give. Media convergence and message coherence are key to achieving this.

The main point to keep in mind is that the target group we intend to ask to support us financially has already been supporting us with their time, online actions, and even on-the-ground activities. Because they have already been helping us and experiencing a program or campaign journey alongside us, they are already part of the cause. Becoming a donor is just one little step forward. And we find it incredibly exciting that many of them are ready to take that little step. Don't you?

SOME DETAILS TO CONSIDER

In our experience, there are several points that optimize conversion rates. We won't go into the basics of direct marketing, but we do believe that the following conversion factors are particularly useful to keep in mind:

1. **Asking for the right cause:** As social trysumers will support programs through specific pushes, plans, and campaigns, it is very important to emphasize the direct link between issues they have been working on and the appeal.

2. **Funds in action**: The reason for the ask must be as clear as always—nothing new there. Remember to give both a specific reason for why you need the money and its purpose. We must show people that their money will be transferred to the cause.

3. **Social trysumers give to people:** Let's assume that we've been using e-mail to stay in contact with social trysumers. The same person from a specific program, such as the program manager or program director, sent all of those e-mails. When it comes to the conversion, this same person must do the ask. If you need to change the person whom these supporters have been in contact with, you need a good reason for this change. People give to people, not to organizations. If your contact with social trysumers is via SMS, we suggest that all messages be signed by the same contact person, too.

4. **Be persistent and win!** In any conversion campaign, we want to be persistent. The main ask should be supported by several reminders, no matter what the appeal channel is. If the cause is of particular interest to social trysumers, then they need to be informed. If they have already joined the cause, emphasize this. Don't lose potential donors because they don't see the ask or because they need to receive several asks before they make up their mind to take a little step forward.

5. **Hello!** Although telemarketing is very expensive, it does have a much higher conversion rate than e-mail campaigns, sometimes up to 20 times higher. Because telemarketing campaigns are diverse and have many different components, they enable us to carry out a lot of testing and make changes on the fly. We can test which times of the day it is best to call, different scripts, different telemarketers, and how many times we should call.

6. **ASAP:** When it comes to timing, it is very important to define a critical moment for your program, organization, or cause. We would expect the Red Cross to run an appeal following a disaster. We would expect a university to run an appeal to graduates before budgeting for the following year's scholarship program. We would expect Greenpeace to ask for funds following the sinking of an oil tanker or the approval of an important law to defend whales or forests, or to stop a specific industry from polluting.

7. **Show me the money:** We can run financial asks when we lose a campaign, when we win, or whenever something occurs that is relevant to our current program. The point is that we must tell people that we need the money to continue our work because current funds are insufficient for what we hope to achieve.

COMPARISON WITH OTHER RECRUITMENT TECHNIQUES

Some e-mail campaigns have a 120 percent ROI in the first year. However, some face-to-face programs, including many street teams, have to wait up to two and a half years before breaking even.

Social-trysumer models are much more economically efficient. They are not based on random recruitment and center on a two-step program: experience an organization for free and be inspired to become a financial supporter.

Quick Note on Attrition

"Attrition" is a horrible word for fundraisers, especially for those in organizations that base their income on individual donors. "Attrition," though, is nothing more than the rate at which donors stop supporting an organization.

When people are asked to join an organization by someone in the street, they have no emotional track record with that organization, and attrition rates for those organizations can therefore rise to around 80 percent per year. This means that 80 percent of new donors recruited in this way will leave an organization within the first 12 months of giving.

Because social trysumers already have an emotional attachment to an organization when they become donors, they tend to stay on longer. In our experience, the attrition rates go from less than 5 percent in the first year to less than 10 percent after three years of continuous giving (of course, this depends on how well you continue to treat your financial supporters).

SOCIAL TRYSUMER CASE STUDIES

Greenpeace Argentina and the Forest Law Campaign

In mid-2007, Greenpeace Argentina was locked in a battle for the full approval of a forest law. The law, which would end the destruction of ancient forestland, had already been approved by the lower house of Congress but was stuck in the Senate. Several direct actions had been taken to raise awareness of the law and expose the Senate, but none had been particularly successful.

At the time, Greenpeace Argentina boasted a database of around 200,000 cyberactivists (social trysumers!), which had been built up over 10 years. The database had been used to generate pressure on several political and corporate targets by sending demands and petitions and by carrying out other cyberactions, phone calls, and so on.

One of those actions involved sending an alarm clock (an animated GIF file) to the senators involved in approving the forest law and asking them to "wake up" and "not put the law to bed." Although this action managed to crack the Senate's server, it proved politically ineffective.

One day, during a brainstorming session, someone came up with a novel idea. At the time, Argentina's First Lady Cristina Fernández was both a senator and the most powerful presidential candidate for the 2007 elections. Political analysis suggested that the rest of the Senate would quickly back any move by Fernández on any issue. It was therefore decided that she should be the target of the Greenpeace campaign. However, because she had a good public image and a positive approach to politics, Greenpeace could not attack her directly. A new approach would be needed to persuade her to vote for the forest law.

And so the concept for a massive public campaign arose: to raise 1 million votes for the forest law and send them to Fernández, asking her to vote for it, too, just like the Argentine people were going to do. It would be very difficult for her to say no to 1 million people just before the presidential elections.

Greenpeace Argentina went on to launch the campaign. The ask was simple: Vote for the forest law. It was easy to understand, positive, empowering, and just what we needed both Fernández and the Senate to do. And in the election year, the word "vote" had additional clout and meaning.

Within 51 days of relentless small pushes to the 200,000-strong cyberactivist database and to slightly more than 30,000 donors (who also participated in online actions), as well as television ads, AdWords campaigns, and the collection of offline votes by Greenpeace staff and volunteers, Greenpeace Argentina reached one million votes. Then, 65 days after the campaign was launched, more than 1.5 million votes had been collected and the net number of online activists in our database had increased from 200,000 to 800,000.

It is important to highlight that this public push was combined with traditional campaigning activities and that, fewer than four months after the public campaign was launched, the Senate approved the forest law.

Following this successful campaign, we launched a massive e-mail fundraising campaign. Each prospect received four e-mails within the first few months following the approval of the law. This was then preceded by a seven-month telemarketing campaign, during which more than 170,000 people were targeted. The final outcome after seven months was 22,000 new monthly donors with an average gift of more than US$4.5 per month.

The Greenpeace campaign is a typical example of a social trysumer model in which people are invited to participate in an activity and then asked to become donors. The model has become almost the exclusive recruitment strategy for Greenpeace Argentina since March 2006 (when the face-to-face program was dismantled, making it the only office in the world without a Direct Dialogue program). In four years, the number of donors increased from 23,000 to 70,000, and the organization's annual income has increased by 450 percent.

It took 11 months for the fundraising campaign to break even (including all gifts, print newsletters, and mailing costs). The ROI was 1.11 percent in the first year and 3.72 percent in the third.

Greenpeace India: Turtles versus Tata

Prior to August 2007, Greenpeace India had no cyberactivists whatsoever. The organization's income was based on a massive, and very successful, face-to-face program, and after five years, the number of donors was already around 30,000.

Despite this success, however, the executive director, the fundraising director, and the communications director all felt that something was missing—people power!

With barely 10,000 e-mail addresses and an enthusiastic campaign director, Greenpeace India began a campaign to prevent a port from being constructed along India's East Coast that would have seriously threatened olive ridley turtles.

The campaign focused on various calls to action (including asking supporters to send flowers, candles, and other asks to Ratan Tata, head of the Tata Group, which was involved in constructing the port). Supporters were asked to spread the word through social networks and make the campaign as viral as possible. In fewer than six months, almost 100,000 cyberactivists had been recruited to the cause. And after just one year, Greenpeace India had achieved the following:

- It recruited 115,000 cyberactivists.
- Of the cyberactivists polled, 17 percent intended to support the organization financially in the future.
- Of Tata customers polled, 98 percent wanted construction of the port to be halted.
- Tata ordered its employees to stop supporting Greenpeace.
- BNP Paribas, which was financing the port, pulled out of the project.
- Tata filed for a restraining order against Greenpeace, although the court ruled in favor of Greenpeace.
- After five years, Greenpeace campaigners were finally received for a meeting with Tata's top executives.

As far as the fundraising campaign was concerned, 160,000 e-mail were sent. The e-mail campaign had a 15 percent open rate and a 24 percent click-through rate. Of the cyberactivists, 4 percent became financial supporters. Although 281 new donors may not seem like much, "Getting India's most respected and powerful corporation to meet us at the negotiating table [was] priceless!" says Gene Hashmi, Greenpeace India's public campaigns manager.

MOBILE SOCIAL-TRYSUMER CASE STUDIES

Mobile social-trysumer programs are slowly gaining popularity throughout the world. Organizations in Africa, Europe, Asia, and the Americas have all had success stories with this model.

UNHCR Spain—Ringtones and Monthly Givers

Francesco Sciacca, the fundraising director for the UN High Commissioner for Refugees (UNHCR) in Spain began a successful mobile social-trysumer program in 2008. This program is based on generating mobile content to raise awareness of the plight of refugees. The program received support from one of UNHCR's ambassadors, the television presenter Jesús Vásquez, who took advantage of one of his visits to Africa to record a children's song with a group of young people from a local refugee camp. The song was then transformed into a ringtone for mobile phones.

Vásquez publicized the ringtone on his television program and invited people to download it to their mobile phones. The results were phenomenal. Not only did the organization raise funds from the downloads, but the UNHCR used the contact details obtained from people downloading the ringtone to run a telemarketing conversion campaign. The conversion rate for the first telemarketing campaign was greater than 8 percent. The UNHCR continues to work with this model because of its initial success.

Greenpeace Argentina—Mobile Social-Trysumer Pioneers

Greenpeace Argentina has always been a new media pioneer in the sector. Greenpeace's mobile activist program first emerged at the beginning of 2002 with the compilation of a mobile contact database. In 2004, the organization designed its own mass "guerilla" SMS platform with help from a local telecom company, BCGS & Associates. Thanks to this platform, the organization was able to send and receive SMS at a lower cost and to implement creative mobile activism campaigns. It soon became a global pioneer of this kind of public mobilization, and in 2006, it won an international award for Best Activism Campaign from the British organization 160characters.org.

Greenpeace Argentina's mobile activism program now has more than 50,000 members and involves far more sophisticated commercial platforms to send and receive SMS with short codes. In 2008, the organization carried out a campaign to recruit more mobile activists to the fight against climate change. The campaign was publicized using posters, flyers, press ads, and online advertisements, and 6,500 new mobile social trysumers signed on as mobile activists. Greenpeace initiated a telemarketing campaign to invite the new supporters to get involved in the direct-debit donation program. The campaign had a conversion rate of 9.19 percent, and 450 new members signed on as monthly donors.

Amnesty Norway: 80,000 Mobile Activists!

In a recent interview published on Marceloiniarra.com, the secretary-general of Amnesty Norway, Jon Petter Egenes discusses his mobile activism program and the impact that it has had on the organization's fundraising program:

> [Approximately] 80,000 Norwegian citizens are part of our SMS action network. We send them an action twice a month and they reply by sending their name to be put on a petition for a particular cause that we could then send to the Russian or Brazilian President or to the United States embassy. Normally, between 25 and 30 thousand Norwegians take action by replying to the SMS with their name that we then send on to help create change. And more often than not, it works! This is a huge network for a country of 4 million people. It is more than 2% of our population taking action twice per month to change human rights situations around the world. And what's even better than that is that we can contact them again and ask them to join Amnesty. More and more of our SMS activists are ultimately becoming members, drawing their activism from SMS into other areas. I think that this is the future of activism.

As we can see, this two-step program is also being used by Amnesty Norway. Supporters are invited to have a remarkable first experience of the organization for free and are then invited to donate via a telemarketing campaign.

IF THE PYRAMID CHANGES, SHOULD FUNDRAISING CHANGE?

Various versions of the new pyramid are being used by organizations in which digital fundraising is a main component of the marketing mix—not only Greenpeace, but organizations all over the world. These organizations have all raised the question of how to most effectively manage nonfinancial supporters: Which department should be in charge of managing the database? These supporters are not just nonfinancial supporters, but newsletter subscribers, cyberactivists, online volunteers, and so on, depending on the organization.

The communications area can manage the e-mail or SMS information from supporters. The campaign department looks after digital actions and their impact on the organization's political objectives or programs and is responsible for taking the lead. The fundraising department wants to invite the nonfinancial supporters to donate to achieve organizational objectives.

A WHOLE NEW ORGANIZATIONAL MODEL

Depending on the mission, type, and style of the organization, social try-sumers will eventually have an impact on diverse organizational objectives. They will become a political power in some cases, will spread the word in others, will change habits and generate change in their homes and neighborhoods—all because they work with us and don't just give us money to do the job ourselves.

We should therefore expect that, in most cases, organizations that develop a social trysumer recruitment model will have a greater impact on their program or campaign work, as well as a higher income and ROI. However, if we wish to develop this paradigm, we must consider new approaches as far as the various areas of an organization are concerned:

1. The communications area will have to make some changes. The organization will be not only informing but also having a dialogue with its audience. If we are going to do things together, there are some things that we have to discuss.

2. Campaigns or programs will start to include the influence of supporters who are already involved in the organization's programs in their power analyses. People will become a campaigning force as well as a financial one.

3. Management will no longer be the same. If supporters are to be allocated specific tasks, then all departments must sit down together and agree on what the supporters should do, how they will be informed, what tools they will need, who will provide internal funding, what kind of outcome will be expected, and how the audiences will be informed of, and thanked for, the outcome. This type of model requires more integration and more leadership, and it could spell the end of the silo model.

4. The fundraising model will still change dramatically. There will be an additional focus on what people are doing and on how much money they are giving. Constructing this model implies generating communities of social trysumers, and this in turn requires various marketing and direct marketing activities as well as conversion techniques.

CONCLUSION

The model introduced in this chapter, that the first contact with potential donors begins with a new, electronic, nonfinancial entrance, through which hundreds or thousands of people pass in a very short space of time, constitutes a major change in vision for fundraising.

Today, more than ever, fundraising departments should become public mobilization or supporter mobilization departments, integrally leading nonfinancial relationships with the organization. This constitutes a significant change to fundraising, especially because many people will never choose the path of donation and will remain members of an electronic community of activists or friends of the organization, whereas others will enter the traditional donor cycle.

Given the new paradigms introduced by electronic media, perhaps Heraclitus, who lived in Turkey more than 2,000 years ago and couldn't possibly have imagined that his wise advice would still apply today, was very right in his assumption that "there is nothing permanent except change."

Marcelo Iniarra Iraegui is the tribe chief of his own international public mobilization, marketing, and fundraising organization, Marceloiniarra.com, which focuses on developing strategies powered by innovation. Iniarra has more than 20 years of experience in the social sector and is Greenpeace International's former international fundraising and campaign innovation manager. He was one of the international pioneers of online mobilization, and mobile marketing is his new obsession.

Alfredo Botti worked as the public campaigning executive for Greenpeace International since July 2007 until July 2009. He entered the organization as fundraising director for Greenpeace Argentina in 2005, where he developed and coordinated the forest law public campaign, which obtained 1.5 million signatures and 22,000 donors. In August 2006, he became Greenpeace International's marketing manager for the I-go project, a global, online community that fights to defend whales. He has also worked as a fundraising and new media management trainer, developing public campaigns in the Indian, British, Dutch, Italian, and New Zealand offices. Today Alfredo leads his own NGO, We-Me.org, an organization that promotes long-term civic action through the generation of a directly managed campaigns portfolio and the design of campaigns for other organizations.

ACKNOWLEDGMENTS

The authors would like to thank Ashley Baldwin (Marceloiniarra.com), Gene Hashmi (Greenpeace India), Francesco Sciacca (UNHCR, Spain), Jon Petter Egenes (Amnesty Norway), and the teams at Greenpeace International and Greenpeace Argentina for their help compiling this chapter.

CHAPTER 11

Social Networks

GETTING YOUR ORGANIZATION WORKING
FOR THEM!

PHILIP KING

There is a lot of talk about online social networks, and at times it can be hard to separate the chatter from truly valuable insight. As a leader in a nonprofit organization, one of the key questions on your mind must be, how much time and energy should we be spending on X? Fill in the blank with the social media brand du jour. Throughout this chapter, I will refer to sites like Twitter and Facebook as archetypal consumer social networks, knowing full well that when you read this text you will need to find and replace one or the other with a newer name that doesn't yet exist. One thing that is certain about social media is that it is extremely dynamic.

This chapter will tease apart some of the nuances of how nonprofits can leverage digital social networks, but the quick answer to the question on your mind depends on what you are trying to achieve. Fundraising? Friend raising? Awareness? All of the above?

An important mind shift that I would encourage you to consider at the outset of this discussion is provoked by the chapter subtitle. Many nonprofits approach the topic of social networks with the attitude of "How can I make Twitter work for my organization?" This approach implies that social media networks are tools similar to more traditional digital tools such as e-mail management platforms or database software. It would be appropriate to ask, "How can I make this database software work for my organization?" A database product is a tool. Social media networks are not tools; they are collections of people already engaged in conversation, and they require a fundamentally different mind-set and approach from that of traditional tools.

WHY THIS TOPIC?

At times it seems easy to discount some of the social networks as trends or fads that will quickly fade. After all, it would be easier to shrug our shoulders and do nothing about Facebook or Twitter; there's just so much else going on. Also, many more traditional nonprofits believe that "their demographic" doesn't use such networks, so why bother?

Many of us approach our digital strategy with the core assumption that we want to drive people to our web site, and if we're really, really good, we can get those people to donate or register for an account with us. But what about a strategy that is focused on going where people already are spending most of their time online? Using an offline metaphor, is our core assumption that we are trying to get everyone to come to our reception area? Or are we going out to spend time with people in their own living rooms, on their own terms?

LEVERAGING MY SOCIAL NETWORK FOR THIS CHAPTER

As president and CEO of Artez, an online fundraising company, I have the good fortune to spend time with bright, technical, and philanthropic people each day. Throughout this chapter I draw on the expertise and advice from a selection of these people. I have tried to create a good cross section of professionals who can help us all think about the role of social media in nonprofit organizations. Much of this content comes from chats with the following people:

Adrian Bradbury, the founder and executive director of Athletes for Africa, a growing global network of people committed to promoting and protecting human rights and to providing education and opportunities that empower youth in Africa (http://www.athletesforafrica.com).

Misty Meeks, the online communications manager for World Society for the Protection of Animals Canada, with a vision of a world where animal welfare matters and animal cruelty ends. The society has been promoting animal welfare for more than 25 years (http://www.wspa.ca).

Dan Latendre, CEO of Igloo Software. Igloo's community and social software solutions are built on top of a patent-pending Web 2.0 community platform. The platform combines rich social software, collaboration, and content management features with on-demand hosting, consulting, design, e-engagement, and support services necessary for a sustainable and successful deployment (http://www.igloosoftware.com).

Shannon Raybold, Internet director of the UN Foundation, a public charity created in 1998 with the entrepreneur and philanthropist Ted Turner's historic $1 billion gift to support UN causes and activities. The foundation advocates for the United Nations and is a platform for connecting people, ideas, and resources to help the United Nations solve global problems (http://www.unfoundation.org).

Jono Smith, vice president of nonprofit marketing for Network for Good, a nonprofit organization with the simple mission of helping other nonprofits raise money and supporters online. Founded in 2001, it has raised more than $300 million for more than 45,000 organizations. Network for Good aims to be the operating system for online fundraising across the Internet. It also processes the online fundraising for Facebook and MySpace (http://www.networkforgood.org).

Ben Alexander, senior developer for HomeMade Digital, a strategy and implementation firm in London that does fantastic work with a variety of nonprofit agencies in the United Kingdom and Europe (http://www.homemadedigital.com).

David Armour, CEO of the Canadian Olympic Foundation, a national charitable organization that provides Canadians with the first opportunity to support the success of high-performance athletes across all Olympic and Paralympic sports (http://www.olympicfoundation.ca).

CONTROLLING THE CONVERSATION AND YOUR BRAND

The loss of control you fear is already in the past.

—CLAY SHIRKY[1]

One of the topics people are most passionate about when considering social media is brand control. In a direct-marketing world of billboards, television advertisements, and mail, the organization has complete control over the message. These are one-to-many models built for a broadcast generation. Because the cost of each impression is so high, as for a television ad, the significant amount of time spent debating the particulars of word choice or font selection makes sense.

How Is Social Media Different?

"We're not dealing with a mass of automated-like consumers anymore, that you just send out messages to and see how they react; you have to be willing to actually engage with people as human beings," says Ben Alexander. "We spend a lot of time with our clients talking about how this is listening rather than broadcasting. What people want in social media interactions is to have a genuine two-way conversation."

Jono Smith puts it even more bluntly: "When you participate in social media, you have to let go of your message. You're engaging in conversations that are already occurring without you. You can throw up your hands in frustration or you can participate. The biggest risk is that organizations shy away from conversations because they can't control them 100 percent."

"We don't treat everyone the same. The day of the mass monthly newsletter is really fading for us. We talk to our audience only when we have something to say, and we have different conversations with different groups. For example, we have a bunch of annual walkers. We wouldn't go to them and ask them to be a monthly donor. We think that would be insensitive and that they wouldn't appreciate the way they've chosen to support us. So with that group we spend our time talking about the upcoming walk and how they can support that," says Adrian Bradbury.

This loss of control is challenging for many organizations, particularly those that have spent years and large sums of money building up brand awareness in traditional media channels. In fact, one of the advantages I see for smaller, newer nonprofits is the relative lack of baggage they have as they leverage social media.

But even groups that have big, global brands are jumping in with both feet. "It's exciting for us since we have one of the best brands in the world—the Olympic rings—and a number of organizations who depend on us including TV stations," says David Armour. "We're going to take some risks. We're live-feeding our donor comments straight to our web front page in the lead up to the 2010 Games in Vancouver. It's part of the discussion" (see Figure 11.1).

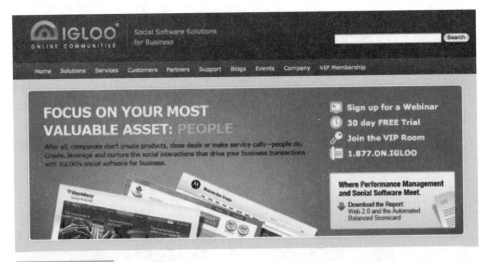

FIGURE 11.1   **The Canadian Olympic Foundation Web Site**

What about Negative Comments?

David Armour notes, "It'll give participants in the online community a chance to self-moderate. From my work in the non-profit sector I've met many volunteers who have the fluency and ability to articulate the mission of the organizations as well as any paid staff member. And keep in mind, there's nothing better than a negative comment to stimulate a positive discussion!"

Jono Smith takes a similar approach at Network for Good: "We actively monitor the social media space for comments about Network for Good. We'll occasionally see negative comments, and most often it's an honest mistake. If we engage quickly, people will often retract their comments, but only if we engage."

"I think there are lots of nonprofits who are afraid that if they let go of the message their fans may say the wrong thing," says Adrian Bradbury. "But I also think you stunt the opportunity to grow your network. The only way to grow is to have your supporters feel like they own it.

"Consider the fact that we operate a volunteer-led event in 100 cities around the world," continues Bradbury. "We've never had a problem giving away control of our message, globally, never! I thought for sure we'd get that e-mail that said, 'Someone told me the money was going to go there and it didn't or that someone had offended the media or someone in the community . . . but not once. These volunteers are doing it because they're passionate about it, and they are doing it with the same intentions that we're doing it. They care about our cause as much as we do."

How Do You Do It ? Use Common Sense

In my discussions with a wide variety of nonprofits on the topic of social media, I find there is often the temptation to overcomplicate the subject. The nuances of the technology sometimes lead people to lose sight of the strategic plan.

Jono Smith underscores this perspective: "It's important to recognize the difference between an online tactic and an online strategy. Having a web site, using Twitter, et cetera, are all tactics that can be used to achieve specific goals. A lot of organizations start with tactics . . . not strategies. We really encourage groups to articulate a strategy first, with measurable goals, and then figure out which of these shiny objects like Facebook or Twitter they might want to test to try and achieve their plan."

It's not hard to get lost in the shiny objects. I've spent many minutes (or hours?) as I write this chapter clicking on links in Facebook and checking on news items and posted photos. Part of me feels that I've wasted time, but the other part realizes that I'm just interacting differently than I did before. Now rather than spend as much time on newspaper web sites, I rely more on my friends to link to articles or blogs they find interesting. In this respect, I'm broadening my sources for information and relying on my network to filter information for me.

One of the real conveniences of sites like Facebook or Twitter is that they allow me to consolidate my digital life. Whereas in the past I would go to one site to blog, another site to upload photos, a different site to upload videos, I can now do all of these activities on Facebook or Twitter.

I recently attended my son's graduation from primary school. Because he was delivering a short speech, I couldn't resist the urge to switch my digital camera into video mode. Later that evening, I uploaded the video and linked it to a Facebook status update.

It was one of those—too-often elusive—technology rapture moments! The next day I received so many comments from my friends, my relatives, and my coworkers that they had watched and enjoyed the video. In the past, it would have been a chore to distribute video using DVDs or links in e-mail to download sites.

Dan Latendre of Igloo Software helps his clients by providing a template for social networks. "We've created a Community Playbook for our clients. You have to start by looking at the demographics of your audience. Are they Gen X or Y? Are they comfortable using the tools you are considering? Most importantly, do you have champions who will get online and stimulate the audience and get the community discussion going?"

You Climb a Mountain by Taking a First Step

"Like everyone else we're learning by doing" says David Armour. "And we're learning and trying to evolve as quickly as the field of social media is evolving. If you're setting up a new foundation right now, you can go straight where you want to go. It's like putting a phone system in the developing world: you don't mess with copper wires . . . you go straight to cellular. We're going straight to online and specifically online communities."

Some of the best advice is also the simplest and most commonsense. Shannon Raybold organizes Facebook "blitzes" at the UN Foundation with interns. "We create talking points and approved messages and then send our interns looking for groups on Facebook who share a similar pro-peace perspective to ours. A lot of smaller groups on these social networks are looking for actions they can take. I used to be surprised when a group organizer would say 'Yes, I'll send this message to my group!' but I'm not anymore. We can also help them grow by linking their Group or Fan Page from our web site" (see Figure 11.2).

This seems too simple to be true, doesn't it? Treat Facebook (or any of the social media networks) like a collection of real people some of whom are interested in making real impact. It's very similar to community organizing in an offline community, only much more efficient. With networks like Facebook,

| FIGURE 11.2 | The UN Foundation Uses Interns to Hold Facebook Blitzes and Encourages Smaller Groups to Link to the Foundation's Fan Page |

a team such as the UN Foundation can meet like-minded people and groups across the globe in far less time than it would take offline.

GLOBAL COMMUNITIES

One tantalizing and intimidating aspect of online social networks is that they are global. With offices around the planet, the World Society for the Protection of Animals (WSPA) decided it was best to have one point person manage the global fan page in Facebook and then have country fan pages branch from that, each managed by a person in that country (see Figure 11.3). Misty Meeks has the honor and challenge of coordinating WSPA's global fan page. "We have almost seventy thousand fans worldwide on Facebook," notes Meeks. Those numbers are likely much higher as you read this printed page. "Most of our fans speak English, and come from the United States, Denmark, Australia, the United Kingdom, and Canada. What I find noticeable is the gender split. Approximately

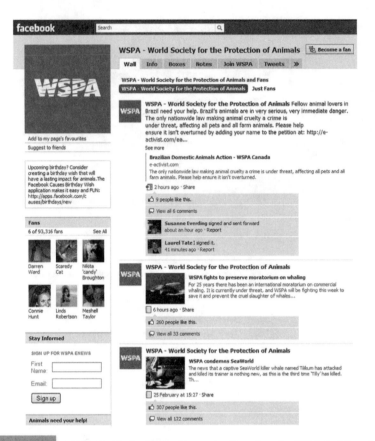

FIGURE 11.3   **WSPA Global Fan Page in Facebook, Which Blends Twitter "Tweets" with Facebook Status Updates**

seventy-five percent are females, and over eighty-five percent of our interactions come from females.

"It's such a great communications resource for us at WSPA," continues Meeks. "We can push out stories, like our recent one about the world's first release of bonobos, and we receive immediate feedback from our fans. Some want to comment, others just give us the 'thumbs-up' that they like this."

At Athletes for Africa, home to GuluWalk, Bradbury realizes he couldn't have done it without his online community (see Figure 11.4). "We are a small office. When our main campaign took off we only had one and a half people working at our charity. Coordinating volunteers in one hundred cities in sixteen countries, it's been incredible to see the reach, scope and opportunity that a small team can have using online tools. You don't need a big megaphone from head office anymore. If you can give little megaphones to your supporters and let them be the voice, you can engage an audience on a global scale.

"When I think about organizing globally, there's was an expectation that everybody is online and everyone has Facebook and is Twittering, and we can

FIGURE 11.4   **The GuluWalk Home Page, Which Prominently Features the Blog for a Fresh, Up-to-Date Feel**

just push our message out there like we did in Toronto or New York City," says Bradbury. "We've stopped making those assumptions. There are people who are going to catch the message and come to you who could be your champions, no matter what city they live in. Without those champions and without the local touch it's really difficult to have an international audience.

"One thing we've learned is that you can't allow online to be the be-all and end-all," cautions Bradbury. "There is still tremendous value in the personal touch. I don't think there's any replacement for face to face or hopping on the phone. I think this gets devalued in this online world."

ELEPHANT IN THE CHAT ROOM—HOW SOON CAN YOU FUNDRAISE?

It's easy to see how social media and online communities can be an effective platform to share stories and get feedback from supporters, but what about the money? As soon as a fundraiser gets involved, that person is going to want to know how to convert the conversations into donations.

Many believe that there is a risk of moving too fast. Jono Smith says: "When we think about social media it is focused on people using tools to share content and have conversations online. It's about listening and having a conversation.

It's about community building first, fundraising second. The golden rule of any online outreach is that on average it takes five to seven different touch points for an online supporter to become an online donor. Don't jump the gun."

This sentiment is echoed by the team at WSPA. "Our approach to social media at this point is that it isn't about generating donations today but developing relationships with people for donations in the future. We're nurturing tomorrow's donors," states Meeks.

Others, however, see it differently. For the Canadian Olympic Foundation it's a two-part process. "Direct online fundraising on our web site and online donations are the first part," says David Armour. "Then we have a need to provide stickiness to that donor or online fundraiser. Everything the nonprofit sector has learned about donor stewardship can be achieved through online communities. We see it as the opportunity to provide a continuous call to action. In our case, there are lots of places to watch the Olympics but we want to be the destination when someone wants to take action either by making a donation or setting up a fundraising page themselves."

So in the case of Canadian Olympic Foundation, donations and fundraising form the core of the online community. Another example of the successful combination of social media with giving is Twestival.

Twestival started as a grassroots initiative in London in the fall of 2008 (see Figure 11.5). By February 2009, more than two hundred cities around the world held Twestivals, which were offline meet-ups organized via Twitter, and

Tweet. Meet. Give.

Announcing...

Twestival Local : Saturday 12 September 2009

Twestival Global : Thursday 4 February 2010

FIGURE 11.5   **Twestival, an Example of Fundraising Using Twitter in 2009**

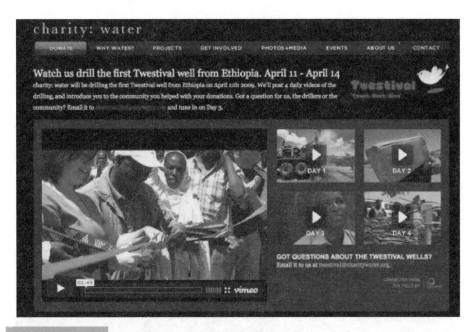

FIGURE 11.6   **Donors Could Watch Live Video as Their Donations Helped Build a Well in Ethiopia**

collectively raised more than US$250,000. The funds were donated to an organization "charity: water," which then broadcast online the drilling of clean-water wells two months later live from Ethiopia (see Figure 11.6). From start to finish, the entire fundraising campaign took only a few months, and participants received near-time video feedback about how their donations were making an impact. The success of this fundraising campaign was a direct result of how well it fit the immediacy of the Twitter community.

The UN Foundation also benefitted from Twitter in a recent campaign. In April 2009, Ashton Kutcher challenged Ted Turner to see who could first hit the million-follower mark on Twitter. The bet was a donation of 10,000 bed nets to campaigns such as Nothing but Nets, which is run by the UN Foundation.

In addition to driving media and public awareness of the online fundraising campaign, Kutcher and Turner exchanged remarks on YouTube, driving additional traffic to the fundraising site (see Figure 11.7). If you search for "Ted Turner" and "Twitter" on YouTube, you'll quickly find the video of Ted saying: "Congratulations, Ashton. Your Twitter followers really came through for you. But World Malaria Day is only the beginning. We need to send more nets to save more lives. And you don't have to be Bill Gates or Oprah Winfrey to make a difference. You just need ten dollars. If ten thousand more people join the UN Foundation's Nothing but Nets campaign. I'll have you and Demi over for lunch at Ted's Montana grill in Atlanta. Hope you like Bison Burgers!" At the end of the video was a link to the online fundraising campaign (see Figure 11.8).

FIGURE 11.7   **Using Twitter, Then YouTube, to Drive Fundraising Traffic**

At Artez, we're seeing more and more traffic to our online donation and online fundraising servers coming from social media networks. YouTube, Twitter, and Facebook are all growing in popularity as referral sites because of campaigns such as Ted Turner's (see Figure 11.9). Many participants in walkathons and bikeathons have naturally started linking their personal fundraising pages to their Facebook profiles, status updates, and "tweets."

In many respects, online fundraisers are using social media channels to augment, or in some cases replace, e-mail. Teams such as Artez and other providers of online fundraising technology are responding by making it easier for people to cross-link their social media spaces and their online fundraising places.

WHO HAS TIME FOR THIS?

There is unanimous agreement that success in social media it requires more than a Twitter account; it requires human talent. But where does this talent come from, and how much does an organization need?

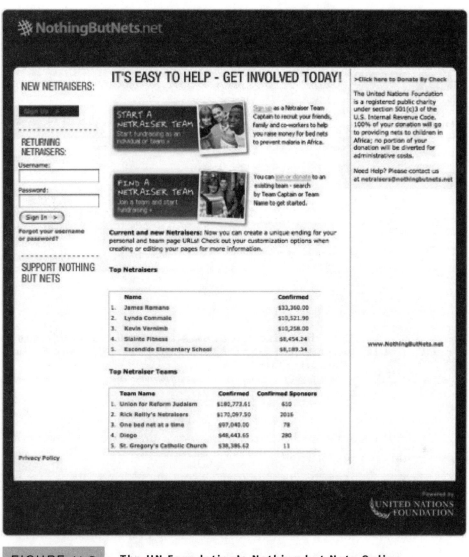

FIGURE 11.8   **The UN Foundation's Nothing but Nets Online Fundraising Campaign: The Home Page Features Top "Netraisers" and Top Netraiser Teams**

"The number-one question I get about social media staff is, 'Where are we going to find these people?'" says Jono Smith. "I think the answer really varies based on whether the organization is conducting a simple test or trying to compete in one of the big fundraising contests on Facebook."

The WSPA uses a global team to push its social media strategy. "I facilitate the global pages on Facebook and Twitter, and we have regional people in each office to manage their country-specific pages," states Misty Meeks. "In terms of content there is one person in the U.K. creating good web content. She distributes

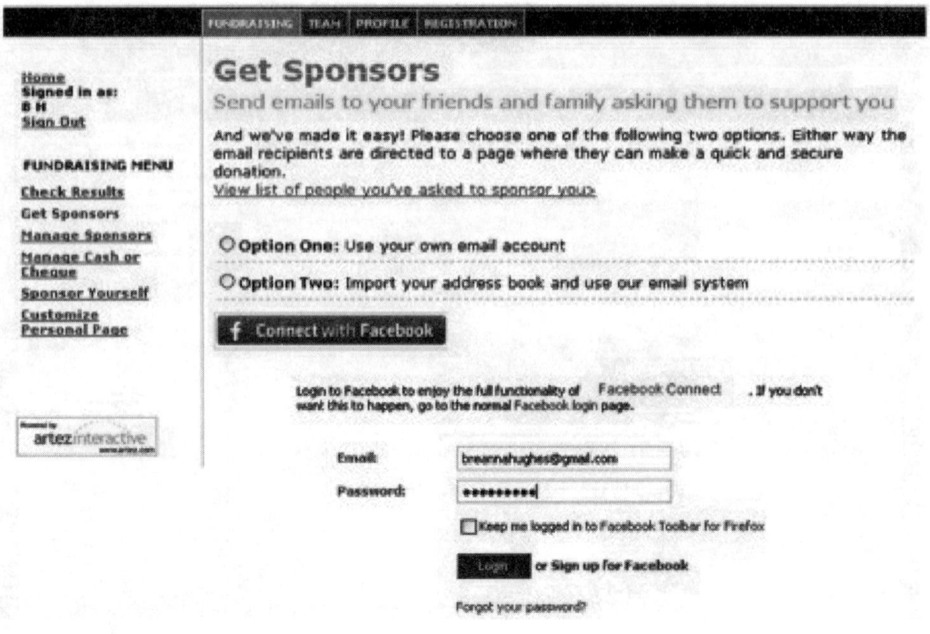

FIGURE 11.9   **Solutions Like Artez Now Allow Online Fundraisers to Supplement E-Mail Appeals with Cross-Links to Social Network Spaces**

it out to all regional people and they post it as they see fit. If I see a conversation on our global page that applies to someone else I direct it to the appropriate person within our organization.

"At first we didn't need a lot of resource," continues Meeks. "When we first launched on Twitter and Facebook we didn't have a lot of followers or fans. But as the audience grew we needed to spend more time having conversations. It's not my full time job right now, but more than 50 percent of my time and growing."

"It's on our wish list to have full time person focus on social media at the United Nations Foundation," says Raybold. "Even though we're a larger foundation, we don't have enough resources to make it full time job yet—hopefully soon we will. We've realized that people want to have genuine conversations with us in this medium, and it will require more resource to have those conversations. It's not like writing an e-mail and sending it out to our list."

For the Canadian Olympic Foundation, talent starts at the top. "My Board is totally on board with this social media conversation. They're rolling up their sleeves to get this broad-based as possible. They're starting with their personal networks and moving on from there" says David Armour.

Many organizations are finding a new and important role for young digital natives who want to volunteer for their cause. Rather than asking them to lick envelopes in the back room, more and more groups are asking them to participate in conversations online and tell stories about the good work of organization ... volunteer work that can be done at any time and from any Internet browser. Armour often assures nonprofit executives that "it's OK you don't have a Facebook or Twitter account, just make sure you surround yourself with people who do!"

WHAT ARE THE RISKS?

Clearly there are risks associated with social media. Risks arise from jumping in with both feet and from standing meekly on the shore.

"I can see how it's perceived as risk, but it should be seen as an opportunity," observes Ben Alexander. "The truth will come out in any case. If you're out there you can manage risk better since you'll have credibility. I think there is actually a big risk to not listening.

"There was a bike lock company here in the U.K. that was very popular, but people started posting online how to easily break the lock," continues Alexander. "It did a lot of damage to their brand. If an organization doesn't engage with online social networks there is risk. I think in the end organizations aren't going to have a choice. They're going to have to have conversations with their audience rather than viewing their supporters as a big list that they message to and measure response from."

"There's a huge risk thinking that 'If we build it they will come,'" says Dan Latendre. "Organizations who will be successful with social media will already have a community of interest or practice. People come together online because of common interest, then you simply apply social software to that community. You provide faces to what used to be just e-mail addresses or names. If you don't already have a community of interest it becomes very difficult to succeed online."

"I think another big risk is that people are spending too much time talking about consumer social software," continues Latendre. "I think there's a pause coming there. I've already met all my old college buddies, and now I'm looking for real value. When I receive so much information on topics I'm not interested in and silly contests, I become disengaged. We think the next frontier will be corporate or branded social software so each community will look and feel different from the next."

Shannon Raybold at the UN Foundation worries about the risk of not participating: "If we're not out there other people will be. If we don't put our foot out there we're going to miss out on a lot of relationships that will benefit us in the future."

This is similar logic to the team at WSPA. "Organizations shouldn't wait," warns Misty Meeks. "They should jump on the social media topic now because soon it will be oversaturated. The risk really is being left behind. At minimum, if the organization can't do it, they should try to get their supporters to do it on their behalf."

But don't spread your resources too thinly. "A risk people take without even realizing it is that they dabble too much and then they don't have any resonance, and the stories don't come across as authentic," notes Adrian Bradbury. "People in these online communities are going to catch on to that very fast. In this social media arena it's about making a decision and drilling down. It's easy to say yes to a lot of things, but if you're doing little bits of everything, you'll do nothing well. For us at Athletes for Africa, we've made a decision to become better bloggers. We have a real face and real name of someone on our team who represents us in the blogosphere."

Jono Smith, at Network for Good, sees a risk in what he calls the shiny-object syndrome: "Groups shouldn't do Web 2.0 at the expense of doing Web 1.0. I see organizations tweeting and blogging, but you can't even find a donation button on their web site, and there's no easy way to leave your e-mail address to learn more. Without a strategy in place, it's easy to lose your way in the tactics—particularly when everybody wants to talk about the new, new thing like Twitter."

One refrain is clear in all of the voices: Strategy trumps tactics and measurements trump technologies. Social networking should have concrete and measurable goals, as would any other important program in your organization. You may not divine the right measurements or the right quantities when you first start, but at least you'll have a reference point. You can use this reference point to recalibrate your social media strategy as you learn more.

CONCLUSION

As you decide to embark on your social networking journey or continue to advance with the progress you've made, here are some parting words of wisdom from the crowd.

> *Find out where your people are, or most likely to be. Go to where they are. Tap into the conversation that is already taking place. Start with simple community building goals such as: "I'm going to add 100 new e-mail addresses."*
>
> —JONO SMITH, NETWORK FOR GOOD

> *My advice for people just starting: Set up a page on Facebook, or a page on Twitter, or a channel on YouTube, and promote it on your web site. I learn a lot by attending conferences like Social Tech Training. Also, I subscribe to the Mashable.com blog.*
>
> —MISTY MEEKS, WSPA

A word of advice? Don't confuse consumer social networking with professional or corporate social networking. They are different.

—DAN LATENDRE, IGLOO SOFTWARE

Understand where your community fits in the ecosystem of the communities around it. Ours will be a supporter community for those who want to take action. For others who want live video, we'll send them to the television network site; for those who want the history of the games, we'll send them to a different site. We want to be really good about sending people where they need to go and not trying to do all things.

—DAVID ARMOUR, CANADIAN OLYMPIC FOUNDATION

This does need to be resourced. It needs content. Someone needs to answer. You shouldn't just put up a page and ignore it. Be open to the fact that it is a long term process, and be willing to learn from each mini-campaign. Don't expect it to deliver huge amount of value up front.

—BEN ALEXANDER, HOMEMADE DIGITAL

The most important thing is to make a choice and try something—one thing. If it's a bit scary or you're worried, do a small test and minimize the risk. If you can commit more resources and dive deep you can do a better job. You can also evaluate it. If you do five or six different things, it's hard to evaluate impact when they're all over. Dig in and drill down.

—ADRIAN BRADBURY, ATHLETES FOR AFRICA

Clearly, social media and the human networks they produce, such as Facebook, Twitter, and YouTube, are exciting ways for organizations to form new relationships and sustain existing ones. But social media is constantly evolving and brings with it risks as well as benefits. Not all groups are a good cultural match to leverage the potential of social media, so it's important for an organization to look itself in the mirror and provide an honest self-assessment before it devotes many resources to the area. If the conversation around your boardroom table focuses primarily on trying to prevent open commentary about your brand and the work of your organization, the time and the team probably aren't right.

For others who are more willing to experiment with the new forms of conversation presented by social media, there has never been a more exciting time. Groups who are thriving in this new world understand that social media isn't just a new piece of technology; therefore, they don't delegate it to only the IT team. It isn't about controlling the brand and the message; it's about actively participating in conversations that are meaningful and about seeking raw feedback. It isn't about making social networks work for them; it's about learning how to make organizations fit better into those existing human networks.

Philip King has been president and CEO of Artez Interactive (http://www.artez.com) since 2002, and it just keeps getting more interesting. He is fulfilled each day by striving to surf the technology curve, fostering a culture of fanatical client delight and continuous fundraising innovation. He and his team have been at the forefront of Artez's expansion into the United Kingdom, Europe, Australia, the United States, Facebook, Twitter, and mobile—all while keeping an eye on the core values of a group dedicated to making the world a better place. King grew up in Tennessee, received a history degree from Harvard, worked in Manhattan for the Edison Project, and then settled in the wonderful city of Toronto, where he rests and plays with his wife and their two sons, ages 12 and 9.

CHAPTER 12

Prospect Modeling, Prospect Research

USING DATA MINING FOR SMARTER FUNDRAISING

LAWRENCE C. HENZE

Data mining and quantitative analysis are increasingly popular exercises and tools available to fundraising practitioners and related professionals in the nonprofit and higher education worlds. About 10 to 15 years ago, a chapter addressing this subject matter would've been largely ignored: online giving was in its infancy, and data mining and predictive modeling were just beginning to find traction among development professionals.

Today, online giving is widely practiced, its impact is growing annually, and data mining and predictive modeling are universally accepted as necessary for assessing and refining fundraising activities. Combining the art of online giving with the science (and some art) of fundraising analytics is the fundamental purpose of this chapter. Specifically, I will seek to do the following:

- Explain online giving analytics as a component of comprehensive fundraising analytics

- Identify appropriate sources of data to be included in fundraising analytics

- Provide an overview of the analytical tools available to you and your colleagues as you seek to evaluate the effectiveness of your online giving program

- Offer suggestions on the best analytical strategies to employ and the questions to ask as you evaluate your online giving program

- Offer actual examples of analyses of online giving programs and provide interpretation of the results, as well as suggest fundraising strategies flowing from the analysis

- Discuss the analytical tools and their relationship to more comprehensive analytical studies that seek to identify the paths of donor development in your organization

- Provide a brief summary of what we know about online donors, as their characteristics and attributes may or may not distinguish them from other types of contributors through more typical channels such as direct mail, special events, and telemarketing programs.

Finally, this chapter focuses on analytics related to membership and/or giving to nonprofit organizations, and not, for example, on analytics related to contributions to political or advocacy groups. It is true that much of what I write applies to this field as well, but there are nuances that are beyond my scope here. Nor will I discuss analytics applied to the use of social media and social networking web sites. I concentrate on analytics that fit within a comprehensive fundraising plan, which now includes e-mail solicitations and online giving through a web site.

Online Giving Analytics and Comprehensive Fundraising

The primary purpose of this chapter is not to offer my perspective on the practice of fundraising, principally in the United States and Canada, or to continue my push for an integrated, comprehensive approach to fund development. However, I am remiss if I do not state definitively that online giving analytics should be practiced as part of a larger schematic to understand comprehensive donor development for your organization.

Figure 12.1 is a diagram of a donor development pyramid to aid in the visualization and understanding of integrated analytics as well as to introduce a concept that I call ultimate giving.

Ultimate giving is the search for the lifetime value of each and every donor and each and every prospect. If some or many of our prospects have a lifetime value of zero, or perhaps even less than zero (getting one or two gifts totaling less than what we spent to acquire and resolicit or steward them), identifying such individuals allows us to successfully reallocate time and resources to those prospects with positive lifetime value. We solicit less, reduce costs, and increase our response and conversion rate in the process.

In the pyramid, potential donors enter as suspects (acquired names, usually from lists) or as prospects (names that come to your database through a preexisting relationship (e.g., alumni, patients, volunteers). Of course, donors may give as their first interaction with you, and their name becomes part of the donor

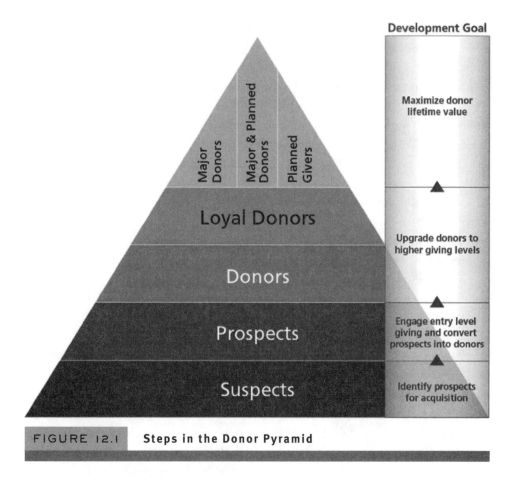

Development Goal

Maximize donor
lifetime value

Major Donors

Major & Planned Donors

Planned Givers

Loyal Donors

Donors

Prospects

Suspects

Upgrade donors to
higher giving levels

Engage entry level
giving and convert
prospects into donors

Identify prospects
for acquisition

FIGURE 12.1   **Steps in the Donor Pyramid**

development pyramid as well. Each of these paths into the pyramid correlates directly with online giving acquisition and solicitation activities.

If our goal is to pump as many donors into the pipeline as possible in the bottom third of the pyramid, and not to seek to create as many loyal donors as possible, we will thwart the objective of ultimate giving as it pertains to lifetime value. A strategy of acquisition first and retention second will put incredible pressure on acquisition and increase your cost-per-dollar-raised ratio. It will significantly reduce upgrade, transitional, major, and planned giving opportunities in the future. A primary reason that organizations relying on direct marketing acquisition for donors and dollars struggle to successfully engage donors in larger gift commitments flows directly from a lack of commitment to the middle of the pyramid.

Donor loyalty is the key to comprehensive fundraising success. Although everyone can point out donors who did not follow the steps of the pyramid in Figure 12.1, those donors are an exception to the rule. Loyalty, as contained in the pyramid, is represented by people who give at least 60 percent of the time, or three out of every five years. Clearly, donors who give every year are preferable, but my research indicates that we do not want to ignore people who contribute more often than not, as they frequently behave like individuals who give annually. Although it is impossible to state how important loyal giving is to your specific organization, for most organizations loyal donors are eight or nine times more likely to reach the top levels of the ultimate giving pyramid than are contributors with infrequent or nonexistent giving patterns.

As online giving brings more and more first-time contributors and points of entry to the donor-development pyramid, it is critical to ensure that online giving analytics not only track success in attracting new donors to your organization but also describe and predict online donors with additional giving potential within the context of the ultimate giving pyramid. For example, once we have a few years of experience in data associated with online giving behavior, through predictive modeling, we can create profiles of those individuals and more successfully predict their ultimate giving capacity. And knowing that donor A is a major giving prospect and donor B is more likely to be a bequest giving prospect opens up new and targeted strategies for the cultivation and solicitation of those donors, whether through further online activities or more traditional face-to-face donor cultivation and solicitation strategies.

On the face of it, it would seem natural that we analyze donor activity from a comprehensive perspective, but I know from experience as a development officer and a fundraising and marketing consultant that such comprehensive analysis is less likely to occur than we may hope. Once a development program has at least three fundraising professionals, it is more likely that the development enterprise is segmented by functional area, such as annual giving, database management, major giving, annual giving, and donor relations. This tendency is described in fundraising literature, and here as well, as the silo approach to development. As we place these functional areas of fundraising into silos, we decrease interaction among professionals who should be seeking the same goal, which is donor development that focuses on the needs of the contributors and provides assistance to loyal donors in reaching their philanthropic goals. By segmenting functionality, we create a disjunctive process that appears to our donors to lack coordination, because it does!

So heed my cautionary advice and practice online giving analytics in the context of the big picture of fund development for your organization. Doing so enables you to not create analytical measures that demonstrate success in short-term online giving efforts, such as the number of new donors during the past year, without also considering and reviewing longer-term rates for retention and upgrading. It amazes me how many annual giving programs—direct-mail, telemarketing, e-mail, and web site efforts—look at acquisition rates in a veritable vacuum, as if they existed on their own. This shortsightedness increases the likelihood that we will pursue activities without the greatest long-term benefit for our organization and miss opportunities to begin to specialize cultivation activities with our best alternative giving prospects at an earlier point in the donor development cycle.

The source of the problems wrought by the silo approach to development is shared throughout almost all levels of fundraising practice, from the beginning professional to the long-term veteran. I am most hopeful, however, that enlightened annual and online giving professionals with an eye to the complete donor development spectrum will successfully eliminate fundraising silos and promote free-range fundraising as they collect and share data that reinforces the donor-development pyramid represented previously in this section.

VITAL DATA OR DATA WITH VITALITY?

Simply put, there are two types of data available to you: internal and external. Internal or organizational data pertains to constituents and their relationships with the nonprofit and is captured in constituent relationship management (CRM) software programs. External data is collected on constituents by outside agencies, such as marketing firms and the U.S. census, and is purchased and appended to the file for inclusion in the analysis.

Internal Data

Internal data, at least in some minimal form, is required for descriptive or predictive analysis, which is described later in the chapter. Describing or predicting donor or member behavior requires past and current giving behavior on which to base the analysis, and such data are a prime example of internal data. At a minimum, demographic data including home address and historical data that relates directly to the question to be answered is essential. Answering the question, Who is most likely to contribute online? requires data on individuals who give online as well as data on those who do not give online. The latter point is surprising to many, so think of the term giving history broadly and inclusive of individuals declining to give as well. The absence of giving is their history.

Over the years, certain internal data variables yield fruitful insights more frequently than others. These variables include, but are not limited to the following:

- Age
- Relationship to the organization
- Participation in organizational activities or special events

- Volunteerism or other indicators of loyalty to the organization
- Giving history
  - Includes, for example, dollar value of each gift or membership, number of years, consecutive years, and total giving
  - Giving by solicitation type (e.g., direct mail, telemarketing, e-mail, special events)

Some of the variables are specific to the type of institution, such as higher education or health care. For example, data variables specific to higher education include the following:

- Degree or major
- Participation in student activities
- Participation in alumni activities
- Legacy (part of multiple generations attending this institution)
- Highest level of education
- Additional constituent relationships (parent or friend)

For each organizational type or specific organization, there are variables that may warrant unique consideration. Variables that are present in a small subset of the organizational database, such as membership on the governing board, are typically of little importance in creating predictive models. Because board membership is limited by its very nature, it is not a variable that will apply to a significant proportion of the population, nor can you add enough new board members to make it statistically valid for predictive purposes. Angela Bradham, a colleague of mine who creates predictive models daily, suggests that a variable should be present in at least 5 percent of the database before it is considered part of the potential mix of predictive factors. Of course, there are always exceptions, but that is a good standard for a starting point.

Do not miss the opportunity to create your own variables from existing fields in your database. For example, you may know which constituents have attended special events and, to take a deeper cut, the specific events they attended. The total number of events attended or the specific event attended may be correlated to giving or membership activity. However, if these variables do not exhibit strong correlations, a simple dichotomous variable (yes or no, attended or did not attend) may work fine. In recalling the earlier discussion on loyal giving, you may create variables for giving behavior over the past 10 years, such as gave in each of the past 10 years, loyal (at least 6 years of giving but not all 10), multiple gifts (at least 2 years but less than 6), one gift, and no gifts.

In addition to demographic and giving data, there are transactional and relational variables that add to the potential predictive and descriptive variables that will assist you in discovering your best online and traditional giving prospects. Ticket-buying practices, subscriptions, and the number of relationships with the institution are potentially powerful attributes for inclusion in the analysis. And remember to not let your assumptions rule the day, or you may miss potentially meaningful trends. For example, higher education fundraisers have speculated that older, long-term season-ticket holders with premium seats are the best planned-giving prospects. Predictive modeling and data mining reveals that although some of these individuals may be planned-giving prospects, there are many more prospects for bequests and annuities sitting in the moderately to lower-priced seats. Fiscal conservatism and loyalty to the institution are powerful planned-giving predictors.

Of course, there are metrics of online and e-mail activity that are useful as well, beyond knowing whether people are giving in response to an e-mail or a visit to your web site. Various authors included in this book provide greater detail on the metrics and data available from online transactions. This type of data fits neatly, if not cleanly, into the category of internal data, as it comes directly from prospect and donor interaction with your organization. As such, we know that data can be critical to online giving analytics. We worry about clean data, because if it is not clear that the data are accurate, they may be misleading in subsequent analyses. If a hit is a metric you collect and analyze but the calculation of a hit results in inflated totals (see Steve McLaughlin's chapter herein for more on this issue), the data as a descriptive or predictive tool are suspect.

Online metrics are intriguing and will be the focal point of online giving analytics as we take that practice beyond a calculation of the amount we raise online and how that compares to the online dollars raised by peer organizations. The ultimate focus of online giving is determining the potential we have to raise through that medium by understanding the profiles and motivations of donors, and as I discuss earlier and later in this chapter, it is ascertaining the short- and long-term paths that donors will take with the organization, or identifying those donors who will not sustain a relationship with us. Online data that intrigue me include the following:

- Unique identified visitors
- Click-through rate
- Conversion rate
- Deliverability rate
- Open rate
- Form-completion rate

Correlating these activities with ultimate giving performance and donor retention and combining demographic and financial data with these transactional fields to further refine profiles are the future of online giving analytics within the framework of the larger organizational fundraising picture.

Finally, there is another source of data that is frequently ignored in data-mining exercises or collected in a manner that renders it almost useless in analytical efforts. I speak of attitudinal and survey data that empowers us to build stronger relationships with our donors and prospects. And e-mail, the Internet, and other social networking venues offer you an opportunity to survey your constituents effectively and inexpensively.

Jump Start If you want to jump-start or revitalize your donor relations efforts, then asking your constituents direct questions through surveys is the best way to accomplish this goal, short of highly personalized activities such as personal meetings and phone calls. Most everyone talks about donor-centered fundraising, but few truly practice it. Surveys ask constituents for feedback that helps your organization evaluate your services, elevate your stewardship and donor relations, and provide data that may be invaluable in determining the future strength of the philanthropic relationship. My research and observations demonstrate that individual respondents to surveys will increase their gift or membership support more rapidly after they participate in survey activities. Furthermore, if you tailor your communication stream to reflect the interests and wishes of your best prospects and donors, their affinity for your organization and their financial support is more likely to approach their ultimate giving potential.

For purposes of this chapter, we are most interested in the data that we can gather from surveys as opposed to the survey process or mechanism itself. However, I would like to share with you a few quick recommendations for the preparations of surveys:

1. Keep the survey tool simple and easy to complete.
2. Limit the number of questions asked, and minimize the time needed to complete the entire questionnaire.
3. Do not ask questions that respondents might consider too personal, such as household income inquiries.
4. To be able to use the data in analytical exercises, limit or eliminate open-ended response questions and instead opt for multiple-choice responses.
5. To keep balance in the survey responses, make sure that the multiple choices offer an equal number of positive and negative replies to avoid skewing the potential responses, such as "How would you rate the content of our quarterly newsletter?" (very good, good, average, poor, or very poor).

Asking questions similar to the example in point 5 allows you to collect and aggregate data that can be used to determine meaningful relationships in your database. By using some of the data-mining and statistical techniques that will be explained later in this chapter, you can analyze the relationship between certain response choices and giving or membership behavior, which will help you target prospects for upgrades or transitional gifts. Specific answers or combinations of answers may provide the information you need to identify online donors with additional gift potential.

I have two final points to make about the collection of survey data. First, when you ask your best constituents to provide you with information and they honor that request, make sure that you use that information to improve your fundraising and communication efforts. Ensure that the collected data is added to your constituent database once individual or household-specific replies are received. Second, create a report with the aggregated survey data and share it with your constituents so that they know you appreciate their input and use the data for the benefit of your organization. If the survey is transmitted online or through e-mail, publish the results on your web site and send e-mail to respondents directing them to the results and thanking them for their participation. Send a different e-mail to nonrespondents briefly summarizing the survey results, allowing them to connect to the full report on the web site, and reminding them that their participation in responses is still appreciated. This may boost your response rate and open doors for relationship building.

At the end of the day, which internal data items should you collect for effective data mining or predictive modeling? The answer starts with the obvious, such as valid home address (use the National Change of Address service to keep current on changing addresses), an accurate name for the prospect or prospects, employment information (e.g., job title, business address), and information about the family (e.g., relationship or marital status, number of children in the household). Next, you want information that identifies the relationship the individual has with your organization, such as the constituency to which he or she belongs (e.g., alumni, members, friends, staff), and you really want to know whether the relationship to your organization spans multiple constituency groupings.

Now that we know who they are, their family information, and perhaps what they do for a living, it is most helpful to know how often we are in touch with each individual prospect. Which solicitation methods do we use and, if at all possible, to which solicitation did they respond favorably with a gift? How often do they give, how many years have they given, and at what level and through which vehicles have they given? Do they attend events? If they do, which events do they attend, and how many in a year? These data will help us understand whether our relationship-building and communication efforts are working and perhaps even give us insights into whether our efforts are too intrusive in the lives of our donors.

If you have these data available to you, you are on the inside track for doing valuable data analysis. If you have only some of this data available, make plans to initiate data collection efforts to increase the width in the depths of your CRM database. Do not forgo data analyis because your database is not perfect; in truth, it never will be. The analytical process usually triggers better data collection efforts, and in the end, your organization and its constituents can benefit from this exercise.

This is a good time for a helpful hint I have gleaned from the many excellent data specialists with whom I have worked: One of the biggest issues in data collection is ensuring that new or updated information is entered in a consistent manner. Establish rules for how data are entered into each separate field. Minimize the choices available to data entry personnel by using tools such as drop-down menus.

External Data

A simple definition of external data is information that exists outside of your normal information-gathering practices for your organization. There is no clear-cut definition of the differences between external and internal data, as data that are external to one organization, such as age, may be part of internal data for another institution. For example, educational institutions readily have age information available for their alumni, whereas most nonprofit institutions cannot easily collect age information on their constituents without relying on an outside source. The point is that you will know the data that are currently external to your CRM, and you will have two ways to collect it: engage in an effort to get that information from your constituents or acquire the data from commercial or governmental sources.

I could dedicate the remaining words in this chapter to a discussion of data sources, and its critical importance to fundraising analytics would warrant that concentration. However, I need to link data to analytics, and therefore I'll will concentrate on three sources or types of external data.

U.S. Census Data   As you know, the U.S. Census Bureau conducts a national census every 10 years, and the next version of that is here in 2010. From discussions I've had with fundraisers across the entire country, there is significant skepticism at the data compiled through the census and the strength of this information when it's used as input for descriptive or predictive modeling. However, the statisticians with whom I have worked over the past 16 years believe that the census data offers valuable insights into the individuals and families that comprise a database.

Census data is compiled and marketed by companies such as Easy Analytic Software Inc. (EASI)[1] In general, this data is updated annually by statisticians and demographers. My colleagues find that the data retain their viability during the 10-year period between the national censuses and add descriptive and predictive substance to the internal data we currently collect. Census data is significantly less expensive than most other external data sources and is a great alternative for your organization if you have decided to pursue fundraising analytics or data mining on your own. If you decide later that contracting for statistical analyses is the best solution for your organization, your data investment is minimal, and you may be able to make the data you have purchased available to the statistical consultant.

Over the years, we observe that there are many census variables that demonstrate measureable statistical significance in building predictive models. The following list is merely suggestive, not exhaustive, of these important variables, and I offer these examples as a taste of the contents of the census database:

- Number of persons in a household
- Owner-occupied housing
- Quality-of-life index, created from a combination of several other variables
- Proportion of households in certain age groups, such as ages 45–54, based on head of household data
- Education, specifically proportion with graduate school
- Consumer Price Index
- Proportion enrolled in private K–12 school
- Home value
- Length of residence
- Per capita income

Although census data is not reported at the household level—it is aggregated into groupings of households—it enhances the data in your CRM and enables additional segmentation opportunities among your donors, lapsed donors, and prospects. The simple fact that data in your electronic database is reported at the individual or household level means that, even when using aggregated data, the scores you create in your analytical profiling can be unique by individual or household.

Demographic or Lifestyle Cluster Data   Cluster codes began as a tool for market segmentation based on a desire to group people with similar characteristics. The underlying assumption is that people with similar characteristics will exhibit similar needs or desires in consuming goods and services or, in the case on philanthropy, in the causes or missions that they support.

Cluster codes were originally based on geodemography, which is the practice of assigning similar or predominant characteristics of individuals or households located within a defined geographic area, such as a five- or nine-digit (called zip + 4) zip code or block group. The applicable geographic grouping is assigned a code, which in turn links to the characteristics of the group. Improvements in the creation of marketing clusters now permit the assignment of codes at a household level. Some of the best-known clustering systems are: Niches, offered by Equifax; PRIZM, created by Claritas Inc. and owned by the Nielsen Company; and PersonicX, created by Acxiom. Because I am most familiar with Niches—we use it in our data analysis—I will use that clustering system as an example.

Equifax created 26 marketing niches from an analysis of the predominant characteristics of its database of more than 115 million individuals. The niches combine variables such as age, income, buying behavior, and interests through a proprietary statistical analysis and assign a distinct niche for each household. The system further segments the niches into 108 super niches that provide greater detail and specificity. The following is a niche description from the explanatory material shared by Equifax with its clients and customers.

> Niche A—Already Affluent
> Average Age: 29
> Average Income: $166K
>
> The households in this Niche are extremely upscale, both with respect to their earnings and their propensity to spend. The household typically consists of two adults between the ages of 18 and 34 with no children. They own their homes with an average value of $221,000 and are more likely to have a length of residence less than 5 years. They are highly educated with most completing college or graduate school.
>
> The majority of the households are employed in professional, technical, managerial and sales/service occupations. They own credit cards and are known to be mail responsive and purchase items thru the mail. They purchase more electronics than the population and they are very enthusiastic about moneymaking opportunities, real estate investments and stock and bond investments.
>
> These households enjoy the pleasures of high society: wines, gourmet foods, fashion, travel and cultural events. They are extremely fitness conscious and are heavily into exercise and self improvement. This Niche

enjoys active outdoor sports such as snow skiing, tennis, golf, running, jogging and biking. They also enjoy reading, photography and casino gambling.

Clustering systems are another valuable source of external data for use in fundraising and online analytics. The descriptive nature of the clusters may be very insightful as you seek to identify appropriate messaging for various segments in your database. Used in this way, the analytical component is already done for you—the process of appending clusters to your database includes the analysis done by the statisticians creating the system. Your primary task is to evaluate the meaning of each marketing cluster as it relates to your mission and then translate that into an action plan for your online giving program.

Zip + 4 Summarized Credit Data   Privacy concerns, professional ethics, and government regulations control the availability of many types of data that would have high predictive content. Bank transactions, Internal Revenue Service files, and credit reports are protected, as well they should be.

Fortunately, zip + 4 summarized credit data offer tremendous predictive capacities and behavioral insights that satisfy the concerns of privacy, ethics, and the law. The source data for this file is actual credit data, but all personal information is compiled within a zip + 4, the individual identifiers are removed, and statistical averages are created for each of the credit report variables. Each household in the zip + 4, typically comprising between 7 and 10 households in total, receives the same value for each of the compiled variables.

Your initial reaction may be that the aggregated and averaged data is far less predictive than credit-specific data. We know, however, after using these data in constructing thousands of models that the loss in predictive power is not statistically significant. In other words, the compiled variables combined with the household or individual specific data in your internal CRM form a great team in predicting the behavior of donors and prospects across the spectrum of philanthropic behavior: online giving and membership, direct-mail and telemarketing responsiveness, major giving, planned giving, and other related activities. We know that these data, when used with accepted and tested predictive modeling techniques, yield better information on donor behavior than hard asset or wealth data do on their own.

The zip + 4 summarized credit data available through Equifax (our data source), Experian, TransUnion, and other commercial vendors is wide and deep in its coverage, providing hundreds of data variables on all credit consumers in the United States. Many of the zip + 4 summarized variables have predictive value in fundraising analytics, but over the years, certain variables used in concert with others emerge as strong elements in the giving equation, including the following:

- Household income
- Home equity
- Ratio of credit balance to available credit
- Mortgage value
- Length of residence
- Age
- Credit card usage
- Mail-responsive-buyer indicator
- Mail-responsive-donor indicator

Using internal data with most or all of the external sources of data results in models with greater predictive strength in almost all instances, but the external data comes with costs to your organization However, licensing these data and performing the analysis on behalf of your organization may actually be more expensive than contracting with a nonprofit consultant or predictive modeling specialty firm.

THE WORLD OF THE POSSIBLE–STATISTICAL METHODOLOGIES AND APPLICATIONS

To successfully apply the results of data mining or statistical modeling, you do not need to be conversant in statistical methodologies. You need to frame the question to be answered and supply the data to be analyzed, but in the industry there are numerous resources to call on to assist in the analysis. Once that is done, honor your commitment to the analytical process by interpreting the data and acting on the results in a timely and dedicated manner. Follow this strategy, and you increase your chance of successful implementation significantly.

There are other pitfalls to be aware of, and I identify those through the use of a few quotes about statistics:

1. "The only science that enables different experts using the same figures to draw different conclusions."[2] Using a sports analogy, the same outfielder last on your team in batting average may also be the hottest hitter on the team, based on his recent 9-for-12 hitting spree. In this case, it is the depth of the data that changes the analysis. In fundraising, you may have data from an e-mail vendor that demonstrates that sending more e-mail

to your prospects generates additional giving revenue. The vendor's recommendation is to increase e-mail solicitations. A different consultant, for example, may agree that in the short-term that is indeed the result, but he or she may encourage a long-term analysis of donor retention and upgrading behavior to see whether there is an inverse relationship between the number of solicitations and donor loyalty and growth.

2. "Then there is the man who drowned crossing a stream with an average depth of six inches."[3] However, that may mean that the range of the water's depth is from one inch to twelve feet! Certain statistical measures are both valuable and misleading, depending on the application of the measure. For example, the average gift for all donors may be skewed by a few extremely large gifts, whereas the average gift for an e-mail solicitation is likely to yield a more meaningful measure. In addition to the average (or mean) gift, other useful measures are median (the middle value in gifts made), mode (the most common or frequent value), and range (the dispersion of gift values from lowest to highest). Using these measures in combination offers greater insights and prevents you from being misled by one statistic.

3. "Smoking is one of the leading causes of statistics."[4] Knebel, author of *Seven Days in May*, one of my favorite books, introduces the concept of causality in this funny quote. Jennifer Key, a longtime colleague, friend, and statistics mentor, first introduced the statistical maxim "correlation does not imply causality" to me, and it is a valuable lesson to remember. Two variables may seem highly correlated, but it can't be assumed or perhaps proved that one causes the other. It is possible that a third variable influences the first two variables; that the relationship is totally coincidental; or that the cause is related to a larger issue, such as data collection. My favorite example of "correlation does not imply causality" is related to the topic of this chapter. Using descriptive statistics, you discover that most of your best annual donors also have e-mail addresses in your database. Someone, not you, concludes that people with e-mail addresses are more likely to give. Wrong! The most likely conclusion is that donors are more likely to provide an e-mail address to you than nondonors are as you collect data in the giving process through such means as completed response cards.

4. "He uses statistics as a drunken man uses a lamppost—for support, rather than illumination."[5] Data mining and predictive analytics work best when approached with an open mind and a willingness to let the data drive the results rather than trying to seek a specific answer. If you hope to prove a particular point, it is possible that the data collection and analysis reflect the bias of the answer you seek. For example, for many years, fundraising research into the characteristics of planned giving donors concluded that

these contributors were older and wealthy individuals, and that fit the consensus in the industry, because it was observed behavior from top prospects. When we study planned-giving behavior without that bias and take a comprehensive look at all types of planned-giving donors, we realize that the historical belief fits only a small number of actual donors and is really the exception, not the rule. If you are willing to have your beliefs or assumptions proved wrong, you will likely find the true path in your data.

5. "To improve quality and productivity from current levels, changes must be made in the way you are presently doing things. We should like to have good data to serve as a rational basis on which to make these changes. The following questions must then be addressed: What data should be collected? and, Once collected, how should they be analyzed? Statistics is the science that addresses these questions."[6] Enough said—let's review some of our statistical options.

Definitions

There are three top-level definitions to discuss first: data mining, descriptive statistics, and predictive modeling:

Data mining: Data mining is not an analytical procedure; it is the identification of relevant or insightful data from a database search, particularly your constituent database. The mining activity uncovers data to be used in descriptive and predictive statistics. Data mining may reveal holes in your database that you can repair through better data acquisition and maintenance practices.

Descriptive statistics: Descriptive statistics derive from the application of mathematical procedures to describe the characteristics of a group. Common math tools such as average or mean, mode, median, range, and standard deviation are examples of descriptive statistics. The statistics are applicable to the population on which they are created and cannot be used to correctly infer a characteristic or characteristics of a different population.

Predictive modeling: Also known as statistical modeling, predictive modeling seeks to identify meaningful relationships between the dependent variable (the action you are trying to predict, such as giving) and independent variables (e.g., age, income, gender, home ownership). Modeling explores current and historical data to determine the variables that best fit and predict the identified behavior. Because it looks at characteristics that correlate with giving other than giving itself, it may be applied to score or rate prospects who are not currently giving. "Regression analysis," "logistic regression," "probit regression," and "neural networks" are terms that describe predictive modeling procedures.

The following brief discussion may help clarify the distinctions among data mining, predictive statistics, and predictive modeling. To conduct online giving analysis, your first step is to mine your database for information that may be important to your effort, such as the online metrics that your software system collects and the demographics available for each prospect and donor. From this, you create a descriptive statistic, such as the average age of donors who are making their first gift online. It is relevant only in the description of online donors and, of course, may suggest strategies for messaging content. Predictive modeling is used to determine the likelihood of any prospect making a gift online, on the basis of the profile of your online donors, and it uses combinations of multiple variables to create the algorithm (equation) that generates that score.

Descriptive Statistics—Single Variable or Univariate Analysis

The statistical term for analyzing one variable at a time is "univariate analysis." Compared to predictive statistics and multiple regression modeling this is a simpler method for analyzing meaningful relationships on your database. Although the analysis focuses on a single factor at a time, it may uncover a relationship that reveals definitive action plans. Univariate analysis describes trends on your database, and this knowledge is often actionable.

Age of Online Donors   The first example is an analysis of the age of individuals making their first online gift compared to the age of first-time direct-mail donors. Of course, you can look at the distribution of age by giving medium separately, but I think it is valuable to visually compare and contrast the ages of donors giving through e-mail, direct mail, special events, and telemarketing.

Age is such a highly descriptive and predictive variable that, if it is unavailable to you, I strongly recommend that you purchase what is known in the nonprofit community as an age append. These data are available from database vendors, list vendors, and marketing research databases. I know from personal experience that not all the data is completely accurate, and I would never recommend sending birthday cards to your constituents based on purchased age data, but for analytical purposes, it is extremely valuable.

Figure 12.2 tracks the age of online donors versus the age of direct-mail contributors. Please note that this data set does not represent any one organization and is not necessarily indicative of current trends in the nonprofit industry,

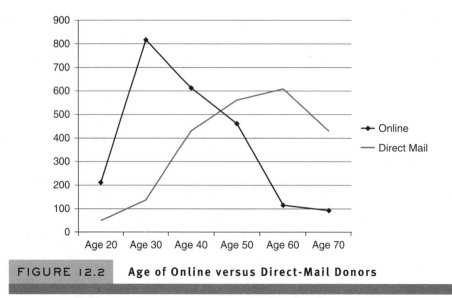

FIGURE 12.2   **Age of Online versus Direct-Mail Donors**

although I have derived the data from my experience with actual clients. Please do not use this graph as a benchmark for your own organization, as it is not created to serve that purpose.

Although Figure 12.2 does not represent findings that apply to your organization, I recommend that you perform age analysis on direct-mail, e-mail, and telemarketing donors. The results will help you refine your target audience for each solicitation method and provide insights into message content. There is no doubt that age is frequently an important variable in analyzing philanthropic behavior.

We all know that the cost of soliciting donors and prospects via e-mail is most attractive compared to the cost of expensive direct-mail packages and telemarketing efforts. We know, in general, that individuals giving online are likely to be transacting other business and personal activities online, as well. With this in mind, as the online giving population ages, you will want to continue to track the age of first respondents by type of solicitation, as well as the age of ongoing or loyal donors by type of solicitation. It is this type of longitudinal analysis—the evaluation of statistical data on the same subject matter over a period of time—that provides us with the best trend analysis specific to our organization.

Years to Give $1,000   The next example is an analysis of the number of years a donor has contributed to your organization before making a gift of a significant amount. The actual amount is a figure that is significant to your organization, but in this example I have used the $1,000 threshold as the measuring factor.

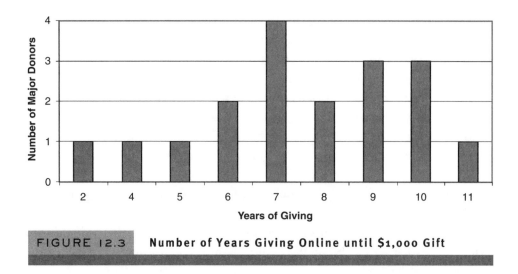

FIGURE 12.3   **Number of Years Giving Online until $1,ooo Gift**

I have found in my work with hundreds of organizations that $1,000 is often a launching pad for major giving behavior. Use an appropriate gift amount for your organization. In Figure 12.3, I have used a sample of actual nonprofit giving data to illustrate this point.

This is a simple example with only eighteen donor observations. Calculate the average (7.5 years of giving), the median (falls between 7 and 8), the mode (7 years), and the range (from 2 to 11 years). In this instance, I suggest that the range is not very useful to you, although the other measures are.

The analytical techniques I use to calculate these measures are easy, but interpreting the results and acting on the findings may be more difficult. Using the statistics and visualizing the chart shows that around year 5 or 6 giving increases and that year 7 is almost magical (although this is a small sample size just used for illustration). What do you do with these data?

This analysis reveals that most $1,000 donors develop over time, or in other words, you will see them coming before they make the larger gift. Establish a threshold number of years of giving – such as five years, in the current example – and establish a policy that your donor relations and stewardship activities will become highly targeted once a donor reaches the threshold. This proactive step encourages the development of a donor relationship that often accelerates the giving process.

Cluster Analysis   In an earlier section, I discussed cluster data and how they could become one of the arrows that you have available in your data quiver. A quick, easy, and effective way to use cluster data in your online giving analytics is to append these data to the entire database you will solicit through a variety of different means and strategies. Once the data have been appended, you can begin the analysis by looking at which cluster groups are dominant in the respondent or donor group. It is equally beneficial to look at the dominant clusters in the nonrespondent or nondonor group.

So, let's assume that you discover that 48 percent of your online donors fall into two of the Equifax niche clusters, that 56 percent of those solicited via e-mail who do not respond fall into three distinct niche clusters, and that the clusters that describe e-mail nonrespondents overlap significantly with the clusters that describe direct-mail respondents. Perhaps this may not be the result for your organization, but whatever the results might be, the following thinking about implementation will be helpful to you.

Your e-mail donors cluster most readily into Niche A, Already Affluent, and Niche F, Feathering the Nest. We've already read about Niche A, and here's a description of Niche F:

> **Niche F, Feathering the Nest:** The households in this niche are mostly young, although some are just young at heart. There is a very high incidence of children in this niche. These households are one and a half times more likely to be employed in professional, technical, or managerial occupations than the general population. The majority of the households in this niche are highly educated and own their homes, valued at about $218,000. They have shorter length of residence, typically six years or less. In addition to buying items for their children, they use their many credit cards to buy electronics (like video recorders), videos, books, CDs, fashion clothing, and home workshop products. They are mail responsive and purchase items through all mediums: retail, mail, catalog, and Internet. This niche is into physical fitness and is overall very active.

These descriptions are edited versions from an Equifax document, but I've included elements of the descriptions that provide insight into possible marketing, cultivation, and messaging strategies. Both of these cluster groups represent younger populations, which correlates with existing research on online donors. They are financially successful, highly educated groups who are likely to own their own homes. Niche F, however, represents households beginning to build their families, and that creates a whole new set of interests, as well as different buying and saving patterns.

So what do we do with this information? This simple cluster analysis is insightful, but it also serves as a reminder that it is worth doing only if it causes us to review our current behavior, consider improvements in messaging and targeting, and test or act on the ideas suggested by the analysis. In the foregoing example, I want to look at additional descriptive statistics, such as average gift, giving frequency, mode and median gifts, and giving range, to determine how the clustering characteristics manifest in actual giving behavior. If the additional analysis indicates that households in Niche F are more consistent in their giving but contribute, on average, far less money than Niche A, then I have data that may lead me to adjust ask amounts to the respective clusters. Furthermore, the contents of the e-mail package or message could be adjusted to reflect the areas of interest of each cluster. As I stated earlier in this chapter, cluster data are not always accurate for each and every household with that clustering score, but they offer a chance to deliver a message more appropriate for the majority of that group.

Taking the application of the analysis a step further, as we seek to engage donors in a stronger relationship with our organization, we might explore recognition events designed to feed into their interests and make them more likely to attend and participate. Special recognition events targeted to Niche F would take into consideration the likely presence of children in the household, perhaps an event that allows for donors to participate with their children. Both Niche A and Niche F households are interested in outdoor activities, so an activity or event such as a walkathon may appeal to both groups.

In addition, looking at the cluster characteristics of nondonors to e-mail solicitations and identifying, in this instance, that the clusters overlap significantly with direct-mail respondents suggests that e-mail solicitations for these households may not be the preferred method of engagement. Don't let the low costs of e-mail solicitations drive you to an ongoing barrage of online contacts with an audience unlikely to positively respond. You may be undermining your donor relations and stewardship connections with these households simply because the e-mail solicitations are so inexpensive. In my opinion, that scenario constitutes cost-centered donor relations, not donor-centered stewardship. Donor-centered stewardship is essential to a successful ultimate or lifetime giving strategy.

Predictive or Statistical Modeling

I admit to having a strong bias toward statistical modeling and its application for analyzing giving potential for nonprofit organizations. It has been the foundation of my work for nonprofits over the past 20 years, and I am convinced that not only do I want to know applicable descriptive statistics on my constituents, donors, and prospects, but also I really want to know which individuals will follow certain paths in their donor development. Predictive modeling enables the greatest insights into the types of gifts the best prospects will consider. The days of concentrating our best fundraising efforts on only the identified wealthy in our constituency are over.

As I considered the scope of this chapter, I made the decision to focus on the applications of predictive modeling rather than any lengthy discussions of the different modeling techniques available to nonprofit professionals. For most organizations, the key decision is a determination of whether you will build the predictive model or models or retain an outside expert or firm specializing in statistical modeling and predictive analytics for nonprofits. If you choose the latter route, the expert makes a decision on the technique to be used on the basis of his or her experience and the type of question to be answered.

If you or a colleague have statistical expertise and want to conduct the analysis on your own, please be aware that the practice of predictive modeling is time intensive; it is unlikely that your current job requirements will be lessened; the acquisition of supplementary data may be costly; and certain models, such as major giving or planned-giving likelihood, are more difficult to construct. In addition, as more and better data become available on web site giving, such as the aforementioned click-through and unique-identified-visitor categories, determining how to handle these variables in the modeling process may be most problematic for individuals who are not full-time statisticians. In fact, it is the knowledge of how to treat data and perform necessary data transformations that differentiates experienced and successful statisticians from the rest or, conversely, that causes significant problems for the inexperienced.

The model-building process creates an algorithm, a mathematical equation that indicates which variables, usually selected from a group of hundreds of variables, are most strongly correlated with the activity you want to predict. Let's use a major gift model for illustration. A major gift model may contain the following three variables: age, household income, and size of mortgage. Household income is found to have a positive correlation with major giving, so that an individual's likelihood of making a major gift increases as household income rises. In contrast, likelihood to make a major gift may decrease as the size of the household mortgage increases, and this is a negative correlation. Finally, age may exhibit a quadratic relationship with major giving, so that as prospects age, perhaps through the ages of 40 to 60, their likelihood of making a major gift increases and then plateaus between the ages of 60 and 70 and finally begins to decrease beyond the age of 70. Each of these variables may have a different value or weight in the calculation of the comprehensive modeling score that likely includes additional variables. This weighting concept is more readily understood in the pie charts to follow later in this chapter.

Continuing with this example, for each individual in the database to be analyzed, the model creates a score that ranks that person's likelihood of making a major gift. The score ranks the probability of that action occurring, and in the system I am accustomed to using, scores are distributed from 0 to 1,000, with higher scores correlating with greater likelihood. A perfect score is not a guarantee that the person will give; rather, it is an indication that the individual possesses identical characteristics to the profile of a major donor to your organization. It is also possible, and indeed likely, that some of your best major donors receive scores lower than expected on the basis of their giving history. It is important to remember that a predictive model will show that some individuals do not fit the common profile of the majority of major donors to your institution. This creates an important rule to remember: Although predictive modeling is very accurate at assessing likelihood of giving, low scores may be assigned to current donors who do not resemble the created profile for your organization, so giving history is always a reality check on a predictive modeling score.

As we will see in the following illustrations, predictive models and the corresponding probability or likelihood scores yield clearer pictures of the characteristics of donors and permit the development of more sophisticated cultivation and solicitation strategies.

Predictive Models for Online Giving   The most relevant initial question to be addressed in predictive modeling for online giving is the overall profile of individuals contributing to your organization through online methods. The question could be general in nature, seeking the characteristics of anyone who contributes through your web site, or more specific, identifying the attributes of individuals solicited first by e-mail who then click through to your web site to make a donation. If your organization also continues to solicit annual gifts through more traditional methods such as direct mail, a predictive model identifying the characteristics of those donors will be useful as well.

Let's examine the creation of the model for individuals who give through your web site on receipt of an e-mail. To build the model, you will need data on those who were solicited, including both respondents and nonrespondents. Internal data, such as relationship to your organization and prior giving behavior, may be combined with external factors, such as household income and occupation, and the statistical software will sort through all the potential combinations of variables to identify a group that best predicts online giving behavior to your organization. Statisticians agree that one of the best ways to determine the viability of the model is to construct the model using a random sample (model sample) of half of your file and to hold out the other half (known as a holdout sample) for model testing. A model created on the first file is applied to the holdout sample to determine how accurately that model predicts past giving behavior of that group. There are various statistical tests to determine how well the model fits and predicts, and those are used to provide the best candidate model for your implementation purposes.

Figure 12.4 is a pie chart representing a theoretical e-mail giving model for a college or university. This model includes six variables that best predict future e-mail giving activity on the basis of the profile of individuals who already give online to your organization.

The story behind the six variables, or the interpretation of the model, is as follows: Alumni most likely to give by responding to an e-mail solicitation by this

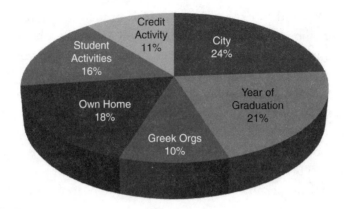

| FIGURE 12.4 | Higher Education Online Giving Model |

university live in certain cities within 200 miles of campus, graduated between 5 and 20 years ago, own their home, participated in student activities during their college years, are active consumers of credit instruments, and belonged to a Greek organization as a student. An individual closely fitting those characteristics receives a score closer to 1,000; conversely, an older alumnus living 1,000 miles from campus in a retirement home receives a significantly lower score.

For me, the beauty of predictive modeling is that the characteristics described here allow for the identification of e-mail–responsive prospects who have not previously given, and are far more valuable than descriptive statistics in identifying the best prospects among the non-donor population. The ability to know individuals most likely to give to you in the future allows for fine-tuning the application of your limited or strained fundraising resources.

Going one step further, let's now look at the model built to predict direct-mail contributors to the university. Figure 12.5 represents a model constructed on donors to the direct-mail campaigns conducted over the past 12 months.

The interpretation of the model in Figure 12.5 is as follows: Alumni most likely to give in response to a direct-mail solicitation are members of the alumni association, live in certain cities or states, graduated between 20 and 40 years ago, are employed in professional positions, and have at least two children still living at home. In addition to giving to their university, they also actively support health-care institutions and initiatives.

As you can see, the models offer different profiles of donors by type of solicitation effort. Applying both models to your database produces two scores that offer easy-to-implement segmentation strategies for your e-mail and direct-mail solicitation programs. Using the 0 to 1,000 scoring framework, you may decide to e-mail anyone who previously gave to an e-mail request or with a likelihood score in excess of 500, regardless of past giving behavior. You may

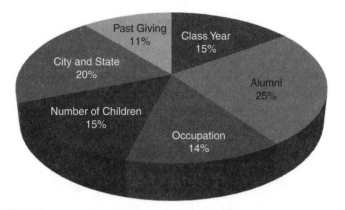

FIGURE 12.5   **Higher Education Direct-Mail Giving**

employ the same strategy for direct mail, and perhaps use a combined approach for nondonors scoring greater than 500 on both models. The interpretation of the actual models allows for more detailed segmentation strategies that are too numerous to mention in this chapter.

As your online giving program grows in sophistication and experiential data, modeling opportunities increase. An interesting topic to explore will be the growth in giving by online donors, so that you can build model to predict which of your lower-level online donors resemble other donors who have begun to make transitional annual gifts online. The pie chart in Figure 12.6 represents a theoretical model identifying the characteristics of transitional online donors (in this instance described as gifts of $1,000 or more).

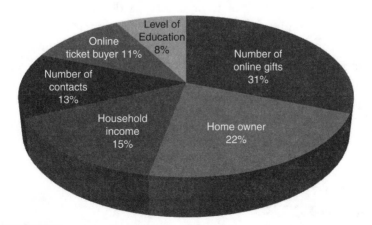

FIGURE 12.6   **Transitional Giving Model**

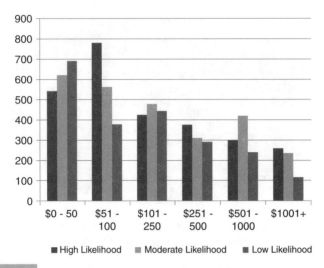

FIGURE 12.7   **Likelihood and Capacity of Giving Online**

Using this model to score your entire pool of online donors identifies individual donors with the greatest upgrade potential. Your packaging, e-mail messaging, and web site can be tailored so that you direct information supporting increased giving opportunities to the very prospects who are most likely to upgrade their current levels of support. In other words, the right message gets to the people who are most likely to act on the request.

Finally, one of the more difficult models to build is a target gift range model that assigns a projected annual gift amount to donors and prospects on the basis of past giving characteristics and financial and demographic attributes. The model allows you to drill down into more specific ask amounts or gift arrays, and perhaps most important, to stop asking all of your donors for the same contribution regardless of their ability to do so. An added benefit of this model is that implementation experience has shown that some prospects have remained nondonors in part because of an incorrect (low) gift ask that fails to motivate a charitable gift reaction. Subsequent requests with higher ask amounts have generated new donors with limited risk. (How much do you worry about possibly offending nondonors by asking for too much?) The chart in Figure 12.7 combines online giving and target gift range scores to reveal growth potential.

THE FUTURE OF ONLINE GIVING ANALYTICS

The future of online giving analytics begins with the adaption of even the simplest data-mining and analytical strategies by organizations that are currently starting and expanding their e-mail and web site giving programs. The thirst for knowledge and greater understanding of online donors, and specifically the path these donors take in a relationship to an organization to hopefully reach their ultimate gift potential, starts with data collection and intellectual curiosity. It continues with an interest in determining the best online or Internet strategies to result in long-term donor development, because we know that donor retention leads to enhanced lifetime donor value.

I have had the good fortune of living through and participating in a tremendous expansion of fundraising analytics in the past 20 years. What we do now in analyzing the giving potential on nonprofit databases is light-years beyond what we practiced two decades ago, in large part because of the intellectual curiosity driving the collection of better data to add to our analytical mix. One of the noticeable improvements in data collection is the validity of transactional data captured by nonprofit organizations. In the online giving arena, those transactional data will allow us to track the path our donors follow in making a gift online. In turn, those data enable us to further adjust and refine our messaging and our web pages and to improve on the cultivation and stewardship of this emerging class of philanthropic donors.

Lawrence C. Henze has worked in the nonprofit sector for the past 29 years, the first 13 of which focused on development and marketing positions in the not-for-profit sector, primarily in higher education. In October 1998, Henze formed Core Data Services, a market research and quantitative analysis firm specializing in the application of predictive modeling services to the nonprofit marketplace. Blackbaud Inc. purchased Core Data on March 1, 2001, and created a new business unit, Blackbaud Analytics, which was renamed Target Analytics in 2008. Henze frequently speaks at nonprofit conferences in the United States and Canada, works with a variety of Target Analytics' clients as a senior consultant, and helps develop new services for the company. In the process of working with clients at Blackbaud and in his previous positions at Econometrics and Noel Levitz, he has accumulated a wealth of knowledge on the financial, demographic, and attitudinal characteristics of philanthropic donors in the United States. He has pioneered the application of statistical analysis to fundraising in North America. Henze earned his bachelor of arts degree in political science from Wisconsin's Carroll University and a master of arts in public policy and administration and a juris doctor from the University of Wisconsin-Madison.

CHAPTER 13

No Borders

LEVERAGING THE INTERNET TO FUNDRAISE INTERNATIONALLY

ANDREW MOSAWI AND ANITA YUEN

In 1989, a young British man, Dave Gotts, visited an orphanage in China and was profoundly moved by what he saw. Wondering why more was not being done, he decided to take it on himself to do something. He started a charity, International China Concern, dedicated to working with the Chinese government to support disabled and abandoned children in the region. He learned Mandarin and started to volunteer at orphanages, eventually bringing in teams of doctors and nurses for months at a time.

Over the years, International China Concern has cared for hundreds of children in China and has run programs in the community that are designed to reduce the stigma associated with disability. Gotts is based in Vancouver, although the organization has charitable status in Canada, the United Kingdom, the United States, and Australia.

As a small charity supported primarily through volunteers, the organization's approach to fundraising is extremely focused. There is, of course, a significant Asian community in Vancouver, which provides a good source of major donors and some large corporations with interests in the region. That was originally enough to fund the programs.

However, as the need for the organization's services increased, it realized that it needed to expand. It was turning away children because there simply was not space. An opportunity arose to buy a building that would serve as another orphanage, so the charity needed to find an additional stream of revenue.

International China Concern decided to have a walkathon event to raise money. It would consist of teams of people in more than six countries all walking 10 kilometers which, combined, would add up to the length of the Great Wall of China. They called the event Walk the Wall (http://www.walkthewall.org).

It was a creative concept, and one that resonated with a lot of people. The organization set up a simple online service that allowed people to register and donate, and by leveraging the viral nature of the web, the group raised awareness, interest and ultimately money. More than 1,000 people from around the world took part, and the charity raised almost $200,000, enough to buy the building.

This true story demonstrates the ever-evolving relationship among globalization, philanthropy, and technology:

1. Consider the charity itself: an almost completely virtual organization with offices around the world, staffed predominantly with English-speaking personnel providing services in China.

2. Consider the way the organization benefits from the increased mobility that globalization has brought.

3. Consider the way technology facilitated and enhanced fundraising activities and achieved something that only a few years before would have been impossible.

Globalization is a combination of economic, technological, sociocultural, and political forces.[1] Philanthropy touches each one of these quite directly, and as a result, it can be argued that no other sector will be affected as greatly by this trend. In this chapter, we will look at the current status of globalization and philanthropy and at how technology plays a part in both affecting and influencing our behavior. We will demonstrate ways that organizations are taking advantage of this trend and leveraging the latest tools to fundraise internationally, some with great success. We will then outline specific ways that you can prepare your organization to take advantage of the Internet to fundraise internationally.

Although there is no silver bullet to fundraising, especially international fundraising, our goal is to provide insight into the wonderful world of global philanthropy and the tools that make it possible.

WORLDWIDE TECHNOLOGY USAGE AND TRENDS

The radical growth of the Internet is well documented, and yet it is hard to overstate its impact. There were approximately 1.6 billion Internet users around the world in 2009, compared to 360 million in 2000 (see Figure 13.1).

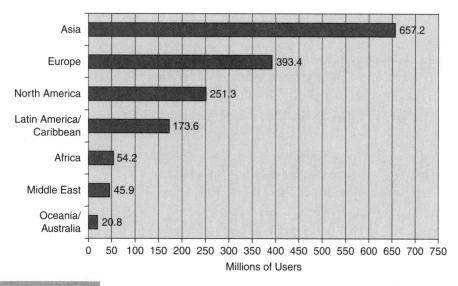

FIGURE 13.1   **Internet Users in the World by Geographic Regions**
Source: http://www.internetworldstats.com.

Productivity without connectivity now seems counterintuitive. We take for granted that a tool that was not available when many of us went to college now defines every part of our day. In 2002, 70 percent of Americans already claimed that they "couldn't live" without the Internet.[2] In Hong Kong, where 77 percent of residents have Internet access (compared to 48 percent in Europe), only 14 percent said they could live without the Internet.[3]

Access to computers and the Internet is now pervasive and in many cases a necessary part of daily life. Indeed, according to the One Laptop per Child project, "When children have access to this type of tool they get engaged in their own education. They learn, share, create, and collaborate. They become connected to each other, to the world and to a brighter future."

However, the growth in technology consumption is not limited to computers and the Internet. Cell phone usage has increased at a much higher rate. There are now 2.7 billion mobile phones in use, and by 2006, more than 30 countries had exceeded 100 percent per capita mobile phone use. Globally, there are twice as many active users of short text messaging (SMS) as there are active e-mail accounts. Interestingly, although 65 percent of global e-mail is spam, only 10 percent of SMS is spam. As much as 62 percent of people with cell phones state that they primarily use SMS as a way to connect with their friends.[4]

Consumers in some countries, India for example, leapfrog PC-based technologies altogether and buy only cell phones, either because of the expense of a computer or because cell technology has advanced so much that a computer is redundant.

The innovative ways that nonprofits use available technologies is fascinating. In 2008, through a pilot project, a nonprofit looking for ways to support poor farmers in Ethiopia and protect them from fraud provided them with cell phones and sent them daily market prices for grain through SMS. Immediately, the farmers were empowered with this information to negotiate better prices for their stock when dealing with wholesalers, who until then could give them incorrect (and unverifiable) information about grain prices.

The Grameen Foundation has also found an ingenious way of using mobile phones to alleviate poverty. They provide a cell phone to an individual in a village and allow that person to rent it out to other villagers, thus providing both a job and a source of communication that the village would otherwise not have. Grameen is now the largest mobile phone operator in Bangladesh.

Hilmi Quraishi is one of the growing number of social entrepreneurs that has used technology as both business and a way to effect change. He distributes extremely popular games for mobile phones that teach players about AIDS.

Since he started distributing the games in 2005, Quraishi has reached tens of millions of young people, first in India and now in Africa—regions especially hard hit by HIV/AIDS and where cell phones are nearly ubiquitous—with games designed to appeal to their passions for gaming and technology.

And in a more direct use of cellular technology to bring about positive change, tuberculosis patients in Thailand are given cell phones and sent a text message when it is time for them to take their medication.

That these types of technology are becoming modern necessities is nothing new. How they are changing the way we interact with one another, however, has significant implications.

MOBILITY AND GLOBAL AWARENESS

According to the Institute for Public Policy Research, 5.5 million U.K. residents (or approximately 10 percent) opted to live abroad in 2006. In 2001 (the last time a census was taken), more than 250,000 of those had immigrated to Canada. In Dubai, the population is made up predominantly of expatriates, from countries such as India, Pakistan, Bangladesh, and the Philippines, with only 20 percent of the population made up of citizens of the United Arab Emirates.[5] Clearly, as increasingly global citizens, we no longer spend our lives in one job, town, or even country. This poses a challenge and, more often than not, an opportunity for nonprofit organizations.

Diaspora fundraising describes the work that some organizations are doing to target a specific community (usually of a certain nationality or ethnic

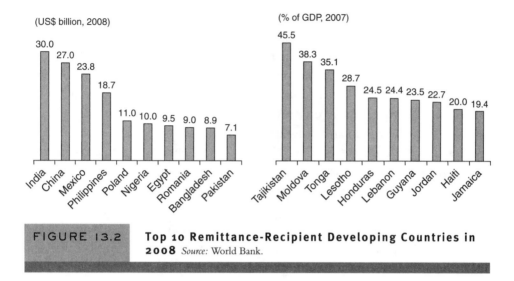

(US$ billion, 2008)

(% of GDP, 2007)

30.0
27.0
23.8
18.7
11.0 10.0 9.5 9.0 8.9 7.1
India China Mexico Philippines Poland Nigeria Egypt Romania Bangladesh Pakistan

45.5
38.3 35.1
28.7
24.5 24.4 23.5 22.7 20.0 19.4
Tajikistan Moldova Tonga Lesotho Honduras Lebanon Guyana Jordan Haiti Jamaica

FIGURE 13.2   **Top 10 Remittance-Recipient Developing Countries in 2008** *Source:* World Bank.

background) within a country. The word "diaspora" comes from Greek, meaning "the scattering of seeds."[6] The volume of the remittances from people living abroad is quite astounding; the World Bank estimated them at US$283 billion in 2008. A breakdown of where this money is going can be seen in Figure 13.2.

An example of diaspora fundraising would be Reconnect (http://www.reconnect.org.ph), a giving portal launched in 2008 in the Philippines. The aim of the site is to link nongovernmental organizations (NGOs) in that country with the huge Filipino diaspora around the world. More than 9 million people from the Philippines live and work abroad.[7]

The tremendous outpouring of support and money for international causes can be statistically proven (the 2008 Giving USA report had giving to international causes as the highest growth area from 2007), but more often it can be seen circumstantially. From Live Aid back in the 1980s to the Haiti earthquake in 2010, we are constantly reminded of people's increasing global awareness and their desire to support those in need.

Thomas Fuller, a 17th century English historian, said that charity begins at home. The interesting question now for us as donors, charities, and foundations is where exactly home is.

INTERACTION

Technology has always been the driving force in facilitating communication. Hundreds of years ago we were able to connect only with those who were within walking distance or, if for the rich enough, horseback. The Industrial

Revolution changed the way we think about distance, and today many of us think nothing of jumping on a plane and traveling several thousands of miles for a meeting. The world started to shrink.

However, this didn't fundamentally change the way we interacted with people. The telephone didn't extend our circle of friends; it just gave us a way to communicate with existing ones. Air travel gave us access to new cultures and countries but did not in and of itself make us friends.

The Internet changed all that. The average Facebook user has 120 friends, and those friends are just as likely to be in another country as in the next street.[8] Although this might or might not translate into more face-to-face relationships, it undoubtedly extends our networks, allows us to stay in touch with people we have not seen in years (and who might not live where we live anymore), and allows us to forge new contacts based not just on live interaction but also (and most important to the fundraiser) on common interests and beliefs.

THE WORLD AROUND US

Why do you rob banks? Because that's where the money is.

—WILLY SUTTON

Many organizations are looking outside their own markets to fundraise. What does philanthropy look like around the world, and what trends are emerging that make it so attractive?

To truly understand today's international opportunities, it is necessary to look at the philanthropic landscape around the world (see Figure 13.3). Myriad of political, legislative, cultural, and socioeconomic variables have to align to make fundraising an option in any country. Here we give an overview and sampling of a few countries to demonstrate the vast differences between them. A great way to provide a view on a country's approach to philanthropy is to analyze what tax relief is available for charitable donations. Some examples follow:[9]

- **The Netherlands**: Donations between 1- and 10 percent of gross income are eligible.
- **Ireland**: There is a minimum threshold of €250, but no upper limit on eligible donations.
- **Germany**: Donations up to 5 percent of annual taxable income are eligible.
- **France**: Donors can deduct up to 60 percent of the value of their donations.
- **South Africa**: 5 percent of a donor's taxable income is deductible.

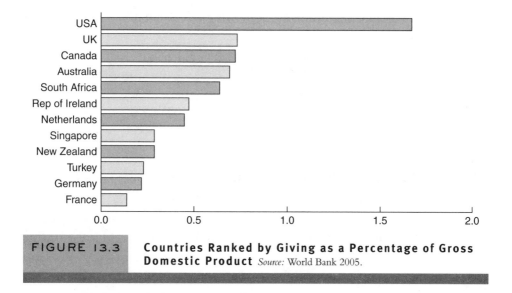

FIGURE 13.3   **Countries Ranked by Giving as a Percentage of Gross Domestic Product** *Source:* World Bank 2005.

- **Canada**: Variable tax credit depending on the size of the gift. A gift of $200 or less attracts a 17 percent tax credit, and higher-value gifts attract as much as 29 percent.

- **United States**: Aims to boost philanthropy by making all charitable donations fully tax deductible for those who itemize tax returns.

Taxes, of course, are not the only measure of maturity or opportunity within a country, nor are tax credits necessarily the driving force behind most donations. There are wonderful examples of innovative fundraising that represent the growing philanthropic sector around the world.

Singapore is a great example of a country that historically had challenges for international fundraising. There was a law that required organizations to spend at least 80 percent of the money raised in Singapore in Singapore. That law has since been amended, making it an extremely attractive proposition for many international NGOs, primarily because the small country has more millionaires than any other in the region.[10] The growing sector has had some remarkable success stories: The National University of Singapore set its annual fundraising goal at $7 million back in 2003 and ultimately brought in 11 times that amount.

Dubai Cares, launched in September 2007, has as its mission to "bring the community of Dubai together to focus on raising funds to provide one million children with access to primary education." Although the campaign's original fundraising target was AED 200 million, the 2007 campaign exceeded expectations and raised AED 1.7 billion through donations. At the closing event on November 25, 2007, H. H. Sheikh Mohammed announced he would match every dirham raised during the campaign, bringing the total to AED 3.4 billion (or approximately US$1 billion).[11]

The underlying theme here is, of course, that people, no matter which country they live in or come from, want to participate. They want to give back. They want to make a difference. Technology is helping them do just that.

Impact

The Internet is not only allowing people from around the world to give back to organizations and causes they care about but it also is allowing donors to get a much clearer sense of where their donation is actually being spent. The use of technology is enabling the increasing demand of donors to track the impact they are having when they support a cause or organization. There is an emerging trend among many of those who use the Internet to want to see the immediate impact they are having on a campaign, a program or the people that they are supporting. Digital technologies are now allowing supporters to get an inside view into the impact that they are having by providing rich storytelling and immediate feedback to the donor.

The tremendous success of Kiva demonstrates this point excellently. Kiva.org is a nonprofit organization that has taken the concept of micro-lending to the web. Instead of donating money to an organization that serves a region, a user can log on to Kiva and lend money to a specific individual who needs a specific sum of money for a specific purpose. It may be a farmer who needs money to buy a tool or a tailor who needs a new sewing machine. That beneficiary, facilitated by Kiva, builds the profile and "ask," and a community of lenders can choose to support them.

As of June 2009 Kiva.org had received more than US$77 million dollars in loans from half a million lenders (see Figure 13.4).[12] Much of Kiva's success has stemmed from the high degree of impact it allows its lenders to have on the lives of the beneficiaries it features and the high level of transparency its web site enables by connecting lenders directly with beneficiaries. What is extraordinary is that the repayment rates of the loans is higher than 98 percent. That is an impressive and telling trend.

Turning Donors into Fundraisers

Just as the web is helping to enable people to track exactly where and how their money is spent, the Internet is also allowing donors to do more than simply donate, allowing people to fundraise themselves on the organization's behalf.

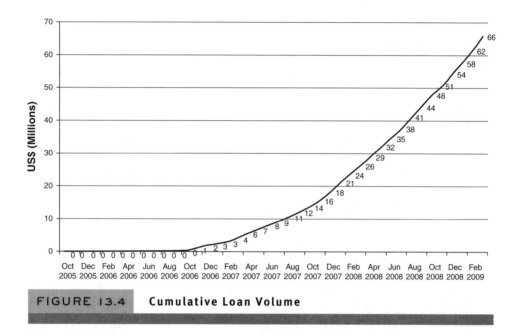

FIGURE 13.4   **Cumulative Loan Volume**

Gone are the days when you would take a piece of paper and knock on doors to get your neighbors to sponsor you. Now sophisticated online tools dedicated only to raising money are available that make it extremely easy to raise money. The book *People to People Fundraising* has some excellent examples of running these kinds of events and how to leverage technology to do so.[13]

The critical concept here is not how technology helps organizations build, run, and manage fundraising events, but how it has helped turn the donor into a fundraiser. A donor may on his or her own contribute only $10 to a charity but that same donor may reach out to a network of friends and family, ask for their support on behalf of the cause, and raise $5,000. So the question is, how do you treat that donor? Did he or she really contribute only $10, or is he or she actually responsible for a $5,000 contribution? If so, then, is that donor a major donor?

The opportunity to leverage the power of an individual donor's network has enormous potential when we consider online networks. Donors now not only are a source of individual donations but also can become our advocates and spokespeople to their circle of friends, generating support, awareness, and funds for an organization's cause from people who might otherwise not have an interest in our mission, much less our specific organization. That most individuals are part of diverse (and often border-crossing) networks only expands this potential that much more.

DISSIPATING BORDERS—EMERGING OPPORTUNITIES

On June 20, 2009, a small group of schoolchildren in Silicon Valley were performing songs they had recently practiced in their music class. On the surface, there wasn't anything particularly special about this performance. What made it unique, however, was that the primary audience for this recital was a group of young children in a refugee camp in Chad—all watching the whole event online. Once the American students had finished their performance, the young refugees from Darfur responded with a drum routine for the children in the United States. Perhaps most remarkable, the entire event was witnessed by a global audience through a live feed on the Internet.

This unlikely encounter of a group of youngsters in an affluent suburb in the United States with a group of refugees in Chad was organized by the UN High Commissioner for Refugees (UNHCR) in celebration of World Refugee Day. In an innovative attempt to bring attention to the plight of refugees, UNHCR arranged a 12-hour live webcast linking some of its global operations to the rest of the world through the Internet (see Figure 13.5).

The live feed allowed viewers from all around the world to get an inside glimpse into a refugee camp in eastern Chad, meet internally displaced people in Colombia, and interact with UNHCR staff in Pakistan and Syria. Viewers were

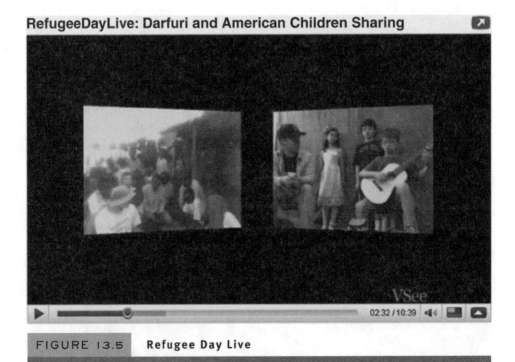

FIGURE 13.5   **Refugee Day Live**

able to ask questions to refugees and UNHCR field staff through moderators in the United States. In addition to the live feed, there were interactive elements to the webcast, such as an online chat so that viewers could comment on what they were witnessing as well as connect with one another. In this pioneering initiative, the live feed not only made the plight of refugees a very real and tangible problem to viewers but also brought home the reality that it would take very little for donors in wealthier parts of the world to assist UNHCR and ultimately help refugees.[14] In this way, technology brought potential donors closer to the plight of refugees.

The growing development of philanthropic giving around the world, the increasing mobility of people, and the rapid growth of Internet usage has opened up new and exciting opportunities for charities. Nonprofit organizations, like UNHCR today not only have the ability to use interactive technologies to reach audiences in more compelling and innovative ways; the Internet has made it relatively easy for charities to reach entirely new and more global audiences. Local, national, and international organizations can broaden their base of support by acquiring new donors and accessing additional funds through the Internet.

The rapid development of Internet technologies has reinforced the realization that local issues can have global appeal. This has opened up opportunities for underexposed causes to get increased attention and for organizations to begin to raise funds online from outside the borders of where an organization is based. The next question is, how do we as organizations leverage these opportunities and take action? In the next section of this chapter, we will explore just that.

New-Market Entry

Typically, when organizations have looked to expand their base of support by fundraising in new markets, it has been a lengthy and costly process. The extensive compilation of market research; the consultants who are brought in to produce a market-entry plan; and the time-consuming process of opening offices, recruiting staff, and setting up a board of directors has meant that accessing new donors in new markets has had very high up-front investments. Today, organizations seeking to enter new markets and generate additional income have the amazing possibility of cutting out all of these traditional steps and saving a lot of time and money by simply setting up a central online operation to target, acquire, and retain donors remotely.

Human Rights Watch (HRW) is an excellent example of an organization extending its geographical reach using its web site (see Figure 13.6). Human Rights Watch is an independent organization dedicated to defending and protecting human rights. Founded more than 30 years ago, HRW has headquarters in New York City, although it also has offices and runs programs around

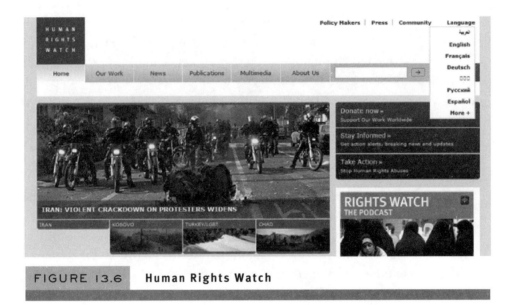

FIGURE 13.6 **Human Rights Watch**

the world. The HRW online presence offers more than 10 language options and allows donations in more than 20 currencies.

Heston Williams from HRW notes that approximately 80 percent of online donations come from the United States, although the amount raised from other countries is increasing steadily: "Not only are we seeing a trend that international giving is increasing, but we are also proactively focusing on international as a growth area online."

Williams believes that HRW is only just beginning to realize the opportunity of fundraising internationally. "We started by proving the most basic tools to allow those in other countries to engage and donate in their language and currency. We have seen a significant increase in donations just by doing that. Now though, we are at the stage where are we approaching this opportunity more strategically and laying down a path for our international aspirations."

Another convincing example of an organization that has accessed new donors in new markets through the Internet is the World Society for the Protection of Animals (WSPA). In September 2007, the WSPA, an animal welfare organization based in London, decided to begin testing remote new-market entry in Argentina and Mexico via the Internet. WSPA decided to use banner-ad creative and landing pages developed by its office in Australia and to set up a payment gateway to take in donations in pesos via a bank account in London (see Figure 13.7). After a one-month test, the organization had gained useful insights into the potential of fundraising online in both countries. The team had discovered that the test in Argentina failed with a return on investment of only 0.4, whereas the test in Mexico produced results that were nearly three times better. In one month, WSPA had successfully recruited approximately 550 monthly

| FIGURE 13.7 | **World Society for the Protection of Animals** |

givers with an average gift of more than $10 per month in Mexico; the results were approximately half that in Argentina.[15]

For an organization with no in-country presence and absolutely no brand recognition in either country, WSPA had successfully acquired new donors and was able to break-even in the first year with a net recruitment cost of zero. Perhaps more important, however, the organization had avoided all of the bureaucratic and legal headaches of setting up fundraising operations in both Mexico and Argentina and had a good sense of the fundraising potential in both countries based on results. These results have allowed the organization to make more informed investment decisions when entering a new market.[15]

TURNING DIGITAL OPPORTUNITIES INTO REALITY

So how does an organization embark on broadening its supporter base and begin to access new markets through the Internet? Below we outline some very basic steps that an organization should consider when entering a new market online.

Step 1: Understand the Activity and Define Objectives

Setting clear objectives for any digital activity always makes for a sound and effective strategy. When considering fundraising in a market that you may have little or no experience in, setting objectives for your activities is critical, as it will help define how you measure success. For instance, if the primary goal of running digital fundraising campaigns in new markets is to test the fundraising feasibility of setting up an in-country fundraising operation, then running tests in multiple markets with a long-term view might be advisable. This will help your organization make informed investment decisions and decide whether to develop a local presence. If your objective is to use the Internet to simply access additional income remotely, then you may want to set out an acceptable return on investment in a shorter period of time. If your activities are to better serve a particular group of international or diaspora donors, then you might deem the required investment as a necessary part of your overall online strategy. Defining objectives up front will help not only shape the type of digital activities you undertake but also determine the level of investment and establish the key performance indicators needed to measure success.

Step 2: Target Markets

To truly understand the potential your organization may have to raise funds in new markets, it is important to map out which countries might provide you with a good testing ground for acquiring donors. Looking at elements such as your cause, your current online donors, and market research can all help you make some educated guesses as to which markets might yield positive results.

With fundraising operations in more than 60 different countries, UNICEF has been tremendously successful in generating income from virtually every corner of the globe. Much of the organization's fundraising infrastructure was developed decades ago, at a time when the Internet didn't exist and supporters would never have even dreamed of making a donation online. Today UNICEF's fundraising is run from nationally based operations with local staff that fundraise for its global programs to assist children. However, with the rapid development of global Internet usage and the organization's global appeal to donors, the organization takes in an increasing amount of online income from countries where UNICEF has no in-country fundraising presence. On the basis of previous years of experience with unsolicited online donations, the organization already has some insight into which markets could be good testing grounds for new-market expansion for UNICEF via the Internet.

Reflecting on your organization's cause and the kind of people that your mission might appeal to is a good starting point. Many organizations like UNICEF may already have relevant information that may indicate which countries have high online fundraising potential based on where current online donations are already coming from (see Figure 13.8).

Market research is another tool that can help you evaluate which countries or regions hold the highest online fundraising potential. Awareness of the level

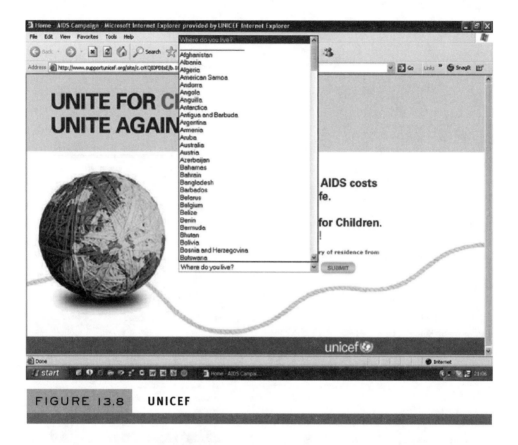

FIGURE 13.8   UNICEF

of Internet access and the development of e-commerce in markets where you are considering running online fundraising campaigns will help you assess how comfortable potential donors might be with giving to your organization online. UNICEF recently undertook an e-readiness assessment survey of 47 individual countries to better understand the relative market maturity, growth patterns, and underlying digital trends in each market (see Figure 13.9). Part of the value of such research is that it will allow the organization to make informed investment decisions related to digital fundraising activities and gain insight into digital recruitment methods that would be most effective for the recruitment of donors online. By evaluating the drivers, barriers, and key trends of Internet usage, e-commerce, and digital marketing, UNICEF is able to gauge which markets might hold the most promise for using the Internet to acquire and retain new donors.

Step 3: Set Up a Global, Online Fundraising Infrastructure

Once you have identified your objectives and assessed your target markets, the next step is to establish the necessary tools and technology to support online

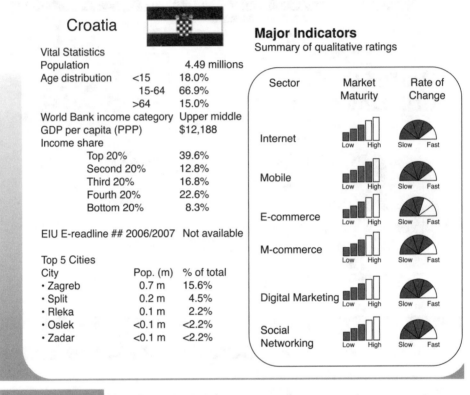

Croatia

Vital Statistics

Population		4.49 millions
Age distribution	<15	18.0%
	15-64	66.9%
	>64	15.0%
World Bank income category		Upper middle
GDP per capita (PPP)		$12,188
Income share		
	Top 20%	39.6%
	Second 20%	12.8%
	Third 20%	16.8%
	Fourth 20%	22.6%
	Bottom 20%	8.3%

EIU E-readline ## 2006/2007 Not available

Top 5 Cities

City	Pop. (m)	% of total
• Zagreb	0.7 m	15.6%
• Split	0.2 m	4.5%
• Rleka	0.1 m	2.2%
• Oslek	<0.1 m	<2.2%
• Zadar	<0.1 m	<2.2%

Major Indicators

Summary of qualitative ratings

Sector	Market Maturity	Rate of Change
Internet	Low — High	Slow — Fast
Mobile	Low — High	Slow — Fast
E-commerce	Low — High	Slow — Fast
M-commerce	Low — High	Slow — Fast
Digital Marketing	Low — High	Slow — Fast
Social Networking	Low — High	Slow — Fast

FIGURE 13.9   UNICEF, Croatia

fundraising activities abroad. The temptation might be to simply use your current online giving systems and tools that work for you domestically— processing donations in your own domestic currency and languages. However, the ability to process online donations in local languages and currencies and to facilitate the use of local payment methods such as debit cards, credit cards, and other locally preferred payment methods such as PayPal will help improve the online giving experience for new donors and ultimately increase the number of single and regular donations you are likely to generate. Human Rights Watch offers donors the ability to donate in a variety of languages and currencies, which provides an enhanced online experience for its supporters (see Figure 13.10).

By customizing donation forms and allowing for local language and data capture, you can provide a more localized look and feel to acquisition campaigns in new markets. Likewise, donation confirmation pages, web pages, and e-mail correspondence should ideally be customizable in the language used in order to cultivate a particular donor. Finally, many countries have the possibility of tax deductions or other governmental incentives to encourage people to donate.

FIGURE 13.10   **Human Rights Watch**

To better serve donors in new countries, it is important to ensure that you facilitate and take advantage of any local incentives by offering these online or providing the appropriate type of receipts to your donors.

Step 4: Test

Once you have set up the necessary online fundraising infrastructure, you are ready to begin testing online acquisition campaigns. An online acquisition test may involve one or more countries; using similar or slightly different creative approaches and messaging; and a range of digital techniques, such as display advertising, e-mail marketing, search engine marketing, and so on. If purchasing or bidding on ad space one approach might be to use one agency that can help you to coordinate your campaigns by doing the media buying centrally. As your campaigns mature you may eventually want to draw upon local expertise to help with purchasing and placement of online ad inventory or other initiatives. There are many different approaches to running online fundraising campaigns, but the critical point is that only a series of robust tests allowing you to try different approaches and capture the results will provide you with hands-on knowledge as to what techniques and messaging will work for your organization. Finally, having a system that can adequately provide real-time reports as well as analytics is critical to running an insightful test. Whatever your approach to testing or your specific digital tactics, you will be able to gather results almost immediately. On this basis, you can optimize your campaigns and ultimately make informed decisions about which digital tactics work best for your organization.

IDENTIFYING THE NECESSARY LEVEL OF INVESTMENT

For organizations considering expanding their reach and generating income outside their own borders, it is often difficult to determine the level of required investment and human resources. There is often a misperception that Internet activities are free. Although using the Internet to attract international donors can be far more cost effective and efficient than setting up local infrastructure, the implementation of a toolset for international Internet fundraising and the running of digital campaigns abroad does require some investment.

The price tag to set up tools to launch Internet campaigns in new markets will vary greatly depending on the level of customization and functionality you require. However the upfront costs for digital campaigns can be relatively low compared to some other types of offline acquisition activity and the ability of organizations to closely monitor the performance of their campaigns means that charities can increase or decrease investment based on performance relatively easily. Finally, one often overlooked consideration when assessing the necessary level of investment in digital campaigning is the need to have a human resource available to manage and drive the development of an international online donor program. Many organizations that are currently recruiting international donors online have an internal resource, if not a team inside the organization to manage the entire process. One thing that cannot be overly stated is that having a dedicated human resource is a necessary element to effectively leveraging the Internet to fundraise internationally.

CONCLUSION

Although tapping into global philanthropy may at first seem like an attempt to boil the ocean, there is a clear systematic approach that can be taken and duplicated to produce results. By identifying your objectives, targeting which markets you want to access, setting up global online fundraising tools, and running robust tests, you will begin to gain a solid insight into which markets might yield new donors and ultimately provide additional income cost-effectively for your organization.

As donors become increasingly global citizens, there is an expectation that we as organizations must follow suit. With the rapid growth of Internet penetration and the development of e-commerce around the world, people are now using technology to actively support, advocate for, and donate to their preferred causes. The rise of the Internet has dawned a new era in global philanthropy, allowing organizations to access donors from all over the world. Individuals are already showing a strong desire to give online to causes they care about—are you ready?

Andrew Mosawi is the vice president of international business development at Blackbaud Inc., the leading provider of software and services to nonprofit organizations worldwide. In his role, Andrew leads the company's efforts in serving the international nonprofit community.

Anita Yuen has been advising national and international nonprofits on the use of interactive media for fundraising, advocacy, and marketing campaigns for over 10 years. In her current role, Anita is responsible for leading UNICEF's global digital fundraising initiatives and maximizing income through its network of national offices. Prior to joining UNICEF, Anita directed digital fundraising program at the World Food Programme and the International Red Cross.

PART III

Making Technology Work for Your Organization

CHAPTER 14

Effective Web Design

ALLAN PRESSEL

In this chapter, you will learn how to create and manage an e-philanthropy web site that has a lot for your web site visitors not only to see but also, more important, a lot for them to do. You'll learn about the five site criteria you should strive for in your site. We'll analyze the seven effective components of an effective web site. We'll discuss what to implement and how—along with key goals and management techniques. We'll examine specifically what you want your web site visitors to do—to support you, not just read about you—and how to structure your web site and Internet strategy to maximize the number of people who do those things. Some of these transactions are related to fundraising, and others are not, but all can provide a high degree of interactivity; site traffic; stickiness; return visitors; search engine rankings; and most important, results for your nonprofit. We'll analyze tools to help you accomplish all of this, and we'll talk about how to use and manage them.

FIVE SITE CRITERIA TO STRIVE FOR

Almost everything you do to build and maintain your web site should be done with the goal of achieving one or more of the following site criteria:

1. **Findability:** People should be able to find your site easily, using search engines or in other ways. Otherwise, even if you have a top-notch web site, it won't do you much good unless people can find it.

2. **Stickiness:** Most visitors probably spend fewer than 30 seconds on your web site. If so, there's almost no way that they have the time to do anything to support you. A sticky site keeps web site visitors on it for at least the two to three minutes they need to consummate a transaction, and hopefully for much longer.

3. **Loyalty:** Visitors are more likely to support you after they have visited your site multiple times than they are on their first visit to your site.

Therefore, your site should foster loyalty or return visits. One way to do this is to have a site and, particularly, a home page that is dynamic. Many nonprofits have a web site that changes little, if at all, over time. If so, it's unlikely that people will return to such a site.

4. **Referability:** You want your web site visitors to refer your site, or particular pages or transactions, to their friends, family, neighbors, and colleagues. You should try to have a site that not only encourages people to do this but also makes it easy for them to share electronically. You may even provide creative incentives for them to do so. This can help you launch a type of viral marketing campaign that has the potential to grow your support base exponentially.

5. **High conversion rate:** Your site's conversion rate is the percentage of web site visitors who are converted into donors, volunteers, event attendees, or whatever it is you want from them. If your site is a brochureware or information-only site, then, by definition, its conversion rate is zero. Even nonprofits that offer some form of online transactions (e.g., donations) typically have a very low conversion rate—much less than 1 percent—because they have implemented online donations in an ineffective way. We'll discuss how to remedy that here.

In the remainder of this chapter, you'll learn a number of ways to make your site more findable, sticky, loyal, and referable, along with how to achieve a high conversion rate.

SEVEN KEY COMPONENTS OF AN EFFECTIVE WEB SITE

Figure 14.1 depicts the seven key components of an effective web site. For each component, we'll examine what you should consider incorporating into your web site and how to manage it, both initially and on an ongoing basis.

1. Look and Feel

You have only one chance to make a good first impression on your web site visitor, and people will come to that impression within the first few seconds they visit your site—much as they do in social situations when meeting another person. Many nonprofits are not putting their best foot forward with respect to their web site. The web site should instantly convey an air of credibility, professionalism, and confidence.

Your home page should pass the 10-second test. That is, a visitor who has no idea what your nonprofit does should be able to accurately summarize what you

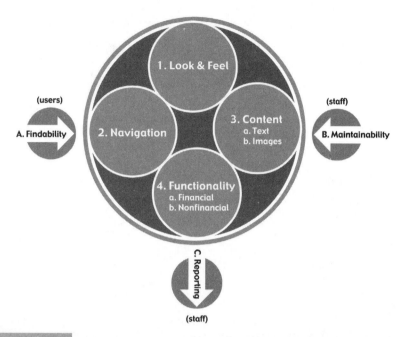

FIGURE 14.1   **Seven Components of an Effective Web Site**

do after only 10 seconds on your home page. You should try this with several folks!

Along with the site looking visually attractive, each page on the site should be designed so that any important information or functionality is above the fold. In other words, users should not have to scroll down to see it. Of course, the fold appears in different places for different users because of different monitor sizes, screen resolutions, window sizes, and so on.

Key Goals   Most nonprofits could benefit from having a graphic designer create a new look and feel for their site that is more of the following:

- Professional
- Attractive
- Modern
- Well branded
- Consistent across the site

Management Techniques   Here are some additional techniques to effectively manage your site's look and feel.

Create a marketing strategy. With or without the help of a marketing consultant, you should create an overall marketing strategy for your nonprofit, with your web site being an important piece of the strategy, and the look and feel being an important piece of the web site. Here are some key elements to consider in your marketing strategy:

- Web site
- Branding
- Messaging
- Identity (e.g., logo, business cards, letterhead)
- Brochure (paper and electronic)
- Search engine optimization, search engine marketing, and pay per click (PPC)
- Public relations
- Testimonials
- Success stories
- Speaking and writing engagements
- Communications (e.g., e-newsletters, e-mail blasts, urgent action alerts)
- Advertising
- Social media

Reflect your marketing strategy in your creative brief. If you are creating a site from scratch, or redesigning the global look and feel of your existing site, you should write a creative brief that lets your graphic designer know what your needs are for your web site design. Let the designer know what you like and dislike regarding web site design and include examples of overall layout, colors, fonts, sizes, images, animation, menu placement and style, and branding. You should also provide your specific requirements for messaging, content, functionality, and anything else you feel may be relevant for the designer. Make sure to include links to sites that incorporate some of the things you like or dislike. Give the designer as much guidance as possible, to maximize the likelihood that he or she will provide a design you like on the first try.

Select the right marketing agency or graphic designer. The most important way to select an agency or designer is to look at examples of the web sites they have created. Also, check to see how many of those are actually live sites. Sometimes agencies and designers show work that a client never actually used. Remember also that a great designer of print materials won't necessarily make a good web designer, so be sure to look for someone with lots of web site design experience. Finally, most web designers approach their work primarily or entirely from an aesthetic perspective. As important as looks are, there are other important skills a good web designer should bring to the table when designing an e-philanthropy site, including the following:

- **Marketing skills:** The designer should view your web site project as an integral part of your overall marketing efforts, and it should be designed to be consistent with and complement those efforts.
- **Fundraising skills:** After all, you're probably going to be trying to raise lots of money through your site!
- **Communications skills:** It is essential that your web site effectively communicate your message. Bear in mind, your web site is the most foundational element of your communications plan.
- **Content skills:** The content on your site, particularly your home page, will help to get your site recognized by search engines, reinforce the message created by your design, and contribute to the visitor's impression of your site and organization.
- **Search engine skills:** Your site's design can have a significant role in its search engine ranking.

This combination of skills can be difficult to find in a marketing or web site agency, but with some searching, particularly by looking at the designers of nonprofit (or even for-profit) sites you like, you should be able to find one.

Provide graphic design guidelines. It can be helpful to you and the designer if you agree in advance on your graphic design guidelines. These guidelines should be based on the types of visitors you expect to draw to your site. We'll discuss that further in the "Navigation" section. Most important, ensure that your design is created to fit your content, not vice versa.

2. Navigation

Many nonprofits have valuable content on their sites, but it can be difficult for users to navigate through the site to find the information they need. Your users should be able to easily find what they're looking for on your site and should ideally be able to get from any page of your site to any other page with just one click.

Key Goals   Your site's navigation should

- Be simple
- Be intuitive
- Enable users to get from any page to any other page with one click

Management Techniques

- **Navigation review:** Periodically review navigation structure to make sure all information on all pages is easily accessible.
- **Exercise:** Here's an exercise that you can do to help think about what should be on your site.
  - The first part of the exercise is to think about the different types of visitors who might come to your site. For example, you might have donors and prospective donors, volunteers and prospective volunteers, staff and board members, prospective employees, event attendees, foundations, corporations, government agencies, clients, partner agencies, members of the local community, members of the press, and so on.
  - Next, step into the shoes of each type of visitor. For example, put on your donor hat and answer these two questions: As a donor, what do I want to see on the web site? What would I want to do on your site?
  - You'll find that the answers to these questions are likely to be quite different from one type of web site visitor to another and are also probably very different from what you have on your site today. The answer to what people want to do on your site is not an intuitive one. In the "Functionality" section herein, we'll discuss a number of examples.

3. Content

Many nonprofits assume that a visitor to their home page already knows what the nonprofit does. However, many first-time site visitors will have either no idea or an inaccurate or incomplete understanding of your mission. Some nonprofits have no description of what they do on their home page—or at least one that's meaningful and easy to find. Still others display a lengthy description that takes up valuable screen real estate with information that is essentially static. Instead, you should display a brief description—one sentence or less—and invite users to click to drill down into greater levels of detail.

Many nonprofit web sites have at least some good content, but often it's rather text heavy. Most sites could benefit from having more images. We'll discuss the specifics in the subsequent sections.

Text   Here are just a few things that people may want to see on your site:

- Home page
- Mission statement
- Services and programs
- Goals
- What's new

- Accomplishments
- Brief history
- Issues or causes
- Message from executive director
- Press releases
- Past events
- Urgent action alerts
- Testimonials
- Photo album
- Endorsements or awards
- Donor hall of fame
- Privacy and security policy
- Annual report
- IRS Form 990
- Documents to download
- How your organization can help
- Frequently asked questions
- Links
- Staff list and bios
- Board list and bios
- Contact information

You are likely to have some of these on our site already. Over time, your web site stickiness and findability will improve as you add new information and make your site more content rich.

Key Goals   Your site's content should be

- Well written
- Accurate
- Up to date
- Broken into small, bite-sized chunks (this may require breaking lengthy pages into several smaller ones)
- Dynamic (your home page content in particular should change at least monthly)
- Filled with calls to action, which hopefully will enable users to easily complete those actions on your web site

Management Techniques

- **Private areas:** You might want to have one or more private areas of your site, a board-only section, a staff-only section, or a members-only section. It could be password protected or not.

- **Foreign-language sites:** If you have a significant number of constituents who speak Spanish or other foreign languages, consider having a mirror image of your site in one or more foreign languages.

- **Online writing:** Accommodate the differences between writing for the web versus offline. For example:
  - Keep text short. Use bullet points. Keep paragraphs short. People tend to scan web sites, not read them.
  - Text that you post on your site should be interesting, credible, present your nonprofit and cause in a positive light, motivate the reader to take action (e.g., donate, volunteer, sign up for an event), well written, error free, and up to date.
  - Bear in mind that readers may skip around a particular page but typically start with content on the upper left and move in the shape of a "z" toward the lower right.
  - For long documents, create Adobe Acrobat PDF files or Word files and enable users to view, print, or download them.
  - Ask for donations wherever appropriate, but tie your request to content. For example, when describing a program, finish by saying something like, "Click here to help us provide food for those in our homeless shelter." Give people a reason to donate, not just because you are asking. Let people know what their donations will help you to accomplish.
  - Transparently and proactively let web site visitors know about your results, such as "Here's what we plan to do with your donation," "Here's what we are doing versus what we said we would do," and "Here's what we did."
  - Determine the presentation style for all text on your site, including font, size, style, foreground and background color, and so on. This decision might also be made by your web site designer.

- **Get feedback:** Solicit feedback from various types of users.

- **Be creative:** You can add cool items to your home page or other pages on your site, including quotes, news, jokes, horoscopes, YouTube, games, and more.

- **Accessibility:** Make your site accessible for users with disabilities. In the United States, your site should conform to the standards of the World Wide Web Consortium's Web Accessibility Initiative (see http://www.w3.org/WAI). Different countries might have different accessibility standards. You can test your site's compliance at http://webxact. watchfire.com.

- **Copyright:** If your web site displays a copyright statement, including the year, be sure to change it at the beginning of each year.

- **Compatibility with offline marketing:** Integrate and ensure compatibility between offline and online content.

- **Work flow:** Develop a work flow for planning, drafting, editing, proofreading, approving, and posting web site content. Be sure that all web site content is perfect. Even one misspelled word can give a negative impression.

- **Intellectual property:** Be sure to protect your intellectual property through copyrights, trademarks, patents, and other techniques.

- **Get permission:** Get permission when you use others' content.

- **Grant permission:** Have a consistent way to grant permission for others to use your content.

- **Private access:** Have procedures for granting and revoking access to private areas of your site.

Images   You probably have some images on your site, but you may need more. The adage "a picture says a thousand words" is especially true on the Internet. Images can be a powerful way to help convey the emotions you want to elicit from your web site visitors and get them to do the things you want them to do on your site—especially pictures of cute children and animals. In addition to your overall site's look and feel, page-specific images can powerfully convey and accentuate your message in ways that text alone cannot. You should strive to achieve a good balance between text and image content because search engines don't rank a site well if it is too image heavy. Accordingly, you should consider adding more images to your site, including the following:

- Photos
- Graphics
- Animation (e.g., animated GIF, Flash)
- Audio
- Video

Key Goals   Make your site more engaging and interesting by adding attractive, meaningful images. Provide visitors with more opportunity to gain a deeper understanding of your organization by viewing videos and listening to audio (e.g., podcasts).

Management Techniques

- **Free or low-cost images:** Here are some sites offering millions of free or low-cost, quality images for your web site:
  - For free photos, http://www.sxc.hu
  - For free or low-cost photos, http://community.webshots.com
  - For low-cost images, http://www.stockxpert.com
  - For royalty-free images by subscription, http://www.ablestock.com
  - For stock photos by subscription, http://www.photos.com
  - For 500 million searchable photos, images, and artwork, http://www.ditto.com
  - To search stock photography, http://www.randomeye.com
- **Free or low-cost templates and animation:** Here are sites offering low-cost or free web site templates and animation, including Flash. Warning: Unless you are extremely cash strapped, it is always best to have a custom-designed web site. Template sites typically look like templates and thus convey a poorer impression:
  - http://www.templatesbox.com
  - http://www.toseeka.com
  - http://www.ez4search.com
  - http://www.e-zekiel.com
  - http://www.freewebsitedesigns.net
- **Creating images:** Create your own photos and videos. Most people now have digital cameras or cell phones that take pictures and/or videos. FlipVideo—a mini camcorder—is also a quick and easy way to create videos and even provides direct upload into YouTube. Encourage your staff, board, and volunteers to take lots of pictures—of your events, programs, services, facility, personnel, and so on. Crop, resize, and post the best ones on your site. Be sure to get permission from people depicted in your images, especially if they are children (in which case you need to get permission from the parents).
- **Minimize the file size of each image:** Most images can be compressed with little to no sacrifice in image quality. This can reduce the load time for your web pages, the storage required to host your site, and your monthly bandwidth usage.

- **Buy custom images:** You can contract others to create your own images. Professional graphic designers, photographers, and videographers can create high quality images for your web site, often at special nonprofit rates.

- **Image tools:** Adobe Photoshop Album Starter Edition is a free tool that allows you to put your photos in a PDF document that you can upload to your web site just like any other PDF document. By using a link or menu, you can allow visitors to view all the images one at a time or in a slide show. Another tool, SnagIt, also enables you to resize images.

- **Zoho:** Zoho.com has loads of free, useful tools for you, including one enabling you to embed your own PowerPoint slide show in a site.

4. Functionality

Your web site should offer a lot for the web site visitor to do, not just see. Let's say you had a choice between these two hypothetical scenarios: (1) You had 10 million web site visitors per month visiting your web site, reading every word on your site but taking no action, and (2) you had not 10 million but 10 web site visitors per month, each spending only three minutes on your site, but each one taking some action to support you, such as donating, volunteering, buying event tickets, and so on. Which scenario would you prefer? Clearly, the second scenario is preferable. Even better would be a combination or the two scenarios: lots of visitors offering lots of support.

The point of all this is that you want people who visit your web site not only to read about you but also to engage with you and support you. Unfortunately, even today, most nonprofits offer little or nothing for their web site visitors to do.

So, what should people be able to do on your web site? Let's explore two categories of transactions. First, we'll examine financial or fundraising transactions. Then we'll discuss nonfinancial transactions.

Fundraising Transactions   Here are some financial transactions that you may want to have on your web site:

- Cash donations
- Events
- In-kind donations
- Membership
- E-store
- Auctions
- Walkathons or other such events

- Affiliate marketing
- Investment donations
- Planned giving

Cash Donations   When it comes to e-philanthropy, the most common thing people think of is online cash donations. However, most nonprofits collect few if any donations through their web site. There are many reasons why. Here are a few:

- Most nonprofits approach online donations in a way that is simplistic and ineffective. That is, they create a donation page and then cross their fingers hoping people will actually find it, and when they do, they are simply asked, How much would you like to donate, and what's your credit card information? You can certainly raise some money that way, but it's likely to be a lot less than you could. Your home page, and probably most or all other pages of your site, should have a clear, compelling call to action encouraging people to donate.

- The donation process should be easy—ideally one to two pages, without kicking the user off of your web site.

- The donation function can offer a number of features. These include recurring donations, the ability to pay by credit card or e-check, targeting donations toward a particular program or service or making them unrestricted, making the gift in someone else's name or in memory of a selected person, choosing from preset donation amounts, and more.

Other Ways to Support Your Organization

Give users choices about how to support you. After all, not everyone will want to take out their credit card or make a cash donation. Let's talk about some of the other options you may want to offer.

You may want to sell tickets to fundraising events, conferences, educational events, or other types of events. There are some good ways to solicit in-kind donations through your site. You may want people to pay or renew membership dues. You can sell things in an e-store, including items that pertain to your mission, promotional items, items from your bricks-and-mortar store, or in-kind donations you can't use.

You can conduct online auctions, perhaps in conjunction with a live, silent auction. This way, Internet bidders can bid against live bidders before or possibly even during your live auction. You could even have a 365-day-per-year auction, in which you periodically put items up for bidding (perhaps in-kind donations you're not using), leave them up for 7 to 10 days, and then sell them to the highest bidder.

You can offer walkathons and other similar events, races, or contests. For example, for a walkathon, walkers should be able to register online and perhaps pay an entry fee. They should receive a confirmation e-mail, plus a solicitation e-mail that they can then customize (or not) and forward to their friends and family, who can sponsor the walker a certain number of dollars per mile or a certain number of dollars overall.

You can also do affiliate marketing, in which you refer your web site visitors to other sites of interest and then collect commissions on any resulting sale. Also, you should solicit investment donations and various types of planned gifts through your site

Nonfinancial Transactions   Here are some nonfinancial transactions to consider for your web site:

- E-mail list sign-up
- Volunteer opportunities
- Employment
- E-newsletter
- E-advocacy
- Petitions
- E-cards
- Forms
- Public opinion poll
- Questionnaire
- Referrals
- User feedback
- Web 2.0 tools (e.g., discussion or message board, chat room, podcast, RSS, blog, wiki)

You may want people to sign up for your e-mail list, even indicating their specific areas of interest. In fact, research shows that your in-house list provides the highest return on investment in generating leads (e.g., donations, volunteers) That way, the information they get from you is pertinent to their needs, not just one size fits all. People should be able to volunteer, either by indicating their general interest or by applying for a specific volunteer position online. Similarly, people should be able to apply for specific jobs online by submitting their résumé and cover letter.

You may want to send out one or more types of e-newsletters. E-newsletters have many advantages over paper newsletters, including low cost, ability to create multiple different types of newsletters easily, ability to click through, the driving of people back to your web site, the ability to be easily forwarded to friends and family, and much more.

E-advocacy enables your web site visitors to write to their elected representatives and, potentially, complete e-petitions. Electronic greeting cards are another good way to drive more traffic to your site. Any form that people currently fill in on paper can now be completed online with online forms, not PDFs or Word attachments. Among the many advantages is the fact that users now do any data entry for these forms, not you, which effectively saves you nonprofit time and money.

You can use questionnaires or public opinion polls to gauge people's thoughts and feelings through your site. You can ask for referrals. This can be an effective way to initiate a form of viral marketing. Think about when you receive e-mail from friends or family asking you to support a nonprofit they care about. Often, if the recipients of those e-mails can provide that support (e.g., donations, walkathon sponsorships) easily and online, they will do so. Remember, people are always more likely to do something when it is easy, quick, and simple.

You can let people provide you feedback on your organization, your programs and services, your events, your facility, even on your web site and social networking presence. Of course, there are various types of social networking and communication tools that can enable you to create online communities of people with common interests, hopefully in ways that will add value both to them and to you. Some of these are external to your site, like Facebook, MySpace, LinkedIn, and Twitter.

Others tools can and probably should be on your site, like blogs and discussion forums. If you don't already have a blog, you should consider adding one to your site. It could be a short, weekly blog written by your executive director or board chair to provide an update about what's new with your nonprofit. You could even have one or more blogs written by a volunteer, staff member, or a client.

Key Goals   Ensure that you offer visitors not only a lot to see but more important a lot to do—financially and nonfinancially.

Management Techniques

- **Positive return on investment:** Set a goal that your web site should pay for itself, probably within the first year. This can be accomplished by increasing revenue, decreasing costs, or a combination of both. There are numerous ways to accomplish both through your site. Also, don't ignore the many intangible or less quantifiable benefits your site can provide, such as increased volunteers, planned gifts, in-kind donations, clients, and more.

- **Security:** If you are collecting personal information, particularly sensitive information such as credit card data, you must make sure that the pages where you collect that information are completely secure. This means that users should be able to see "https" (where the "s" stands for "secure") at the beginning of your web site address (URL) for those pages. You may also need to comply with other security requirements, such as Payment Card Industry Data Security Standard.

- **Privacy and security policy:** Once you collect personal information, you must post a privacy and security policy and, preferably, link to it from every page of your site. People will be more likely to donate to your nonprofit if they trust that their money will get to you and that their personal and financial information will not be misused or compromised. The Direct Marketing Association offers a free policy builder at http://www.the-dma.org/privacy/creating.shtml.

- **Reporting:** There are a number of reports you should be able to track to decide which transactions are working, how well, which you should continue or discontinue, and the impact of your efforts to drive more traffic to your site and promote specific transactions there. For more information, see the "Reporting and Analysis" section that follows.

- **Reconciliation:** Your accounting personnel may wish to reconcile the financial transactions flowing through your web site.

- **Online merchant account:** To process financial transactions securely on your site, you must have an online merchant account. Some nonprofits already have an offline merchant account, but this will not process online transactions. However, most online merchant accounts will handle both online and offline transactions. Of course, you must also comply with your merchant account provider's technical specifications.

- **Integration:** You should be able to share data between your web site and most other applications or databases. You should also be able to import or export virtually any data in any of a number of standard formats (e.g., comma delimited, tab delimited, extensible markup language).

5. Findability

Even if you were doing everything we've just talked about and you have a world-class, interactive web site, it still won't do you much good unless people are able to find it. So the concept of findability is critical. Perhaps the most effective techniques you can use to drive more traffic to your site are search engine optimization (SEO), search engine marketing (SEM), and pay per click (PPC). With SEO, you attempt to list your site at the top of the search engine's "natural" links, whereas SEM enables you to implement other ways to show up organically in search engines via interactive press releases, directories, videos, and so on. In contrast, PPC enables you to buy your way to the top by paying for specific keywords to be listed as a sponsored link at the top or to the right of natural links. There are literally dozens of SEO, SEM, and PPC techniques to help you get more traffic to your site—far too many to discuss here. Let's discuss just a few.

Perhaps the most effective way to boost your search engine ranking is to have lots of other sites link to yours. First, let's look at one way you can easily determine how many and which sites link to yours. Go to Google and in the search box, type "link:www.yournonprofit.org" and hit enter. You'll see which sites link to yours (called back links), and you can click through to each to determine exactly where those sites link to yours and what they are saying about you. It's likely that some of those sites have information about you that is incorrect. If so, contact them and ask them to correct it, probably by supplying them with the correct wording. Obviously, you want the number of sites that link to yours to be as high as possible. Therefore, you should think about which other organizations—relevant, reputable ones—might consent to linking from their site to yours. You should also have lots of links from your site to other sites. This should be easy for you to do, but limit the number of outgoing links to 100.

Another effective way to boost your search engine standing is to optimize your keywords and content. You need to identify keywords that sell for you and that are descriptive terms. You can get help selecting appropriate, popular keywords at the following sites:

- Google Zeitgeist, at http://www.google.com/press/zeitgeist
- Google AdWords Keyword Tool, at https://adwords.google.com/select/KeywordToolExternal
- Google Trends, at http://www.google.com/trends
- MSN Search Insider, at http://www.imagine-msn.com/insider
- Yahoo! Buzz Index, at http://buzz.yahoo.com

You can optimize keywords into the following three places: site content, metatags, and URLs. Metatags are simply pieces of HTML code embedded in your site that identify various characteristics of your site to search engines. There are about 15 types of metatags, but only two you should care about. Metadescriptions are a brief description of, say, your nonprofit or some aspect of it. Keyword metatags are words or phrases you want people to search for and then find your site. The following is sample HTML code for description and keyword metatags: <meta name="Keywords" content="keyword 1, keyword 2, keyword 3"> and <meta name="Description" content="This should be a 150 character or less description of your nonprofit">.

Let's first look at how you can find your metatags. From your home page, click "View" and then "Source" to see the HTML code behind your home page (this may vary from browser to browser). You can search for your keyword metatags by hitting "Control + F" and then typing the word "keyword." You may find that you don't have any metatags or that they are ineffective for several reasons. This will somewhat hinder the ability of search engine visitors to find your site. The good news is that you can easily implement effective metatags and even have different metatags on different pages of your site to help drive traffic directly to those pages.

You should also make sure that the content on any given page is relevant to the keywords embedded on that page. It is also helpful to include key-words in the URL for each page of your web site. For example, the URL http://www.nonprofitsite.org/abuse_victims is better for search optimization than the URL http://www.nonprofitsite.org/how_we_help, particularly if that page has "abuse victims" as a keyword metatag.

When using SEM or PPC, be sure to create one or more landing pages that cater to the specific reason that a user clicked on your ad. Typically, you should not link users to your home page, because that page usually caters to many different types of visitors who are looking to see and do a variety of things. Instead, direct users to a landing page that has only content that is directly related to the keywords and ad content that enticed them to click to your site in the first place. That landing page should probably feature one (or a few) calls to action. Some landing pages have little to no navigation to avoid confusing the user.

Key Goals

- Drive as many visitors as possible to your site.
- Maximize the relevance of those visitors to you; for example, you may not be interested in someone in Cambodia searching Google for information tangentially related to your mission.
- Use SEO to boost your search engine ranking.
- Use SEM to boost your search engine ranking.

Management Techniques

- **Website Grader:** You can run your site through an analyzer at http://www.websitegrader.com, which grades your site from 0 to 100 in terms of search engine effectiveness. The score is actually a percentile, so if your score is 90, that means that your site ranks in the 90th percentile of all sites in terms of search engine effectiveness. The average nonprofit scores about 55. If your score is less than 50, that means that it's somewhat difficult for users to find your site—but there's a lot of room for improvement!

- **Google PageRank:** Google has its own measure of the importance of each web page, called PageRank, and that rank is a number from 0 to 10. You can calculate the PageRank of your own pages or others' by downloading Google's free toolbar at http://toolbar.google.com or by checking individual pages at http://www.prchecker.info/check_page_rank.php.

- **Google Grants:** Google Grants (http://www.google.com/grants) is a service where you can apply for free Google AdWords for up to one year. Most nonprofits are accepted. Google values the service at around $10,000. What it doesn't tell you is that if you actively use the service, Google is likely to extend the free period indefinitely!

- **Social Media:** Use social media to boost your search engine ranking. Social media not only builds a following for your organization but also creates additional links to your site.

- **Track dead links:** You can identify any dead links at your site (which hurt your search engine standing and credibility with users) at http://www.dead-links.com.

6. Maintainability

Anyone in your organization—with permission, of course—should be able to build or change any aspect of your site quickly and with no training or technical skills. Tools are available that permit this level of maintainability.

Key Goals

- Anyone in your organization (with no training) should be able to build new pages and functionality while also maintaining a world-class, e-philanthropy web site—quickly and easily.

Management Techniques

- **Site maintenance permissions:** You should enable different personnel to have different access privileges to maintain your site. For example, you may want the development director to maintain the development section of your site and the programs or services director to maintain that portion.

- **Granting and revoking:** Develop procedures for granting and revoking access to your web site.

- **Work flow:** You may want to designate the procedures to follow for all web site changes. For example, you may have one person or group who proposes changes, another who edits them, another who approves them, and another who posts them to the site. This can ensure consistency of content, functionality, and look and feel across your site.

- **Soft launch versus hard launch:** Consider a soft launch instead of a hard launch. In a soft launch, you create your site but do not publicize it. You invite a controlled group of people—staff, board members, volunteers, and donors—to use it for a specified period of time. During this time, they can perform an intensive review and provide feedback, and you can add or modify features and perfect your content. With a hard launch, you pull out all the stops to promote your site and attach it to your URL. You may consider a soft launch followed by a hard launch about a month later.

- **Other management considerations:** Table 14.1 provides some key questions you may ask about the management of your site and typical answers given by nonprofits (of course, your answers may vary from these) along with ideal answers that you should strive to achieve.

7. Reporting and Analysis

Activity on your site generates a lot of valuable data. You should be able to report on the data, analyze it, and strategically use it. For example, you should be able to track your web site traffic. You should know how many people visited your site, when, and how they found your site? Did they find it through search engines? If so, which ones, and what keywords did they type in to find your site? Or did they find it through links from other sites? Which pages of your site did they visit? How long did they spend there?

Also, for each transaction on your site, you should be able to report on that transaction. For example, if you accept online donations, you should be able to analyze how many people gave you $100 or more last year but nothing yet this year, and then send those people an e-mail that essentially says, "Thanks for your generous donation last year, please click here to repeat or increase it this year." These are just two examples of reporting and analysis. Of course, there are many others.

TABLE 14.1   KEY QUESTIONS

Question	Typical Answer	Ideal Answer (Strive to Achieve This)	Explanation
Who maintains your site?	One person—an employee, volunteer, or paid web site developer	Anyone (with permission)	Most nonprofits are forced to rely on one or more people to maintain their site, which usually requires some level of technical skill (e.g., Dreamweaver, FrontPage, HTML). Instead, business considerations, not technical ones, should drive the decision as to who maintains your site. For example, you may want the development director to maintain the development section of your site and the program director to maintain that portion.
How long does it take for you to get a typical change made?	Days or weeks—perhaps longer	Minutes	If your web site person is sick, busy, on vacation, or (worse yet) decides not to support your organization, your site will likely stagnate. Even if that person is available, he or she often has other job responsibilities and may need time to make your site changes. Also, you need more time to proofread and go over the changes carefully. If there's even one punctuation mark that's incorrect, you need to reinitiate the process, perhaps several times, until the change has been made perfectly. Instead, you should be able to make almost any change to your site in minutes and, presumably, do it right the first time.
How much do you pay this person to maintain your site?	$0 if he or she is a volunteer or employee), and between $50 and $400 (or higher) per month otherwise	$0	Some organizations mistakenly believe that having an employee spend hours each month maintaining their site does not cost them anything. In fact, their time does cost money, in salary, taxes, and benefits, and this can add up quickly. Even a volunteer webmaster can cost the nonprofit money, given the staff time required to request and verify web site changes and to manage volunteers. Paid web site developers usually work on an hourly rate of $30-$100 per hour or occasionally maintain a site on a flat-fee monthly basis. Instead, if staff (or volunteers) can make changes themselves, in minutes, the cost of the changes becomes negligible.

TABLE 14.1	KEY QUESTIONS *(Continued)*

Question	Typical Answer	Ideal Answer (Strive to Achieve This)	Explanation
How much do you pay for hosting?	$0–$400 per month	$0–$20 per month	Some nonprofits get free hosting services donated to them. Those that do pay often pay too much, sometimes up to several hundred dollars per month.
How much did you pay for your site?	$0 if built by a volunteer or employee; $5,000–$20,000, give or take a few thousand dollars on either end, for a brochure-ware site, and $20,000–$200,000, give or take a lot, for an e-philanthropy site	$1,000–$10,000 for an e-philanthropy site	The adage "you get what you pay for" often applies to nonprofit web sites. It's tempting for an executive director to accept an offer to build a site for free, but often the result is a subpar, brochure-ware site that takes months to complete, requires the person who built the site (or someone with similar technical skills) to maintain it, and is somewhat static. Paying for a brochure-ware site often produces somewhat-better results but still yields a brochure-ware site. Building an e-philanthropy site by hand is so complex that it is almost never available on a pro bono basis and is prohibitively expensive for most nonprofits.

Key Goals

- Cultivate data from your site activity.

Management Techniques

- You should determine what data should be tracked, by whom, how often, how to analyze those data, and the actions you should take as a result.
- To get the best results from your web site, you should develop an effective Internet strategy, revise it periodically, and manage your web site and organization in accordance with it. Table 14.2 provides a few of the many components of an effective Internet strategy.

In addition to the information in Table 14.2, you might also consider domain names, legal and tax issues, creating a communications strategy, and integrating online and offline fundraising initiatives.

You should create an effective Internet strategy, reflect it in your web site, and periodically reevaluate and revise your strategy. The web site traffic, transactional, and other reports you review and analyze will help this process.

TABLE 14.2	SOME COMPONENTS OF AN EFFECTIVE INTERNET STRATEGY

Internet Strategy Component	Description
Set objectives for your site like what you want to achieve with the site.	Your site has two overriding strategic objectives: The first is to inform the web site visitor about your organization and its mission. The second, and more important, objective is to get the web site visitor to support you. You want a site that has a lot for the user to see and do. Examples of specific, measurable objectives include the following: • Accept at least $6,000 in online donations in the next 12 months. • Recruit at least 10 volunteers online in the next 12 months. • Get at least 100 people to join your e-mail list in the next 12 months. • Increase brand awareness across Southern California, and get at least 500 people from Southern California to register on the site within 12 months.
How will you measure actual results and compare them against objectives?	Options include the following: • Online activity reports • Exporting data to another application • E-mail confirmations • Monthly statements • Online merchant account statements • Bank statements
Collect e-mail addresses.	Collect e-mail addresses for as many constituents as possible.
Designate someone to be in charge of your nonprofit's Internet strategy and implementation.	Designate someone to take responsibility for each of the following (in many cases, the same person can take care of these): • Developing your Internet strategy • Overseeing the implementation of the Internet strategy (you may assign individual tasks to different people) • Creating your web site • Maintaining and administering your web site • Responding to web site and e-mail inquiries. Many nonprofits, particularly larger ones, should allocate a half-time or full-time equivalent to run the Internet aspects of the nonprofit. Typically, during the early phases of Internet adoption, a nonprofit will incur additional work, but later, the net effect could be reduced workload. Clearly, the workload can be distributed among several people. Make sure you provide these people with the time, budgets, authority, and management support to accomplish their jobs! Also, set clear expectations for these people—specific, measurable, time-specific objectives.

TABLE 14.2	SOME COMPONENTS OF AN EFFECTIVE INTERNET STRATEGY *(Continued)*

Internet Strategy Component	Description
Allocate sufficient budget dollars to maximize the likelihood of success.	Costs to include are the following: • Software, active server pages, and software-as-a-service fees • Graphic design fees • Online merchant account fees • Personnel • Consulting • Enhancements • Publicity • Domain name registration • Campaigns

CONCLUSION

You can have a world-class, interactive web site that enables visitors not only to read about you but also to engage and interact with you and one another and to support you in various financial and nonfinancial ways. E-philanthropy tools can help you quickly and easily implement most of the ideas we've discussed in this chapter. You can find more information about these tools at http://www.techsoup.org/servicedirectory or http://www.nonprofitmatrix.com.

Allan Pressel is founder and CEO of CharityFinders, which helps nonprofits use the Internet to further their mission. CharityFinders' NonprofitSite123 tool enables any nonprofit to build its own world-class web site quickly, affordably, and without training. Pressel has done hundreds of presentations for the nonprofit community nationwide, almost always to rave reviews. In fact, the ePhilanthropy Foundation has designated Pressel as an e-philanthropy master trainer. He received the Volunteer Service Award from President George W. Bush. Pressel has served as founder and board member for a number of nonprofits. He previously cofounded i-Cube, which had a highly successful initial public offering and was later acquired by Razorfish. Before founding i-Cube, Pressel was a technology strategy consultant at Arthur Andersen and First Consulting Group. He holds an M.B.A. from the Anderson School of Management at UCLA.

CHAPTER 15

Multichannel Fundraising

INTEGRATING TOOLS THAT INCREASE RESULTS

MICHAEL JOHNSTON AND MATTHEW BARR

It has many names, and it can be a bit of a buzz term: it's "integrated fundraising" or "multichannel fundraising." Whatever its name, the definition is the same: using multiple channels to raise money. However, it's not the name or the definition that is debated but whether multichannel fundraising leads to better results and better donor relationships.

This chapter has as its task two clear deliverables: first, to present an analysis of multichannel effectiveness with accompanying case studies; second, to present the human resource issues and prospective solutions to deliver more effective multichannel fundraising to your nonprofit organization.

THE BIGGER PICTURE

The furious adoption of the Internet for fundraising has brought the issue of multichannel marketing to the forefront. In the past, direct mail, television, and the telephone have been effectively combined to help improve fundraising results. In general, the evidence from multichannel marketing before the emergence of online giving was that using a more active channel (e.g., the human voice of a phone call) was an effective way to upgrade donors who were regularly swimming in the channels of a more passive medium like direct mail.

Why does this happen? A wonderful colleague, David Love, once said, "No one has ever made a wet dash out of the bathtub to open a letter, but they have to answer a ringing telephone." And that's the difference between active and passive channels. The phone is much more active and more human, and it still has a place in multichannel fundraising.

At the outset of this chapter, it's important to show how multichannel fundraising is connected to online giving. Unequivocally, the examples that follow in this chapter (which show a combination of online and traditional channels, especially the telephone) can make huge improvements to online fundraising. The web is a passive medium and can often be helped by more active media like the telephone.

One of the most frequently asked questions about multichannel marketing is the question of whether donors who come in on one channel (e.g., direct mail) are most likely to stay in that same channel or choose another channel to make a donation. The answer is mainly anecdotal, and here we endeavor to give the reader some larger cross-channel statistics to help in the decision to invest more in multichannel fundraising.

Cornerstone Group of Companies, Canada's leading provider of outsourced donation processing and donor database-management services, each year provides clients with detailed historical trend analyses of their donor activity. In 2008, it provided clients with a benchmark study based on the combined historical results of many of the leading fundraising organizations in Canada (see Figure 15.1).

Cornerstone's analysis looked at close to $400 million dollars worth of giving by dozens of charities over five years. It's as good a study as we have seen, and its results need dissection. The main result shown in Figure 15.1 is that both direct mail and web donors have similarly low conversion rates to other channels. After five years, donors who first came in by those two channels remain in the same channel (95.6 percent for direct mail and 95.1 percent for the web).

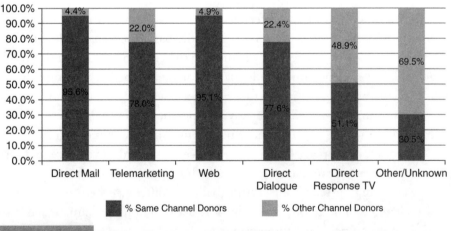

One-Time Gift Donors across Channels (2004–2008)

FIGURE 15.1   **Will One-Time Donors Who Come in on One Channel Move to Another Channel over Time?**

George Irish, an online fundraiser for almost 15 years, offered his very tren-
chant perspective in commenting that those percentages don't necessarily mean
that first-time donors in either channel want to remain in those channels. Instead, charities have constructed direct-mail and web fundraising channels as are
silos, with little cross-channel solicitation for either kind of donor. Without a
doubt, many direct-mail and web donors want to stay in the channel they first
gave to, but examples later in this chapter show that, when offered compelling
opportunities to give in other channels, many donors do so.

So, we believe that the jury is still out on whether direct-mail and web donors
want to stay in their first gift channel. Only with proper cross-channel testing
can we know whether donors from the two channels want to live in splendid
isolation.

With other channels, there is a higher crossover from the channel donors who
first gave through another channel (78 percent, 77.6 percent, and 51.1 percent
for telemarketing, street fundraising, and direct-response television [DRTV],
respectively). The initial offer for some charities, like DRTV's offer to use the
telephone for initial entry, often occurs through another channel, and therefore
cross-channel usage is immediately high.

Cornerstone's analysis in Figure 15.2 looks at all donors (not just one-time
donors but also the important category of monthly donors) and whether they
use multiple channels. It's obvious that the most mature channel, direct mail,
keeps most of its donors in the same channel.

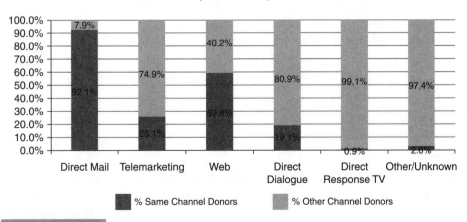

**6+ Years on Database across Channels
(2004–2008)**

% Same Channel Donors   % Other Channel Donors

| FIGURE 15.2 | **Do Donors (Including Regular Monthly Direct Bank Debit Card Donors) Who Come In on One Channel Make Gifts through Other Channels As Well?** |

In some ways, this is self-fulfilling, in that the programs are often not linked to other giving channels, and the customer service model, upgrade system, and resolicitation programs are complete, sophisticated, and isolated. We have constructed direct mail to be self-enclosed and have received donor results that prove that it has worked.

In addition, DRTV programs often follow up with direct mail, which leads to the use of other channels for giving. And direct dialogue (or face-to-face or door-to-door giving) is the same. We have often followed up door-to-door giving with a telephone call and then direct mail. Donors respond to multichannel solicitation by giving through multiple channels.

Finally, web donors are no different. Many organizations put web donors into the direct-mail stream, and Figure 15.2 shows that 40.2 percent of web donors do give through other channels, too (most likely direct mail).

Overall, Cornerstone's analysis is very important in that it provides real-world data sourced from many charities. It highlights that donors in direct-mail and web channels tend to stay in the same channel over time; those in other channels do so less often.

All in all, we urge each organization to construct, and test, more multichannel solicitation programs to find out the right combination of online and offline giving to make the most money and lead to the happiest donors.

AN ENCOURAGING INTEGRATION RESULT

For many organizations, the place to begin integrated fundraising is to connect and test direct-mail fundraising with online giving. Following up from the case study presented by Frédéric Fournier in this book, we want to outline a direct-mail and online test conducted by Optimus on behalf of its client Fondation 30 Millions d'Amis. The foundation, an animal welfare organization that draws its strength from a cobranded television show that has been on the air for years in France, drives a huge amount of traffic to its web site. The landing page and web site are focused on the foundation, which tries to get people to adopt animals, give, and take action.

Optimus created a three-part test structure for people who had filled out an online petition including their email address and had also given their direct mailing address through a campaign specific URL. The results were as follows:

- Group 1: Received only mailing. 4,982 petition signers, 107 donations, 2.15 percent response; average donation of 29.63 euros, and return on investment (ROI) of 1.20:1.

- Group 2: Received e-mail before the mailing. 7,504 petition signers, 172 donations, 2.29 percent response, average donation of 26.19 euros, and ROI of 1:1.

- Group 3: Received e-mail after the mailing. 7,504 petition signers, 196 donations, 2.61 percent response, average donation of 26.98 euros, and ROI of 1.17:1.

The results are close, but the direct-mail package and the e-mail after the mailing were a winning combination, with the highest response rate (the organization wants to get as many donors as possible) and the ROI close to the best result as well (see Figure 15.3).

FIGURE 15.3   **The E-Mail Sent after the Direct-Mail Package**

This example shows charities that they should be creating offline and online tests to find the right combination for the best fundraising results. With the extreme silos in the Cornerstone studies, it is obvious that most charities have not yet done this kind of sophisticated cross-channel testing to get better fundraising results.

It's important to note that this is an acquisition example that is different from cross-channel solicitations to past donors. It may be that cross-channel fundraising is even more important in acquisition than in donor renewal. This will be explored in more detail later in this chapter.

ALTERNATIVE GIVING

In 2005, a small but very capable overseas development charity, CHF (formerly known as the Canadian Hunger Foundation), created an online alternative gift catalog with only one gift, a donkey. The alternative gift campaign was called Gifts That Matter (http://www.giftsthatmatter.ca). Donors could buy a donkey for someone at holiday time and send a cute, playful e-card. The money for a donkey then goes directly to CHF uniquely, delivering a real donkey to where it was needed.

The program was a success: It earned $39,000 online with limited investment. In 2006, a paper version of the online catalog was created, and an 8.5-by-7-inch insert. It just so happened that CHF sent out a paper newsletter that October to approximately 6,000 direct-mail donors. Everyone agreed that a paper alternative giving catalog should be inserted in the 2006 October newsletter. The commitment was made to add more alternative giving gifts beyond the donkey (see Figure 15.4).

The results were extremely encouraging: $59,435 came in through the catalog. That was approximately $10 earned for every mail package sent out (with both newsletter and catalog).

There was a subsequent holiday direct-mail package sent in November 2006, and the organization wanted to know whether the October catalog would have a subsequently depressing result on the November appeal. There was indeed a slight depression in results (of approximately $13,000), but the $136,000 brought in by the print catalog more than made up for that.

The cross-channel question has been: how many online catalog buyers go over to direct mail, and vice versa, how many print catalog buyers go over to the online environment? In the print catalog, online gift buying is highlighted, and online, alternative giving is highlighted (see Table 15.1).

An analysis was done of Gifts That Matter (GTM) alternative gifts over the 2007 and 2008 holiday periods, which showed a healthy crossover between online and offline donors. In total, 3,176 direct-mail alternative gift donors from

Give a Gift That Matters
Change a life this school year!

Seeds $10 — Help farmers grow crops

Chicks $25 — Provide families with nourishing eggs

Stove $30 — Smoke-free stoves prevent cataracts and respiratory disease in women

Goat $40 — Provides rich milk to drink and meat to sell

Home Garden $50 — Rebuild home gardens for tsunami-affected families

Natural Fertilizer $65 — Indigenous, organic fertilizer to improve crops

Water $80 — Clean drinking water for a family (or $4,000 for an entire village)

Improved-breed Ram $100 — Improve breeding and produce disease-resistant lambs

Rickshaw $100 — Increase a family's income

Malaria Kits $150 — Protect a whole community

Post-Tsunami Livelihood Kit $300 — Restore a family's livelihood

Nutrition Garden for Orphans $500 — Provides food and agricultural training for AIDS orphans

For an updated list and for complete descriptions of each item please visit us at www.giftthatmatters.ca

For each order, we will send you a **Gifts That Matter greeting card.** You can send this card to a special someone at your school, or to family, friends or colleagues to tell them that a special gift has been purchased on their behalf.

Gift	Amount	Quantity	Total
Seeds	$10	____	____
Chicks	$25	____	____
Smoke-free Stove	$30	____	____
Goat	$40	____	____
Home Garden	$50	____	____
Natural Fertilizer	$65	____	____
Clean Water (for a family)	$80	____	____
Improved-breed Ram	$100	____	____
Rickshaw	$100	____	____
Malaria Kits	$150	____	____
Post-Tsunami Livelihood Kit	$300	____	____
Nutrition Garden for Orphans	$500	____	____
Clean Water (for a village)	$4000	____	____
Total:		____	____

Thank you for shopping with CHF Gifts That Matter.
You've just bought a gift that can change a life!

To order directly from this catalogue, please complete both sides of this form, tear it along the dotted line and mail it back to CHF.

When you buy a CHF Gift That Matters, here's how it works...

The cost of your gift takes into consideration all the factors needed to ensure that it has the greatest possible impact on the lives of people living in poverty. Each item in the catalogue is needed for one or more current CHF projects overseas. Your donation will be applied to one of them. Once enough funds are raised for the specific type of gift you selected, CHF will apply your donation to another aspect of our projects providing livelihoods for people challenged by poverty.

FIGURE 15.4   A Simple Offline Catalog to Support an Online Catalog

TABLE 15.1   A HEALTHY CROSS-CHANNEL MOVEMENT BETWEEN ONLINE AND DIRECT-MAIL ALTERNATIVE GIFT DONORS

Giving Year	Giving Channel	Number of Donors	Percentage
2007/2008	Mail GTM specific	3,176	
Tracking specifically these 3,176 mail 07/08 GTM donors by channel in 08/09			
2008/2009	Online GTM specific	39	1.23%
	Mail GTM specific	1,073	33.78%
Combined both channels, GTM specific		1,112	35.01%

Giving Year	Giving Channel	Number of Donors	Percentage
2007/2008	Online GTM specific	400	
Tracking specifically these 400 online 07/08 GTM donors by channel in 08/09			
2008/2009	Online GTM specific	146	36.50%
	Mail GTM specific	16	4.00%
GTM specific, both mail online and mail		162	40.50%

2007 were subsequently tracked in 2008. A few—1.23 percent—gave online only in the second year. A solid 35 percent gave in more than one channel (at least two gifts), and 33.78 percent stayed in the mail.

Similarly, online-only alternative gift donors in 2007 moved around. A small percentage (1.23 percent) moved to direct mail; a solid 36.5 percent stayed online, and 40.50 percent gave through both channels. It's important to note that online alternative gift donors received the print catalog the year after, and then gave through both channels.

At a minimum, this example shows that alternative gift donors should be given multiple channel opportunities to give. If an online alternative gift donor gives on one holiday, put him or her into the mail program for alternative giving, too. Make sure that print catalogs also mention online giving.

To remind readers of how online and offline integration can lead to a higher-value donor, we would be remiss if the groundbreaking study by Convio wasn't mentioned. In a study done with the American Society for the Prevention of Cruelty to Animals (ASPCA) from June 2003 through June 2007, traditional channel donors with e-mail (who knew they would be solicited both online and offline) gave twice as many single gifts in a year, for almost double the average revenue of a donor contacted in one channel only.

A Lovely, Integrated Fundraising Test

An important (and intriguing) test was conducted by the Humane Society of the United States (HSUS) from May through June 2006 that gives evidence of the value of integrated, offline and online fundraising. The campaign concentrated on the U.S. Pets Evacuation and Transportation Standards (PETS) Act and was designed to raise money for the legislative arm of HSUS, the Humane Society Legislative Fund.

The issue focused on the events surrounding Hurricane Katrina. During that disaster, none of the local, federal, or state authorities formally agreed to marshal their resources to help save pets and other animals starving to death in the areas affected by the hurricane. A series of e-mails were sent to internal contact lists, asking them to use online advocacy tools to urge their congressional representatives and senators to support the PETS Act. The act would require state and local authorities to take the needs of individuals with pets and service animals into consideration in disaster plans. The HSUS set up four communications streams:

- E-mail appeal only
- Direct-mail piece only
- Pre-e-mail postcard, followed by direct-mail piece
- Direct-mail piece, followed by e-mail appeal

The HSUS made sure to test integrated, cross-channel results by the original entry source of the donor: whether they were direct-mail–acquired, Internet-acquired (during Katrina), or PETS activists (nondonor). It also tested by the last gift date (e.g., whether they were previous donors from the 0–6 month period versus donors from the previous 6–12 months). These streams created six overall test categories:

- Direct-mail donors 0–6 months
- Direct-mail donors 7–12 months
- Internet donors 0–6 months
- Internet donors 7–12 months
- Katrina donors 0–12 months
- PETS action nondonors

With four different streams and six categories of donors, there were 24 groups to be analyzed. The results? Of the direct-mail–acquired donors (with gift dates in the previous zero to six months), those who received only an e-mail had the highest net return per 1,000, and those who received a direct-mail piece and then a post-e-mail had the highest gross net income. Similarly, of the Internet-acquired donors, those who received only an e-mail had the highest net return per 1,000, and the donors who received a direct-mail package and then a post-e-mail had the highest gross net revenue. The HSUS learned that the cross-channel combination of direct mail and a subsequent e-mail had the highest net income for both direct-mail– and Internet-acquired donors. However, the highest net income per 1,000 was the e-mail–only approach.

What does this mean for your organization as you contemplate more integrated online and offline fundraising? First, within budget and reason, create test cells of online and offline integrated fundraising to see what works best for your organization. Second, you may cut to the chase with this test and make direct mail in combination with a follow-up e-mail the standard way to run your integrated fundraising. The only caveat to jumping to the HSUS model is that every organization is unique. What works for one organization's donors may not work for another's. Adopt the testing culture exhibited by HSUS to find the best approach for your organization.

MASS MEDIA INTEGRATION

Up to this point, this chapter has emphasized donor-focused channels like direct mail, e-mail, and the telephone to be integrated for fundraising. But there is also opportunity for the integration between fundraising and mass media channels for online and offline fundraising.

Once again, we draw on a symbolic giving campaign, Oxfam Unwrapped, by Oxfam Canada. The Unwrapped campaign is active in multiple countries, including the United States, Canada, Australia, the United Kingdom, the Netherlands, and a number of others.

Like the pioneering work of Heifer International in the area of overseas development symbolic giving, the Unwrapped site offers individuals the chance to buy the symbolic gift of a donkey, chicken, goat, or other sustainable livelihood items. When Oxfam Canada launched its online fundraising site in 2006, the organization not only used its internal lists but also looked to mass media to help carry the message about the new symbolic giving site.

The mass media effort included radio ads and public relations to get the story picked up by the media. When anyone made an online gift during the holiday campaign, the bounce-back confirmation e-mail would urge donors to fill out a quick survey by clicking on a link. A solid 15 percent to 20 percent of donors filled out this survey, and the responses helped Oxfam Canada understand the top media drivers for online giving. Figure 15.5 shows the breakdown of the major media channels and highlights some of the biggest drivers, including *The Ellen DeGeneres Show*.

Figure 15.5 displays a week of survey answers that were heavily influenced by a mention of the Unwrapped campaign by British actress Minnie Driver on *The Ellen DeGeneres Show*. What's most amazing is that Canadians watching this U.S. show still found their way online to the Canadian site to give. The power of celebrity through traditional mass media to drive online donations should never be underestimated and always planned for, if possible.

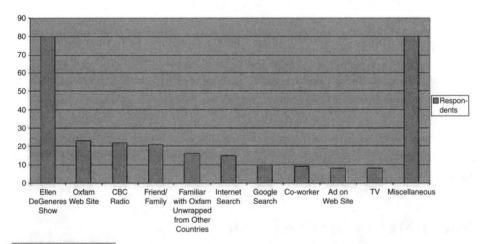

FIGURE 15.5 **The Top-10 Channel Drivers to Online Giving for Oxfam Unwrapped for One Week in the 2006 Campaign**
Source: Oxfam Canada

In addition, it's interesting to note that Canada's CBC radio (the equivalent of National Public Radio in the United States or the BBC in the United Kingdom) was a strong driver also, and many of the miscellaneous answers at the far right of the survey chart mentioned radio ads. All in all, traditional mass media through celebrity, television, and radio journalism and ads drove a high percentage of online donations. The future integration of mass media (and public relations) with online fundraising will be essential for many campaigns.

In fact, we believe that a strong integration must be made between non-fundraising media departments and fundraising departments for future integrated fundraising.

The example of Oxfam Unwrapped's use of traditional mass media to drive online donations highlights the role of radio in integrated fundraising. From health-related walkathons to symbolic gift campaigns, radio is a proven, cost-effective driver of donations and should be considered part of an integrated offline and online fundraising mix.

How Integrated Media Relations and Fundraising Can Help Raise More Money Online

Beyond the use of mass media tools, the internal integration of different departments should also be a part of an organization's mix for integrated fundraising.

A number of years ago, we sat down with the hardworking staff at Mothers against Drunk Driving USA (MADD) in Irving, Texas. The integrated fundraising session began with nonfundraising and fundraising staff sitting some physical distance from one another. A way to bring them together—both literally and figuratively—was devised.

We began by pointing out that, because the tragedy of drunk driving kills and maims people every single day across the United States, there is a daily stream of tragic and riveting news stories online. The author then emphasized that MADD needed to ensure that media-responsible staff members deepen their partnerships (and online fundraising opportunities) with organizations that have online news services.

To make that point more powerful, we had a draft example drawn up from CNN online, including a story on six individuals who had been killed by a drunk driver. CNN attaches a set of "story tools" to every online story that give readers the opportunity to save, print, and e-mail the story. We had the graphics department add an additional piece to the story tool set—a MADD link that said, "Don't let it happen again" (see Figure 15.6). The link was created to have the same font and style as the other story-tool links and would link directly to an online giving form.

FIGURE 15.6   **MADD Story-Tool Link with Online Media**

The reaction was positive and physical. The two groups moved closer together, and we launched into the next step for more integrated cooperation—asking for a chart of how staff could find common, integrated ground to put their mass media connection together with fundraising endeavors online.

The simple graphic in Figure 15.6 led to more dialogue about the kinds of media opportunities available online. The general consensus was that online dialogue was possible, but someone needed to take staff time to attempt to build such relationships online. There was also discussion that the media could be interested in a partnership that emphasizes the idea of why MADD is still reporting on this story.

The media relations staff came up with an excellent idea of taking press clippings on a daily basis and pushing them into timely, regionally focused, solicitations online. This then led to the discussion of interdepartmental sharing of

TABLE 15.2   Online News Media Links to Fundraising

Online News Source	Existing Relationship	E-Philanthropy Story Button?
CNN.COM	?	?
USATODAY.COM		
NYTIMES.COM		
AOL.COM		
MSN.COM		

a rented media-tracking resource, like LexisNexis. Finally, there was agreement that the departments would take stock of who could provide online story links (see Table 15.2). In addition, fundraising and nonfundraising staff agreed that, before the development or implementation of an improved and integrated marketing strategy, it would be necessary for MADD to review, identify, and list the online media sources it had already worked with in the past. Staff came up with a simple chart (see Table 15.2).

How the Integration of Offline Media and an Online Destination Led to Fundraising Success

In the spring of 2003, two women from northern Nigeria were to be executed under the Muslim sharia law. There was global outrage at the idea that two women who had had children out of wedlock were being sentenced to death, while the men involved would not even be punished. In response to the human rights debacle, Amnesty International Spain created a web campaign that asked Spanish citizens to leave their e-mail addresses as signatures on an online petition protesting the human rights abuse against these two young women.

Amnesty Spain used traditional offline media, including direct mail, to drive hundreds of thousands of individuals online to sign a petition. Figure 15.7 is an example of the multichannel approach Amnesty Spain took to drive traffic to the web site.

One powerful offline channel for this campaign was direct mail. Amnesty Spain sent a rock (as would be used to stone these women to death) to university students and urged them to go online and sign the petition.

The Spanish citizenry responded, and in a matter of weeks, more than 240,000 e-mail addresses were collected. After 20,000 e-mail addresses were rejected through purging, 220,000 e-mails were sent to individuals who had signed the online petition page and had agreed to be contacted again.

The results were better than Amnesty Spain expected. A subsequent e-mail solicitation, seeking to convert petition signers, yielded 1,022 monthly

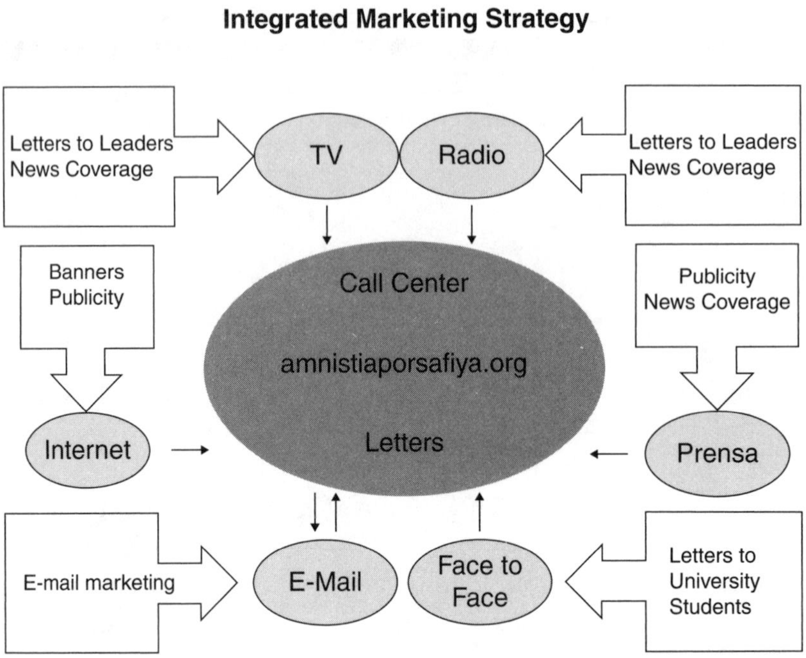

Integrated Marketing Strategy

FIGURE 15.7   **Amnesty Spain's Integrated Campaign**

committed donors (a 0.46 percent response rate) giving 13 euros a month, for a yearly total of approximately €159,000. There were also 688 single-gift donors (a 0.31 percent response rate) who gave an average of 50 euros each, for a total of €37,840. With a total cost of approximately €10,000, the ROI was very impressive for an acquisition campaign.

An important test was conducted during this acquisition and conversion campaign. Half of the warm (recent monthly donor) list was sent a text-only appeal, and the other half received an HTML version that added a picture of one of the Nigerian women holding her child. The Amnesty logo was also added as a stylized graphic (see Figure 15.8). The HTML version received a 50 percent higher response rate and was clearly the winning solicitation.

Two months after the first acquisition solicitation, Amnesty Spain ran the petition campaign again and gathered another 200,000 e-mail addresses. The group subsequently e-mailed another conversion e-mail to the 180,000 that survived a purging. This time, an HTML-only version was sent out. The results were even better than the first appeal:

- 1,478 committed monthly donors giving 14 euros a month, for a yearly total of approximately €250,000

- 977 single-gift donors giving 44 euros, for a total of approximately €45,000

AMNESTY
INTERNATIONAL

| FIGURE 15.8 | Amnesty International Logo |

The results show that when there is a high-profile event connected to an organization's core mission, online acquisition techniques like contests, quizzes, and petitions can gather large warm lists, which can be subsequently converted to online donors. Every organization should take inspiration from this example and try to duplicate its ROI success for the same kind of 20:1 return.

THE TELEPHONE AND ONLINE FUNDRAISING TOOLS

The fundraising world has been transformed by social network fundraising tools, and other chapters in this book outline how personal and team pages have allowed nonprofits to create effective, profitable fundraising sources that rely on the cost-effective marketing of individuals and teams to their own social networks.

As much as these social network tools are effective in raising money through technology alone, we have found that the tactical and strategic use of the phone further accelerates and improves fundraising results.

The Princess Margaret Hospital Foundation in Toronto is a cancer-related hospital foundation on par with Sloan Kettering Memorial in the size and sophistication of its fundraising—though in online giving it is probably the most capable in the world.

The organization was intrigued by how the telephone could help improve personal-page fundraising results, and the Harry Rosen Spring Run Off was chosen as a test. This event has been going on for more than 20 years and was founded by the Canadian men's clothier Harry Rosen.

In 2007, a test was conducted on 200 individuals who had made personal fundraising pages. Using an even split, 100 of the individuals were contacted by telephone. The callers thanked the individual for making a page and asked whether they needed any help in raising money online with their social network tool. The other 100 individuals were not called.

The results were encouraging: Individuals who were given a quick (three minutes on average) call got 20 percent closer ($75 more per registrant) to their fundraising goal than did those individuals who were not called. The calling test was repeated in 2008, and the results were again encouraging and profitable. A call in 2008 improved personal-page fundraising by $131.42 per participant reached.

This example shows the value of testing and rolling out calling for social network fundraising. E-mailing participants is not enough; it is passive, and the human voice is active and more effective.

Keep in mind a few key investment issues:

1. What will it cost to train internal or external callers to provide expert service to those called? Will that initial investment be recouped by the improved results?

2. Should the calling happen in-house or externally? The answer may be based on the issue of scale. If the organization knows that a successful test would lead to a high number of calls in the future, then an outside solution may be best.

With statistical evidence that a brief call can improve the bottom line results of social network fundraising, a charity needs to think of what to say and when to call. Here are some script ideas in any phone conversation to help stimulate social network online fundraising:

- Thank you for registering.
- Can I help at all?
- You're doing a great job! Is the technology working for you? Any questions on how to use it?
- One week until race day!
- You've reached your fundraising goal! Let's raise it.

As indicated in that list, a phone call to stimulate fundraising can come at different times during a campaign. If you can call more than once, then there are three key points at which to call: at the beginning, middle, and end of a campaign. A social network fundraising campaign has a natural momentum—the ball starts rolling at the beginning, picks up speed and urgency in the middle, and accelerates to the conclusion (event day).

A phone call at the beginning to welcome people and get them comfortable with the technology is key; then a call in the middle of the campaign urging the individual to keep raising money (or to get started because it's not too late!) or to keep raising money to reach a certain incentive is also important. Finally, a final call close to the event to stimulate someone to meet their final goal or exceed it is a natural denouement to any call campaign. Organizations should investigate how this can be done—and how they can afford it.

At a minimum, if an organization can afford to call only once, it should be a welcoming, introductory call when someone first makes their social network fundraising page.

Making Your Own Online and Offline Testing Schedule

Every nonprofit organization is different in the way it raises money, requests an action from its supporters, and gives tools to users to do either of these. With that in mind, we present a testing schedule (Figure 15.9) that has been crafted for more activist-minded organizations but shows how test cells are created that integrate online activism, social network fundraising (with personal pages), send-to-a-friend action (conscript other petition signers), and follow up with a telephone call to donate.

The idea behind this plan is to move people along what's often called the ladder of engagement. Four different ladders of engagement are outlined. They all start with the simplest and quickest activity to show their support, which in this case is the signing of an online petition. The test schedule then introduces a number of different second and third activities to test the best ways to get a prospective donor more involved with the organization, and to ultimately make a donation

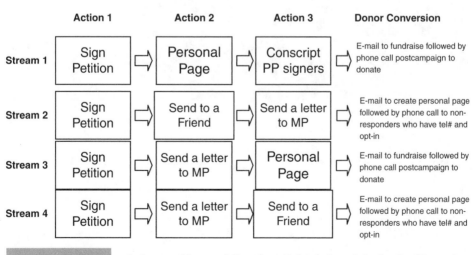

	Action 1	Action 2	Action 3	Donor Conversion
Stream 1	Sign Petition	Personal Page	Conscript PP signers	E-mail to fundraise followed by phone call postcampaign to donate
Stream 2	Sign Petition	Send to a Friend	Send a letter to MP	E-mail to create personal page followed by phone call to non-responders who have tel# and opt-in
Stream 3	Sign Petition	Send a letter to MP	Personal Page	E-mail to fundraise followed by phone call postcampaign to donate
Stream 4	Sign Petition	Send a letter to MP	Send to a Friend	E-mail to create personal page followed by phone call to non-responders who have tel# and opt-in

FIGURE 15.9   **A Cross-Channel Testing Schedule with the Ladder of Engagement in Mind**

and become a donor. In the schedule outlined, an organization would run the tests through to the call conversion to give. Of course, there could be different criteria for success for other situations. Straightforward fundraising criteria would look at the number of donors found and dollars raised to determine the most successful cross-channel sequence, but a more activist bent organization might look at the number of petition signers and activists found.

LIVE CHAT

A new technology is now at hand that could transform social network fundraising: online live chat. More and more, commercial enterprises are offering prospective consumers the opportunity to click on a link to live voice or live text customer service on their web sites to help make a sale.

This technology is now available for nonprofits and should be tested to see whether it can help raise more money (Figure 15.10).

In Figure 15.10, imagine that the International Fund for Animal Welfare (IFAW) is running an online campaign asking individuals to make a personal or team page to raise money to stop seal hunting. When people go to the campaign page to make a social network page, they see a place to click for immediate

FIGURE 15.10   **Online Customer Service via Text or Live Voice to Help Stimulate Fundraising**

customer service. Perhaps they don't know how to download their e-mail list and send a fundraising appeal to friends, or perhaps they want to upload a class or team photo but don't know how. Questions could immediately be answered by live text or live voice via Skype. Modern philanthropy demands great and immediate customer service, and this kind of integrated approach of a human voice or live text with social network online tools is, and will be, successful.

How Do You Staff for an Integrated Fundraising Program?

Over the past 10 years, charities have often been allocating online fundraising responsibilities to a part-time staff person. The amount of money that online giving has brought in (traditionally a small percentage of overall giving) has historically made it difficult to justify the budget for a full-time position.

But that time has come and gone. Online giving is one of the few areas of growth in fundraising for charities, and every organization should make an immediate investment in a full-time e-philanthropy position to take advantage of that fact.

In our experience with dozens of charities over the past six years, there has been one overwhelming human resources recommendation: to create a full-time e-philanthropy, or integrated fundraising position. That position could be occupied by a present charity staff person if he or she possesses the skill set required for the position.

Currently, for most charities, there are a number of staff positions that touch on e-philanthropy and integrated fundraising, but none are fully committed to tying online and offline together. We have consistently found that building internal skill sets and internal expertise is the best way to guarantee the success of online and integrated fundraising. Your outside vendors are important resources for any new e-philanthropy and integrated-focused staff person, but those people are still outsiders. They may not be your vendor in a few years, yet you would have a significant online donor base. In addition, an internal expert will be able to adapt to quick changes in technology (e.g., social media).

Many charities have web-related committees with both volunteers and staff. The e-philanthropy and/or integrated fundraising staff person can provide leadership to such committees. For example, if a staff person were to direct a web committee, then the committee would have to include the following high-priority tasks:

1. Create a one-year plan for online fundraising that outlines integration tactics, media tactics, testing schedules, technology testing, and goal setting

2. Provide creative and testing direction to an application service provider (ASP) to maximize use of technology for integrated fundraising

3. Provide an integrated stewardship plan for existing and future donors

4. Coordinate with public relations and other departments to obtain online and offline media to support online fundraising

5. Coordinate with the IT and marketing departments on online fundraising

What could this new position look like? The e-philanthropy manager or integrated manager would be a full-time staff position. The manager would be responsible for delivery of the entire e-philanthropy program and areas of online and offline fundraising integration, which includes maximizing the following:

-   Online and offline marketing and media relationships that relate to online giving
-   Primary person for interacting with ASP on maximizing the use of the technology for online and integrated fundraising
-   Integration of social network fundraising with online and offline channels
-   Integration of all direct response media as it relates to online fundraising

This position would have middle management, nondirector status; would report to the director of fundraising; and would be independent of the public relations, marketing, IT, and communications departments. This new staff person should also have the following qualifications:

-   Reasonable technical background (especially in ASP implementation)
-   Good interpersonal skills
-   Good communication skills
-   Experience working in directorship positions
-   A leader with experience in the field
-   A track record of success
-   A team player
-   Good blender
-   Online marketing experience
-   Experience in other area of direct-response fundraising

It is vital that this position be seen as—and be allowed to be—a connecting position. The point is not to create another silo in fundraising but to be open and collaborative.

An e-philanthropy or integrated fundraising position allows for open channels of frequent communication among other departments and development teams and a new, additional, resource of expertise on matters that brings together fundraising, the Internet, and new marketing.

How the Staff Person Can Create a Successful Model of Cooperation

The earlier example of excellent integrated testing from the Humane Society of the United States did not come easily and without a structure of cooperation in the organization. Geoff Handy, the director of Internet fundraising for HSUS, was kind enough to describe how his organization has created something he calls the "nooner," which is a daily communications meeting that works as follows:

1. At noon every day for nine minutes (to not interfere with most other meetings)
2. Features all communications managers (public relations, online, video, pubs, and member services)
3. Features campaigns and program staff when events warrant it

The meetings ensure the following:

1. All communication channels are in sync on messaging, timing, and so on.
2. A response to breaking news is immediate and effective
3. Effective campaign planning
4. Easy communication for program and campaign staff to share their ideas, goals, and events to drive the mission forward

This outline should inspire integrated fundraising staff to get the most out of an integrated fundraising plan for their organization.

Conclusion

It's as clear as mud. The idea of combining online and offline fundraising to make more money and improve donor relations has not been definitively proved. The start of this chapter revealed through a huge giving study that many direct-mail and web donors stay in their channel, never leaving, and after six years of giving, continue to give the way they did at the start.

But the waters are muddied when you realize that many direct-mail and web donor programs have remained in separate silos for the past six or seven years, and the evidence that donors stay in their channels is, in part, constructed by the walls we've put around channels.

Furthermore, when channels like telephone, street fundraising, or DRTV are studied, those channels have much higher crossover than the web or direct mail. A reason for that is that cross-channel solicitation is much stronger in those channels, often by design.

We have tried to show in this chapter that the thoughtful combination of mail, phone, and the web can increase average donations, response rates, and net income. But individual case studies do not forge a broad definitive study that everyone can rely on. The only way you will discover whether integrated fundraising can be effective for your charity is to create a testing model appropriate for the organization.

If your organization is good at pledge events, then it makes sense to test how the telephone can support online pledge pages. If your organization has a strong direct-mail program, then it makes sense to investigate how e-mail and web activities can work in conjunction with the mail to increase net revenue. And if your organization has a symbolic gift campaign, then the combination of online and offline giving will lead to a larger gross and net income, as with CHF.

But even if you have a test structure for integrated fundraising and are ready to execute a program, who will do it? Do you have the internal resources and skill sets to run an online and offline fundraising program?

So, clear as mud. However, there's one thing that's clear—the only way your organization will discover whether it's the way to raise more money and improve donor relations is to find the right staff person to relentlessly test the best combination of online and offline channels.

In the spirit of inspiring action and creating a sense of urgency, organizations should have started an integrated fundraising strategy yesterday. But there's still time. Good luck!

Michael Johnston is president and founder of the global fundraising consultancy Hewitt and Johnston Consultants and cofounder of two New York–based companies, Global Legacy Giving Group and ProAm Global. He has been a fundraiser for 21 years and has worked with hundreds of nonprofit organizations around the world. Johnston is an expert in direct-response fundraising innovation and integrated campaigning, especially the use of new media technologies and their integration with traditional direct-response methods. He is author of *The Fund Raiser's Guide to the Internet* and *The Nonprofit Guide to the Internet* and is editor of *Internet Strategies: Best Practices for Marketing* and *Direct Response Fund Raising: Mastering New Trends for Results*. Johnston is also a contributor to *People to People Fundraising: Social Networking and Web 2.0 for Charities*. Johnston was a founding board member of the e-Philanthropy Foundation and was first chair of the Education Committee. In addition, he was founding foundation chair for the first global charity online lottery, http://www.globelot.com.

Matthew Barr is an online fundraising innovation consultant at Hewitt and Johnston Consultants (HJC), where he works with a diverse range of local and global nonprofits. He is HJC's resident expert on charities' web site and online donation usability, which incorporates organization-specific user data and internal and external best practices to create the most effective design for fundraising and organizational success. In addition, he has completed the Humber College postgraduate certificate in fundraising and volunteer management under the direction of Ken Wyman.

Competency Profile of a Manager or Director of Integrated Fundraising

Effective integrated fundraising requires working across organizational structures, the ability to adapt existing fundraising programs to new audiences and media, operational expertise in multiple fundraising channels, and a clear understanding of the marketing and donor relations principles that drive such adaptations. It also requires flexibility, exceptional leadership, teamwork and communications skills, and an ability to comprehend the possibilities behind newly developing technologies and fundraising strategies. Self-awareness and continuous learning for self-improvement is a necessary prerequisite for success in integrated fundraising.

This competency profile is intended for a fundraising manager who reports to the director of development operations and direct-response marketing but who interacts frequently with the communications team and between the two teams. It is assumed this individual has a fair level of accountability for fundraising results.

Technical/Operational Competencies

- Significant, proven fundraising track record
- Demonstrates detailed knowledge at an operational level of multiple fundraising channels, particularly direct mail, telegiving, and e-philanthropy
- Collects and analyses qualitative and numerical data to measure effectiveness of fundraising initiatives
- Superior knowledge of database segmentation techniques
- Fluent in current computer technology
- Ability to understand new developments in technology as they may affect fundraising strategies, program development, and channel operations

- Demonstrates superior knowledge of marketing and donor relations principles
- Innovates to expand or initiate new fundraising programs on the basis of an understanding of these principles
- Consistently seeks to improve her or his knowledge of fundraising strategy and the market and technological trends that may affect the development of fundraising strategy

Leadership Competencies

- Retains a strategic and operational focus on the full range of donors and all segments of a donor database
- Consistently advocates for effective integrated fundraising programs and solutions within the broader organization
- Probes for deeper understanding of nonobvious issues or relationships and seeks additional information about a situation other than what has been given; consults available resources
- Acts assertively as required to encourage, promote, or protect the measurable success of integrated fundraising programs
- Manages relationships between internal and external stakeholders
- Encourages experimentation to maximize the potential for innovation, within an ROI framework
- Actively seeks and responds to constructive feedback; teaches and learns from others.
- Fosters enthusiasm and a sense of common purpose.
- Follows through on commitments.
- Communicates vision and information with clarity and impact.
- Takes calculated risks and evaluates progress, success, or failure openly and transparently
- Gets the job done

Teamwork Competencies

- Focuses on team objectives and helps others achieve those objectives
- Supports and celebrates team accomplishments
- Promotes a friendly climate by maintaining cooperation, pride, trust, and team spirit
- Expresses positive expectations for others, speaks of team members in positive terms, shows respect for others
- Supports creativity in others

- Accepts and delivers constructive feedback
- Applies negotiation, persuasion, and other conflict resolution techniques to achieve team goals, and solve disputes and problems
- Demonstrates an ability to negotiate the needs and goals of the home team versus the needs and goals of other cross-functional teams when these may come into open or unspoken conflict

Communications Competencies

- Actively listens; seeks opportunity for dialogue to fully understand communicator's message or needs
- Clearly articulates thoughts and ideas in language appropriate to the listener; checks level of understanding by asking for feedback
- Effectively communicates organized and accurate information in writing
- Makes effective presentations to groups; presentations reflect appropriate preparation, organization, use of language, gestures, and visual aids
- Presents oneself confidently and effectively to donors and internal stakeholders.

Interpersonal Competencies

- Establishes trust, respect, and rapport
- Demonstrates diplomacy, tact, skill and discretion when dealing with others; uses behaviors that are appropriate for the workplace and situations
- Constructively interacts with others by listening and observing to predict and prepare for others' reactions
- Responds to people's concerns by altering own behavior in a helpful, responsive manner
- Uses influence strategies tailored to individual situations, jobs, or changing organizational structure to encourage desired behavior
- Acts assertively as required
- Demonstrates an ability to meet and socialize with people at all levels
- Manages disagreements with others in ways that preserve ongoing working relationships

Thinking Competencies

- Uses good judgment and practices effective problem-solving skills
- Challenges and uses other team members for input to see new approaches
- Carefully thinks through complicated assignments or situations; demonstrates logical thought and attention to detail

- Demonstrates ability to break down problems into simple lists of tasks or activities
- Applies innovative solutions and insights to problems and assignments
- Generates creative ideas and approaches to achieve organizational and team objectives
- Commits to action once solutions or paths forward are identified

Organizational Competencies

- Effectively plans work to fit the available resources
- Ability to work in the organization to secure the necessary resources for a task or project
- Understands the vision, mission, functions, business strategies, and structure of the organization
- Proactively expands his or her knowledge of what is going on in other parts of the organization
- Supports and provides input to the development of organizational objectives and plans
- Adheres to appropriate confidentiality requirements and codes of ethics
- In a crisis, maintains calm demeanor and actively works with others to seek solutions
- Makes decisions with adequate information and without unnecessary delays
- Meets expense budgets and revenue goals

Donor Relations Competencies

- Develops strategy and plans with a donor-focused perspective, reaching all segments of a donor database with appropriate approaches
- Is accessible to donors as appropriate and provides for prompt, attentive service
- Develops and maintains strong relationships with donors; develops trust and credibility with the donor
- Anticipates donor needs and quickly responds with appropriate and helpful solutions
- Demonstrates understanding of issues from the donor's perspective
- Consistently applies creativity to find new ways to meet donor needs

Self-Management Competencies

- Effectively balances stressful demands

- Demonstrates ability to be self-directed and motivated to ensure that expectations are met
- Understands the need to balance work, family, and personal time
- Participates willingly in training and development programs to improve personal skills and knowledge; develops a personal plan for continuing professional development
- Applies ethical principals and standards in accomplishing work
- Uses caution to avoid actions or statements that would compromise his or her professional integrity and/or that of the organization
- Takes responsibility for his or her failures and mistakes without blaming others or the circumstances
- Models and encourages high standards of behavior that is consistent with the organization's core values
- Assumes personal accountability for achieving goals, outcomes, and deadlines
- Consistently demonstrates enthusiasm and a positive attitude toward the organization, donors, and work in general
- Demonstrates the ability to make the best use of available time and resources
- Organizes and prioritizes work effectively, making the best use of time and resources for higher-prioritized tasks while maintaining timeliness on other projects

Measurement and Evaluation Competencies

- Regularly engages in brainstorming and other means to generate creative new solutions, programs, and approaches to organizational or team issues
- Builds on the ideas of others to come up with new ways to address organizational issues or problems
- Documents processes and collects performance measurement data to determine where improvements can be made
- Takes calculated risks to help the organization advance toward its strategic goals

CHAPTER 16

12 Steps to Protect Your Organization and Donors from Fraud and Identity Theft

CATHERINE N. PAGLIARO

The Internet is a powerful communication tool that enables nonprofit merchants to fundraise locally, nationally, and internationally at a fraction of the cost of traditional communication mediums such as television, radio, and print to reach existing and new donors. The cyberspace frontier enables nonprofits to cost-effectively offer their donors a variety of innovative ways to donate with their credit or debit cards to projects that aid those in need throughout the world.

Online payment application tools for donation management are an easy and convenient way for donors to give to causes that they believe in from anywhere in the world. Within minutes from home or the office, a donor can give through single and monthly gift forms with real-time e-tax receipts. Alternative gift-giving programs such as Oxfam Unwrapped (at http://www.oxfamunwrapped. ca) allow donors to buy goats, chickens, donkeys, and training to help families create permanent sustainable incomes. Donors can use social networking of peer-to-peer systems enabling friends, family members, or corporate sponsors to participate in events to raise money for their favorite charities or projects.

These and many other types of online donation-management tools are providing billions of dollars to nonprofits throughout the world. This massive flow of transactions is also making digital merchants potential new targets for financial crime. Insufficient information technology and physical security of some merchants, service providers, software developers, data-storage hosting facilities, and financial institutions provide criminals with the opportunity to easily steal and use a donor's personal financial information from credit card transactions and processing systems.

Cybercrime is a serious and growing problem. The Aberdeen Group estimates that more than $221 billion is lost globally every year to identity theft! In 2007, more than $52 billion was lost to fraud in the United States alone. Criminals can expect to receive at least $1 per credit card number. The low risk of being caught combined with the high profit potential is an intoxicating invitation to individuals and organized crime syndicates today.

Cybercrime is difficult to investigate and prosecute because it is borderless. Cybercrime can and is committed from anywhere using different computers and servers all over the world. For example, a criminal or a criminal network can be set up in New Zealand and steal money and data in any country using compromised home and office computers and servers. Law enforcement agencies are still bound by jurisdiction, which effectively ties their hands in some cases. Fortunately, new laws are being enacted to ensure that global task forces are able to work in real time to fight this worldwide threat.

Resolving the rapid rise of electronic criminal activity will take a cooperative and collaborative commitment from merchants, consumers, law enforcement, credit card associations, government, financial institutions, and security professionals. It means that every one of us must take responsibility for our office environments and our home computer and technology to effectively reduce the criminal penetration of the Internet environment!

The purpose of this chapter is to provide you with an overview of the mandatory global security requirements for merchants doing business or fundraising using cardholder data. This chapter will help you understand and implement security best practices, to fulfill the mandatory Payment Card Industry Data Security Standard (PCI DSS) and to comply with the Payment Application Data Security Standard (PA-DSS) in your organization. This will help you prevent the compromise of confidential information. Compliance with the 12 requirements of the data security standards will protect your organization and donors from fraud and identity theft!

PCI security standards are technical and operational requirements set by the PCI Security Standards Council [PCI SSC] to protect cardholder data. The standards apply to all organizations that store, process, and transmit cardholder data—with guidance for software developers and manufacturers of applications and devices used in those transactions. If you are a merchant who accepts or processes payment cards, you must comply with the PCI DSS.

The PA-DSS is for software developers and integrators of payment applications that store, process, or transmit cardholder data as part of the authorization or settlement when these applications are sold, distributed, or licensed to third parties. These are databases or online management tools that you use to fundraise online. The applications must be hosted within your PCI DSS–compliant facility or with a PCI DSS–compliant service provider or vendor.

All payment applications must be PA-DSS validated by summer 2010. Check with your financial institutions to find out whether the dates for validation have changed.

The PCI SSC is responsible for managing security standards, and compliance with the PCI standards is enforced by the founding members of the council, such as American Express, Discover Financial Services, JCB International, MasterCard Worldwide, and Visa Inc.

Step I: Questions to Consider

While you read this chapter, consider the following questions:

- Do your service providers have valid PCI DSS and PA-DSS certificates that are required today to process credit card transactions through payment applications?
- Do all of your third-party suppliers and vendors that handle credit card transactions for you have valid PCI DSS or PA-DSS certificates?
- How do you protect your donor's confidential data in your organization?
- Are your organization's databases that store, transmit, or process cardholder data encrypted to PCI DSS standards?
- Who in your organization has access to sensitive donor information and cardholder data?
- Is all cardholder data locked up, or is it left out so that unauthorized staff has access?
- Do all people handling cardholder data have criminal and credit checks done as part of your hiring practice?
- Is cardholder data processed, stored, or transmitted on or between computers in your office or from call-center staff without proper encryption?
- If cardholder data is stored, does it need to be?
- How is cardholder data handled when collected by phone or in the field?
- In times of disaster-relief campaigns, how is cardholder data transported between offices or collection offices?
- How long do you store cardholder data?
- Are your web site and other applications coded to the security standards of the Open Web Application Security Project (http://www.owasp.org)?
- Do you have written security policies outlining procedures and processes?
- Do you provide security education for all staff and volunteers?

STEP 2: UNDERSTANDING WHY PCI DSS AND PA-DSS COMPLIANCE IS MANDATORY FOR ALL MERCHANTS THAT PROCESS CREDIT CARDS

The Internet was first created by the U.S. military in the 1960s and gained prominence when universities began using it to transmit data between campuses. The Internet expanded into a global system of interconnected computer networks in the early 1990s.[1]

A survey by the International Telecommunications Union estimates that nearly a quarter of the world's population uses the Internet today.[2] The vast commercial opportunities of the mid-1990s created explosive growth from the global private sector, which was keen to profit from the new cyberspace frontier. People rushed to create online businesses, payment applications, and network systems with little or no thought to security best practices, thus making it easy for criminals to steal personal financial information for profit.

By 2001, online criminal activity was increasing rapidly and the cost of fraud was in the billions. Visa developed the Account Information Security Program and Card Information Security Program (AIS and CISP) to provide a framework of security requirements for all payment application service providers to adhere to. Visa began the pilot in 2002, and by 2003 there were a handful of payment-application service providers compliant with the new regulations.

In 2004 MasterCard International launched its secured data protection (SDP) regulations and American Express and Discover followed shortly after with their own requirements. Although credit card companies required their own independent compliance program to avoid antitrust issues, they recognized that merchants worldwide should be assessed against one set of global standards.

Consistent regulations, policies, procedures, and methodologies are the only way we can move from the reactive security environment we have today to the proactive fight against crime.

STEP 3: UNDERSTANDING HOW FRAUD HAPPENS

Social engineering is the act of manipulating people into performing actions or divulging confidential information. Although similar to a confidence trick or simple fraud, the term typically applies to "trickery or deception for the purpose of information gathering, fraud, or access to computer systems; in most cases, the attacker never comes face-to-face with the victim."[3]

Once upon a time, most social engineers were brilliant high school and university students having fun or looking to show vulnerabilities in applications and network systems. Today, social engineers are sophisticated business types, organized crime syndicates, and terrorists.

RISKY BEHAVIOR

A survey of businesses in the U.S. and Europe reveals activities that may put cardholder data at risk.

81% store payment card numbers

73% store payment card expiration dates

71% store payment card verification codes

57% store customer data from the payment card magnetic stripe

16% store other personal data

Source: Forrester Consulting: The State of PCI Compliance (commissioned by RSA/EMC)

FIGURE 16.1   **Risky Behavior** *Source*: PCI SSC.

The Most Common Ways to Commit Crime

Social engineering is a serious problem, and people are usually the weakest link in the crime. Social engineers prey on the qualities of human nature such as the tendency to trust people and fear of getting into trouble. The most targeted staff members:

- Can access an abundance of private and confidential information
- Communicate with many customers and the public
- Are uneducated about social engineering threats

The staff positions most at risk to social engineering attacks include the following:

- Receptionists and executive assistants
- Database, system, and network administrators
- Computer operators
- Call-center operators
- Help-desk support staff
- General users in possession of confidential data

There are two types of social engineering, human based and computer based. The following lists provide details on each one.

Human-Based Social Engineering

- **Impersonation**: A person pretends to be someone important in the organization to gain passwords or access to private data.

- **Important user**: A person pretends to be a manager or supervisor and threatens an employee's position if he or she doesn't gain access to sensitive data.

- **Third-party authorization**: A person pretends to be an outside valued source with authorization to gain access to sensitive data.

- **Tech support**: A person pretends to be someone from the technical department with a legitimate reason for gaining access to passwords or sensitive data.

- **Dumpster diving**: A person goes through the garbage for cardholder data.

- **Shoulder surfing**: A person looks over your shoulder to gain access to sensitive data.

- **Reverse social engineering**: A person sabotages someone else's equipment and then offers to fix the problem.

Computer-Based Social Engineering

- **Botnet**: A group of computers that hackers have taken over and used to launch attacks against Internet servers

- **Phishing**: The fraudulent attempt to acquire user names, passwords, and credit card details by pretending to be a trustworthy organization in an e-mail or instant message.

- **Pop-up windows**: A web browser window that asks for sensitive information

- **Mail attachments**: A computer file or image, such as a virus or worm, sent with an e-mail message

- **Spam, chain letters, and hoaxes**: E-mail that may harm your computer or ask for personal information to steal your personal financial information or passwords

- **Web sites**: Fake web sites can be used to obtain personal financial information and passwords

- **Denial of service**: An attack intended to make a computer system unavailable to its users

- **Trojans**: Malware installed on a user's machine that facilitates unauthorized use by a hacker.
- **Pharming**: Modification of a PC with a virus or Trojan so that access to the correct URLs goes to the wrong server.

STEP 4: HOW TO PREVENT HUMAN AND COMPUTER SOCIAL ENGINEERING

There are numerous ways that nonprofit organizations can help to prevent social engineering including the following:

Actions to Prevent Human Social Engineering

- Do not give out confidential information or reset passwords without following approved security policy procedures.
- Implement strict policies and training that outlines that staff should never share passwords with coworkers or friends—then change passwords every 30 to 90 days.
- Be aware of anyone who does not have the proper authorization to be in the workplace.
- Follow security policy procedures on crosscut shredding or a PCI DSS compliant shredding and disposal company to dispose of all confidential data and media such as disks, CDs, DVDs, and backup tapes.
- Shred any phone lists, e-mail lists, or other important documents before recycling them or throwing them in the trash.
- Give extra security training to the people on the company's perimeter—security guards, help-desk workers, and receptionists.
- Have procedures in place on what to do if someone calls needing assistance with a password, user ID, or other form of authentication.
- Train all of your employees and let them know they all have a role in protecting the company and, thus, they're own jobs.

Actions to Take throughout the Workday

- Lock sensitive confidential documents and computer media in drawers or filing cabinets.
- Physically secure laptops with security cables.
- Secure your workstation before walking away.
- Ensure that you are logged off your terminal when you leave it unattended.
- If no locking desk or file cabinet exists, store sensitive or confidential documents and computer media in a filing cabinet or desk drawer and

then lock the work environment or room before leaving to ensure that no unauthorized personnel can access sensitive or confidential data.

- Do not disclose or publish sensitive data such as:

  - User IDs and passwords
  - IP addresses
  - Contracts
  - Account numbers
  - Checks
  - Client lists
  - Intellectual property
  - Employee records
  - Anything you wouldn't want disclosed

- At the end of the day, take a moment to tidy up and secure sensitive material; lock drawers, file cabinets, and offices; and secure expensive equipment (e.g., laptops, PDAs).

Actions to Prevent Computer-Based Social Engineering

- Have your organization become PCI DSS and/or PA-DSS compliant
- Ensure that all web applications are coded to Open Web Application Security Project standards.
- Ensure that your computers use and regularly update the latest in anti-spyware, anti-spam, anti-malware, and anti-virus software.
- Do not follow e-mail instructions. If in doubt, forward the e-mail to the actual organization (e.g., a bank) for review and further instructions. Report the e-mail to the appropriate authority.
- Do not open any attachments at work or at home that you do not expect from a trusted and authorized person, as hackers usually impersonate trusted people.
- Do not open or respond to anything or anyone you don't know personally. If in doubt check with authorities.
- Be sure to check out a web site and make sure it is legitimate before you give any personal financial information or passwords. If you are in doubt check with authorities.
- Report any unusual behavior, phone calls, or activities that could fall into the previously outlined activities to the appropriate person in charge.

- Check a site's SSL certificate to verify the site's validity. Remember that SSL is encryption that is required but in no way guarantees that the web site, payment applications, and hosting system are secured.

- Ask the webmaster for a valid PCI DSS or PA-DSS certification, as that is the only way to guarantee that the site you give your cardholder data to is secured to industry requirements.

STEP 5: UNDERSTANDING THE DANGER OF NONCOMPLIANCE

The following examples show the damage created when organizations do not maintain a PCI DSS compliant environment:

In 2005, the UK charity Aid to the Church in Need had its online security systems breached. The addresses of more than 200,000 online donors were compromised. The security breach prompted the UK Charity Commission to issue a warning for organizations about the dangers of Internet fraud. Andrew Hind, CEO at the Charity Commission, said, "All charities need to regularly review web site security and make sure they stay ahead of the hackers and fraudsters."[4]

Security breaches have been on the rise since the 2005 incident in the United Kingdom. The Open Source Foundation gathers information about events involving the loss, theft, and exposure of Personally Identifiable Information (PII). The amount of incidents and records affected is alarming (see Table 16.1) [5]

The security breaches have also been widespread across a variety of sectors. This illustrates that no organization is immune to attacks or data integrity problems. Figures 16.2 and 16.3 show data-loss incidents by sector and by data type.

Third Parties and Data Loss

Figure 16.3 highlights a trend that indicates that data-loss incidents involving third parties, on average, result in a greater number of records lost. This may be

TABLE 16.1   TRADITIONAL ROI PROCESS, STEP BY STEP

Year	Total Incidents	Total Records Affected
2009	235	6,112,606
2008	644	84,745,058
2007	467	164,509,706
2006	509	51,099,584
2005	140	55,988,256

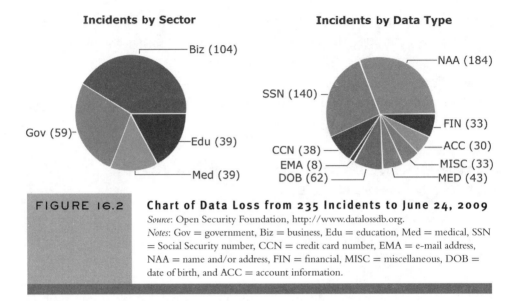

FIGURE 16.2	**Chart of Data Loss from 235 Incidents to June 24, 2009**

Source: Open Security Foundation, http://www.datalossdb.org.

Notes: Gov = government, Biz = business, Edu = education, Med = medical, SSN = Social Security number, CCN = credit card number, EMA = e-mail address, NAA = name and/or address, FIN = financial, MISC = miscellaneous, DOB = date of birth, and ACC = account information.

as a result of the type of data handled by third parties or the process of transferring the data between organizations. The trend is concerning—and the reason that all third-party vendors and suppliers must be PCI DSS and/or PA-DSS compliant.

STEP 6: UNDERSTANDING HOW IDENTITY THEFT HAPPENS

Every year, millions of people worldwide fall victim to identity theft, which costs billions of dollars. Identity theft occurs when an imposter or criminal gang steals your personal information such as a Social Security number, driver's license information, and/ or credit card information to secure credit, merchandise, and

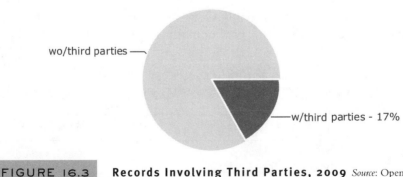

FIGURE 16.3	**Records Involving Third Parties, 2009** *Source*: Open Source Foundation, http://www.datalossdb.org.

services in the victim's name. People also use the stolen information to provide false credentials, which if given to the police, can create a criminal record or arrest warrants for the victim.

There are two main kinds of identity theft. First is true name and account takeover, in which someone uses your personal information to create new credit card accounts, contract cellular phone service, buy cars or furniture, and obtain mortgages or a new bank account to create debt in the victim's name. Second is account takeover, which occurs when a criminal accesses existing accounts in the victim's name and racks up huge debts before the victim realizes what has happened.

Identity theft is costly to repair. According to the web site Spam Laws, repairing identity theft takes a victim an average of 330 hours, and it can exceed $15,000 in business costs, personal wage loss of between $1,800 and $14,000, and personal expenses between $850 and $1,350.[6] A victim can also experience trouble securing credit or loans; problems getting a new job; and stress, anxiety, and frustration with a system that makes it difficult to repair identity-theft damage, even if the victim has proof. You want to ensure that you are taking all security precautions necessary to protect your donors' confidential information and avoid that they experience identity theft from a data breach of your organization's systems.

STEP 7: HOW TO PREVENT THEFT OF YOUR DONORS' INFORMATION

There are several preventative measures that organizations can take to help prevent the theft of donor information including the following:

- Have your organization become PCI DSS compliant.
- Ensure that all third-party service providers, vendors, and suppliers have a valid PCI DSS certificate.
- Ensure that all in-house software that stores, transmits, or processes cardholder data and was purchased from a third-party vendor has a current PA-DSS validation or will have one by July 2010. If the software application is a customized solution, it may require only a PCI DSS certification. Check the validation required with your qualified security assessor and/or acquiring merchant bank.
- Educate and train all staff and volunteers on how to prevent identity theft.

Personal Prevention of Identity Theft

There are also specific steps that staff members can take to prevent identity theft including the following:

- Be careful who you give your personal information out to unless you initiated the contact for a specific purpose.
- Always ask how your personal information will be used and protected.
- Only give out your Social Security number or social insurance number (in Canada) for employment or taxes.
- If you use your credit card over the phone or voice mail, know the company, the person, and how your credit card number is protected.
- Never send your credit card number or other sensitive data over unencrypted e-mail.
- Ensure that personal computers have up-to-date anti-virus, anti-malware, and anti-spyware software that is used continually.
- Guard your pin numbers from shoulder surfers and hidden video cameras.
- Shred all personal and financial documents.
- Never share your cards, pin numbers, or passwords with coworkers, friends, or family.
- Create difficult passwords, memorize them without writing them down, and change them regularly every 30 to 90 days.
- Never use the same password for all accounts
- Call police and your financial institute immediately if you believe that you have been a victim of identity theft.

STEP 8: HOW TO PROTECT YOUR DONORS' CARDHOLDER DATA

The Payment Card Industry Security Standards Council (PCI SSC) was founded as a global body by Visa, MasterCard Worldwide, American Express, Discover Financial Services, and JCB International in 2006. The council's mandate was to create one global security standard based on commonsense security best practices to assess all merchants worldwide. This global standard applies to all organizations that store, process, or transmit cardholder data. The current standard is in version 1.2 and is due to be upgraded in 2010.

There are three ongoing steps to adhere to PCI DSS:

1. **Assess**: Identify cardholder data, take an inventory of your IT assets and business processes for card processing, and analyze them for vulnerabilities that could expose cardholder data.

2. **Remediate**: Fix vulnerabilities and do not store cardholder data unless you need it.

3. **Report**: Compile and submit required remediation validation records (if applicable), and submit compliance reports to the acquiring bank and card brands you do business with.

The PCI DSS and PA-DSS are standards that require merchants to validate annually. The annual certification is not like a Girl Scout badge that once attained can be forgotten. Although you validate only once a year, including quarterly scans, your organization's physical and network security must be carefully maintained on a daily basis to maintain your compliance and avoid being hacked.

Step 9: Attaining and Maintaining the 12 PCI DSS Requirements

The current version of the PCI DSS requirements is based on 12 key requirements, with various subrequirements to secure and protect cardholder data. The requirements are commonsense steps that mirror best practices. The standard is to be upgraded about every two years. Table 16.2 presents the goals and requirements.

If you store, transmit, or process credit card data, then you must become PCI DSS compliant and recertify annually. By the summer of 2010, the payment application software you use in your organization must have a PA-DSS validation certification. In some cases, a custom payment application created and sold as a one-off application will qualify under vendors' PCI DSS certification. Your payment-application software vendor that provides you with online donation-management tools must provide you with either a valid PCI DSS and/or PA-DSS certification annually. If you need clarification, call a qualified security assessor or your bank for clarification.

PCI compliance applies to every

- Acquiring bank
- Merchant

TABLE 16.2   PCI DSS COMPLIANCE GOALS AND REQUIREMENTS

Goals	PCI DSS Requirements
Build and maintain a secure network	1. Install and maintain a firewall configuration to protect cardholder data. 2. Do not use vendor-supplied defaults for system passwords and other security parameters.
Protect cardholder data	3. Protect stored cardholder data. 4. Encrypt transmission of cardholder data across open, public networks.
Maintain a vulnerability management program	5. Use and regularly update anti-virus software or programs. 6. Develop and maintain secure systems and applications.
Implement strong access control measures	7. Restrict access to cardholder data to those who need to know. 8. Assign a unique ID to each person with computer access. 9. Restrict physical access to cardholder data.
Regularly monitor and test networks	10. Track and monitor all access to network resources and cardholder data. 11. Regularly test security systems and processes.
Maintain an information security policy	12. Maintain a policy that addresses information security for employees and contractors.

Source: PCI SSC.

- Every third party that accepts, processes, stores, or transmits payment cards, which may include resellers, software application providers, acquirers, payment service providers, card-processing bureaus, data-storage entities, web-hosting providers, shopping cart providers, miscellaneous third-party agents (e.g., call centers), and software vendors.

STEP 10: UNDERSTANDING THE BENEFITS TO YOUR ORGANIZATION

Some organizations may be wondering if all the work to achieve compliance is worth the effort. The following are some important benefits:

- Minimizes the data security risk to your organization
- Data security is a consideration, if not a requirement, for every organization.
- Global expectation and legal requirement for data protection
- Common sense for all organizations
- Fulfills any donor bill of rights or ethical obligations
- Implementation identifies any risks in how you store, process, or transmit card data

- Provides a clear outline for action and remediation to address any data security risks
- Ensures that your service providers and third-party suppliers do not put your business at data security risk

By minimizing your organization's risk of data compromise, you do the following:

- Protect against potential financial liabilities if found compliant at time of breach.
- Protect against the risk of investigative and legal costs.
- Protect against the risk of invasive media attention.
- Protect against loss of donor revenue.
- Demonstrate to donors that you are serious about their data security.

Qualified Security Assessor

Qualified security assessor (QSA) companies are organizations that have been qualified by the PCI Security Standards Council. Qualified security assessors are employees of those organizations who are PCI SSC–certified to validate an entity's adherence to the PCI DSS. The council has qualified more than 100 companies and trained and certified more than 1,500 assessors. All QSAs are required to adhere to strict guidelines maintaining independence and the quality assurance program requirements for validating merchants.

The self-assessment questionnaire (SAQ) is a validation tool for organizations not requiring an on-site audit. In Canada, for example, all merchants must have a certified QSA validate their SAQ to achieve compliance. You must check with your acquiring institution to determine your merchant level and which SAQ you will complete. Your QSA can also assist you in determining which SAQ you are required to complete (see Table 16.3).

Quarterly Scans Conducted by Accredited Scanning Vendors

Scans must be conducted on all externally facing Internet protocols (IPs) connected to the Internet by PCI SSC–certified accredited scanning vendors (ASVs). The ASVs are certified annually and monitored by a quality assurance program to ensure that the merchant's network systems are scanned. If any vulnerabilities are found, they are remediated on a consistent basis worldwide.

Merchants receive an executive summary and report of their scan that shows an overall pass or fail for their IP addresses. The report outlines any required

TABLE 16.3   LIST OF VALIDATION TYPES

SAQ Validation Type	SAQ
1. Card-not-present (e-commerce) or Mail Order / Telephone Order MO/TO merchants, all cardholder data functions outsourced. This never applies to face-to-face merchants.	A
2. Imprint-only merchants with no cardholder data storage.	B
3. Stand-alone dial-up terminal merchants with no cardholder data storage.	B
4. Merchants with payment application systems connected to the Internet, no cardholder data storage.	C
5. All other merchants (not included in descriptions for SAQs A, B, or C), and all service providers defined by a card brand as eligible to complete a SAQ.	D

Source: PCI SSC, https://www.pcisecuritystandards.org/.

remediation of vulnerabilities. Merchants can consult with their QSA or an independent QSA for support and advice

Although quarterly scans are the minimum required today, they provide only a snapshot of the state of an organization's network systems at the time of scanning. It is important that an organization scan daily, weekly, or monthly to ensure that all web applications and systems are free of vulnerabilities that could allow hackers to steal cardholder data (see Table 6.4).

Safe-Harbor Provisions

There are some safe-harbor provisions to provide protection against financial and legal costs if an organization is breached and cardholder data stolen. Level 1 merchants and service providers are granted safe harbor only from compromises that take place during their annual PCI DSS certification. Level 2, 3, 4 merchants are granted safe harbor from a breach if the investigative team deems they were following PCI DSS and requirements during the breach.

Each credit company—Visa, MasterCard Worldwide, American Express, Discover, and JCB—has its own compliance program but uses the PCI DSS and PA-DSS requirements to enforce its program. Tables 16.5 and 16.6 define

TABLE 16.4   SEVERITY LEVELS FOR VULNERABILITY SCANNING

5: Urgent	Trojan horses, file read-and-write exploit, remote command execution
4: Critical	Potential Trojan horses, file read exploit
3: High	Limited exploit of read, directory browsing, denial of service
2: Medium	Sensitive configuration information can be obtained by hackers
1: Low	Information can be obtained by hackers on configuration

Source: PCI SSC.
Notes: To be considered compliant, a component must not contain level 3, 4, or 5 vulnerabilities. Moreover, all components in the customer infrastructure must be compliant. The scan report must not include any vulnerabilities that indicate features or configurations that violate PCI DSS requirements.

TABLE 16.5   VISA MERCHANT LEVELS

Level	Merchant Criteria	Date
1	Merchants processing more than 6 million Visa transactions annually (all channels) or global merchants identified as level 1 by any Visa region. Service providers processing more than 300,000 transactions annually	Annual onsite report on compliance by QSA Quarterly network scan by ASV Attestation of compliance form
2	Merchants processing 1 million to 6 million Visa transactions annually (all channels) Service providers processing less fewer than 300,000 transactions annually	Annual self-assessment questionnaire (SAQ) Quarterly network scan by ASV Attestation of compliance form
3	Merchants processing 20,000 to 1 million Visa e-commerce transactions	Same as level 2
4	Merchants processing less fewer than 20,000 Visa e-commerce transactions annually and all other merchants processing up to 1 million Visa transactions annually	Same as level 2

Source: Visa Inc.

merchant levels for Visa and MasterCard. Acquirers are responsible for determining the compliance validation levels of their merchants

Step 11: How to Begin Your Organization's PCI DSS Compliance Action Plan

- Creating an action plan is an effective way to start down the path of achieving PCI DSS compliance. Review and familiarize yourself with the PCI DSS requirements.
- Contact the PCI SSC if you want to send any management, staff, system administrators, or other IT staff for PCI DSS training.
- Determine your merchant level from your acquiring merchant bank.
- Review the certified QSAs and ASVs from the list available at the PCI SSC web site.
- Decide whether you will contact a QSA and ASV from the beginning of the process to help you or whether you will prepare before hiring them.
- Identify where cardholder data is processed, stored, or transmitted through the organization's systems
- Identify third parties that store, process, or transmit cardholder data.

TABLE 16.6   MASTERCARD MERCHANT LEVEL DESCRIPTION AND VALIDATION SUMMARY

Merchant Level	Criteria	Date and Requirements
1	All merchants, including e-commerce merchants, with more than 6 million total MasterCard transactions annually All merchants that experienced an account compromise All merchants meeting the level 1 criteria of a competing payment brand Any merchant that MasterCard, at its sole discretion, determines should meet level 1 requirements	Onsite review, quarterly network scans, report on compliance validation must be completed by June 30, 2005
2	All merchants with more than 1 million but fewer than 6 million total MasterCard transactions annually All merchants meeting the level 2 criteria of a competing payment brand	On-site review by December 31, 2010 Annual SAQ Quarterly scans Validation date: December 2010
3	All merchants with more than 20,000 but fewer than 1 million annual MasterCard e-commerce transactions All merchants meeting the level 3 criteria of a competing payment brand	Annual SAQ Quarterly scans Validation date: June 20, 2005
4	All other merchants	Annual SAQ Quarterly scans Consult acquirer for validation date

Source: http://www.mastercard.com/us/sdp/merchants/merchant_levels.html.
Notes: For level 1 merchants, the annual onsite review may be conducted by either the merchant's internal auditor or a QSA. To fulfill the scanning requirement, all merchants must conduct scans on a quarterly basis using an ASV. Level 4 merchants are required to comply with PCI DSS. Level 4 merchants should consult their acquirer to determine whether compliance validation is required.

- Identify the extent to which third parties that work on your behalf can process, store, or transmit any cardholder's account data.
- Identify any software vendors requiring PA–DSS certification.
- If required, complete your SAQ on your own or with the help of your QSA.
- Schedule your scan and prepare a remediation action, implementation, and enforcement plan to fix any vulnerabilities. Make sure you schedule the remaining three quarterly scans with your ASV.
- Have your QSA or chief security officer or chief information officer prepare a security gap analysis.

- Prepare any remediation, implementation, and enforcement action plans to ensure that all PCI DSS requirements are met for validation.
- Prepare and conduct education and training for all staff and volunteers to make sure that they understand and can follow all security policies, procedures, and methodologies.
- Prepare and conduct a quarterly review for all staff and volunteers to outline any issues or problems in maintaining compliance, outline any new security requirements to be implemented, and maintain a quarterly snapshot of the state of security of your organization.
- Have your QSA conduct compliance validation as required by the card brands in your region.
- Receive your PCI DSS compliance on implementation of all PCI requirements.
- Report to your merchant acquiring bank and the credit card companies as required.

Cost of Becoming PCI DSS Compliant

The cost of the PCI DSS–compliant assessment and certification varies on the basis of your merchant level and the certified QSA and ASV you hire for validation and scanning. Compliance validation fees can range from $150 for a level 4 merchant that requires no remediation of security vulnerabilities to more than $100,000 for level 1 merchants and service providers. You should get several price quotes from QSAs and ASVs listed at the PCI SSC web site.

Costs to Consider for Your Budget

The following items will impact the cost to become PCI DSS compliant

- Internal human resource time
- Criminal and credit background checks for all staff and volunteers who handle cardholder data
- Hardware
- Software
- Outside security consultants

Compliance Equipment You'll Need

There are some potential pieces of equipment that will be needed by your organization including the following:

- Crosscutting shredders
- Visitor badges

- Biometric equipment
- Locking file drawers or cabinets
- Video cameras
- Compliant shredding or data-storage facilities

Step 12: Understanding PA-DSS

The PA-DSS requirements originated with Visa's payment-application best practices and are based on the PCI DSS requirements. The PA-DSS is a requirement for all software vendors that process, store, or transmit cardholder data. As part of your PCI DSS compliance, any software that you have on your computer, server, and network systems must be certified to PA-DSS standards by July 2010 (see Figure 16.4). The third-party PA-DSS validations will be required for you to be PCI DSS compliant after the deadline date. Check with your acquiring merchant bank for final dates of inclusion for your PCI DSS compliance. All PA-DSS certified software must be hosted in a PCI DSS–compliant environment.

The PA-DSS applies to software vendors and others who develop payment applications that store, process, or transmit cardholder data as part of authorization or settlement, where these payment applications are sold or distributed to third parties. Payment applications validated by PA-DSS and implemented in a PCI DSS–compliant environment will minimize the potential for security breaches leading to compromises of full magnetic-strip data, card validation

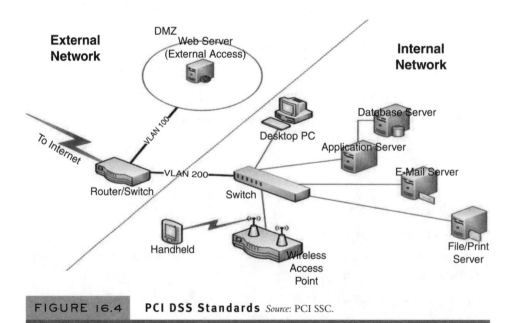

FIGURE 16.4   **PCI DSS Standards** *Source*: PCI SSC.

codes and values (e.g., CAV2, CID, CVC2, CVV2), PINs and PIN blocks, and the damaging fraud resulting from such breaches. Internally developed applications that are not sold or distributed to third parties are not subject to PCI PA-DSS but are subject to PCI DSS.

These programs apply to all merchants worldwide and in conjunction with one another (e.g., Verified by Visa, Securecode by MasterCard, iDeal in the Netherlands) to reduce criminal activity.

It is important for you to understand how to securely program your web site and any application that will store, process, or transmit cardholder data. The Open Web Application Security Project (OWASP) provides the top-10 web security flaws that are essential to consider when developing applications. At http://www.owasp.org, you'll also find a checklist for senior executives to ensure that any purchased donation-management tool applications are in fact securely created. To maintain PCI DSS and PA-DSS compliance, all applications must be coded to OWASP's specifications.

CONCLUSION

The low-cost delivery of the Internet and wireless communication through-out the world is causing the convergence of traditional communication media, television, radio, and print—revolutionizing how we live. Social media tools such as Facebook and Twitter and myriad other Internet applications have created a borderless global village to conduct both business and philanthropic commerce. Well-organized criminal syndicates are taking advantage of the current state of jurisdictional law that law enforcement agencies must adhere to. Together, by collaborating and cooperating, we can educate and train ourselves, our staff, and our volunteers to implement, monitor, and enforce security best practices in our offices and homes. This committed action will turn the current reactive approach toward criminal activity into a proactive strategic attack plan to defeat criminal organizations and syndicates.

Catherine N. Pagliaro, B.B.A., is CEO of C. N. Wylie Group Inc., which she founded in 1994, envisioning an internationally based group of companies. With a focus on security and privacy, Pagliaro and her team have created a proprietary infrastructure of web applications, network systems, and educational workshops for businesses and charities around the world while combining profit and social responsibility to facilitate positive changes in the global village. The solutions are offered through several companies including PayPaq Solutions Inc., a leader in innovative payment applications; HelpFor Charities.com Inc., which provides global online donation-management tools;

SPI-guard Security Solutions Inc., which provides PCI DSS–compliance services for merchants; Strategic Profits Inc., which offers strategic marketing programs; and Communitystorefronts Inc., which offers solutions to nongovernmental organizations. As an online development pioneer, Pagliaro enjoys sharing her knowledge, experience, and expertise in speaking engagements, publications, workshops, and presentations.

CHAPTER 17

Mobile Technology

CHARITIES' BRIDGE FROM REAL TO VIRTUAL

BEN RIGBY

Let's look ahead 10 years. Data is everywhere. It's streaming out of physical objects and into your consciousness. You look at a can of beans on the supermarket shelf, and its secrets are revealed to you: place of origin, manufacturing technique, materials used, and a warning from Greenpeace that this product is on its do-not-buy list. As you drive home, your speed and location are transmitted to your personal location monitor, which updates a dashboard that reviews your carbon footprint for the week—and will alert emergency personnel if it detects a crash. When you arrive home, you turn on your news wall, a 10-foot-by-10-foot surface in your home that displays your recent path through the neighborhood along with news articles corresponding to locations that you've passed. You peruse a story about the edible garden being installed at your child's school—and select "locate child" just to see where your youngest is located at the moment. She's safe at school, currently in the lunchroom seated next to someone you don't recognize. You'll remember to ask her about her new lunch mate when she gets home.

As excited or as fearful as you are about this future, it is coming. Although there are many mobile technologies emerging, mobile phones are the most commonly used and widespread mobile device – and they are harbingers of the uber-connected world described above. Mobile phones connect us to one another, to organizations, and to the physical environment that surrounds us. They bridge the real world to the virtual world and will soon make the two indistinguishable. For change makers, mobile phone expertise and familiarity will become a must-have capacity.

Across every nation, mobile phone ownership rates have skyrocketed. Even in the most destitute countries you'll find that a majority of the population has this device in his or her pocket. A recent UN report notes that 6 in 10 people now have mobile phone subscriptions—and increasing ownership rates are driven by developing nations.[1]

These devices enable much more than voice calls—they are data-empowered devices that retrieve and send data via the Internet as capably as any personal computer. If you're a change maker, your organization can connect with, deliver information to, fundraise from, and empower a majority of the world's population via the mobile phone. There's no other method of communication that has such broad reach and ability to bring your cause directly into the hands, pockets, purses, and minds of the world's population.

How Organizations Use Mobile Technology

So far, the most successful mobile phone campaigns have relied on text messaging. A text message is a series of up to 160 characters, typed on the keypad of the sender's mobile device, which travels through wireless networks and arrives on the screen of the recipient's mobile phone. The term "SMS" stands for "short messaging system" and is used interchangeably with "text messaging." You might also hear people refer to it as texting or just text. The growth of text messaging has been explosive. In the United States, more than 63 percent of mobile phone users send texts, compared to 90 percent in Germany, 83 percent in Spain, 85 percent in Britain, and 65 percent on average across Australia, Hong Kong, Malaysia, China, Singapore, South Korea, and Taiwan.

In developing countries, social change campaigns rely almost exclusively on text messaging and voice communication. In developed nations, where so-called smart phones are becoming more popular, we're starting to see the information-ubiquitous landscape described in the opening paragraphs. Over the past several years, the uses to which mobile phones have been put are as varied as human activity itself.

In Malawi, mobile phones enable UNICEF to increase child health and nutrition-reporting rates. Before making a one-day trek to the market, remote farmers in Uganda are able to check prices to determine whether they should go to that market or another. In the United States, teens are able to access information about sexually transmitted diseases at the bus stop, and volunteers are able to do work for their favorite nonprofits while sitting at the airport. And in Argentina, Greenpeace uses mobile phones to coordinate protesters with militarylike efficiency.

This chapter explores how these mobile technologies work along with use cases by a range of organizations from across the world. The examples presented herein are not exhaustive but illustrative, aiming to give the reader a sense of the wide variety of uses and deep integration of mobile devices in almost all regions of the world.[2]

How Mobile Phone Technologies Work

Although smart-phone campaigns are proliferating rapidly, most organizations and campaigns rely on text messaging exclusively or on a combination of text and voice. Here's a top-level summary of the configurations that are commonly used to power a mobile device campaign.

Two-Way Texting

With two-way texting, all interaction occurs via text messaging. It's a conversation between a supporter and text-enabled software that is configured to ask a series of short questions. Most event-based campaigns use this approach. The performer or speaker asks supporters to text in, and the texting software receives the incoming texts and replies with a preconfigured response, such as a request for additional information or a thank-you message. This entire conversation is scripted beforehand.

Text Alerts

Text alerts are a series of recurring texts similar to a mailing list but for text messages. Supporters first request to join the alerts campaign, either by texting in or by filling out a form on a web site. The organization then decides when to send messages to the list. Asthma UK used this approach to send texts to its list whenever pollen count exceeded a certain limit. Most text software will allow you to segment your group according to demographic data such as zip code, area code, or other information you have compiled about your supporters.

Text to Voice

Using the text-to-voice tactic, a phone number is texted to supporters along with a compelling short message that encourages someone to call the number. In most cases, the number leads to a call center or an interactive voice response (IVR) system, the systems that ask you to "Press 1 for X or 2 for Y."

Programmatic Texting

Text messages travel from mobile phones to software applications that process the messages and send replies. In a sense, the text message is akin to a mouse. Instead of clicking, however, the user is required to send a particular keyword. In the Blue Ocean Institute's campaign, for example, texting the name of a fish returns information about that fish. This type of texting campaign exhibits more intelligence than other types, as complex decisions are based on the contents of a text message. The software application is controlled by text message.

Sending a Ringtone

Methods for installing ringtones vary widely among different types of mobile phones. Ringtone service providers have made a business of understanding the differences among handsets and offering universal ringtone delivery services. If you want to send a ringtone to supporters, the easiest route is to hire one of these vendors to do it for you.

Sending a Photo

Most mobile phones store photos like a personal computer. Using the phone's mobile web browser, you can select the photo from the phone's memory and upload it to a photo-sharing site, such as Flickr. On phones that support e-mail, a photo can be sent as an attachment to any e-mail address. In both cases, sending photos from mobile phones requires a high degree of mobile phone proficiency. Sending a photo by text message is not possible. However, an alternate (but less and less used) variant of text messaging, called MMS or Multimedia Messaging Service, can be employed to send multimedia files such as photos.

Smart-Phone Applications

Most smart phones allow developers to create software specifically for these devices. The software works just like software on your personal computer. You download it, install it, and then use it. Smart-phone software has the advantage of being tightly tied to the mobile device's functions, such as the camera, GPS locator, address book, SMS system, e-mail system, and more. The Extraordinaries, for example, offers smart-phone software for the iPhone. It's an application for microvolunteering that takes advantage of all of the built-in iPhone functions: watching video, listening to audio, reading documents, visiting web pages, transmitting GPS location, taking photos, recording audio, writing text documents, and more.

Text to Screen

For text-to-screen applications, an organization sets up a large screen in a public location. The screen will typically display a text-in number and a call to action such as, "What do you think about Bloomberg's recycling plan? Text 54444." Incoming messages are then displayed on the screen. "Text to screen allows people in remote locations to interact in a meaningful way with one location," says Jed Alpert, of Mobile Commons, a vendor providing a text-to-screen platform.[3] MobileActive.org has a great resource that explains how to set up a text-to-screen system (http://mobileactive.org/how-run-text-screen-campaigns-mobileactive-guide-ngos).

Unstructured Supplementary Service Data

The abbreviation USSD stands for unstructured supplementary service data. This rather wonky term refers to real-time or instant messaging on mobile phones. One of the advantages of using USSD is that sending and receiving messages is often free or close to free (unlike SMS). Use of USSD has been particularly popular in Africa to advertise products—and by nonprofits running so-called please-call-me campaigns. In these campaigns, a call to action is sent out over USSD, such as "Please call me 07255444 No one suffers alone. We can deal with HIV & AIDS. HIV911 helpline." If this call to action interests the recipient, he or she can then make the call and incur the charge.[4] SocialTxt is one of the leading vendors to offer such campaigns (http://www.praekeltfoundation.org/socialtxt.html).

How to Get Started

You can start a text (or text-and-voice) campaign in four ways: by hiring a text vendor; by hiring a self-service, web-based service provider; by setting up an account at an aggregator; or by using a laptop-based system. The field is quite new, so vendors and providers are still figuring out the balance of price, service, and features. Their offerings change frequently, so it's in your best interest to do some comparison shopping. If you're operating in a country in which smart phones are prevalent, you might consider building a smart-phone application.

Text Vendors

Hiring a text vendor is the easiest way to set up a text campaign. These specialists can get a new campaign started in a couple of days. Most have built proprietary systems for managing incoming and outgoing messages. If you want a customized solution, they can usually build it for you or help you configure a set of tools. Text vendors will offer you support, tracking, and strategic advice. Typically, they can charge for setup, monthly usage, and per-message usage.

Self-Service, Web-Based Service Providers

If you don't need a guide to walk you through the process and you're not expecting a lot of traffic, a web-based provider may be the way to go. To get started, head to the provider's web site, decide which of its plans works best for you, fill out a few forms, leave your credit card number, and you'll be up and running within several minutes. Most providers offer a wide range of services, ranging from sending out a one-time message to a list of phone numbers to integrating texting into a software application that you already own and operate.

This option isn't completely self-service, as most providers offer telephone support. However, you won't get the same level of attention and expertise that you'll get from a text vendor. You'll also pay a premium on per-message fees. Most providers make it easy to sign up and charge little up front, and then they earn their money from messaging fees. If you plan to send a lot of messages, a text vendor may end up being less expensive. Some of these providers are adding higher levels of service and the ability to craft custom campaigns, blurring the line between them and the other vendors.

Desktop- or Laptop-Based SMS

A new breed of software allows you to set up a service to send and receive text messages directly from your personal computer or laptop. It's like running your own custom text-messaging center. Using a simple cable from your mobile phone to your PC, along with this software, you'll have your own personal text-messaging system set up in less than an hour. The downside is that you'll need a technical person to configure the system, and throughput rates are often slow— -allowing you to process only about 30 messages every minute. If these rates are acceptable for your case and you have a technical person on staff, desktop SMS software is a great solution. FrontlineSMS and RapidSMS are two market leaders.

Do It Yourself

If you've got a highly technical staff, ample financial resources, and long-term texting goals, building an in-house texting application will give you maximum control over functionality and cost. Be warned that working with the carriers and their intermediaries can be a trying experience, however. Pursue this route only after a careful cost-benefit analysis. Doing things yourself typically requires the following steps:

- Reserving of a short code
- Purchase of an account with an aggregator

- A wait of two to six months for all of the wireless carriers to approve your application;
- Coding of the software application that handles incoming and outgoing messages
- Ongoing maintenance and carrier compliance (they change their rules frequently).
- Need for an aggregator, someone who works with all of the carriers to centralize and coordinate sending and receiving messages. Even if you do things yourself, you'll need to work with an aggregator. The carriers don't want to negotiate deals with thousands of small organizations. They've chosen a handful of aggregators to take on that responsibility.

Strategic Considerations

The following are some of the considerations in developing relationships and conducting a successful campaign.

The Old Advertising Rules Still Apply

Each supporter needs to opt in to your campaign, according to carrier policies. This means you'll need to promote your campaign. You might use announcements from stage and on event screens, web site promotions, and newspaper and outdoor advertising. In all of these scenarios, the old rules of advertising apply. Higher frequency and greater reach result in better response rates. Promote your call to action far and wide.

Use a Trusted Messenger at Live Events

If your organization is not well known, you face an obstacle in persuading people to text your short code, as most young people know their numbers are captured when they text in. Ask someone who is known and trusted among your community of supporters to make the announcement. In trials of our texting software at events, we found that when a person unknown to the community asked people to text in, response rates were around 1 percent, but rates increased to between 15 percent and 45 percent when a well-known person made the request.

To maintain this level of trust, you'll need to treat your supporters' personal information with respect, which means giving them an easy method for opting out of the text campaign and not selling their numbers to third parties, unless they grant you permission to do so.

Incentives

What does a person get in return for texting your short code and giving you their personal information? In the case of the musician Bono's concerts, participants' names scrolled across a giant screen. Some organizations give away backstage passes, coupon codes, bumper stickers, or ringtones. Such incentives may work, but they're a weak incentive. They are tantamount to saying, "Our texting campaign is so lame that we have to give you something extra to sign up. We have to pay you to participate." Devise incentives that support your cause while making use of the mobile phone as a medium.

For example, San Francisco Health's SexInfo campaign offered valuable and confidential information in return for participating in their bus-stop advertised campaign (sexual disease information in the privacy of one's own mobile phone screen). The incentive was a relevant message at the location where the campaign was advertised.[5] Instead of relying on gimmicks, the health department offered something of real value to its constituency.

Timeliness and Relevance

Timeliness is counted in hours, not days. Relevancy is measured in terms of the value of information in a given place.

Being timely is easy. Avoid sending messages that refer to events that occur in more than 24 hours.[6] Ask your supporter to make a call now or to come to an event in an hour. Don't tell them about a speech taking place the next evening. Text messages are ephemeral—take advantage of the near term.

Relevancy is a lot more difficult to achieve because it depends largely on a supporter's location. If the person is at home and you send information about environmentally friendly fish, it's not very relevant. If that person is running errands, the information is more relevant. And if you send it while that person is at the market, it's incredibly relevant. The best way to achieve relevancy is to encourage your supporters to request information from you when they're at a location that fits your campaign.

A Clear Call to Action

Confusing language hampers many texting campaigns. With only 160 characters at their disposal, organizations take numerous liberties and shortcuts with language. Consider this message from John Edwards's 2008 presidential campaign: "John Edwards wants 2 talk 2 you! Hit Reply. Type 'CALL' & hit Send. John will call YOU right back! OR call 202-350-9749. txt STOP 2 unsub." This call to action seems jumbled. Just because it's a text message doesn't mean that you have to forsake clarity.

Texting as an Initial Hook

Texting is great for reaching a large number of people in an instant. Conversely, it works well in situations when you want many people to be able to simultaneously reach you, such as at a concert. But it's also a shallow medium. If your campaign isn't suited to delivering extremely valuable information in the space of 160 characters, consider moving the supporter to a more immersive medium such as voice. Use texting for its strengths: immediacy, timeliness, and ubiquity.

Campaign Integration

If you're operating a mobile phone program that features texting, photos, or ringtones, integrate the effort into your broader campaign efforts. Standing alone, any of these mobile-only touch points is weak. Interactions on the mobile device become more powerful when used in tandem with richer forms of communication, such as in-person meet-ups or voice, or when followed up with e-mail.

Localization

As with any other social change campaign, something that works in one area or among one community may not work in another. It's important to develop the messaging, processes, and user-experience design in collaboration with or assisted by the people who will end up using it.

Sustainability

As we're still in the early days of mobile social change campaigns, many campaigns are run as pilots. Pilots are great for testing assumptions, usage patterns, and evaluating usefulness. However, one factor that is often left out of pilot programs is pricing. It's important to develop the pricing structure during the pilot phase to understand whether the project is sustainable over the long term—and to build the expectation that the service costs money—if the end users are to be charged for it. It is, of course, difficult to charge for a mobile service after it has been free for some time. Several promising mobile services have been shuttered after the funded pilot phase—despite delivering value—partly as the result of an insufficient pricing model.

EXAMPLE USE CASES

Immediate Information—Making Markets More Efficient Worldwide

In an age of global markets, farmers are forced to enhance production, improve the quality of their yield, and access markets in short time frames. Small-scale farmers, in particular, face even greater challenges, such as lack of access to weather and market information. Without good information, these farmers are left to the mercy of often-usurious intermediaries. With the advent of mobile technology, governments and nongovernmental organizations (NGOs) are helping farmers gain greater control of their economic destinies.

In Uganda, the Women of Uganda Network (Wougnet), a local NGO, is helping more than 400 rural farmers in the Apac district in northern Uganda access information about market prices through text messaging.

"The use of SMS has attracted a lot of interest from farmers because information can easily be accessed. Mobile phones are affordable to many people even in rural areas," explains Wougnet's executive director, Dorothy Okello.[7]

Through the system, information officers from Wougnet collect market-price information through physical visits to markets and from web research. They translate the information to Luo, the local language, before sending it to the farmers via an SMS alert. If they desire additional information, farmers can send text direct questions to the NGO. According to Wougnet, the project has improved farmers' access to markets, which has, in turn, increased sales and income. Two other organizations, FoodNet and the Busoga Rural Open Source and Development Initiative (BROSDI) are running similar projects in different regions in Uganda.

In a similar program, and one that has greater potential for sustainability, Kenya's SMS Sokoni project provides agricultural information through SMS for a fee. The project is run by the Kenya Agricultural Commodities Exchange (KACE), a private firm, in partnership with African mobile service provider Safaricom. Information kiosks are located near places where agricultural commodity buyers and sellers meet, to provide low-cost access to farmers. The KACE workers collect information on prices from the kiosks and then send it to the farmers, buyers, and exporters through SMS.

According to the KACE web site, farmers have quadrupled their earnings because they have access to information about potential buyers and prices. The partnership with a mobile service provider has given SMS Sokoni a wider reach and has helped reduce costs, which largely explains why it is popular. Charging user fees may ensure sustainability after the donor phase as opposed to Wougnet's donor-supported venture.

Another project in Africa offering SMS messaging service for farmers is Xam Marsé in Senegal. Launched by Manobi in 2001, Xam Marsé provides market information about various products to Senegalese farmers, traders, hoteliers, and others via Internet and free daily SMS. According to the Manobi web site, the information has enabled farmers to increase their sale prices negotiated from their fields or on the markets by more than 50 percent per year.

TradeNet in Ghana is another example. It was started in 2004 as one of several software projects undertaken by the Ghanaian software company BusyLab. "On the TradeNet web site are more than eight hundred thousand prices from hundreds of markets, spanning a range of time periods and countries. The price offers are available to search and compare over time, and across markets and countries."

Because only a small percentage of its users are active on the computer-based Internet, TradeNet has an SMS service at its core. Users can sign up to receive weekly automatic SMS alerts on certain commodities in particular markets, upload offers to buy and sell products via mobile phone, request current prices for a commodity in a country, and receive an SMS with the information.

Many studies have revealed that access to good market information can increase revenues for everyone along the supply chain—producers, collectors, traders, transporters, and exporters. According to OneWorld Africa (2008) in Chipata, Zambia, mobile phones assisted three area associations in selling their produce at better market prices.

There is growing evidence that mobile phones allow better access to market opportunities and allow farmers to work more efficiently as a result. "In the Indian village of Kerala, fishermen would generally return to their 'home' markets with their catch. Oversupply meant that fish had to be routinely dumped into the sea. After mobile phones were introduced, the practice of dumping fish overboard stopped; fishermen's profit rose by eight percent and consumer prices fell on average by four percent," according to a study by Robert Jensen in 2007.

By offering farmers faster and cheaper communication, mobile phones often substitute for costly and risky journeys. (id21 Insights 69, 2007). These projects have demonstrated how mobile telephony has given farmers a chance to access information more quickly and thus reduce losses. Information about markets and prices gives farmers more options for selling their produce and helps them make informed decisions.

However, challenges do exist. Illiteracy prevents many rural farmers from receiving the benefits of mobile phone technology. "Many rural farmers in Africa are illiterate . . . [which] rules out the delivery of complex technical information that would traditionally be delivered through training, booklets and manuals."[8] With experience gained by partners and pilot projects run by TradeNet in Ghana, it has become clear that strong distribution networks are needed to deliver relevant information to everyone along the supply chain, especially rural farmers. This means creating networks to upload the data and training village operators to provide support. This will go a long way in solving the illiteracy problem, as information can be translated and interpreted by those who understand.

This subsection was adapted from the blog post by Esther Nasikye titled "Mobile Telephony Makes a Difference" from MobileActive.org.[9]

Text in Strategy—Recruiting at Events in the United States

The crowd simmers with excitement as the rock band U2 launches into its second set. Bono, the band's charismatic front man, tells the crowd to raise their mobile phones in the air. Thousands of little lights flicker in the night sky. An impassioned Bono describes the horrors of AIDS and poverty in Africa and says, "Time to do a magic trick. These little devices—these cell phones—they can do all sorts of things."

The immense screen above the stage displays the phrase "UNITE. 86483." Bono asks the crowd to type their names, addresses, and the keyword "UNITE" into their cell phones and send it to the number on screen. As they text in, their names scroll across the giant display. By the end of the evening, more than 10,000 people had joined Bono's cause. More than 250,000 had signed up by the end of his tour.

It doesn't hurt to have an international superstar stump for your cause, but even if all you've got is a crowd of people, texting offers an inexpensive and effective method for gathering contact information. To use this method, you have to persuade people to send a text to what is known as a short code. A short code is a five- or six-digit number that works a lot like a web address. Texts sent to it are routed to a computer that records the sender's phone number and whatever other information you've requested from him or her.

The initial text-in will serve as your first point of contact. It's the beginning of a dialogue with a potential new supporter. Subsequently, you can send additional texts to request more information or direct the person to another medium, such as voice-based calls. I will share examples of this type of redirection later in this chapter. One of the primary advantages of gathering contact information in this way is that it's instantly centralized and digitized. You don't have to transcribe names and numbers from a sign-up sheet; they're instantly stored in a spreadsheet-friendly format.

Bono promoted his short code with an announcement from stage and then reinforced the message on screen. The common rules of advertising apply to short-code marketing: for the best results, show your message as often as possible and in as many different media as possible. Talk about it at events, print it on ads and fliers, and show it on computer screens.

Jed Alpert, the CEO of Mobile Commons, one of the leading text-messaging vendors, reports that live events frequently generate initial response rates in the 50 percent range; of those respondents, 20 percent to 40 percent typically provide additional information, such as an e-mail address. At very large events, text messaging has the potential to serve as a highly efficient recruiting mechanism.

Delivering Timely, Relevant, and Private Information: United States and United Kingdom

Young people live mobile lives. They're on the move between home, school, work, cafes, and friends' homes, among other places. Text campaigns work well when they deliver timely and personal information of value to someone who is on the go.

For example, Asthma UK launched a text-alert campaign to warn asthma sufferers about high-pollen-count days so that they could take extra precautions. The organization's web site advertises the service and provides the forms necessary to sign up.

This campaign delivers time-sensitive and useful information to people who may not have had access to the information otherwise. It makes extremely good use of texting as a medium by addressing the needs of a mobile constituency. One problem with the campaign, however, is that asthma sufferers are required to sign up for the service on a web site. It takes advantage of texting to push out relevant information, but it doesn't use the same model to pull in potential asthma sufferers. Asthma UK might increase its number of participants if it were to advertise its service outdoors, where people tend to experience asthma the most.

One of texting's primary benefits is that it can be inserted into a relevant place. The San Francisco Department of Public Health in partnership with the sex education organization Internet Sexuality Information Services, took advantage of this opportunity to deliver sexual health information through its SexInfo campaign, which offered facts and resources about sexually transmitted diseases, condoms, and pregnancy. It was advertised on billboards around the city.

The campaign focused on privacy. The Department of Public Health understood that young people have few avenues for privately learning about sex. Mobile phones, however, are perfect devices for having private conversations. The campaign advertised the service at bus stops and enabled young people to request, read, and delete information on their terms. It made optimal use of text messaging because it selected a relevant place to promote the service and to deliver information.

Fundraising: United States

The special type of text message called premium SMS, or PSMS, allows an organization to place a charge on a supporter's phone bill. The funds are then passed from the carrier to the organization every month. For example, in the wake of Hurricane Katrina, the Red Cross conducted a campaign called Text 2HELP in which it asked supporters to text the keyword "HELP" to a short code. After texting in, a $5 tax-deductible donation was charged to the supporter's phone bill and paid to the American Red Cross for disaster-relief efforts. The carriers agreed to completely eliminate their commission, and the Red Cross raised more than $100,000. And more recently, after the Haiti earthquake over $30 million (and counting) was raised via a similar text-in fundraising campaign.

The caveat with mobile fundraising campaigns is that, in most countries, wireless carriers charge a hefty commission on transactions (up to 50 percent) and limit the amount of each donation (to $5 or $10 in the United States, for example). In the United States, the Mobile Giving Foundation allows nonprofits to register for an exemption to this fee. However, getting set up with Mobile Giving often takes a good deal of time and still requires a 10 percent fee.

Make Data Accessible—On-Demand Advocacy Worldwide

The Blue Ocean Institute was launching a text-messaging campaign called Name the Fish that has subtle but important distinctions from the foregoing examples. The institute maintains a database of ocean-friendly seafood, meaning seafood that is relatively abundant and harvested using environmentally responsible techniques. The group has now made its database accessible via text message.

Text the name of a fish to 30644 and you'll receive details about that species on your cell phone. For example, if you text "orange roughy," you'll learn that the fish is typically caught using habitat-damaging trawl gear and that fishing also catches threatened deep-sea sharks. Skipping that option on the market shelf, you might then text "striped bass," which has a high rating on the ocean-friendly scorecard.

Like the Asthma UK and SexInfo campaigns, this program delivers timely and relevant information. The key difference is that it's intended to be used as an ongoing, on-demand service. Whenever you're in the fish market, the institute wants you to remember to text in. Unfortunately, marketing this type of service is difficult. The best place to promote the service (at the market) is also the least likely to accept advertising. The institute doesn't have the location advantages of the SexInfo campaign or the ability to know when its information is relevant, like the Asthma UK campaign. It's a valuable service that will be tough to effectively promote.

Like a Flock of Birds—Coordinating Protesters Worldwide

Since the early 2000s, text-enabled political movements have erupted throughout the world. In 2002, text messaging was instrumental in the election of South Korean President Roh Moo-hyun. When Election Day polls showed that Roh's opponent was winning, hundreds of thousands of Roh's supporters mobilized friends via text messaging. Roh edged out a victory. After the 2004 bombings in Madrid, Spain, officials banned demonstrations in the 24 hours preceding the election. In defiance of the ban, Spanish citizens used text messaging to organize impromptu demonstrations against the government. Most believed that the government lied about key facts related to the bombing. Thousands arrived, and the incumbent, who had been ahead in the polls, lost the election.

Such spontaneous mobilizations are now recognized as a potent political force. Texting changes the dynamics of mass political movements: Like a flock of birds synchronizing themselves through silent signals, crowds respond dynamically to compelling texts. They gather in a flash, disperse in an instant, and shift the balance of power.

Organizers have taken advantage of these dynamics to coordinate smaller-scale mobilizations. For example, Greenpeace Argentina recently won a campaign to save the Pizarro reserve on behalf of the Wichí people thanks to a campaign that used text messaging to coordinate activists. Situated in Argentina's northwestern province of Salta, the reserve came under threat when the local government sold some of the Wichí's land without the tribe's consultation or approval.

Greenpeace gave mobile phones to Wichí leaders, instructing them to text Greenpeace organizers whenever the developers approached with their bulldozers. Once alerted, Greenpeace organizers would send texts en masse to their volunteers. Those who were available at the moment could hop on a motorbike, ride to the designated area, and chain themselves to the bulldozers. Others would arrive with video cameras to film the intervention. The activists would stay on the site until sentries at the park entrances alerted them that police were on the way. At this point, those with video footage would make a quick exit, before the others were arrested.

Greenpeace was therefore able to deliver compelling and regular footage to supporters and the news media. After a 20-month battle, the reserve regained its protected status.[10] Oscar Soria, one of the Greenpeace leaders, says of the effort, "Using short message service [texting] to mobilize people on the ground, in the forests, and in the cities is an extremely powerful tool, because you are able to reach so many people in one moment."[11]

Texting enabled Greenpeace to coordinate a nimble team that stayed one step ahead of its antagonists. Activists across the world have used the same militarylike tactics to evade police and organize flash mobs of protesters.

Timely Mobilizations: United States

Greenpeace's Wichí campaign involved a complex web of coordination. Much simpler text-messaging campaigns have also proved effective. In 2006, I had the good providence to partner with Working Assets, the Student PIRGs, and a team of academic researchers to conduct a campaign to test the effectiveness of text messaging in getting out the vote for the upcoming November elections.[12]

Leading up to the election, we registered young people to vote online and on the ground. In addition to the standard information that the Federal Election Commission requires, we asked whether registrants would mind receiving a text-message reminder to vote. We compiled a list of about 12,000 phone numbers through this method. The day before Election Day, we sent text reminders to half of these numbers (leaving the other half to serve as the control group). The messages said: "A friendly reminder that TOMORROW is Election Day. Democracy depends on citizens like you—so please vote! PIRG/TxtVoter.org."[13]

When the voter files later became available, the research team was able to see how many people voted in both the experimental and the control group. Text reminders increased an individual's likelihood to vote by four to five percentage points. Past studies have shown that this rate is about the same as a professional-quality phone call. This response rate is promising because it hints that groups doing voter registration can spend less money to get out the vote. In this instance, it's difficult to compare costs because the studies don't do an apples-to-apples cost comparison, but in theory, a phone call by a human should be less expensive than a text by an automated system.

Text-mobilization campaigns that don't require as much effort as getting voters to the polls have shown even higher participation rates. In late 2006, a series of legislation was proposed in the U.S. Congress. Working Assets felt that the passage of several bills was important to the organization, and it set up a text campaign that was responsive to the unpredictable and time-sensitive nature of the legislative process.

When a high-priority bill came up for a vote, Working Assets sent a text message to its network of activists that contained a short note about the upcoming legislation as well as a phone number to call to take action. When supporters called the number, they heard a recorded message describing what was at stake in the legislation. Callers were then automatically transferred to the congressional switchboard and from there on to their representative's office. Each time the messages went out, supporters responded enthusiastically: 28.8 percent responded to the first batch of messages, 31.4 percent to the second, and 18.3 percent to the third.[14]

This campaign relied on the ability of text messaging to make an immediate connection among a large group of people. Working Assets then moved people quickly to voice, which has a much greater persuasive capacity.

On-Demand Volunteerism by Smart Phone Worldwide

Over the past year, I have been fortunate to collaborate on the Extraordinaries, a project that brings volunteerism to mobile phones. We've been calling this form of action microvolunteerism, and it allows people to volunteer on demand and on the spot—whenever and wherever they have the time. For nonprofits, it's a new way to engage supporters and to make use of volunteer talent.

For most people, finding time to give back is a challenge. With 60-hour workweeks, kids, errands, and the stress of everything else, most people don't volunteer.[15] Overwhelmingly, the reason cited is lack of time. But although most people don't have several hours each week to volunteer, they do have a few minutes here and there. Despite busy schedules, we often find ourselves with idle time: waiting for the metro, in line at the bank, at the doctor's office, watching television commercials, and more.

The Extraordinaries lowers barriers to giving back by enabling people to volunteer during these idle minutes. The system delivers microtasks on behalf of nonprofits that can be accomplished on the spot via mobile phones. The system is not appropriate for every type of task. Some tasks are better suited to distributed work than others, but we are discovering new types every day. Thus far in our early experiments, we've found that following task categories work well:

- Language translation
- Audio transcription
- Digitization of nonscannable texts
- Film subtitling
- Photographing
- Document review and commenting
- Member relationship management

- Call banking
- Surveys
- Research
- Image and video tagging (categorization/archiving)
- GPS transmission (for route tracking and aggregation)

Early results are promising. In our image-tagging experiments (cataloging media archives), volunteers have submitted more than 90,000 tags in just a few months. During the recent Haiti quake, we asked volunteers to tag images coming in from the news with phrases such as "can see a person's face" "female" or "male." These images were then matched up against photos of missing people and the volunteers were then asked to find missing people. Tens of thousands of volunteers responded and as this chapter goes to print, we're in the process of verifying over 550 potential matches.

Traditional volunteer management requires a high degree of overhead, such as training, vetting, and application processing. These high costs prevent most organizations from making significant use of volunteer labor. In practice, many skilled and enthusiastic supporters are turned away.

Using the Extraordinaries, organizations can systematically distribute work to volunteers with little overhead. It allows nontechnical staff members to create tasks, publish tasks, and receive completed work from thousands of volunteers.

As a corollary benefit, the process strengthens relationships with supporters while providing opportunities to recruit new members and solicit donations.

CONCLUSION

Most of the world's population already owns a mobile device. It is the dominant communication channel between organizations and their constituencies. If your organization can navigate the often-overwhelming variety of options, the mobile device holds tremendous promise as a tool for recruitment, advocacy, mobilization, and information. Few other technologies have such wide reach and deep integration into the social fabric of our lives.

Mobile devices will bring the power of social computing to real-world spaces. They will create opportunities for supporters to meet, discuss, and mobilize offline. In the hands, pockets, and purses of a majority of the world's population, these diminutive devices are redefining what it means to be connected to the Internet and to one another.

In the future, these devices will stop looking like phones—they will first follow the form of the iPhone and then will simply connect every object in our lives directly to the network. Untethered from our desks, we will have more freedom to act on inspiration and heightened emotion. As change makers, it's our task to create these moments or to be there at the right time—and then to put the tools of action in the hands of our supporters.

Ben Rigby graduated from Stanford University with Honors, Distinction, and Phi Beta Kappa. He cofounded Akimbo Design, a web design firm that created and managed consumer web sites for The North Face, Beringer Vineyards, and California Pizza Kitchen and completed award-winning projects for Nokia, Sony Pictures, MGM, Calvin Klein, and Macromedia. His company produced three web design books, won dozens of awards, and was featured in *Newsweek*, the *New York Times, Washington Post*, and *USA Today*. As CTO of DFILM, he managed the launch of a youth-focused communication platform in partnership with KPN. He also launched a viral "MovieMaker" application licensed by Yahoo!, Sam Adams, IBM, the Sierra Club, and Old Navy. In 2004, he founded Mobile Voter, the first organization in the United States to engage young voters via text messaging. Rigby is the author of *Mobilizing Generation 2.0: A Practical Guide to Using Web2.0 Technologies to Recruit, Organize and Engage Youth* (2007). In 2008, Rigby cofounded The Extraordinaries, a project to deliver microvolunteer on-demand and on-the-spot.opportunities to mobile phones.

Transforming Activists into Donors—Nicolas Hulot Foundation Case Study

FRÉDÉRIC FOURNIER, ePMT - OPTIMUS

Since its creation in 1990, the Nicolas Hulot Foundation (http://www.fondation-nicolas-hulot.org) has made it its mission to change the individual and collective behaviors of the French in order to protect our planet. As a registered charity, the foundation implements every possible effort to initiate a new type of society based on awareness of the interdependence of humans and all living organisms.

Early on, the foundation was financed in preference and priority by corporations, and it never, or seldom, appealed to the generosity of the public. Individual gifts did not represent a significant portion of the organization's financial support.

Two events led the foundation to turn toward the public to raise funds: In May 2005, the foundation in partnership with ADEME (http://www2.ademe.fr) launched the project Le Défi pour la Terre (Challenge for the Earth) (http://www.defipourlaterre.org) and invited the French people to join them in selecting a series of ecological activities against global warming. At the end of 2008, nearly 800,000 people added their signatures and became involved. At the end of 2006, following the great success of Défi pour la Terre, Nicolas Hulot, president of the foundation, as well as celebrity animator of a TV show on the environment, decided to run for the presidential elections in France. He launched a Pacte Ecologique (http://www.pacte-ecologique.org) so that ecology would take center stage in political activities. Within a few months, nearly 700,000 French citizens, including the major presidential election candidates, signed the pact.

With nearly 1 million activists, other charities may feel envious. It is with this capital, with this huge potential, that we started work at the foundation at

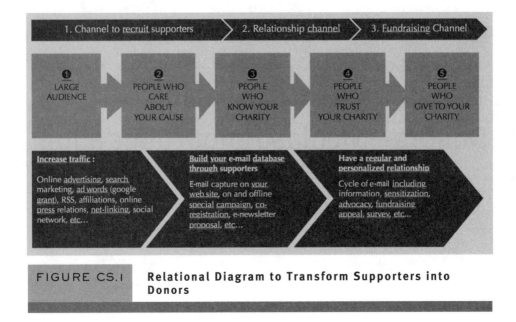

| FIGURE CS.1 | **Relational Diagram to Transform Supporters into Donors** |

the beginning of 2008 to raise funds for the Nicolas Hulot Foundation from individuals—with the Internet as our primary tool.

First, the strategy recommended by Optimus and implemented in conjunction with the foundation consisted of a combination of advocacy and fundraising campaign using a completely clean database. Figure CS.1 summarize the strategy in a diagram.

At the end of 2008, fundraising needed to be greatly developed for two reasons:

1. To increase private resources of the foundation to finance more projects
2. To increase the number of contributors, the principal element for the Nicolas Hulot Foundation to be considered a privileged contact of the government.

It is in this context that Optimus came up with the Eco-Actor project.

About the Eco-Actor Campaign

The community of friends of the foundation (mainly activists involved in activities to protect the environment) is not a community of donors. This is often the case for environment charities. Thus, the challenge for Optimus and the foundation consisted of mobilizing this community within a short period, right in the middle of the end-of-year holidays. France offered a tax deduction for contributions made before December 31, which was a reason for the urgency of this campaign.

The objectives of the campaign were as follows:

- Transform supporters of the foundation into donors to reach a minimum of 10,000 donors, the threshold required to represent the foundation in front of governmental boards
- Collect funds to finance projects
- Enliven the community and send a message that financial support is important, even primary
- Achieve a positive return on investment

To meet those objectives, we proposed implementing the concept of eco-actors. We proposed to supporters that they become actors of change themselves. By signing a petition and by supporting the foundation, mobilizing their surroundings, making changes to their environmental behavior, and providing the foundation with the possibility to be heard by public authorities.

We offered a privileged and separate status to those who wished to become involved more deeply in the activities of the foundation through an event web site. The web site presented a video of the foundation's president, Nicolas Hulot, and chief executive, Cécile Ostria. Both reminded members of the community of the urgency and importance of the activities and contributions. The tone of the eco-actor campaign was quite urgent, with a reminder of the challenges involved in activities for the planet, and thus the importance of supporting the foundation. An urgency to act was created at year-end, and a countdown was launched a few days before December 31, the deadline to benefit from the tax relief. The campaign took place from December 18, 2008, through January 5, 2009 (see Figure CS.2).

DEDICATED EVENT WEB SITE

The first step was to create an event web site dedicated to the campaign, where people could obtain information on becoming eco-actors, make a contribution, and—most important—mobilize people around them and give their opinions about the campaign or the foundation.

The web site was very simple and centered on a video that started automatically and presented Hulot's message on mobilization (see Figure CS.3).

The call to action was clear and easy to understand, whether through the web site or the video: "Become an eco-actor by supporting the Nicolas Hulot Foundation."

The site proposed the following actions for mobilization:

- First priority: Making a gift of at least 10 euros to encourage a greater number of donors (see Figure CS.3)

FIGURE CS.2   **Overall Online Campaign: How to Draw People to the Event's Web Site**

FIGURE CS.3   **Eco-Actor Event Web Site Home Page**

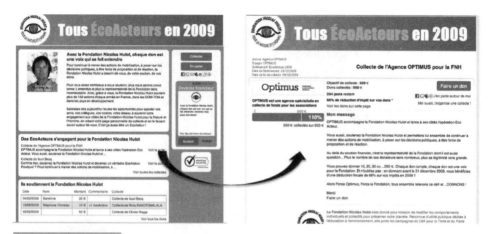

FIGURE CS.4   **Peer-to-Peer Fundraising Pages**

- Second priority:
  - Raising funds for the foundation yourself (peer-to-peer) (see Figure CS.4)
  - Sharing opinions (see Figure CS.5)
  - Telling a friend (see Figure CS.6)

FIGURE CS.5   **Share Opinions Page**

FIGURE CS.6   **"Tell a Friend" Page**

A counter was set up at the beginning of the project with the objective to bring onboard 10,000 eco-actors. The concept behind this challenge allowed individuals to see concretely that they were participating in this project. We later realized that such logic behind a challenge is one of the key elements to keep in mind in the framework of any project.

What's more, to highlight the campaign's urgency, before December 31, we also implemented a countdown to encourage everyone to contribute as soon as possible.

As you can see on the home page of the web site (see CS.3), the major theme was to encourage a visitor to make a donation. This main proposal was repeated three times on the web site: in a gift button (the biggest button) on the right side of the video, a link on the left side of the video, and another in the web site navigation area. Visitors could not have (or should not have) misunderstood what we expected of them.

Other mobilization elements also worked very well even though we did not wish to place them at the forefront. That was true for peer-to-peer fundraising (see Figure CS.4).

Why didn't we want to overly promote this proposition? Simply because the main objective was to transform supporters into donors. Overpromoting this peer-to-peer call to action could have distracted our supporters from making gifts. There was a risk that they would try (with or without success) to find new donors without actually making a gift themselves!

It's all about the strategy and objective. Just because peer-to-peer is so popular now does not mean that your organization needs to start such a campaign at any given stage of developing its online strategy.

This experience was an excellent test: Without promotion and with just a self-administrated technical platform, nearly 100 personal fundraising pages were created (see Figure CS.4), including the Optimus agency's fundraising page, of course. This was a good sign for the next steps of the foundation's online strategy—everything in its time though!

The number of people who visited the site during the three weeks of the campaign was moderately successful. What is interesting is that the community moderated itself. Except for two offensive messages, removed by the web site moderator, there was no attack made on the foundation or its president. All the messages contained words of encouragement, ideas to change the world, propositions, and so on. When a web site visitor left a message that was less than positive, it was the community itself that answered rather than the foundation's moderator. That is an important lesson. Trust in those who support you. In the case of a black sheep, the community will intervene. Try it for yourself.

People give to people—and for people. Never forget this in your campaign. Whether it be on fundraising personal pages or "tell a friend," this principle was effective. Admit it—you would open a e-mail from a friend relaying the message of a television personality such as Nicholas Hulot regarding the environment, right? We'll see the results on this point later.

Finally, the campaign's web site included the fundamental elements of this type of project:

- A link to the foundation's Facebook group that posted information on the campaign (see Figure CS.7)
- A link to the Dailymotion web site (French YouTube)
- The proposal to receive the foundation newsletter for free
- Various information on the reasons for the campaign and the foundation

These elements are important. For more than 100,000 pages viewed, 4 percent of the visitors read the "Reasons for This Campaign" page. You may think that 4 percent is a small number. That is true, but if all the people who see this page later make a gift, then doesn't that make this page essential? Of course!

Creating a web site is useless if no one visits it. The second part of our task was to promote the web site among the community of supporters of the foundation.

Post about the
« Eco-Actor »
campaign

FIGURE CS.7   **Nicolas Hulot Foundation's Facebook page with Post about the Campaign**

Targeted Promotion Using E-Mail and Various Tools

With nearly 500,000 e-mail addresses of supporters (less than 10 percent of donors at the time), it was not pertinent to launch a wide-ranging promotion campaign. Having the largest possible e-mail database for your organization is a key element. I recommend to all charities to urge launching a strategy to capture e-mail addresses as soon as possible.

Optimus therefore considered and implemented a plan based on the following:

- A series of e-mail to the entire community (see Figures CS.8 and CS.9)
- Promotion of the campaign on the foundation's web site using banners
- A link to the main social network: Facebook
- A link to Dailymotion
- Use of a peer-to-peer fundraising platform

Between December 18 and December 30, we sent out four e-mail messages to 500,000 supporters (see Figures CS.8 and CS.9). The first was sent December 18, 2008 (Thursday), to encourage maximum reading over the weekend (since many people check or reply to their e-mail on weekends). In this first e-mail, we placed Nicolas Hulot at the forefront, given his strong media presence and his role as president of the foundation.

Objet : Devenez EcoActeur avant le 31/12 !
Date : jeudi 18 décembre 2008 20:49
De : Fondation Nicolas Hulot <news@news-fnh.org>
Répondre à : Fondation Nicolas Hulot <news@news-fnh.org>
À : Virginie Gagnaire vgagnaire@optimus.fr
Conversation : Devenez EcoActeur avant le 31/12 !

Si ce message ne s'affiche pas correctement, cliquez ici

Bonjour,

Les crises économiques, écologiques, climatiques et alimentaires qui secouent notre planète sont étroitement liées et interdépendantes.

Elles ne pourront être résolues que par la mobilisation de tous les acteurs politiques et économiques, mais aussi de tous les citoyens. **Y compris de la vôtre, car chaque engagé compte.**

Votre soutien et celui des 746 000 signataires du Pacte Ecologique a déjà permis la prise en compte de nos principales propositions dans le cadre du Grenelle de l'environnement et contribué, fait exceptionnel, au vote à la quasi unanimité, majorité et opposition confondues, de la Loi Grenelle 1 en 1ère lecture à l'Assemblée nationale.

Ce ne sont que les premières étapes. La mobilisation doit s'amplifier.
REGARDEZ CETTE VIDÉO et soutenez-nous - FAITES UN DON

Nous avons devant nous des échéances très importantes qui déterminent notre avenir à tous et celui de nos enfants :
- Suivi de l'application de la Loi Grenelle et adoption de la seconde partie,
- Intégration de mesures permettant de surmonter simultanément la crise économique et la crise écologique,
- Mise en oeuvre par l'Union Européenne du paquet climat-énergie qui vise à réduire significativement les émissions de gaz à effet de serre,
- Conférence des Nations Unies à Copenhague fin 2009 sur le changement climatique pour préparer l'après Kyoto...

Il y a urgence. Le compte à rebours a commencé.

C'est pourquoi, je lance un appel solennel pour que le plus grand nombre possible de personnes s'associe à notre action et devienne EcoActeur avant le 31 décembre 2008. Par votre don, si modeste soit-il, vous nous apporterez un soutien précieux et votre voix pourra être entendue.

Je vous propose 4 façons de nous soutenir, choisissez celle qui vous convient le mieux. Dans tous les cas, j'espère pouvoir compter sur vous dès maintenant

Écologiquement vôtre,

Nicolas Hulot
Président

FIGURE CS.8   **First E-Mail in the Campaign Promotion Plan**

FIGURE CS.9   E-mail 2, 3, and 4

A video produced for the web site was used in the first e-mail. Again, the call to action was clear: "Become an Eco-Actor before December 31." Upon opening the e-mail, Hulot himself invited the recipient to watch a video and support the foundation by the tax deadline. With one click, users found themselves at the event web site, where the video started automatically.

The next step of the plan, a reminder e-mail, was sent out on day D + 4. This e-mail (see Figure CS.9), also signed by Hulot, focused on the number of people who had made a gift. A reminder was included about becoming one of the 10,000 eco-actors (or donors) to launch or relaunch mobilization. A button on the right emphasized users to take action on that day to give a sense of urgency to the e-mail—tomorrow would be too late. This technique of organizations emphasizing urgency usually works well and any charity may find a reason to communicate urgency to donors or supporters. Note that this e-mail was not sent to those who already made a gift. This is a basic but important reminder!

On day 8 after the first e-mail was sent, a third reminder e-mail (see Figure CS.9) was sent to those who hadn't made a gift. A schedule for sending out e-mail was followed (every four days) during the holiday season. The third e-mail came in second in terms of generating contributions. Again, the reminder focused on the incredible mobilization of members of the community (the counter on the web site displayed the mobilization of supporters in real time). We chose to place the video at the forefront in this e-mail and offer the possibility of becoming an eco-actor for 10 euros. The idea of a small gift allowed more people to make gifts.

The last e-mail of the campaign (see Figure CS.9) was sent out on December 30. It was a last chance e-mail: the last chance to make a gift before midnight on December 31 and thus benefit from the tax relief, a last chance to help the foundation reach a minimum of 10,000 contributors before year-end.

We were surprised that this e-mail obtained the best results of the entire campaign. We thought that only a few people would check and read their e-mail the night before New Year's Eve, but the web site access rate was excellent and a large number of contributions were triggered by this e-mail. This is an interesting and important element to remember in your own project. This works as long as the urgency is "justified."

The e-mail strategy was by far the most effective in terms of traffic directed to the event web site. Other elements of the promotion plan were less significant but were good additions. For example, information posted on Facebook (see Figure CS.7) allowed us to create a buzz and announce that the foundation was conducting a campaign.

There was actually much communication on Facebook between group members, which was quite interesting. This demonstrated to the foundation the importance of its method and projects. It was also a way to reach an audience and repeat the message. Supporters who receive an e-mail from the foundation and then a post on Facebook before receiving another e-mail know that they must act!

We now believe that we could have achieved better results if we had reduced the amount of days between e-mail and been able to send one or two more e-mail. Our choice not to oversolicit (four times in three weeks) was still a good choice for us in view of the results we obtained.

The Power of "Thanks"

There is never enough attention given to the power of saying thank-you after a gift. In this campaign, Optimus and the foundation decided to create a specific "thanks system."

It is always very disturbing to see that charities that understand the power of thank-you letters offline seem to forget about this online! But the Internet offers endless possibilities in terms of personalization and technical terms.

In the framework of the eco-actor campaign, we saw that the video of the foundation's president was at the center of mobilization. It was presented in e-mail, automatically launched on the event web site, and posted on web sites of social networks.

Our idea was to use a video to thank people and donors. Thus, we recorded a personal video message from Hulot, who thanked the donors himself. Rather than receive an automatic e-mail signed by the foundation team, the thank-you e-mail for this campaign contained a new video of Hulot (see Figure CS.10).

By clicking on the video, donors could view the message from Hulot as though it had been created specifically for them. This is a much more effective and better relationship-building idea to consider than just an e-mail. In this e-mail we proposed regular support as well as sending the message to others using a "Tell a friend." feature. Whether it be online or offline, in fundraising, the thank-you time is always an occasion to make new proposals to your supporters or donors.

CAMPAIGN RESULTS

The results of our campaign exceeded our expectations:

- We raised nearly 300,000 euros within the three weeks of the campaign and more than 9,000 online gifts.
- The objective of 10,000 eco-actors was surpassed; we had 12,000 by the end of the campaign. Hundreds of personal fundraising pages were created, with average contributions of 93 euros per page.

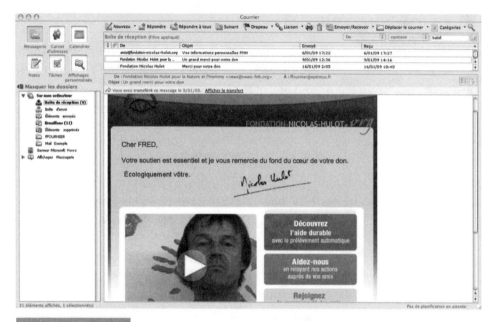

FIGURE CS.10   Thank-You E-Mail with Video from Hulot

- More than 200 contributions and opinions were voiced by members of the community.

- 600 people used "Tell a Friend," which generated nearly 50,000 euros in gifts.

- Of the four e-mail sent, the last two generated 66 percent of the funds collected.

Finally, the project's return on investment was better than 12—a great achievement, especially considering the economic and social crises in France and around the world during the winter of 2008. Table CS.1 shows the campaign results.

TABLE CS.1   Campaign Results

Metric	Result
Visits	> 50,000
Pages Viewed	> 100,000
Unique Visitors	> 45,000
Average Number of Page Views	> 2
Most Viewed Page	"Make A Gift" page

Keys to Success

Our keys to success were a popular cause (protection of the environment), a high-profile and charismatic foundation president (Nicolas Hulot), our recognition in the French nonprofit sector, and one of the biggest e-mail databases of supporters. Beyond these very important points, the marketing success of the Eco-Actor campaign lay in the following elements:

- A strong and clear call to become an eco-actor
- An event web site with a call to action
- A video at the heart of the plan
- Various methods for people to mobilize their friends and family
- A simple and efficient contribution form
- A counter to put mobilization into a concrete form
- A countdown to symbolize urgency
- E-mail as the primary promotion tool

For more information on this campaign, please see the video that presents this project at http://www.optimus.fr/news/realisations/2009/04/20/optimus-pour-la-fondation-nicolas-hulot-une-success-story-on-line/.

Frédéric Fournier is CEO of Optimus in Paris, an independent, leading French fundraising agency. Fred has 15 years of experience in fundraising. Specializing in marketing services, Fred's expertise combines online and offline fundraising programs.

He has helped execute direct mail, telephone, online fundraising and special events for a wide range of organizations – such as French Salvation Army, French Téléthon (AFM), Handicap International, Unicef, Curie Center Care Foundation, Mme Jacques Chirac's Hospital Foundation, French Red Cross, Prince Albert II of Monaco Foundation, World Wildlife Foundation, Nicolas Hulot Foundation, Caritas France, The French Shoah Memorial, and many others. Fred has provided a wide range of fundraising assistance–strategic planning, direct-mail planning, online programs, and so forth.

He has been a board member of the ePhilanthropy Foundation from 2006 until 2008 and became ePmt (ePhilanthropy Master Trainer) in 2008.

He is a regular trainer and speaker for the French fundraisers association, and for universities such as IAE Paris, Panthéon Sorbonne Paris, and the University of Montpellier department of economics. He is married and has two daughters, Violette and Suzanne. You can e-mail Fred at ffournier@optimus.fr.

Notes

CHAPTER 1

1. Li, Charlene, "Future of Social Networks Presentation from SXSW" *Altimeter Blog*, San Mateo, CA (cited April 16, 2009), http://blog.altimetergroup.com/2009/03/future-of-social-networks-presentation-from-sxsw.html.
2. Kanter, Beth, "Measuring the Return on Investment," in *Managing Technology to Meet Your Mission: A Strategic Guide for Nonprofit Leaders*, ed. Holly Ross, Katrin Verclas, and Allison Levine (pp.53–54) San Francisco: (Jossey-Bass/Wiley, 2009).
3. M+R Strategic Services and NTEN. 2009 eNonprofits Benchmarks Study, May 2009. (cited May 15, 2009), http://www.e-benchmarksstudy.com/2009.html; Rubel, Steve, *Micropersuasion Blog*, New York (cited April 16, 2009), http://www.micropersuasion.com/2006/12/the_iminent_dem.html; Falls, Jason, *Social Media Explorer Blog*, Nashville, TN (cited 2009 April 16), http://www.socialmediaexplorer.com/2008/10/28/what-is-the-roi-for-social-media/.
4. Hart, Kim, and Megan Greenwall, "To Nonprofits Seeking Cash, Facebook App Isn't So Green" *Washington Post* (cited April 22, 2009), http://www.washingtonpost.com/wp-dyn/content/article/2009/04/21/AR2009042103786.html?sub=AR.
5. Kanter, Beth, *Beth's Blog*, Los Altos, CA (cited May 15, 2009), http://beth.typepad.com/beths_blog/2009/04/hello-washington-post-dolllars-per-facebook-donor-is-not-the-right-metric-for-success.html
6. Fine, Allison, *A Fine Blog*, New York (cited May 15, 2009), http://afine2.wordpress.com/2009/04/22/wash-post-disses-causes-on-facebook/.
7. Kanter, *Beth's Blog*, http://beth.typepad.com/beths_blog/2009/04/hello-washington-post-dolllars-per-facebook-donor-is-not-the-right-metric-for-success.html.
8. Kanter, *Beth's Blog*, http://beth.typepad.com/beths_blog/2009/04/hello-washington-post-dolllars-per-facebook-donor-is-not-the-right-metric-for-success.html.
9. Kanter, *Beth's Blog*, http://beth.typepad.com/beths_blog/2009/04/hello-washington-post-dolllars-per-facebook-donor-is-not-the-right-metric-for-success.html.
10. Armano, David, *Logic and Emotion Blog*, Chicago, http://darmano.typepad.com/logic_emotion/.
11. Kanter, *Beth's Blog* (cited June 1, 2009), http://beth.typepad.com/beths_blog/2009/01/nonprofit-examples-of-how-listening-returns-valuable-insights-and-impact-.html.
12. Armano, *Logic and Emotion Blog* (cited May 16, 2009), white paper available at http://darmano.typepad.com/files/the_collective.pdf.
13. Paine, K. D., "The ROI of Relationships: Presentation," (cited May 16, 2009), electronic slide show available at http://www.slideshare.net/kdpaine/sob-con-roi-of-relationships-in-social-media?type=presentation.

14. Kanter, *Beth's Blog* (cited May 6, 2009), http://beth.typepad.com/beths_blog/2009/05/twitter-measure-what-counts-to-help-you-improve-what-youre-doing.html.

15. Kanter, *Beth's Blog* (cited June 1, 2009), http://beth.typepad.com/beths_blog/2009/01/nonprofit-examples-of-how-listening-returns-valuable-insights-and-impact-.html.

16. Karnofsky, Holden, *Givewell Blog*, Brooklyn, NY (cited June 1, 2009), http://blog.givewell.net/?p=31.

17. Karnofsky, *Givewell Blog* (cited June 1, 2009), http://blog.givewell.net/?p=33.

18. http://givewell.net/recommended-charities.

19. Kanter, *Beth's Blog* (cited May 16, 2009), http://beth.typepad.com/beths_blog/2009/06/are-you-a-listening-organization-.html.

20. Kanter, *Beth's Blog* (cited 2009 May 16), http://beth.typepad.com/beths_blog/2009/01/listening-literacy-skills-keywords-are-king-what-keywords-or-phrases-have-brought-you-some-insights.html.

21. Lewis, Carie. *Carie's Girls*, Washington, DC (cited June 15, 2009), http://cariegrls.blogspot.com/2009/05/my-free-igoogle-brand-monitoring.html.

22. National Wildlife Federation, Washington, DC (cited June 15, 2009), http://www.nwf.org/playandobserve.

23. *WeAreMedia Wiki*, Portland, OR (cited May 15, 2009), http://www.wearemedia.org/Tool+Box+RSS+Readers.

24. Kanter, Beth, *Beth's Social Media Listening Wiki* (cited June 1, 2009), http://socialmedia-listening.wikispaces.com/Tools.

25. Kanter, *Beth's Blog* (cited June 1, 2009), http://beth.typepad.com/beths_blog/2009/06/what-are-your-nonprofits-super-power-listening-tips-for-using-twitter.html.

26. Kanter, *Beth's Blog* (cited June 1, 2009), http://beth.typepad.com/beths_blog/2008/03/social-media-ro.html.

27. Kanter, *Beth's Blog*, http://beth.typepad.com/beths_blog/2008/03/social-media-ro.html.

28. Kanter, *Beth's Blog* (cited June 1, 2009), http://beth.typepad.com/beths_blog/2008/12/facebook-users.html.

29. Kanter, *Beth's Blog* (cited June 1, 2009), http://beth.typepad.com/beths_blog/2009/05/target-facebook-challenge-ten-large-charities-compete-for-votes-to-divide-the-3-million-pot.html.

30. Norman, Chad, *Chad Norman's Webby Things* Charleston, SC (cited June 1, 2009), http://forums.blackbaud.com/blogs/webbythings/archive/2009/04/27/15-clay-shirky-quotes-that-blew-my-mind-at-ntc.aspx.

31. Kanter, Beth, *Cute Dog Theory Wiki*, Los Altos, CA (cited May 1, 2009), http://cutedogtheory.wikispaces.com/.

32. Kanter, *Beth's Blog* (cited May 1, 2009), http://beth.typepad.com/beths_blog/2009/05/cause-marketing-or-cause-me-to-puke-marketing-interview-with-scott-henderson.html.

33. Kanter, *Beth's Blog* (cited June 1, 2009), http://beth.typepad.com/beths_blog/2009/04/from-nonprofit-social-media-strategist-to-social-media-change-agent-and-beyond.html.

34. Kanter, *Beth's Blog* (cited June 2, 2009), http://www.hsus.org/pets/pet_care/why_you_should_spay_or_neuter_your_pet.html.

35. Kanter, *Beth's Blog* (cited June 2, 2009), http://beth.typepad.com/beths_blog/2007/11/the-flickr-hold.html#comment-90161114

36. Kanter, *Beth's Blog*, (cited February 15, 2009), http://beth.typepad.com/beths_blog/2009/02/how-do-you-measure-the-success-of-dog-to-person-fundraising-on-social-networks-dollars-or-doggie-tre.html

37. Mishra, Gaurav, *Social Media Analytics Blog*, Mumbai (cited June 25, 2009), http://2020webtech.com/blog/approach/.

38. Kanter, *Beth's Blog* (cited June 20, 2009), http://beth.typepad.com/beths_blog/2009/06/future-tech-panel-at-craigslist-nonprofit-bootcamp.html

39. Catone, Josh, *Mashable*, New York, NY (cited June 25, 2009), http://mashable.com/2009/06/23/humane-society/.

Chapter 3

1. "There are many definitions of e-government, and the term itself is not universally used. Definitions . . . range from 'the use of information technology to free movement of information to overcome the physical bounds of traditional paper and physical based systems' to 'the use of technology to enhance the access to and delivery of government services to benefit citizens, business partners and employees.'" Subhajit Basu, *E-Government and Developing Countries: An Overview*, Queen's University Belfast, June 1, 2004, http://www.digitaldivide.net/articles/view.php?ArticleID=594.

2. BoardEffect and Alliance for Nonprofit Management, Survey, June 2008.

3. Bill Bradley and Paul Jansen, "Faster Charity," *McKinsey Quarterly*, 2002.

4. Sandra Hughes, "The Boardroom: Putting the 'Knowledge' in Technology," *Foundation News and Commentary* 44, no. 6 (2003).

5. Rachael King, "Corporate Boards Get Busy Online," *BusinessWeek*, 2007.

6. BoardEffect and Alliance for Nonprofit Management, Survey, June 2008.

7. Matt Perkins, "Board Portals: No Assembly Required," *BusinessWeek*, 2008.

8. Linda Dixon, "Doing Board Business on the Web," *Board Member* 17, no. 2, (2008); John DiConsiglio, "Robo-Board," *Board Member* 13, no. 7 (2004).

9. "Developing a Web Portal for the Board: A Research Paper from the Corporate Practices Committee," Society of Corporate Secretaries and Governance Professionals, conducted originally in 2005 with updated data collected in 2007.

10. King, "Corporate Boards"; Jaclyne Badal, "Goodbye Briefing Books," *Wall Street Journal*, October 2006.

11. For example, Anthony Bernal and Ian Uriarte, "Creating a New Portal: Part 1," IBM, 2005, http://www.ibm.com/developerworks/websphere/library/techarticles/0508_bernal/0508_bernal.html; Jakob Nielsen, "Enterprise Portals Are Popping," *Alertbox 2008*, http://www.useit.com/alertbox/portals.html.

12. BoardEffect Case Study of the Enterprise Center, "Online Governance Reduces Direct and Indirect Costs; Provides over 6 Times Return on Investment," June 2008.

13. Telephone interview conducted by BoardEffect with Della Clark, Philadelphia, PA, June 2008.

14. Telephone interview conducted by BoardEffect with Olivia Selinger, Miquon, PA, June 2009.

15. Telephone interview conducted by BoardEffect with Jonathan Horn, Philadelphia, PA, May 2008.

16. Telephone interview conducted by BoardEffect with Olivia Selinger, Philadelphia, PA, June 2009.

Chapter 4

1. http://en.wikipedia.org/wiki/Web_2.0.

2. http://en.wikipedia.org/wiki/Social_media.

3. http://en.wikipedia.org/wiki/Social_Networking.

4. Kate Adams, and Adey Melissa, "Social Collaboration: Joining Forces on the Digital Frontier," December 2008, http://www.scribd.com/doc/8997505/Whitepaper-Social-Collaboration.

5. Thomas H. Davenport and Laurence Prusak, *Working Knowledge: How Organizations Manage What They Know*. Harvard Business Press, 1998

6. http://www.webex.com/pdf/cs_Positive.pdf.

7. http://www.wildapricot.com/blogs/newsblog/archive/2007/05/17/using-google-docs-as-an-online-collaboration-tool-for-board-members.aspx.

8. http://googleblog.blogspot.com/2009/05/went-walkabout-brought-back-google-wave.html.

9. http://www.theport.com/whitePapers.aspx.

10. http://apps.facebook.com/causes/about.

11. http://www.youtube.com/videovolunteers.

12. http://blog.compete.com/2009/02/09/facebook-myspace-twitter-social-network/

13. Michael C. Gilbert, "Hype, Anxiety, and Hope (HAH!): How to Do Social Media Wrong (and How to Do It Right)," June 22, 2009, http://news.gilbert.org/SocialMediaHAH.

14. http://blog.ning.com/2008/10/nonprofit-know-how-when-networking-on-ning.html.

15. http://www.blackbaud.com/files/resources/industry_analysis/2008_SONI_NorthAmerica.pdf.

16. http://remotecolab.wikispaces.com/Strategies+for+Adoption.

17. http://www.nten.org/blog/2006/12/21/the-building-blocks-for-nonprofit-collaboration.

CHAPTER 5

1. Roger Craver and Tom Belford, "DonorSuperstars," DonorTrends Whitepaper Series, 2008–2009, pp. 2, 3.

CHAPTER 6

1. M+R Strategic Services and Nonprofit Technology Network, *eNonprofit Benchmarks Study*, 2009.

2. M+R Strategic Services and Nonprofit Technology Network, *eNonprofit Benchmarks Study*, 2008–2009.

3. *Summer 2007 Philanthropic Giving Index*, Center on Philanthropy at Indiana University, 2007.

4. *2007 State of the Nonprofit Industry*, Blackbaud, 2007.

5. *2008 donorCentrics Internet Giving Benchmarking Analysis, Target Analytics*, 2009.

6. *Chronicle of Philanthropy*, 2009.

CHAPTER 7

1. http://www.nonprofitsocialnetworksurvey.com.

CHAPTER 8

1. Pidgeon, Walter P., *The Not-for-Profit CEO: Practical Steps to Attaining and Retaining the Corner Office*, John Wiley & Sons, Hoboken, NJ, 2006, p. 127.
2. Fisher, James L., and Gary H. Quehl, *The President and Fund Raising*, Macmillan, New York, 1989, p. 21.
3. Ibid., p. 18.
4. Bremner, Robert H., *American Philanthropy*, University of Chicago Press, Chicago, 1988, p. 7.
5. Madison, James, *A Memorial and Remonstrance on the Religious Rights of Man, To the General Assembly of the State of Virginia*, 1784.
6. Ellis, Susan J., and Katherine H. Noyes, *By the People*, Jossey-Bass, San Francisco, 1990, XII, p. 22.
7. de Tocqueville, Alexis, "Political Associations in the United States," in *Democracy in America*, trans. Francis Bowen, ed. Phillips Bradley, Vintage Books, New York, 1945, pp. 64–73.
8. Pidgeon, Walter P., *Universal Benefits of Volunteering*, John Wiley & Sons, New York, 1998.
9. Pidgeon, *The Not-for-Profit CEO*, p. 19.
10. Mc Kay, Lauren, "Strategy and Social Media," *Customer Relationship Management Magazine*, June 2009, p. 28.
11. Leverus Internet Survey for Associations and Not-for-Profit Organizations, 2004.
12. "After the Flood," *Chronicle of Philanthropy*, June 12, 2008.
13. "Social Media from A to Z," *Customer Relationship Management Magazine*, June 2009, p. 27.
14. http://social-media-optimization.com/2007/09/the-future-of-social-networks.
15. Donordigital, Perfecting Your Page, May 9, 2009.
16. Buggs, Shannon, "Business of Giving: Nonprofits Should Make Use of Social Networking," Houston Chronicle, 2008.
17. "All That Twitters Isn't Gold," *PCMA Convene Magazine*, June 2009, p. 69.
18. Pidgeon, Walter P., *The Legislative Labyrinth: A Map for Not-for-Profits*, John Wiley & Sons, New York, 2001, p. 198.
19. Preparing for a Recovery, *Wall Street Journal*, June 22, 2009.
20. Handy, Geoff, "The Five Basic Steps to Acquiring Donors Online," *Fund Raising Success Magazine*, Philadelphia, May 2009, pp. 24–25.
21. Ellis, Susan J., and Katherine H. Noyes, *By the People*, Jossey-Bass, San Francisco, 1990, XII, pp. 23–24.
22. American Society of Association Executives, *Principles of Association Management*, American Society of Association Executives, Washington, DC, 1975, p. 3.
23. Borum, Regina Ann, "A Comparative Profile: A Study of African-Americans and Caucasians in Institutional Advancement in the United States, Union Institute, Cincinnati, OH, 1991.
24. Karl, Barry D., and Stanley N. Katz, *The American Private Philanthropic Foundation and the Public Sphere, 1890–1930*, Minerba, 1981.
25. Ellis and Noyes, *By the People*, p. 178.
26. Bremner, Robert H., *American Philanthropy*, University of Chicago Press, Chicago, 1987, p. 118.
27. Ibid., p. 118.
28. Ibid., pp. 150–1.

29. Ibid., pp. 215, 244–5, 171.
30. Hesburgh, Theodore M. with Jerry Reedy, *God, Country, Notre Dame*, Doubleday, New York, 1990, pp. 267–270.
31. Hodgkinson, Virginia A., and Murray S. Weitzman, *Giving and Volunteering in the United States*, Independent Sector, Washington, DC, 1990, pp. 267–270.

CHAPTER 11

1. Clay Shirky, *Here Comes Everybody*: The Power of Organizing without Organizations, New York, Penguin Press, 2008.

CHAPTER 12

1. www.easidemographics.com
2. Evan Esar, http://www.quotegarden.com/statistics.html
3. W. I. E. Gates, http://www.quotegarden.com/statistics.html
4. Fletcher Knebel, http://www.quotationspage.com/quote/1017.html
5. Greg Easterbrook, http://www.quotegarden.com/statistics.html
6. W. G. Hunter, http://cqpi.engr.wisc.edu/system/files/r004.pdf

CHAPTER 13

1. Sheila L. Croucher, *Globalization and Belonging: The Politics of Identity in a Changing World*, Rowman & Littlefield, 2004.
2. The Yankee Group, 2002.
3. The Hong Kong Federation of Youth Groups, March 29, 2009.
4. Experian.
5. ExpatForum.com, 2007, http://www.expatforum.com/articles/moving/moving-to-dubai.html (retrieved September 5, 2007).
6. *Oxford English Dictionary.*
7. *Chronicle of Higher Education*, June 7, 2009.
8. Facebook.
9. Source: Charitable Aid Foundation 2006.
10. *Asia Business*, June 26, 2008.
11. http://www.dubaicares.ae.
12. Kiva.org
13. Ted Hart and James Greenfield, *People to People Fundraising: Social Networking and Web 2.0 for Charities*, Wiley, 2007.
14. Leo Dobbs, http://www.unhcr.org/4a3d16416.html.
15. Chris Williams, "Turning Pesos into Pounds," *Professional Fundraising*, March 2008.
16. Williams, "Turning Pesos into Pounds."

CHAPTER 16

1. http://en.wikipedia.org/wiki/Internet
2. http://www.goldsteinreport.com/article.php?article=7430

3. http://en.wikipedia.org/wiki/Social_engineering_(security)

4. http://news.com.com/Hackers+grab+donor+info+from+U.K.+charity/2100-1029_3-5991361.html

5. http://datalossdb.org/reports

6. http://www.spamlaws.com/id-theft-statistics.html

Chapter 17

1. "World's Poor Drive Growth in Global Cell Phone Use," http://www.wirelessweek.com/article.aspx?id=166612.

2. http://mobileactive.org/evaluation-rapidsms-increase-child-nutrition-surveillance-malawi; http://mobileactive.org/preventing-famine-mobile; http://www.mobiledevelopmentsolutions.org/unicef.pdf.

3. "Empowering Women through ICT: Enhancing Access to Information by Rural Women," http://www.egovmonitor.com/node/14541.

4. http://mobileactive.org/Mobile+Telephony+Makes+a+Difference+in+Livelihoods.

5. http://mobileactive.org/Mobile+Telephony+Makes+a+Difference+in+Livelihoods.

6. http://www.personaldemocracy.com/node/756.

7. http://www.personaldemocracy.com/node/756.

8. For the full study, see http://www.newvotersproject.org/uploads/jX/a4/jXa4y7Q3JFWhnPsmdQcGfw/Youth-Vote-and-Text-Messaging.pdf.

9. TxtVoter was the name of our 2006 campaign. The name of the organization that registered the individual was attached to the end of each message.

10. Mobile Commons provided this anecdote and data.

11. Bureau of Labor Statistics, *Volunteering in the United States*, 2008.

12. http://mobileactive.org/how-run-text-screen-campaigns-mobileactive-guide-ngos.

13. http://mobileactive.org/please-call-me-messages-hiv-info-mobile-social-marketing-south-africa.

14. The location was, of course, public but is private in the sense that adults did not mediate. Ironically, being surrounded by strangers at a bus stop can be one of the most private places in urban areas.

15. The astute reader will note that the author's own texting campaign asked voters to vote "Tomorrow," and the campaign delivered positive results. We made this decision because of the unreliable nature of wireless networks. They go down with some frequency. We didn't want to rely on the networks to send messages on Election Day. By sending them the day before, we gave ourselves a one-day buffer. If they went down the day before, we'd try on Election Day.

AFP Code of Ethical Principles and Standards

ETHICAL PRINCIPLES • Adopted 1964; amended Sept. 2007

The Association of Fundraising Professionals (AFP) exists to foster the development and growth of fundraising professionals and the profession, to promote high ethical behavior in the fundraising profession and to preserve and enhance philanthropy and volunteerism. Members of AFP are motivated by an inner drive to improve the quality of life through the causes they serve. They serve the ideal of philanthropy, are committed to the preservation and enhancement of volunteerism; and hold stewardship of these concepts as the overriding direction of their professional life. They recognize their responsibility to ensure that needed resources are vigorously and ethically sought and that the intent of the donor is honestly fulfilled. To these ends, AFP members, both individual and business, embrace certain values that they strive to uphold in performing their responsibilities for generating philanthropic support. AFP business members strive to promote and protect the work and mission of their client organizations.

AFP members both individual and business aspire to:

- practice their profession with integrity, honesty, truthfulness and adherence to the absolute obligation to safeguard the public trust
- act according to the highest goals and visions of their organizations, professions, clients and consciences
- put philanthropic mission above personal gain;
- inspire others through their own sense of dedication and high purpose
- improve their professional knowledge and skills, so that their performance will better serve others
- demonstrate concern for the interests and well-being of individuals affected by their actions
- value the privacy, freedom of choice and interests of all those affected by their actions
- foster cultural diversity and pluralistic values and treat all people with dignity and respect
- affirm, through personal giving, a commitment to philanthropy and its role in society
- adhere to the spirit as well as the letter of all applicable laws and regulations
- advocate within their organizations adherence to all applicable laws and regulations
- avoid even the appearance of any criminal offense or professional misconduct
- bring credit to the fundraising profession by their public demeanor
- encourage colleagues to embrace and practice these ethical principles and standards
- be aware of the codes of ethics promulgated by other professional organizations that serve philanthropy

ETHICAL STANDARDS

Furthermore, while striving to act according to the above values, AFP members, both individual and business, agree to abide (and to ensure, to the best of their ability, that all members of their staff abide) by the AFP standards. Violation of the standards may subject the member to disciplinary sanctions, including expulsion, as provided in the AFP Ethics Enforcement Procedures.

MEMBER OBLIGATIONS

1. Members shall not engage in activities that harm the members' organizations, clients or profession.
2. Members shall not engage in activities that conflict with their fiduciary, ethical and legal obligations to their organizations, clients or profession.
3. Members shall effectively disclose all potential and actual conflicts of interest; such disclosure does not preclude or imply ethical impropriety.
4. Members shall not exploit any relationship with a donor, prospect, volunteer, client or employee for the benefit of the members or the members' organizations.
5. Members shall comply with all applicable local, state, provincial and federal civil and criminal laws.
6. Members recognize their individual boundaries of competence and are forthcoming and truthful about their professional experience and qualifications and will represent their achievements accurately and without exaggeration.
7. Members shall present and supply products and/or services honestly and without misrepresentation and will clearly identify the details of those products, such as availability of the products and/or services and other factors that may affect the suitability of the products and/or services for donors, clients or nonprofit organizations.
8. Members shall establish the nature and purpose of any contractual relationship at the outset and will be responsive and available to organizations and their employing organizations before, during and after any sale of materials and/or services. Members will comply with all fair and reasonable obligations created by the contract.
9. Members shall refrain from knowingly infringing the intellectual property rights of other parties at all times. Members shall address and rectify any inadvertent infringement that may occur.
10. Members shall protect the confidentiality of all privileged information relating to the provider/client relationships.
11. Members shall refrain from any activity designed to disparage competitors untruthfully.

SOLICITATION AND USE OF PHILANTHROPIC FUNDS

12. Members shall take care to ensure that all solicitation and communication materials are accurate and correctly reflect their organizations' mission and use of solicited funds.
13. Members shall take care to ensure that donors receive informed, accurate and ethical advice about the value and tax implications of contributions.
14. Members shall take care to ensure that contributions are used in accordance with donors' intentions.
15. Members shall take care to ensure proper stewardship of all revenue sources, including timely reports on the use and management of such funds.
16. Members shall obtain explicit consent by donors before altering the conditions of financial transactions.

PRESENTATION OF INFORMATION

17. Members shall not disclose privileged or confidential information to unauthorized parties.
18. Members shall adhere to the principle that all donor and prospect information created by, or on behalf of, an organization or a client is the property of that organization or client and shall not be transferred or utilized except on behalf of that organization or client.
19. Members shall give donors and clients the opportunity to have their names removed from lists that are sold to, rented to or exchanged with other organizations.
20. Members shall, when stating fundraising results, use accurate and consistent accounting methods that conform to the appropriate guidelines adopted by the American Institute of Certified Public Accountants (AICPA)* for the type of organization involved. (* In countries outside of the United States, comparable authority should be utilized.)

COMPENSATION AND CONTRACTS

21. Members shall not accept compensation or enter into a contract that is based on a percentage of contributions; nor shall members accept finder's fees or contingent fees. Business members must refrain from receiving compensation from third parties derived from products or services for a client without disclosing that third-party compensation to the client (for example, volume rebates from vendors to business members).
22. Members may accept performance-based compensation, such as bonuses, provided such bonuses are in accord with prevailing practices within the members' own organizations and are not based on a percentage of contributions.
23. Members shall neither offer nor accept payments or special considerations for the purpose of influencing the selection of products or services.
24. Members shall not pay finder's fees, commissions or percentage compensation based on contributions, and shall take care to discourage their organizations from making such payments.
25. Any member receiving funds on behalf of a donor or client must meet the legal requirements for the disbursement of those funds. Any interest or income earned on the funds should be fully disclosed.

A Donor Bill of Rights

PHILANTHROPY is based on voluntary action for the common good. It is a tradition of giving and sharing that is primary to the quality of life. To assure that philanthropy merits the respect and trust of the general public, and that donors and prospective donors can have full confidence in the not-for-profit organizations and causes they are asked to support, we declare that all donors have these rights:

I.

To be informed of the organization's mission, of the way the organization intends to use donated resources, and of its capacity to use donations effectively for their intended purposes.

II.

To be informed of the identity of those serving on the organization's governing board, and to expect the board to exercise prudent judgement in its stewardship responsibilities.

III.

To have access to the organization's most recent financial statements.

IV.

To be assured their gifts will be used for the purposes for which they were given.

V.

To receive appropriate acknowledgement and recognition.

VI.

To be assured that information about their donations is handled with respect and with confidentiality to the extent provided by law.

VII.

To expect that all relationships with individuals representing organizations of interest to the donor will be professional in nature.

VIII.

To be informed whether those seeking donations are volunteers, employees of the organization or hired solicitors.

IX.

To have the opportunity for their names to be deleted from mailing lists that an organization may intend to share.

X.

To feel free to ask questions when making a donation and to receive prompt, truthful and forthright answers.

DEVELOPED BY
Association for Healthcare Philanthropy (AHP)
Association of Fundraising Professionals (AFP)
Council for Advancement and Support of Education (CASE)
Giving Institute: Leading Consultants to Non-Profits

ENDORSED BY
(in formation)
Independent Sector
National Catholic Development Conference (NCDC)
National Committee on Planned Giving (NCPG)
Council for Resource Development (CRD)
United Way of America

Index